Genders and Sexualities in History

Series Editors: **John H. Arnold, Joanna Bourke and Sean Brady**

Palgrave Macmillan's series, Genders and Sexualities in History, aims to accommodate and foster new approaches to historical research in the fields of genders and sexualities. The series will promote world-class scholarship that concentrates upon the interconnected themes of genders, sexualities, religions/religiosity, civil society, class formations, politics and war.

Historical studies of gender and sexuality have often been treated as disconnected fields, while in recent years historical analyses in these two areas have synthesised, creating new departures in historiography. By linking genders and sexualities with questions of religion, civil society, politics and the contexts of war and conflict, this series will reflect recent developments in scholarship, moving away from the previously dominant and narrow histories of science, scientific thought and legal processes. The result brings together scholarship from contemporary, modern, early modern, medieval, classical and non-Western history to provide a diachronic forum for scholarship that incorporates new approaches to genders and sexualities in history

Surviving Hitler's War: Family Life in Germany 1939–48 is a groundbreaking revision of the burgeoning scholarship in history and sociology on the effects of Nazism, war, and post-war reconstruction upon gender and the traditional nuclear family in Germany. In this seminal book, Hester Vaizey provides a meticulously researched, incisive, and moving account of the remarkable tenacity of emotional bonds in the traditional family unit, inspite of the invasiveness of Nazi policy in the private sphere, extended periods of family separation during the war and its aftermath, and the traumas of family reunion. Through examination of the emotional and practical side of family life in Germany, Vaizey deconstructs hugely influential scholarly paradigms in German scholarship for this crucial period, such as the 'Hour of the Woman', and notions that post-Nazi German masculinity was particularly ill equipped to cope with the realities of defeat. The book contrasts evidence of emotional realities, with the institutional, representational, and demographic evidence that has dominated scholarship to date. *Surviving Hitler's War* recasts the history of German families in a radical new light, and repositions our understanding of society in the new West Germany after 1948. In common with all volumes in the 'Genders and Sexualities in History' series, Hester Vaizey's *Surviving Hitler's War* presents a multifaceted and meticulously researched scholarly study, and is a sophisticated contribution to our understanding of the past.

Titles include

Matthew Cook
QUEER DOMESTICITIES
Homosexuality and Home Life in Twentieth-Century London

Jennifer Evans
RECONSTRUCTION SITES
Spaces of Sexual Encounter in Cold War Berlin

Christopher E. Forth and Elinor Accampo *(editors)*
CONFRONTING MODERNITY IN FIN-DE-SIÈCLE FRANCE
Bodies, Minds and Gender

Dagmar Herzog *(editor)*
BRUTALITY AND DESIRE
War and Sexuality in Europe's Twentieth Century

Jessica Meyer
MEN OF WAR
Masculinity and the First World War in Britain

Jennifer D. Thibodeaux *(editor)*
NEGOTIATING CLERICAL IDENTITIES
Priests, Monks and Masculity in the Middle Ages

Hester Vaizey
SURVIVING HITLER'S WAR
Family Life in Germany 1939–48

Genders and Sexualities in History Series
Series Standing Order 978–0–230–55185–5 Hardback 978–0–230–55186–2 Paperback
(outside North America only)

You can receive future titles in this series as they are published by placing a standing order. Please contact your bookseller or, in case of difficulty, write to us at the address below with your name and address, the title of the series and the ISBN quoted above.

Customer Services Department, Macmillan Distribution Ltd, Houndmills, Basingstoke, Hampshire RG21 6XS, England

Surviving Hitler's War

Family Life in Germany, 1939–48

Hester Vaizey

Postdoctoral researcher with a Hanseatic Scholarship courtesy of the Alfred Toepfer Stiftung in Hamburg

First published 2010 by
PALGRAVE MACMILLAN

306. 8509

Palgrave Macmillan in the UK is an imprint of Macmillan Publishers Limited, registered in England, company number 785998, of Houndmills, Basingstoke, Hampshire RG21 6XS.

Palgrave Macmillan in the US is a division of St Martin's Press LLC, 175 Fifth Avenue, New York, NY 10010.

Palgrave Macmillan is the global academic imprint of the above companies and has companies and representatives throughout the world.

Palgrave® and Macmillan® are registered trademarks in the United States, the United Kingdom, Europe and other countries.

ISBN: 978–0–230–25148–9 hardback
ISBN: 978–0–230–25149–6 paperback

This book is printed on paper suitable for recycling and made from fully managed and sustained forest sources. Logging, pulping and manufacturing processes are expected to conform to the environmental regulations of the country of origin.

A catalogue record for this book is available from the British Library.

Library of Congress Cataloging-in-Publication Data

Vaizey, Hester, 1981–
    Surviving Hitler's war : family life in Germany, 1939–48 / Hester Vaizey.
        p. cm.—(Genders and sexualities in history)
    Includes bibliographical references and index.
    ISBN 978–0–230–25148–9 (hbk. : alk. paper)—
    ISBN 978–0–230–25149–6 (pbk. : alk. paper)
        1. Families – Germany – History – 20th century. 2. Sex role –
Germany – History – 20th century. 3. Man-woman relationships –
Germany – History – 20th century. 4. Interpersonal relations –
Germany – History – 20th century. 5. Parent and child – Germany –
History – 20th century. 6. National socialism – Social aspects –
Germany – History. 7. Germany – Social life and customs – 20th century.
8. Germany – Social conditions – 20th century. I. Title.

HQ625.V35 2010
306.850943'09044—dc22   2010011091

10 9 8 7 6 5 4 3 2 1
19 18 17 16 15 14 13 12 11 10

Printed and bound in Great Britain by
CPI Antony Rowe, Chippenham and Eastbourne

In memory of my grandmother, Mary McGlashan,
who nurtured my interest in the past

Contents

List of tables and graphs	ix
List of illustrations	x
Preface	xi
List of abbreviations	xiii

Introduction		1
1.	**Family Life under National Socialism**	**20**
	Destroying the private sphere?	22
	Racial demands	29
	Room for manoeuvre	33
2.	**Staying in Touch**	**36**
	Communication difficulties	36
	On the move	50
	Letter-writing	54
	Radio	60
3.	**Staying in Love**	**62**
	Separation	62
	Material shortages	69
	Endurance	77
4.	**Empowerment or Endurance?**	**93**
	The Hour of the Woman	93
	What remained	98
	Exhaustion	101
	Injured masculinity	113
5.	**Parents and Children**	**123**
	Motherhood on the home front	124
	Fatherhood from afar	131
	Reunion	139
Conclusion		**150**

Appendices	156
Notes	176
Bibliography	212
Index	247

Tables and Graphs

Graphs

3.1 Number of divorces per 1000 inhabitants, in
     West Germany (without West Berlin), Hamburg and
     Berlin, 1946–54   76
4.1 Does the author mention looking forward to reunion?   111
4.2 Physically disabled men with at least 50% reduced
     working capacity, 13 September 1950   119

Tables

4.1 Divorce, 1910–53   100
4.2 'Do you get the impression that German PoWs who
     have been released from Russian captivity since 1949
     still have problems with fitting into normal life today?' 121

Illustrations

2.1   A soldier on the Eastern Front reads a letter from home.
      Source: BA B6–05/A.   58

3.1   A nine-year-old licks cabbage soup from the edge of
      a pot in Berlin. *Source*: Emmy E. Werner, *Through
      the Eyes of Innocents. Children Witness World War II*
      (Oxford, 2000) p.208   73

3.2   A wife portrays the reunion with her husband in
      a picture diary on 20 June 1945. *Source*: DTA Reg.
      Nr. 329/II, Gisela S.   88

4.1   A woman records her sadness at her husband's
      return to the front in a picture diary on 10 April 1944.
      Source: DTA Reg. Nr. 329/II, Gisela S.   105

4.2   Women go to the Friedland arrivals camp to try and
      find out the fates of their husbands from Prisoners of
      War returning from Russia. *Source*: ADW BA/HW   112

4.3   A Prisoner of War returns to Berlin, *circa* 1950.
      Source: *Constanze*, 10 (1950) p.51.   118

5.1   A mother records her son taking his first steps in
      her picture diary on Christmas Day 1944.
      Source: DTA Reg. Nr. 329/II, Gisela S.   133

5.2   A father and daughter meet again at a train station
      after years of wartime separation. *Source*: ADW BA I 1
      Nr. 144/5.   141

Preface

Used to climbing into his mother's bed every morning, a young boy, Rolf, was most put out when one day his father returned home from war and sat on the end of the bed. Perhaps fearful that the close relationship with his mother would be threatened by his father's return, he shouted at his father 'Go away! Go away! Can't you see that this space is taken?' A chance reading of this anecdote got me thinking about the impact of war on family relationships. How did men, women and children in Germany experience wartime separation and postwar reunion? What follows seeks to address this question.

It gives me great pleasure to thank all the people who helped bring this book to fruition. I would like to thank the Arts and Humanities Research Council who supported my doctoral research at Cambridge University and the Alfred Toepfer Stiftung FVS whose generous funding enabled me to turn my PhD into this book. Trips to the archives were also made possible by grants from the German History Society and the Sir John Plumb Memorial Fund.

I owe many thanks to the numerous archivists across Germany whose assistance allowed me to the gather the material for this research. In particular, I should like to mention Gerhard Seitz and the volunteers at the German Diary Archive in Emmendingen, and Thomas Jander at the Field Post Letters Archive in Berlin.

I am thankful for the permission to use some of my research already accepted for publication in *European History Quarterly*, 'Husbands and Wives: An Evaluation of the Emotional Impact of World War Two in Germany', and in the *Journal of Contemporary History*, 'Parents and Children in World War Two Germany: An Inter-Generational Perspective on Wartime Separation'. I am also grateful to the following for granting me permission to quote from material to which they hold the copyright: Das Bundesarchiv Deutschland; Das Archiv des Diakonischen Werkes der EKD, Berlin; Das Deutsches Tagebucharchiv, Emmendingen; Der Allensbach Institut für Demoskopie, Allensbach am Bodensee; Das Statistisches Landesamt, Berlin, Das Statistisches Bundesamt Deutschland, and Emmy Werner. I was unable to trace the copyright holder of picture 8, which I found in the now-folded magazine *Constanze*. To anyone whose copyright I have unwittingly infringed I offer my sincere apologies.

On numerous occasions, input from others has made me think again. Members of the German History Workshop in Cambridge provided an invaluable sounding board for my ideas. Fruitful discussions of my work at the Women's History Group in New York and the Centre for the History of Emotions in Berlin also made me consider the subject from new angles. I would like to thank Christopher Clark, Ute Frevert, Elizabeth Harvey, Mary Nolan and Nick Stargardt, all of whom offered helpful suggestions at various stages of this project. Michelle D'Arcy, Christian Goeschel, Victoria Harris, David Motadel, Tom Neuhaus, Catherine Orme, Astrid Swensen and Elizabeth Wakely also kindly commented on early drafts. Above all, I am hugely indebted to my PhD supervisor, Richard Evans, for whose steadfast support and encouragement I will be forever grateful.

A number of friends took a particular interest in my work. The wise words of Angela Abmeier, Michelle D'Arcy, Catherine Orme, Matilda Smith, Gardner Thompson and Elizabeth Wrangham urged me on when I needed it. Michael Strang and his team at Palgrave have also been extremely supportive of this project.

Throughout this project my partner David Tinnion has been a constant source of wit and wisdom. The bonhomie of my parents and brother too has provided a welcome antidote to the seriousness of the task at hand. Each of the people I have mentioned played an important part in bringing this book together: I am grateful to them all.

Abbreviations

ADW	(*Archiv des Diakonischen Werkes – Innere Mission*, Berlin)
BA	(*Bundesarchiv*, Koblenz)
BDM	(*Bund Deutscher Mädel*, or League of German Girls)
CARE	(Cooperative of American Remittances to Europe)
CRALOG	(Council of Relief Agencies Licensed to Operate in Germany)
DTA	(*Deutsches Tagebucharchiv*, Emmendingen)
DZI	(*Deutsches Zentralinstitut für Soziale Fragen*, Berlin)
HJ	(*Hitler Jugend*, or Hitler Youth)
KA	(*Kempowskiarchiv, Akademie der Kunst*, Berlin)
KdF	(*Kraft durch Freude*, or the Strength Through Joy organization)
KPD	(*Kommunistische Partei Deutschlands* or The Communist Party of Germany)
LAB	(*Landesarchiv*, Berlin)
MKB	(*Museum für Kommunikation*, Berlin)
NSF	(*Nationalsozialistischer Frauenbund* or the German Women's League)
OMGUS	(Office of Military Government, United States)
PoW	(Prisoner of War)
RSHA	(*Reichssicherheitshauptamt* or Reich Security Head Office)
SA	(*Sturmabteilung* or Storm Division)
SD	(*Sicherheitsdienst*, or Security Service)
SED	(*Sozialistische Einheitspartei Deutschlands*, or Socialist Unity Party of Germany)
SPD	(*Sozialdemokratische Partei Deutschlands* or The Social Democratic Party of Germany)
SRS	(Statistical Research Sample)
SS	(*Schutzstaffel* or Nazi Protective Squadron)
StaAH	(*Staatsarchiv*, Hamburg)

Introduction

Looking back on the day that her father left home to join the Army, Elspeth Emmerich remembered pleading with him to stay. She hugged him tightly and listened to her father as he promised that he would be back soon.[1] Elspeth was five when her father left her, her two sisters and her mother in Düsseldorf on 30 November 1939. When the political events of World War Two came hurtling into the private sphere, many families like the Emmerichs were dramatically affected. Throughout the course of the war, 18 million German men left families behind to serve in the Armed Forces.[2] The majority of two-parent families became one-parent families at some stage during the war. This naturally altered the family dynamic within the home. Like Elspeth's mother, many women were forced to take on sole responsibility for the upbringing of their children. Fathers could only attempt to retain their role from a distance. And as the Allied bombing campaigns began in earnest in 1942/43, war became a more immediate and emotional enterprise as the fear of death and the loss of loved ones became an all-round concern. How then, did the external disruptions caused by war affect the family relationships of Germans?

For a variety of reasons, historians have emphasized the crisis of the German family during and after the war. Scholars working in the field have argued that war, by removing husbands for years at a time, strengthened the position of women, reinforced their self-reliance and created a new and independent female type.[3] At the same time, war, it has been claimed, profoundly undermined the structures sustaining German masculinity. Men were not only in many cases physically broken by war and long periods of imprisonment in the Soviet Union, but also psychologically weakened and poorly equipped to return to the routines of peacetime or to cope with the complex demands of a ruined home front in which just surviving called for considerable ingenuity.[4] Many men supposedly returned from the front to find that there was no longer a place for them in the bosom of the families they had left behind.[5] Under these circumstances, many historians have suggested, this period was the 'Hour of the Woman', and thus a crucial moment, not only in the emancipation of women from the structures of patriarchal control, but also in the decline of the nuclear family. The evidence presented in this book questions this portrait. It demonstrates the extraordinary resilience of the nuclear family and the emotional ties that bound its members together, under the extreme pressures of Nazism, war and reconstruction.

How has such a negative picture of 'the German family' at this time emerged? Looking back to Nazi rule, Lisa Pine's *Nazi Family Policy, 1933–1945* examined how National Socialist ideology informed Nazi policies on the family and explored the ways in which the Party tried to imbue families with Nazi values.[6] There can be no doubt that families were extremely important to Nazi leaders intent on physically and psychologically mobilizing the population for war. A whole range of Nazi institutions such as the League of German Girls and the Hitler Youth took children out of the family in the drive to indoctrinate them with the essentials of the Nazi creed. On this basis, some historians have argued that the division between the 'public' and 'private' spheres became blurred.[7] Nazi rule, they contend, amounted to 'an attack on the family' which 'tended to pull the family apart'.[8] By this logic, if 'state policy promoted a submissive family that delivered up its members to the total state', then the outbreak of war could only compound the family's fragility.[9]

This situation, it has been claimed, continued after the war as well. The detention of 11 million German soldiers in enemy Prisoner of War camps after the war meant that many families spent several more years without the father at home. Though most of these men were released by 1948, some German soldiers were held in Soviet camps for over a decade after the war's end.[10] Separated family members had been through quite different but dramatic experiences of the war, and their limited means of communicating these experiences to each other, it has been argued, caused estrangement and difficulty in rebuilding home life together after the war. The resulting historical picture conveys a sense of crisis in the family, with the emphasis on skyrocketing divorce and illegitimacy rates, and irreconcilable adjustments upon reunion.[11] Many studies have accordingly dwelt on the socially disruptive impact of war.[12] Merith Niehuss's *Familie, Frau und Gesellschaft*, which charts variations in marriage, divorce, birth and employment rates between 1945 and 1950, emphasizes the dislocatory effect of war in the private sphere.[13] The quantitative data in Niehuss's study reveals a great deal about the disruptive impact on families of the circumstances in Germany after the war. With the majority of men still away, missing or dead, in the immediate post-war period women outnumbered men at a ratio of seven to one.[14] The higher visibility of females in the workplace and the increased number of households headed by women encouraged the belief that the war had dramatically upset traditional gender roles. As a result, Robert Moeller explains in *Protecting Motherhood*, families, and in particular the role of women, became central to public policy debates. In the wake of defeat, 'the family' was seen as the only possible rock of stability in unstable times. West German family policy intended to reinstate and protect the 'traditional' families, which in turn would provide an essential basis for the general reconstruction of Germany.[15]

The apparent dislocation in established gender roles in the wake of war aroused the attention of so-called 'Second Wave' feminist historians in the 1970s and early 1980s, who set the trend for uncovering the history of women. The oral history project conducted by Margarete Dörr, alongside the projects completed by Eva Schulze and Sibylle Meyer, and the research of Elizabeth Heineman, sought to capture a sense of what women went through during and after the war. Based on a set of oral history interviews with 500 women, Dörr's three volume work *'Wer die Zeit nicht miterlebt hat...' Frauenerfahrungen im Zweiten Weltkrieg und in den Jahren danach,* investigates women's experiences in this era, touching on emotional as well as practical elements of their daily lives.[16] The work of Schulze and Meyer has created two extremely evocative collections of personal material about family life after the war in Berlin. In *Von Liebe Sprach Damals Keine*, they interviewed the husbands and wives from 27 Berlin families, to find out about the typical fates of German families at this time. In *Wie wir das alles geschafft haben*, they talked to 25 women who were 'standing alone' in Berlin at the end of the war, 5 of which are described in great depth in the book. Their research is particularly interested in how wives responded to having more responsibilities and independence while their husbands were away, missing or dead. Elizabeth Heineman's work is preoccupied with the same question. In *What Difference Does a Husband Make?* she argues that most women, regardless of marital status, were 'standing alone' in this period. In these circumstances, she claims, women surprised themselves with their own capabilities.[17] Focusing on female activity and female independence, the research of Heineman, as well as Schulze and

Meyer, emphasizes the so-called 'Hour of the Woman' after the war. This phrase gained common currency with the publication of Christian von Krockow's best-selling book *Stunde der Frauen* (Hour of the Women) in 1988, which he wrote with his sister Libussa Fritz-Krockow, describing her ordeal fleeing Pomerania in 1945.[18] Overall, their research suggests that the experiences of women during and after the Second World War caused conflict in the private sphere post-reunion as women were less willing to defer to their husbands.[19]

The so-called victim discourse which emerged in Germany at the end of the war has also informed our understanding of family life in this period. Germans, it seems, were so preoccupied with their own suffering during and after the war that this sat incongruously with the acts perpetrated by Germans against others. By 'telling stories of the enormity of their own losses' Germans depoliticized their individual experiences and thus were able to side-step accusations of collective guilt.[20] Recent historical research uncovering the suffering of ordinary Germans during the war has further reinforced the victim discourse. Most notably Jörg Friedrich in *Der Brand: Deutschland im Bombenkrieg, 1940–1945* compared German suffering under the Allied air raids as congruous with the violence meted out against the Jews.[21] This was an extremely controversial argument, rejected as hugely distasteful by the academic community and the German population at large. As other historians turned their attention to German suffering, public discussions that had for so long focused on German collective responsibility for the Holocaust broke a taboo by giving voice to the anguish and torment that Germans had experienced in this period.[22] Popular culture in Germany has also played into this narrative, with films like *The Marriage of Maria Braun* (1979), *Germany Pale Mother* (1980) and *The Miracle of Bern* (2003) all focusing on the social fall-out of war in the private sphere. The republication of *Eine Frau in Berlin*, an anonymous diary by a woman living in Berlin in 1945 when the Russians invaded, sold millions of copies in Germany, hitting the best-seller lists for the best part of a year in 2003, and has also enjoyed popularity in the English book market since its translation in 2005.[23] Her account of rape at the hands of Russian soldiers and the subsequent rejection by her partner showed Germans to be as much the victims of the war as its aggressors. All these factors come together to explain the representation of German families as turned to rubble by the war (*Trümmerfamilien*).

Why not accept this picture of the family in crisis? This book suggests that we need answers to new questions before we can assess the strength or otherwise of family relationships in this period. For the Nazi period,

Pine's research showcases Nazi policy intentions rather than their impact. Michelle Mouton's *From Nurturing the Nation to Purifying the Volk* addresses this, demonstrating the disparity between government intentions for the family and the reality of day-to-day life.[24] What follows builds on Pine and Mouton's work, delving deeper into the connection between government action and daily life, with the specific intention of investigating the influence of the Nazi regime on intra-familial relationships. Looking beyond the Nazi era to the reconstitution of the family in war's aftermath, Niehuss's study explains the state of the West German family through statistical trends. But if we want to understand the emotional meaning of such social data for individuals, we need to ask what impact these practical circumstances had on personal relationships within families. Moeller's research deals with the family as an institution, rather than as an ensemble of individuals, and his analysis of the family is based on government actions and debate. What would be interesting to know, however, is what families, but above all women, who were the main targets of these government policies, thought about the situation the government claimed to be addressing. The research by Pine, Mouton, Niehuss and Moeller is extremely important for the family history of this period, demonstrating external factors that influenced family life. This book, by contrast, considers the emotional side of family life by looking at intra-familial relationships. This gives us a rather different picture of the state of the family between 1939 and 1948.

If much of the historiography focuses on political discourse and statistical trends, then the work of Schulze and Meyer and Heineman at least tells us about women's experiences in this period. Why then, should we question the notion of 'The Strong Woman', who they allege, relished the independence thrust upon them by World War Two and its aftermath? Early on in my research I came across women's accounts from this period which seemed to contradict the accepted strong woman narrative. It should come as no surprise that women responded to wartime circumstances in a variety of ways. Yet these women's stories call into question our understanding of how gender relations were shaped by the war. This book revisits the so-called Hour of the Woman, and re-examines the impact of female activity in and after the war on how women viewed established gender roles. Overall then, our current understanding is based either on historical research that does not consider how family members thought and felt, or on a narrative that homogenizes women's experiences to mask a more complex reality, or on the unconscious process by which Germans fashioned themselves as victims at the end of the war. It is thus time for a reassessment.

By studying everyday life in the past we can learn a great deal about the inner workings of family life. Since the late 1980s, advocates of the history of experience, such as Alf Lüdtke, Hans Medick, Lutz Niethammer and Detlev Peukert,[25] have argued that the 'insides' of the 'structures, processes and patterns' of social analysis – 'the daily experiences of people in their concrete life situations' – deserved attention but had previously been left out.[26] This approach is part of a general shift in the historiography away from a focus on structures, to an increased emphasis on experience, in which historians ask after the emotional texture of life for individuals in the past, and historical change and continuity are understood as the outcome of actions by concrete groups and individuals.[27] Structures, historians of experience argued, offered only an abstract sense of day-to-day life in the past, considering neither how actors in the past shaped their own lives nor what they thought and felt. As Konrad Jarausch explains in 'Towards a Social History of Experience',

> *Gesellschaftsgeschichte*'s nominalist abstractions tended to slight individual human beings, since they focused on organizations, trends, or structures as the crucial actors of the past ... This vigorous pursuit of generalization fostered a style of history which portrayed social relations rather mechanically. Every-day historians seek to break out of the armament of theories and analytical concepts in order to get at the so-called 'little people' .... Such a social history of experience promises to uncover the role of individual consciousness in the collective past.[28]

This focus brings the subjective dimension of historical events to the fore.[29] It gives insight 'below, where life is tangible', (*unten, wo das Leben konkret ist*), as Hegel put it.[30]

Sociologists have long recognized the family as 'one of man's most valued possessions'.[31] Historians by contrast, have only latterly come to realize its significance since the rise of social history. 'We have only recently begun to appreciate the overwhelming power of family feelings and ties', observed gender historian Ellen Ross in 1983. To understand the historical parameters of individual's lives, she contended, we need to know more about them as fathers and mothers, sons and daughters, and brothers and sisters.[32] Since the 1960s, prompted by Philippe Ariès' seminal work *Centuries of Childhood*, 'The Family' has been used as a category of analysis in the past.[33] Before this, historians predominantly referred to the family in the context of other institutions or occasionally in terms of changes in customs within society.[34] Aside from biographies, the study of the family remained the domain of sociologists and anthropologists. As Tamara Hareven noted, 'it was symptomatic of historians' general tendency to focus exclusively on public events rather than on private experience, except where biography was concerned...[and] reflected the profession's long-standing indifference to the study of lives of common people in the past and its concentration on elites.'[35] From the very outset, historians of the family have been interested in the relationship between the family and social change. Theorists writing on the family point out that 'the family' as an institution has not been static over the years, but on the whole has reflected its economic circumstances, which have in turn had an impact on relationships within the private sphere.[36] In our quest to better understand how the war influenced family life, the economic circumstances of the period will be important to consider in their effect on family interactions. This book incorporates economic data into the analysis, but looks at them principally in relation to their 'emotional meaning for individuals'.[37]

Historians influenced by post-structuralism have questioned whether we can find out about individuals' thoughts and feelings in the past. Part of the linguistic turn, which took place in the late 1980s and early 1990s, advocates of post-structuralist thought challenged the long-accepted notion of the 'self' as an autonomous and individual entity, arguing instead that the self is in part socially constructed through language and other social influences. This called into question the authority of the subject as a 'free, autonomous author of the text' and therefore cast serious doubt on what ego-documents like letters and diaries could tell us about people's thoughts and feelings in the past.[38] If all experiences are linguistically constructed, critics of social history argued, then testimonies from private sources do not give the historian direct access to the emotions expressed by witnesses. The feminist historian Joan Scott was a particularly ardent supporter of such thinking. In her seminal article 'Gender: A Useful Category of Historical Analysis' (1986), she emphasized the centrality of language in communicating, interpreting and representing gender.[39] Letters and diaries written by women, she argued, could not give us a window into reality in the past, because the contents of these texts were conditioned by the prevailing gender system. On the history of experience, she further argued: 'The evidence of experience...takes meaning as transparent, [and] reproduces rather than contests given ideological systems...The project of making experience visible precludes critical examination of the workings of the ideological system itself.'[40] Like many other so-called 'Second Wave' feminists, Scott had been keen to add women's history or 'Her Story' to the historical narrative. Since women's testimonies from the past were influenced by the male-dominated environments in which they lived, conditioning female attitudes and expectations, Scott and other feminists argued, these documents could not shed light on women's actual experiences. Instead, they contended, women's voices in letters and diaries were revealing mainly in what they could tell us about the prevailing discourses of a particular era.

All of this has had serious implications for how historians approach the discipline. Those interested in emotions in the past, for example, have tackled the subject discursively. Until the 1980s it was widely believed that emotions were psychobiological processes that remained untouched by the social or the cultural.[41] But Peter and Carol Stearns, early contributors to the history of emotions, invented the term 'emotionology' to demonstrate how emotions were classified and recognized within particular cultures.[42] The studies that followed have historicized the development of a particular emotion over time, on the basis that like language, emotions too have a history and are influenced by cultural norms.[43] This book does not historicize one emotion over time, since it is interested in the numerous and varied emotional responses to a particular set of circumstances. It adds to the history of emotions in another sense however, by describing the emotions provoked by war.

Other historians have chosen not to focus on emotion or experience but have instead studied cultural politics and prevailing discourses.[44] Writing about German PoWs returning from Soviet captivity, for example, Frank Biess's *Homecomings* focuses on the reception, treatment and experience of German PoWs returning from Russian captivity. His work shows how the realities of the experience were reported in the public sphere and explains why it was done in this way. As such, *Homecomings* is predominantly interested in how these PoWs were perceived and received, and how their story was manipulated for political purposes, rather than in how they themselves felt. Like Biess's work, this book is concerned with questions of reintegration and adjustment after the war. But while his research is driven by a desire to understand the role played by the prolonged imprisonment of Germans in the East and the visible consequences that followed from this in the subsequent political construction of the two Germanies, this book is interested in returnees' adjustment in terms of what it can tell us about the impact of war on family life.

Discursive representation of the past can be only of limited help if we are looking to learn how individuals experienced daily life in the private sphere. If experiences are purely social and cultural constructs, this leaves no room for individual responses to events. 'Any account of subjectivity where the rational individual constitutes the end-product is at best a partial account', objected Laura Lee Downs, the historian who challenged Joan Scott's arguments in what was one of the most famous and acrimonious historical exchanges of the era.[45] Concurring with Downs, Joanna Bourke argues that removing agency from historical analysis imposes 'an absolute plasticity on the individual'.[46] Lyndal Roper criticizes this approach on similar grounds, arguing that the individual subject cannot be understood as 'a container of discourse'.[47] Individual people recede from centre stage in this mode of analysis, to be replaced by the faceless, nameless and culturally determined masses.[48] Deconstruction, therefore, 'forecloses altogether on the possibility of an authentic, meaningful subjectivity'.[49] How, then, can we gain access to past lives?

Ego-documents like letters and diaries would seem to be an obvious place to start research on the emotional history of the family, yet post-structuralists dismiss such material as discursively constructed texts. In fact, as this book will argue, linguistic representations of the emotions and experiences of ordinary people in Nazi Germany neither simply reproduce Nazi ideology nor preclude us from interrogating such sources. People still have genuine feeling even if these feelings are socially constructed. This book insists on the validity and necessity of trying to access lived experiences in the past, for all the complexities inherent in such an attempt.

These complexities include the interpretation of often difficult source material. Alf Lüdtke notes that regrettably, 'the joys and sufferings, longings and worries of earlier generations have often left little more than a smudged imprint on the material sources that remain'.[50] On this basis, some historians have interviewed people who lived through the war and post-war period to get their account of events. The oral history projects by Ingeborg Bruns, Jürgen Kleindienst and Ulla Roberts have all documented the experiences of children in wartime Germany.[51] These children's testimonies, and the rich personal material about women's experiences, collected in interviews by Dörr, Schulze and Meyer, and Heineman, further add to our understanding of what individual groups went through during and after the war.[52] But oral history is not without its shortcomings. As historians we will never be able to recapture events as they were directly encountered (*Erlebnis*). At best, we will learn how people made sense of such experiences upon reflection (*Erfahrung*).[53] Put another way, emotions are always delivered 'second-hand' because the very act of relaying feeling is different from how the emotion was first felt. With oral history testimonies often collected decades after the event, the difference between experience and memory is particularly marked. This is especially true for the Third Reich, as the changing tone of public discussion undoubtedly influences how people talk about their lives in this period.

This need be no cause for the historian to despair, however, for particularly in immediate sources such as diaries and letters, emotion may be directly expressed through language. Even though written sources might be composed texts, the tone and phraseology of which may be formulaic, 'repeated commonplaces', banal clichés may also convey very real emotions. As Rosenwein argues, in spite of the fact that there are limitations to the genre, and that we will never know how all people felt, through this approach we 'can begin to know how some ... felt or, at least, thought they ought to feel. That is all we can know. But it is quite a lot. How much more do we know about the feelings of the people around us?'[54] This book argues that we can know far more even than this: we can learn not just what people felt they ought to feel, but also how they thought, or remembered, they felt. The act of writing expressed emotions that surely bore some relationship to the ones it recalled. Diaries, for example, did not present sadness as joy, or longing as indifference.[55] Probing individual subjectivity thus remains an achievable and desirable goal.

Since the linguistic turn, historians interested in recovering individual subjectivity have looked for ways to explore what people experience beyond their choice of words.[56] Nicholas Stargardt does this very effectively in *Witnesses of War*, about how German children experienced the Second World War. Through adult eyewitness accounts of children's war games, he argues, we can learn that children were far from passive victims of the war, as is often assumed. Rather, he explains, children actively engaged with the scenarios they found themselves in, incorporating their circumstances into games.[57] By examining the changing division of labour between parents and children during the war, his research further reveals much about the shifting dynamics of relationships in the private sphere.[58] His work shows that studying interactions within the family can be extremely fruitful for showing how emotional dynamics change over time.

What follows considers the interactions between husbands and wives as well as parents and children to give us multiple perspectives on family life at this time. The voices of mothers, fathers, sons and daughters, need to be deployed in conjunction with each other for an overall understanding of the dynamic in the private sphere. As early as 1960, sociologist Ernest Burgess described the family as a 'unit of interacting personalities'.[59] This book places these interacting personalities at the heart of the narrative and focuses on what everyday life was like in the private sphere, both during the war and its aftermath in Germany. In considering the history of the family 'from below', through the interaction between family members themselves, this book recasts the social history of German families in this period in a radical new light.

Looking at correspondence between mothers and children on the home front and fathers at war or later in PoW camps reveals much about the emotional interaction of family members during the war. Indeed between 30 and 40 million letters were exchanged between the Home and the Front during the war. Because telephone connections, particularly over long distances, were often relatively bad, insufficient in quantity or simply not available, letters or cards were the most important source of communication between separated family members. Apart from the very occasional spell of leave from the Front, letters were essentially the only way of keeping in touch.[60] They were thus an important space that people used to express their emotional response to wartime events. Crucially, through such letter-exchanges, we are privy to how families adjusted to living without a father at home for prolonged periods; we can witness the dialogue between men and their families as it unfurls on the page. The letters quoted throughout this book come from private donations held predominantly in three collections: *The Deutsches Tagebucharchiv* in Emmendingen; *the Kempowskiarchiv*, now held in the *Akademie der Kunst* in Berlin, and the *Feldpostbriefarchiv*, housed by the *Museum für Kommunikation* in Berlin. They vividly convey a sense of the atmosphere in which they were written, and build a picture, in the words of contemporaries, of how daily life and relationships within the family were affected by the experience of war.

Until recently historians have been sceptical about how effective letters could be at warding off estrangement. Much has been made of the barriers that censorship presented to keeping in touch.[61] Arguing that the contents of letters were also shaped by a desire on the part of authors to write what the recipient would want to hear, historians have cast doubt on the worth of Field Post Letters (*Feldpostbriefe*), calling sentiments expressed in them 'the product of fantasy'.[62] Only lately have scholars begun to redress this, with important contributions to the field by Martin Humburg, Wolfram Wette, Klaus Latzel, Herta Lange and Benedikt Burkhard.[63] Not only has their work led to a greater recognition of the worth of wartime letters as a source, it has also demonstrated how informative correspondence from this period can be, on topics ranging from attitudes to the Nazi regime to the morale and motivations of soldiers at the Front, from everyday life in wartime to how people made sense of their experiences. Looking at the question of why German soldiers continued to fight on in the East after the situation was clearly hopeless, historians have studied *Feldpostbriefe* to ask what it was that kept these men going. One answer has been ideological conviction;[64] another has been camaraderie among the troops.[65] Here it will be suggested that family ties should be central to understanding the motivations and state of morale of men at the Front, as well as women at home.

Using subjective sources like letters raises the tension between individual and collective experience.[66] In many senses, there was not a 'typical experience' of the war. Indeed one major strength of *Feldpostbriefe* as a source is that they offer a multi-perspective view of the impact of war on the private sphere.[67] Yet even acknowledging the variety of experience, there are certainly some identifiable topics which were regularly discussed in these letters. In almost all letters, subjects covered include letters received and sent, the weather, the well-being of the wife and children or the latest news about the neighbours. Typically, soldiers described the non-violent side to the war. They wrote about their duties, the standard of living-quarters and the standard and quantity of food available; about the soldiers' free time, about the physical demands of long marches, or about illnesses, about homesickness and longing to see relatives and of their hopes for their private and work life for after the war.[68] In a bid to quantify these topics, this book includes a set of statistics created from a sample of husbands' and wives' letters held at the *Feldpostbriefarchiv* in Berlin, with its 60,000 letters from World War Two.[69] These statistics enable us to reconcile individual and general experiences by showing how the content of letters changed over the course of the war.

Throughout the war, wartime letters expressed the longing of separated family members for one another. Photographer Liselotte Orgel-Purper sent the following instructions to her husband, indicative of how keen she was to be reunited with him:

> Take the next air mail stamp, stick it to yourself and address the whole bundle to the photographic reporter Liselotte Purper in Berlin-Schöneberg, Martin-Luther-Strasse 27, at the top of the fourth flight of stairs on the right. One ring should be enough. The enormous parcel will be collected immediately. So, is there any reason to tarry? Come! I'm expecting you![70]

Like Liselotte, numerous letter-writers wrote that their overriding wish was to be reunited with their loved ones. But were relations in the flesh as cordial as they had been via letter? How well did families adjust to reunion after the war? After the war, individuals generally tackled the emotional and practical issues that they faced, rather than bearing witness to them on paper. Trying to gain an insight into the private sphere after the war is thus more difficult as there is not as much contemporary evidence from within the family about day-to-day life at this time. There are however some sources from the period after the war that give us access to the personal experiences of contemporaries. When the post stopped working, many women wrote diaries – quasi unsent letters – to their husbands instead.[71] Writing a diary could be a cathartic process, a way of releasing emotional tension and coping with discontinuity, grief or other traumatic circumstances. Writers poured out their feelings onto the page as an emotional compensation for the toughness of war. For the historian, diaries offer direct access to how contemporaries saw their situation at the time.[72]

Also informative about the inner workings of family life after the war are the sociological studies of German families undertaken by Hilde Thurnwald and Helmut Schelsky.[73] Hilde Thurnwald's study *Gegenwartsprobleme Berliner Familien* is based on information gathered between 1946 and 1947 about 498 Berlin families. Thurnwald believed in the self-healing powers of a newly reinforced traditional value system. Internal family conflicts had to be overcome, in her view, if the successful ethics of 'traditional' middle-class families were to regain their former strength. Helmut Schelsky, often called the father of modern German sociology, looked at 167 so-called '*Schicksalsfamilien*', predominantly from north Germany between 1949 and 1950 in *Wandlungen der Deutschen Familie in der Gegenwart*. Using interviews and eyewitness reports, he charts the structural changes within these families resulting from war. Schelsky keenly pursued the issue of institutional stability in the 'society of collapse' (*Zusammenbruchsgesellschaft*). His results, recorded in his monograph on the family, found that such conditions usually led to an increased importance of and cohesion within families. Through his work on family life, he became interested in the condition of German society after the war in general. He saw the family as a crystallization point for all the social changes that took place following on from the war.[74] With both Thurnwald and Schelsky, it is important to consider their individual motivations. Both sociologists demonstrate a wider resurgence of traditional values in the aftermath of world war, as people tried to put the war firmly behind them. By no means does this render their work unusable, however. Indeed their research provides invaluable data for the period; it merely means that their conclusions regarding the family should be seen within this post-war climate.

Alongside these numerous sociological reports about the state of German families after the war, the *Landesarchiv Berlin* holds 763 eyewitness accounts on the topic 'Berlin after the war', written in 1976 after an advertisement was placed in the *Berliner Morgenpost*. By focusing on the transitional phase from war to peace these accounts show the real impact of conditions after the war on individuals' lives.[75] Some of these accounts were contributed by people who were children at the time. These, alongside children's wartime letters and diaries, as well as Jürgen Kleindienst's edited collections of German children's testimonies about the war and post-war, give us invaluable access to children's voices, to complement the abundant material showing adult responses at this time.[76] Together with the wartime correspondence and women's magazines from the post-war era, these sources allow us to investigate the strengths and weaknesses of family ties during and after the war, from the outbreak of war in 1939 to the return of the majority of German PoWs in 1948.

In looking at the impact of warfare on relationships in the private sphere, the experiences of families in East and West Germany, not to mention any of the combatant countries, certainly have much in common. However the differing priorities of the Western and Soviet powers made, in many senses, for a different experience in the private sphere after the war. Whereas Communist rulers in the East viewed private concerns as obstacles to the realization of socialism, and placed little importance on the family as an emotional support network, the early West German government desperately tried to re-establish and bolster the traditional bourgeois image of the family, viewing the family unit as critical to the reconstruction of West Germany as a whole. There is good reason to believe that the challenges facing German families in the wake of war were greater in the East. As Chapter 4 will show, West governmental efforts to reimpose 'traditional' family structures largely corroborated with popular aspirations for a return to normality, most obviously represented by resuming pre-war gender roles. The Communist government in the East hampered this natural impulse to retreat into the private sphere. Women, regardless of whether they were wives and mothers, were urged into production. This often left them continuing the double burden of employment and domestic duties, since their husbands rarely became more involved with household chores. Other factors too conspired to make circumstances in the East more difficult for families. In contrast to authorities in the Western zones, the Soviets set up no organizations to facilitate the search for missing relatives, with the result that many families were plagued with uncertainty about the fates of their husbands, fathers or brothers. Initially too, the Soviets forbade any contact via letter with relatives in Russian PoW camps, only later on allowing a restricted amount of communication. On top of all this, there were distinct disadvantages to living in the Eastern zone in general. Rape by Russian troops, so often thought only to have occurred in the transition between war and peace in 1945, continued to pose a real threat to German women right up to the founding of the German Democratic Republic on 7 October 1949. Furthermore, while occupation troops in all zones took advantage of their position as victors, Russian occupation troops were particularly and persistently unruly and unpredictable. Thus, though doubtless there were similarities between the emotional reconstruction of families in East and West Germany, the environment in which the private sphere was recreated after the war differed significantly, making it logical to deal with the two sides separately. Donna Harsch's research has recently thoroughly explored the interaction between private sphere and state in Communist East Germany, so the present book confines its attention to West Germany where roughly three-quarters of Germans lived.[77]

This book deals with the nuclear family – a mother, father and children under the age of majority – that would have lived together if the war had not separated it, and, specifically where the post-war era is concerned, it focuses on 'complete' West German families where the father had returned from war. The war had left 3 million German women widowed and 1.25 million children fatherless. But there were also 10,029,000 complete families in the western zones of Germany and the western sectors of Berlin each living under one roof in 1946. Of these families 5,025,000 had children under 14.[78] Since these figures did not include children who were too young to attend school, the number of families that fall into this book's definition is thus certainly higher than 5 million. Given the difficulties of collecting demographic material in the chaotic circumstances of the early post-war years, exact figures are unfortunately not available. Nevertheless, these figures give us an approximation of how many West German families conformed to the chosen definition. Of course there were some types of family that had very particular experiences of the war, such as Jewish families or forced labourer families. However the focus of this research is specifically how *German* families experienced the transition from war to peace.

Before embarking on a study of how separation and reunion affected German families, first, a word on how the average German family looked before Nazism and war intervened. There was, of course, in some senses, no typical German family as there were variations between family life in the town and in the country and differences between middle- and working-class family units. It is possible, however, to make some general points about the structure and emotional dynamics of family life in 1930s Germany. The most common type of set-up was a nuclear family, with a mother and a father and their offspring, all living under one roof. On average, families had two children, though working-class and peasant families tended to have more.[79]

The father stood at the head of the household; his primary task was to be the breadwinner for the family; the mother, by contrast, was in charge of the day-to-day running of the household and care of the children.[80] As a result children tended to build closer relationships with their mothers. For a number of reasons children's relationships with their fathers were more distant: Fathers, who were out at work all day, would often expect to be left in peace on their return home, to allow time to eat, read the newspaper and relax. Some would even spend their evenings in pubs rather than at home. For most men at this time, looking after the children was a task that fell to their wives. In line with their patriarchal position in the home, however, fathers were often charged with punishing their children for bad behaviour. This further contributed to making fathers distant figures of authority to their children.

Broadly speaking, the emotional dynamics within families varied according to their material security. In middle-class families, fathers tended to get more involved in the upbringing of their children, in particular taking an interest in their education, whereas in working-class families, where making ends meet was sometimes a struggle, a father's focus would be on providing for his family materially.[81] In working-class families too, mothers were sometimes forced by economic necessity to work outside the home. This further reduced the time that parents could spend with their children. Before 1933 therefore, though there was not just one family type, the prevailing model was based around firmly established gender roles, whereby the father-figure, as the provider, was engaged in employment outside the home, while the mother-figure, as the nurturer, was responsible for the domestic sphere.

The book opens with a chapter on family life under Nazism prior to the outbreak of war. For the Nazis, intent on physically and psychologically mobilizing its population for war, the family unit was extremely important. A whole range of Nazi organizations such as the League of German Girls and the Hitler Youth took children out of the family in an attempt to inculcate them with the essentials of Nazi dogma. Such measures suggest that the regime exerted a high degree of control over individual behaviour. Investigating the limits of 'total' rule, this chapter considers the power relationship between the regime and the population in the build-up to war. It examines how far the Nazi government was able to reshape the private sphere. And it discusses what impact this had on family cohesion.

The second chapter describes how family members communicated during the lengthy periods of war-enforced separation. After the outbreak of war more and more husbands, fathers and sons were called up to fight and families were forced to replace face-to-face interactions with communication via letter. Far-away soldiers snatched a moment to write home from their often cramped and noisy barracks. And as Allied bombs fell on Germany, women at home penned letters to their husbands and sons from stuffy air-raid shelters. Drawing on detailed eyewitness accounts in the form of diary entries, social worker reports and Allied occupation files, this chapter examines the extent to which families were able to stay in touch with each other during this period of separation. To keep people fighting for their cause, the Nazis knew that it was essential to keep the population in a good mood. Yet paradoxically, though letter-exchanges between loved ones were crucial for maintaining morale, the regime sought to control and limit communication through the heavy censorship of mail. What impact did this have on families trying to keep in touch?

Chapter 3 investigates the emotional realities experienced by couples separated in war. In the early years of war German soldiers came home on leave regularly and casualty figures remained low. In the wake of defeat at Stalingrad, however, Germans began to feel the full effects of the war. For weeks afterwards, page after page in German newspapers was filled with little black crosses, each denoting the death of a soldier. Nazi propaganda could drone on about the enduring commitment to German victory, but as the harsh realities of war became more apparent, support for the Nazi war began to wane. So how did all this affect marital relations? This chapter asks if wartime and post-war circumstances strengthened or weakened emotional bonds within individual marriages.

The question of continuity and change in gender roles from the pre-war to the post-war period is the subject of the fourth chapter. At the end of the war it was women who cleared the debris from the streets of Germany's bomb-damaged cities. When dishevelled and disoriented men returned from war or Prisoner of War camps to a destroyed homeland they had failed to protect, in many ways it appeared as if traditional gender roles had been turned on their head. Men's status had been considerably inflated during the Hitler regime, with the German soldier and fighter at the heart of National Socialist imagery. But Nazi discourse on masculinity did not sit well with defeat. Chapter 4 asks how far women were empowered by their wartime independence from men, and discusses how their experience of independence shaped their experience of reunion with their husbands. It compares contemporary public sphere concerns that the war had dramatically upset traditional gender roles with women's attitudes expressed in letters and diaries at the time.

The final chapter discusses how the relationship between parents and children were affected by war. With fathers away from home, sometimes for as long as a decade, many children grew up without a father being present. This chapter examines how fathers retained an emotional presence in the home during the war in spite of their physical absence. In one correspondence, a son sent his schoolwork to his father, who was very impressed by his son's efforts and frequently answered queries relating to his homework. In another case, a little girl regularly stood in front of her father's photograph at home, talking and gesticulating towards it as if he were really there. This chapter further considers whether war encouraged the erosion of patriarchal models of the family. It also analyses the different experiences of reunion as a family: from the young boy who told his father to go away again to the soldier whose daughter greeted him excitedly and promptly showed off her homework to win his admiration. It is here that we see the importance of the family as a site for reconstruction in war's aftermath.

Looking at the situation of German families 'from below' and focusing on their emotional history raises questions about our current understanding of the war's impact in this sphere. If letters were an effective way to communicate, as recent research has suggested, then surely this boded well for reunion in the flesh? Did estrangement then really pose a big problem for reuniting families? If wives' letters expressed desperate longing for their husbands to return, this would suggest that their wartime experience of independence had not rendered their spouses redundant in a dramatic overturning of traditional gender roles. And what if war had encouraged people to reassess their priorities, and in so doing reinforced the importance of the family? West Germany of the 1950s has often been characterized as a period in which traditional German families were reconstructed and restored. But what if family values had never broken down? If the bonds between family members remained strong in spite of the wartime separation, this raises questions about how the social history of German families in this period has been represented, or rather misrepresented. The accepted picture of the German family in the era of war and reconstruction is thus ripe for revision.

1
Family Life under National Socialism

When war broke out on 1 September 1939, it came as no surprise to ordinary German people. For years prior to its outbreak, Hitler had repeatedly stated that in order for Germans to assume their natural position as world leaders, the nation would need more living space, with access to more agricultural land and natural resources. To this end, the Nazi Party had focused on preparing the nation for war from the moment they came to power in 1933.[1] Germany's defeat in the First World War, the Nazis alleged, was caused by the so-called 'Stab in the Back' by Jews, who had undermined morale on the home front. With this in mind, the Party sought to create a unified nation committed to Germany's success in war. This they set out to achieve in two ways: firstly by mobilizing the minds of the German population to their cause, and secondly by suppressing any independent thoughts or actions that ran counter to the realization of their goals.[2]

The Nazi seizure of power on 30 January 1933 brought significant changes to daily life in Germany. Above all, party leaders were keen to create and enforce national unity. This they did by demanding conformity to newly established Nazi rituals, such as hanging out flags on important days in the Nazi calendar and attending Party parades. The Winter Relief Programme was another of these rituals. Every winter from October to March Nazi officials went knocking from door to door collecting money to pay for Germany's rearmament and Nazi welfare activities. In return donors were given special monthly badges to be displayed on front doors to show that a contribution had been made. The Nazis also invented monthly 'One pot Sundays', *Eintopfsonntage*, which took place during the winter. Families were expected to have only one dish for their Sunday lunch and donate what they had saved to the collectors who came to the door and sometimes even to the kitchen to make sure the ritual was being observed. Observance of these rituals was monitored by the local Party Block Warden and employers. These demonstrations of support contributed to the outward appearance, at the very least, of a national community. Those who failed to conform would be marked down as 'politically unreliable', which could lead to penalties such as promotion blocks, exclusion from welfare or other state benefits, dismissal or worse.[3] And where Nazi Youth Offices discovered that parents held political or religious views which contradicted those of the regime, children could be taken away from their parents and placed in a 'politically reliable' home.[4]

Since unified support was central to Nazi objectives, the Party sought to render opponents powerless to act. Right from the outset the Nazi leadership introduced penalties for failure to tow the Party line. In March 1933 the Decree against Malicious Attacks was brought in against 'whoever purposefully makes or circulates a statement of a factual nature which is untrue or grossly exaggerated or which may seriously harm the welfare of the Reich'.[5] For those who wanted to make a joke at the expense of the regime in public therefore, it was wise to check that the 'air was pure' before proceeding, or one would risk prosecution. In July 1938, for example, a woman was arrested in a café by the Gestapo, because she had been overheard saying 'Mussolini has more political sense in one of his boots than Hitler has in his brain.'[6] That Germans could be prosecuted for what they said in the Nazi special courts certainly extended the feeling that the regime's surveillance was all-pervasive. What counted was not whether or not there really were informers everywhere, but the fact that people thought there were.[7] The widespread belief that every staircase had an informer discouraged individuals from voicing any criticism of the regime. As one factory worker noted in September 1938, 'now one goes into the plant with a heavy heart because one is always afraid of saying a word too many and landing oneself in a spot'.[8] In February 1936 the Gestapo Law was passed which further enabled the Party to silence opposition to its agenda. Through this law, the Gestapo was officially transformed into an independent national agency. According to this law virtually no actions taken by the Gestapo were subject to court review, not even in the event of wrongful arrest. The Gestapo understood its remit to include the correction of acquittals or lenient sentences, and as such it re-arrested those who were acquitted.[9] All of these measures encouraged conformity with the regime.

Not only were new laws created to support the regime's agenda, the principles of a society governed by law were also eroded to allow the government more freedom of action. The principle of 'no penalty without law' had already been violated by the law of 29 March 1933, which authorized prosecution of the Reichstag arsonists on the basis of a law that was passed after the crime was committed. Two years later it was officially stated that anything that violated the 'healthy national spirit' (*gesundes Volksempfinden*) was punishable even if no specific provisions existed that dealt with such violations. The arbitrariness of the leadership was thus made a principle of law.[10] Hitler removed treason cases from the Reich Court and transferred them to a special People's Court, set up on 24 April 1934. It was to deal with political offences speedily and according to National Socialist principles. Judges were expected to be rooted in the *Volk*, which meant being emotionally liberated from desiccated legal procedures. All of these courts adopted one simple rule of thumb, as one newspaper story put it: 'Anyone who offends against the community of the people, must fall!'[11] German citizens were rendered vulnerable and powerless by the Nazi's haphazard and unpredictable application of the law. The costs of opposing the regime could be high and thus many people favoured submitting to Nazi dictates as being the safest option. As a Sopade (Social Democratic Party in Exile) report from Westphalia noted in June 1938, 'wherever one goes one can see that people accept National Socialism as something inevitable... People put up with everything like a fate which they cannot escape.'[12] Such behaviour played into the hands of the regime. With its sights firmly set on territorial expansion, the regime's primary objective was to control the will of the population to this end. All of this meant that there were noticeable changes to daily life in Germany after the Nazis took power.

Destroying the private sphere?

But what did all this mean for families living under Nazi rule? For a government intent on physically and psychologically mobilizing its population for war, the family unit was an extremely important target for its ideology. The legal and less legal measures taken by the regime to encourage conformity suggest that the regime exerted a large amount of control over individual behaviour. But in reality, how far was the Nazi government able to access the private sphere?[13] And what impact did its efforts have on family cohesion?[14] This chapter examines the impact of Nazism on family life between 1933 and 1939 in two ways: first, it shows how the Party tried to undermine family loyalty and privacy to make the regime the ultimate priority; second, it discusses how much people's actions showed commitment or otherwise to Nazi policies.

Many Nazi policies, which affected day-to-day family life, were intended to pave Germany's road to war. As of June 1935, the Reich Labour Service Law made six months of service compulsory for all men aged between 18 and 25. A major motivation for this scheme was the opportunity it would provide to imbue young men with the spirit of National Socialism. After all, these would be the men who would provide the cannon fodder for conflicts in the future. Young men thus had to leave their homes to live in camps and participate in projects such as digging canals and draining marshes.[15] Men were also conscripted into the Army from 1935 onwards. Indeed on the eve of war 2 million men had passed through the *Volk*'s 'school of masculinity'.[16] Also demanding were the implications of the law passed on 25 March 1939, which made membership of the Hitler Youth compulsory. Catching boys and girls from a young age, meetings of the Hitler Youth Movement gave Nazi leaders the occasion to instil the importance of nation and military might in their young protégées.[17] The overall effect of these policies on family life was the amount of time that was demanded of individuals by the Party. Some wives were described as being in a state of 'political widowhood' under Nazi rule: although their husbands were alive, they spent so much time fulfilling the political demands of the Party that they were barely at home at all. And young people, who were required to do labour and military service or attend Hitler Youth camps, also spent long periods of time away from home.[18] A well-known joke at the time was that with the father in the Storm Troopers, the mother a member of the National Socialist Womanhood, a son in the Hitler Youth and a daughter in the League of German Girls, the National Socialist family only crossed paths at the Nuremberg Rally.[19]

But, did the demands of the regime pit family members against each other? The demands of the Party organizations certainly reduced the amount of time families spent together. And this could place family relations under pressure. On the other hand it is not as if the Weimar period had been without its pressures for families either.[20] Furthermore, that children spent time away from home at Hitler Youth camps was not a new concept, for many of its activities were modelled on the long-standing German youth movement, which traditionally involved trips away from home.[21] Given that the Hitler Youth was in many senses very similar to previous youth groups, the fact that young people more often expressed enthusiasm for the activities rather than the ideology, and the fact that so many young people had belonged to youth organizations prior to 1933 (between 5 and 6 million at the start of 1933), this raises the question of whether the introduction of compulsory Hitler Youth membership for youths over ten in March 1939 prompted dramatic change for young people.[22]

For the Thousand Year Reich to be sustainable, the Nazis realized that securing the support of young people would be essential. As such they intended to claim total control of young people's minds, as Hitler's speech in Reichenberg on 4 December 1938 made clear:

> These young people learn nothing else but to think as Germans and to act as Germans; these boys join our organization at the age of ten and get a breath of fresh air for the first time, then, four years later, they move from the *Jungvolk* to the Hitler Youth and ... [then] we take them immediately into the Party, into the Labour Front, into the SA or into the SS.[23]

The Party also sought to influence children in school. A directive issued in January 1934 made it compulsory for schools to educate their pupils 'in the spirit of National Socialism'. Furthermore in every school, non-Nazi literature was removed from libraries and Nazi books were stocked instead.[24] These measures demonstrate that National Socialist policy aimed to gain control over the minds of impressionable German youths.

Yet as with many aspects of Nazi policy, there could be a difference between the government's wishes and the reality of day-to-day life. By 1939 the Hitler Youth encompassed virtually the entirety of German youth, but the extent to which these members were fully enthused is far less certain.[25] To be sure, the regime was keen to trumpet its own successes with propaganda conveying the popularity of its youth movement in a bid to enforce conformity. And some children absorbed and regurgitated the political and racial attitudes of the Party to which they were exposed. However not all young people took on National Socialist ideas enthusiastically. A less well-known scenario is that of the reluctant participant, commonly not athletic, who would have far rather spent his Sunday mornings in bed than in the fresh air. The Hitler Youth was so regimented that as one young person put it 'it was not surprising that some young people began to long for time to spend on their own private pursuits'.[26] Thus a more complex picture emerges in which the claim of the regime about controlling the minds of the youth is brought into question.

Some young people did participate enthusiastically in the Hitler Youth. For many though, it appears that their enthusiasm had far less to do with the regime's ideology, than the fact that the movement gave young people opportunities to do outdoor activities such as camping and playing games in the countryside, just as the youth movements prior to the Nazis had offered.[27] Members recall putting up with the rather tedious ideological lectures, only because the activities were so enjoyable.[28] If young people went along to Hitler Youth meetings for the outdoor activities or the excitement of having and wearing the uniform, it seems unlikely that these motivations would undermine family unity since belonging created no clash of views – the Hitler Youth was just a club. This was particularly the case in the League of German Girls, the equivalent of the Hitler Youth for girls, where the activities themselves were far more the focus than the ideology anyway.[29] In this sense, young people were able to enjoy their involvement with the youth movement without undermining relationships with family members just as they had done with other youth groups in the past. Though some middle-class parents complained about the time their children were forced to spend outside the home in activities organized by Hitler Youth or The League of German Girls, other sectors of society viewed the youth organizations differently: the regime offered exciting activities outside the home, which were especially appealing to children in rural settings who would otherwise have had few opportunities of this kind. In some cases these youth group activities actually took the pressure off mothers and aided family life, particularly in the case of poor families who had lots of children.[30]

Where young people did engage enthusiastically with both the activities and the ideology, this could prompt conflict between the generations where this enthusiasm was not matched by parents. The regime did then prompt ideological disparity within the family in some cases. Renate Finckh was seven when the Nazis came to power in 1933. Writing about her experiences under Nazism, she later recalled how obnoxious she had been when trying to convert a beloved aunt and a respected teacher who made no secret of their hatred of the regime. Finckh wanted desperately to make the people she loved feel and think as she did about her ideals.[31] Some mothers complained that their sons were arrogant, rude and difficult to deal with having been buoyed by a sense of self-importance derived from the 'youth leads youth' principle in the Hitler Youth.[32] But how far was generational conflict in this era a direct result of Nazi attempts to indoctrinate German youth?[33]

Difficult relations between parents and their adolescent offspring in 1930s Germany could well have had as much to do with a commonly problematic phase in the coming of age of teenagers, merely played out in the context of the Third Reich.

What was distinct about life under the Third Reich, however, was that individuals were encouraged to report 'malicious gossip' against the regime. Though the private sphere was difficult to monitor, Nazi officials devised ways to identify opponents to the regime. Denunciations of parents by children were encouraged, not least by school teachers who set essays entitled 'What does your family talk about at home?'[34] as well as urging pupils to speak out against parents who disagreed with the government. When German youths signed up to the values expounded by their Hitler Youth leaders with unreserved, unquestioning enthusiasm and their parents did not, this potentially threatened the balance of power between generations, as young people could wield the threat of 'shopping' or denouncing their parents to the authorities should they deviate from the conformity demanded by the regime.[35] In some senses, parental influence over children was confined to the pre-school years, for once children attended school, the Party could push its agenda very forcefully. On this basis some historians have argued that state intervention hugely decreased the influence of parents over their children.[36]

Nonetheless, we should pause to consider whether the regime did pit parents and children against each other in an ideological struggle. Could the regime undermine family cohesion so easily? Out of fear of denunciation parents might not have shared their political views frankly and openly with their children. But whether parents and children would have talked about such subjects on a day-to-day basis is by no means a certainty. Even under less extreme government, parents pick and choose what is appropriate to talk to their children about. Research on denunciations found that it was predominantly wives from the lower classes of German society who, by reporting on their husbands to the state, took advantage of the possibilities presented by denunciation to shift power relations in the family for personal reasons. Whether or not these denunciations actually undermined family cohesion is questionable as, firstly, in many of these cases, these wives were disgruntled with their husbands anyway, and secondly, because the Gestapo mostly dismissed wives' complaints as petty domestic squabbles. Since most denunciations came from wives who were already unhappy in their marriages, it seems reasonable to question the extent to which fear of denunciation presented problems for relationships within the family. Overall of course, denunciations were not the norm, but rather exceptions to the rule.[37]

Where children had parents who were dead set-against the regime, for example former members of the outlawed Social Democrat and Communist parties, these children might absorb and be at least partially influenced by the values espoused by their parents. The same could be said for children growing up in Catholic households. As the regime tried to undermine Catholicism in Germany, children in Catholic families may well have become aware of the less positive implications of Nazi rule.[38] Adults who had strong religious or political beliefs that were different from National Socialist dogma could thus counteract or dilute the barrage of propaganda with which children were confronted. For children, the environment in which they experience their formative years often informs the values that they espouse in later life. Given that families have a profound impact on each individual's socialization, perhaps the influence of the family home has been underestimated in the light of Nazism.[39]

Sometimes parents and children were united in their opposition to the demands of the regime. In this situation mothers would come up with all sorts of inventive reasons to excuse their children from National Socialist youth activities. As one contemporary explained, 'My mother always tried to send me to The League of German Girls as little as possible. To that end, she would play up the seriousness of a little cough if the leaders came to check on me.'[40] Examples such as this one show that the influence of parents over their children in the context of close and continuous interaction within the family could make the family a powerful 'reservoir of resistance'. And the mother, as guardian of that reservoir, had the potential to create a space apart from the public arena.[41] In fact, contrary to the perception that individuals were powerless against the regime's insistence on conformity, there were many ways in which families could circumvent Nazi control. The regime tried to align the private sphere with the Party's priorities by offering advice and material assistance to families. But families who opposed the Nazi Party could simply choose not to take up these offers, and in so doing avoid the attention and scrutiny that being in the public eye would have entailed. Where there were alternatives to the programmes offered by the regime, families could choose these instead. They could, for example, send their children to nurseries run by local churches or even opt to keep their children at home, as a way of evading Nazi kindergartens. Similarly, women could go to clinics run by the church as opposed to those run by the National Socialist Womanhood. There were thus ways to steer clear of the government's efforts to control the private sphere.[42]

So were parents really rendered superfluous and without influence under the pre-war regime? That the Nazi Party was so keen to infiltrate the private sphere is indicative of the fact that the family represented a refuge from governmental influence. But in spite of the Party's efforts to enforce total conformity to the regime, there remained nonetheless 'islands of separateness' under National Socialism.[43] Though the Party had visions of the ideal German families that would make up its population, in reality variable enforcement of Nazi policy at a local level undermined this. Indeed, the successful mobilization or otherwise of ordinary Germans was very much conditioned by the prevailing values within a particular milieu, and whether these values were compatible with Nazism. Some doctors and lawyers, for example, continued to make decisions on the basis of their own views or according to what was best for the particular area.[44] All of this suggests that a 'popular opinion' independent of the government propaganda machine continued to exist during the Third Reich.[45] There were thus havens from National Socialism that existed despite the government's attempts at total control.

National Socialist policy made the family a priority as Nazi leaders realized it was a serious obstacle to gaining control of the *Volk*. Since the Party aimed at conformity, it sought to infiltrate families with the Party's ideas. As Hans Franck, the Reich Commissar for Justice explained to a Family Law Committee in December 1935, families were at the heart of Nazi policy: 'There is no area of state policy which does not have its foundations in the realm of the family.'[46] The Nazis therefore definitely intended to have a huge effect on the family.[47] However, the extent to which government policy made real changes to family life is a point of discussion amongst historians.[48] Historians Tim Mason and Detlev Peukert have suggestively argued that in Nazi Germany the home provided men with a refuge from the pressure of the outside world. In their home life men could find a source of stability and emotional comfort, a rest from the struggle for survival in the world outside. The intense political pressure that pervaded daily life in the public sphere in fact encouraged individuals to retreat into the private sphere.[49] Interestingly, the fact that the family could function as a refuge from the outside world was no unique product of Nazism, but rather a more gradual response to rapid urbanization which started in the early 1900s. From this time it was more common for family members to find employment outside the household, and as such the home became what has been termed 'a haven in a heartless world'.[50] From the perspective of the Nazi leadership, though widespread enthusiasm for the regime was its ideal, the retreat of families to the private sphere was crucial to the operation and stability of the regime.[51] The passive consensus of numerous families who got on with their daily lives regardless of changes in the public sphere enables us to better understand how such a regime could come to exist and stay in power.

Racial demands

Ordinary Germans were racial as well as ideological targets of the regime. 'Aryan' families were such a focus of Nazi policy because they were crucial to the flourishing of the Germanic race. In the National Socialist idyll, the private sphere was a space for the nurturing of national pride in Germany's youth, under the careful guidance of a stay-at-home mother. If mothers impressed on their young sons the superiority of Germany to other nations, then, Nazi ideologues believed, these boys would grow into men who were eager to fight for their country. But for all their talk of prioritizing the family to such an end, we must consider how far the National Socialist idyll shaped the daily lives of German families in reality. The immediate concerns of daily life were most likely more pressing than the abstract family scenes epitomizing Germandom that the policy makers had envisioned. Whether political speeches urging mothers to pass on what the Party considered the most important aspects of German culture to their children made mothers act differently is hard to say, though it seems likely that the reality fell short of the National Socialist idyll.[52]

Like so many of its other policies that affected families, Nazi population policy was linked to the regime's desire to quite literally conquer the world. Mothers were the incubators of future soldiers for the nation, and thus the population needed to be large to sustain German losses in combat. In 1934 the Ten Commandments for Choosing a Spouse were introduced, encouraging healthy Aryans to choose a good-blooded spouse with the express intention of producing many children. The Nazi divorce law of 1938 also aimed to facilitate a population rise. One clause stated that 'A marriage party can seek a divorce if the other partner has become infertile after marriage'. Another forbade the divorce of fertile Aryan couples.[53] During the war Heinrich Himmler, *Reichsführer* of the SS, issued statements condoning illegitimacy. Sparking some controversy within Nazi leadership circles, on 28 October 1939 Himmler declared that births outside of marriage were deemed acceptable to increase the population, especially in view of anticipated wartime losses: 'Beyond the limits of bourgeois laws and conventions, which are perhaps necessary in other circumstances, it can be a noble task for German women and girls of good blood to become mothers even outside marriage.' Already in 1935 Himmler had established the *Lebensborn* (meaning 'fountain of life') homes to 'further the number of children in SS families, protect and administer to all mothers of good blood, and care for needy mothers and children of good blood'. Himmler hoped that 100,000 abortions per year could be avoided by providing facilities for unwed mothers.[54]

But the limits of Nazi influence on family life were evident in their efforts to boost the German population. Only 5000 illegitimate children were born in Himmler's *Lebensborn* homes, so their demographic effect was minimal. Overall, illegitimacy rates fell from 10.7 illegitimate children per 100 births in 1933 to 7.7 in 1938 further underlining the limits of Nazi control.[55] Most Germans shared traditional moral values, which received powerful reinforcement from the Christian churches. This meant that although these pro-divorce and pro-illegitimacy policies could potentially have had the effect of massively undermining the family as an institution, it is not actually as if Germans just capitulated to these ideas. Old ideas about family values were fairly firmly entrenched and could not be overridden easily.[56] Symptomatic of this is the fact that the divorce rate rose only very marginally in the pre-war Nazi period from 29.7 divorces per 10,000 existing marriages in 1933 to 38.3 in 1938.[57]

The Party also attempted to encourage married couples to produce more children by offering them financial incentives: Maternity benefits were improved; concessions on railway fares were introduced for large families, and family allowances were brought in. Under the terms of the new National Socialist marriage-loans programme introduced in June 1933, newly weds initially received loans of up to 1000 marks and the birth of each of the first four children converted one quarter of that loan into an outright gift.[58] The Reich Mother's Service, founded in May 1934, introduced measures both to persuade women to have large families by offering them support, and also as a means to influence and regulate German mothers. It ran classes and courses relating to motherhood and the family, dealing with matters such as baby hygiene and household budgeting; centres were set up which could provide material aid, such as beds, clothes and food for children, and childcare provision was made available in some areas during harvest time, to ease the difficulties of balancing work and children. However whilst the regime tried to infiltrate the private sphere with its own ideal of how the family should be, many families were happy to take the benefits the regime provided without buying into the ideology or changing their family size. There was thus a marked distinction between Nazi policy intentions and social reality.[59]

The Nazis' drive to boost the 'Aryan' population met with success, some historians have claimed. Indeed the birth rate did rise in the 1930s.[60] However this increase occurred because of improved employment levels rather than any of the proactive attempts made by the Party to foster a population rise.[61] Furthermore couples living in the Third Reich retained the ability to make their decisions privately about how many children they wanted, irrespective of the regime's wish for the hereditarily healthy to produce many offspring. Though the government tried to restrict access to birth control, it could not actually force Aryan women to have more children. Propaganda sought to persuade women of the benefits of having a large family. The Nazi guidebook for women, for example, tried to appeal to women's sense of duty to the nation: 'Marriage is not merely a private matter, but one which directly affects the fate of a nation at its very roots.'[62] But ultimately such government efforts were limited in what they could achieve. The regime never exerted violence against Aryan women who ignored such appeals because these women were seen as a valuable potential source of future soldiers for the Reich.[63]

All the National Socialist rhetoric about the importance of breeding and of mothers staying at home did not decrease the number of married women who worked, for most did so out of financial necessity rather than a desire to be financially independent. Regardless of the Nazi stance against women's employment, those women who needed to work continued to do so.[64] The regime's difficulties in mobilizing married women into the war effort is further indicative of the limits of Nazism's ability to manipulate families for its own ends. It has often been suggested here that the Nazis were the victims of their own success in convincing women of their 'natural place' within the home. Across Europe at this time, however, it was still a widely held belief that a woman's place was at home. A more likely reason for this difficulty was the lack of incentives for women to volunteer, such as cut allowances for earners, no prospects of a pay rise, and little to spend wages on given that goods were rationed. It was thus far from straightforward for the regime to accomplish either its racial or its ideological objectives.[65]

While 'Aryan' families were able to retain a certain amount of autonomy and privacy within their emotional unit, which could act as a protective shell against the invasive efforts of the Nazi regime, for those who fell outside Nazi categories of acceptability, this protective layer was swept away with the coming of the Third Reich. The war that was so central to Nazi policy aims was about race as well as space. If human life boiled down to the survival of the fittest, Nazi ideologues argued,

Germans were not only competing with other European countries for territory, they were also in a struggle for survival with their racial rivals, the Jews. The way that Jews were treated under the Nazis reflected this strongly held belief that Jewish people were the enemy to German prosperity.[66] Despite National Socialist rhetoric about creating a unified 'national community' (*Volksgemeinschaft*) therefore, its impact was actually pretty divisive.

'The family' had many variants in Nazi Germany. For families who were subject to Nazi persecution on an ideological or racial basis, there can be little doubt that the impact of National Socialist policies was extremely invasive of the private sphere. To be acceptable as a 'national comrade' one was required to be of the correct racial type (Aryan), to be hereditarily healthy, to be socially efficient (*leistungsfähig*), and to be ideologically reliable. If unsatisfactory on any of these counts then one was outside the *Volksgemeinschaft* and subject to the various penalties doled out by the agencies charged with protecting the national community from biological or ideological pollution.[67] While Aryan couples were given incentives to have more children, quite the opposite was true for social and racial 'outcasts'. A few examples suffice to demonstrate that the experience of 'outcasts' differed significantly from those deemed acceptable by the regime. For the hereditarily 'unhealthy', measures ranged from compulsory sterilization (July 1933), to government-enforced 'euthanasia' (September 1939).[68] For Jews, who the Nazis considered racial enemies, not to mention responsible for all the difficulties Germany had suffered following from their defeat in World War I, persecution took innumerable forms, from loss of citizenship (September 1935), exclusion from the welfare system (November 1938), to ghettoization in 'Jewish houses' (also November 1938).[69] All of this led the Jewish academic Victor Klemperer to conclude that 'We shall not live to see the end of the Third Reich'.[70] Unlike many other Jews however, Klemperer did outlive the regime.

For all persecuted groups, the outbreak of war gave new impetus to the Nazis' discriminatory measures. In the case of Jews, the introduction of the compulsory yellow star on 1 September 1941 was quickly followed in October 1941 by the beginning of deportations to the East and their subsequent murder.[71] For homosexuals, who had been watched, registered and arrested in Germany pre-1939, the war also heralded more intensive persecution, as they were herded into concentration camps, penalized with the death penalty for homosexual acts, and increasingly put under pressure to be 'voluntarily' castrated.[72] Gypsies too felt the shift towards more radical wartime persecution: starting in May 1940, they were deported in their thousands to Poland where they perished in ghettos and later were murdered in camps.[73] The experience of daily life under National Socialism was therefore very much conditioned by how the individual was perceived in the Nazi world view. The private lives of those whom the regime termed as 'enemies' were ruthlessly invaded in a bid to control or remove those influences that were seen to be inimical to the Party's goals.

Room for manoeuvre

Historians have engaged in heated debates about the extent to which the National Socialist government was able to infiltrate life in the private sphere.[74] Some have argued that the measures imposed by the authoritarian state constituted an attack on the family, which in turn undermined family cohesion.[75] Did government policy, as one historian has argued, 'promote a submissive family that delivered up its members to the total state'?[76]

Robert Ley, leader of the Labour Front, claimed that 'the only person in Germany who still has a private life is a person who's sleeping'.[77] This chapter has presented a rather more complex picture of the private sphere in pre-war Nazi Germany. It has suggested that in spite of government attempts to intrude on family life, the Aryan family unit lost neither its sense of belonging together nor its emotional intimacy in this period.[78] It appears that in the majority of cases, both parents and children knew what to do to satisfy the regime. Thus meeting the demands of the regime did not necessarily cause problems in the home.[79] People who were not active politically only had to alter their behaviour slightly to avoid reprimands from the regime. As an SPD report from South West Germany in the Spring of 1937 explained, 'The private face shows the sharpest criticism of everything that is going on now: the official one beams with optimism and contentment'.[80] People were careful where and with whom they had certain conversations; they may have joined the Party for easier life or simply to keep their job.

Families were aware of what was acceptable to the regime and what was not and therefore were neither totally blind to the regime's attempted influence, nor did they unquestioningly assimilate Party views. Most were simply content to focus on their own immediate and personal concerns with little attention for much beyond their daily routine. At the beginning of 1938 an underground Social Democrat contact man in Saxony reported: 'Never since the overthrow [of the Weimar Republic] has participation in day-to-day political events been so limited as it is now. It seems to us that the indifference, which has gripped large sections of the population, has become the second pillar supporting the system. For these indifferent groups simply want to get by and know nothing about what is going on around them.'[81] What was it that secured this indifference? For some, it was feelings of powerlessness in the face of seemingly pervasive government control. The acquiescence or indeed the support of others was secured through the improved material situation which coincided with the Nazi's early years in power. The Nazi pledge to provide bread and work appeared to have been fulfilled, providing a sense of security for families that had been painfully absent in the Weimar period, with hyperinflation in the early 1920s and mass unemployment later in the decade.[82] On top of this many women were able to visit the advice centres for mothers to benefit from free medical treatment, or for other types of material help, such as infant clothing and supplies. In this way many families gleaned the material benefits offered by the regime and were able to do so without buying into Party ideology.[83] And as such, it was possible for those families who were not persecuted by the regime to live under pre-war National Socialist rule relatively unaffected or at least unharmed.[84]

Perhaps the ultimate litmus test for determining how successfully the regime had mobilized German families for war was their reaction to its outbreak. Few rejoiced at the news that Germany was at war, in a marked contrast to the outbreak of the First World War where crowds Germans went onto the streets to register their support. On 3 September 1939, the first day of the war, there was, William L. Shirer, an American correspondent in Berlin noted in his diary, 'no excitement, no hurrahs, no cheering, no throwing of flowers, no war fever'. Overall, he concluded, 'everybody [was] against the war'.[85] In Munich, Anna Neuber, a middle-aged woman from a humble background, was one of the many who were far from pleased that Germany was at war. Looking back, she recalled that 'all the women in the neighbourhood ... felt so worried and frightened. And the men who were still at home didn't say much.' Above all, she was 'terrified for my boy George' who had been sent straight to the Front with the infantry.[86] Individuals like Anna were clearly resilient to the barrage of propaganda when it ran counter to their interests. In peacetime, Nazi rule had offered numerous types of material support which benefited families. But being at war stripped away the security and protection of the private sphere.

Overall, the regime wielded enormous power, which could and did change daily life significantly. However, individuals in the private sphere were able to retain their own power and influence in the Third

Reich.[87] Where families were not fully in accordance with the regime it was still possible to keep alternative ideas alive within the home. For as much as the regime tried to woo families with special benefits, it was perfectly possible for families to take advantage of these without needing to show more than the minimal requisite signs of conformity to the regime. Furthermore, in families that were on balance relatively content with the regime, it was even easier to continue with daily life relatively unaffected. The harsh realities of war, when family units were torn apart, would be more difficult to circumnavigate.

2
Staying in Touch

Since Germany had been geared up for war from the mid 1930s and the early war years brought a string of victories, in some respects the early years of war did not bring a massive change to life on the home front. Indeed until the second half of 1941, most Germans remained largely unscathed. Military casualties were still relatively low, living standards had not yet declined drastically and German cities and towns had not yet been extensively bombed. Yet in one crucial sense, individuals were affected by the war right from the outset. As more and more husbands, fathers and sons were called up, families were forced to replace face-to-face interactions with communication via letter. To what extent were families able to stay in touch with each other during this period of separation?

Communication difficulties

Wartime separation made it harder for couples to maintain a healthy marriage. The Nazi Security Service regularly compiled reports about the morale of the German population. Despite the fact that these reports often expressed wishful thinking on behalf of the Nazi authors, even as early as 18 November 1943, one such report admitted the damage to familial relations caused by war:

> Many women are concerned that the stability of their marriages and the mutual understanding with their partners is beginning to suffer from the lengthy war. The separation which, with short breaks, has now been going on for years, the transformation in their circumstances through total war and, in addition, the heavy demands

which are nowadays made on every individual are changing people and filling their lives.[1]

Many authors expressed frustration at the inadequacy of letters as a medium for communication. Some writers complained that there was so much to report that it was difficult to know where to start; others found that it was hard to find the words to describe what they had witnessed or how they felt. Authors from different classes, religions and geographical regions lamented that they could not describe their experiences and feelings in person. Communication via letter was limited in comparison with face-to-face interaction, since factors such as tone of voice, gestures and mime were lacking.[2] A typical experience in these respects was that of Heinrich Böll. Born in Cologne, Böll came from a liberal Catholic pacifist family. He had studied for a German degree at his hometown university, before being drafted into the *Wehrmacht*, where he served in France, Romania, Hungary and the Soviet Union. Writing from Russia on 22 June 1944 to his wife of two years, he explained 'In five years of war there have been loads of perverse occurrences, which I would dearly like to explain to you, but which I won't be able to describe through writing'.[3]

Soldier husbands desperately tried to overcome the dangers of estrangement through separation by asking their wives pleadingly to share more about their lives, and in particular, their feelings. Heinz R. was a First Lieutenant who had been serving in the *Wehrmacht* since the outbreak of war. Born in 1912 to a middle-class Protestant family from Heiligendorf, he had trained to be a curate and had joined the SA before the war began. Writing from Russia on 14 September 1941 to his wife, whom he had married on the eve of war, in August 1939, he exhorted her to describe her inner thoughts to him: 'I would really like to know more about your personal feelings, what makes you tick and what's on your mind.'[4] 'You write absolutely nothing about yourself', wrote midshipman Klaus B. to his wife Suse on 18 July 1943, three years after his call-up in 1940. From a middle-class Protestant family in Bad Segeberg, Klaus B. had studied Law at university and joined the Nazi Party prior to the war. Anxious about his wife who was tending to their children on her own he inquired 'How is your health? Have you got any ailments? Or is everything okay? I very much hope so.'[5] With prolonged periods of time apart, couples who could not put their experiences or feelings into words on paper faced the prospect of estrangement.

Letters were overwhelmingly the sole method of communication between family members separated by war, but the conditions of war could make letter-writing difficult. German soldiers stationed in various theatres of war across the globe faced similar problems. Commonly writing from shared barracks, men were often surrounded by other soldiers. Gerhard Udke, a 32-year-old Private First Class, had been a schoolteacher pre-war. He left behind a wife and five children in Berlin when he was called up to fight. Writing to his wife Dorothea from his station in Poland, he apologized if his letter was difficult to read or did not make much sense, explaining that he was pressing on a suitcase balanced between his knees, with a room full of people talking and making jokes around him. Time constraints were also a factor. Udke explained how there was so little time for writing home, that in order to write his letter, he had had to forgo washing and shaving.[6] As important as maintaining contact with home was, lack of time and tiredness often got in the way of letter-writing. Indeed so much so that one soldier wrote 'all this scribbling is such a hassle now'.

German soldiers, who had been fighting in Russia since 22 June 1941, existed in particularly difficult conditions. Twenty-nine-year-old Heinz R., writing from Russia, described how he was writing outside because the bunker was unlit, but that there were many bombers in the air. The situation of many soldiers fighting in the East was even worse than Heinz R.'s account described. In late December 1941, for example, temperatures dropped to 40 degrees below zero in some places. With inadequate winter clothing, soldiers suffered with frostbite and some even died.[7] In these circumstances, men went for weeks on end without washing or changing their clothes, which led to the proliferation of lice amongst the troops. And yet this was the situation facing soldiers who were trying to keep in touch with their families back home.

Particularly from 1942 onwards, when the Allied bombing campaign on Germany began in earnest, it often seemed to be a choice between writing or sleeping – both for soldiers at the Front and also for those on the home front experiencing the bombing raids.[8] At home, even when there were no air raids, they were always threatening in the frequent alarms, which interrupted both daily and nightly life. In Tübingen, for example, hardly a major Allied target, the sirens rang for the two hundred and fiftieth time on 15 January 1945.[9] As Germans on the home front spent yet another night in air raid shelters, they turned to humour to provide some solace. 'Where would we be now if it wasn't for the *Führer*?' one weary Berliner might ask in the middle of the night. 'In bed' a quiet voice might reply, poking fun at Hitler's failure to shield them from the raids.[10] Indicative of the disruption caused by air raids was a diary entry penned by Mathilde Wolff-Monckeberg, a mother of five from Hamburg:

> The days are now so absurd. With the wailing sound of the air raid warning from the previous night still ringing in your ears, you get up and make a plan of what you want to do – and then the siren goes again...And with that, any peace and quiet comes to an end...The situation in the air is now reported every hour, so one exists with a constant ear out for what's happening on the ether.[11]

As the bombing intensified in 1944/45, townsfolk spent so much time in air raid shelters that people referred to 'bunker life' (*das Bunkerleben*). All of this conspired to make it particularly difficult to maintain regular contact with male relatives at the Front.[12]

Another factor making it difficult for some separated family members to keep in touch was letter-writing. Although adult literacy was universal in Germany by the late nineteenth century, some people were poor or unpractised at writing letters in general. Alongside the circumstantial difficulties created by war, some soldiers may have been unaccustomed to expressing themselves via letter. This was particularly true when it came to writing letters of an emotional kind. Time constraints could put particular pressure on those who were less familiar with letter-writing as a medium. Yet how effectively couples were able to communicate undoubtedly affected the extent to which they were able to hold their marriage together during separation.[13]

It was also difficult to communicate during and after the war because the postal service worked only intermittently. As important as post had become in war, wartime conditions hampered its regularity. Though letters theoretically replaced everyday conversations between couples, there were often weeks between the receipt of letters. This was partly due to the wartime situation, which made it impossible to write, partly due to the fact that letters from the field sometimes went missing, and also sometimes due to the lack of writing materials available. Letter-exchanges were increasingly interrupted as the war intensified. Some post got lost, overwhelmingly from the Front to Germany, often because the recipient lived in parts of the Reich occupied by the enemy or because of the military situation in general. In the areas from which the German Army retreated from 1944, the post offices were either vacated or blown up, so that by the winter of 1944/45 hardly any letters got through, and those that did took between two and four weeks to reach the recipients. The postal service was further worsened by the breakdown of the railway service through bomb damage, added to which fuel for such trains when they were possible was also in short supply.[14] Post to and from the Eastern Front depended on air links as well: shortages of aircraft and fuel also played a part in preventing regular letter-exchanges. From the beginning of 1945, as the area of enemy-occupied territory grew, more and more letters were sent back to the sender, marked with the stamp 'Returned – no postal connection at present' (*Zurück – vorläufig keine Postverbindung*).

As Germany's military situation deteriorated, its postal service became less reliable. More and more people commented on this in their letters.[15] Since the postal connection was so unreliable, many authors numbered their letters so that the recipient would know if he or she had received all the sent letters, or whether some were missing. Other writers sent two copies of each letter, in the hope that at least one would get through.[16] Because post was so intermittent, particularly in the latter years of the war, a real exchange of questions and answers between couples was not always easy. Often to be seen in letters were sentiments like 'I still haven't received any post from you and so I can't answer your questions', as one soldier wrote to his wife.[17] Another solider, commenting on the lack of post that had reached him, wrote that constantly writing letter after letter without receiving a response felt like calling out into an empty room.[18] One 26-year-old staff-sergeant rather poetically wrote that he wished his greetings had wings so that they could reach his wife more quickly.[19] The *Völkisch Beobachter-Feldpost,* a magazine published by the Nazi party newspaper and issued by the German Armed Forces for the entertainment of the troops, made the following joke out of the poor postal connection:

> Everyone received many parcels and letters, except Fritz. One time Fritz also received a parcel and stared at it glumly.
>
> The boss: 'Fritz, nothing again?'
>
> Fritz: 'Actually, yes captain.'
>
> The boss: 'Nothing good in it?'
>
> Fritz: 'I don't know. It says on the outside: Open only at Christmas! And it is only the end of March!!!' [20]

In some extreme circumstances, such as when German troops were being surrounded by the Russian Army at Stalingrad, the postal service was halted altogether.[21] Captain Kurt Orgel, formerly a lawyer from

Rügen, who continued to write during this period, reported to his wife that all his fellow soldiers were mocking him for writing, since there was so small a chance that post would make it back home.[22] The uncertainty about whether one would receive mail, or when one would next find the opportunity to write, certainly increased the importance and meaning of the post that did arrive, as was reflected in letters which both regretted the lack of mail or expressed joy at the received post. For the recipient, receiving news from loved ones offered a moment of respite in the threatening conditions of wartime. A letter brought an end, if only a momentary pause, from the nagging worry and uncertainty.[23] 'The summer went by, the spring went by and then news came from my husband', wrote Gertrud Tenniger, a full-time housewife and mother from Berlin describing the relief and joy she felt on finally hearing from her husband:

> Was he alive? Yes, he was alive! The postwoman hugged me. She was pleased for me. I cried with joy – my husband was alive and in an English prisoner of war camp. He would come back and we would see each other again. The terrible being alone, the nagging worry about my husband...would come to an end![24]

The first sight of the postman brought with it great excitement and the prospect of post. Indeed postmen were often surrounded by people, desperate to receive news from their loved ones. Böll described the anticipation with which all the soldiers gathered to wait for the post to arrive:

> The whole booth is full of soldiers waiting for the postman; he broke down again somewhere on the way today and so he is already an hour overdue; everyone is waiting in great suspense and impatience for the brown potato sacks, in which the most precious things – our letters – are transported.[25]

Conversely it could be depressing to receive no post as Böll explained in a letter to his wife on 12 August 1943: 'There was absolutely no post for anyone today...I found this out in the morning, so the whole afternoon was a write-off, because when the hope of receiving post is removed, what else is there in our wretched existence that might brighten things up?'[26]

Those who were waiting for news from the Front did not know whether relatives were alive or dead. When the post was 'suspended' (*gesperrt*), many people were consumed with anxiety. The failure of an expected letter to arrive could easily make people jump to the wrong conclusions. Parents and wives feared the death, wounding, or imprisonment of their relative; soldiers, and sometimes wives too, inferred the indifference of their spouse to their fate, and sometimes suspected unfaithfulness or a loss of affection.[27] Twenty-four-year-old Corporal Martin M. had worked as a clerk in a Berlin bank pre-war. He wrote reproachfully to his wife from Russia in the following letter:

> It is raining outside. And my mood is just as gloomy as the weather, and it is your fault. Why?... Post arrived again today and only for me was there nothing: All the post that arrived was sent up to the 3rd of July. Did you really write me no letters from June 27th to 2nd July? It certainly appears so. I don't think you care about me anymore. How can you leave me waiting like this?[28]

When people failed to receive post, they sometimes fired off letters to their loved ones accusing them of not caring. This was certainly the case in the following letter to army sergeant Wilhelm T. from his wife Ingeborg in Westfalen:

> Why haven't I had any news from you? You promised me! Have I done something wrong or don't you want to be my partner anymore? Would you have preferred it if I had died in the flames? You only need say if the children and I are too much for you. If this is the case, then I would be grateful if you could help transport me to the hereafter.[29]

Such accusations could fuel hurt and acrimony between couples, as Gerda M.'s response to her husband's allegations shows:

> Do you really think that I am leaving you waiting because I don't care about you? I constantly write to you, explaining that it is very difficult to send post to you out there, and that the fact that knowing you receive so few of my greetings has always made me very sad... So it is not true, my Martin, that I have forgotten you – never accuse me of this again. You are right, even when I have lots of work, I always have a quarter of an hour spare for my dear husband. And I have always managed this, because even if it was a short greeting, at least you would know that I am always thinking of you.[30]

Of course some soldiers were able to be more objective and less accusatory about long gaps between letters. They were aware that when none of their comrades received letters either, their lack of post was a result of the postal system not working properly, rather than being down to a negligent partner.[31]

Deliberate government intervention of the mail further hampered communication during the war. The Nazi government encouraged separated families to stay in touch because contact with loved ones was crucial to the morale of both those at the Front and those at home. But fearful that harsh truths about the war would undermine morale and in turn the war effort, the Nazis also wanted to control what individuals wrote in these letters. From April 1940 the department for Army propaganda issued statements to the troops, which gave strict guidelines on writing letters to and from the Front. Headlines included 'the art of letter-writing'; 'rumours'; 'letters as weapons', and 'if you should receive a worrying letter from home'. As Germany's fortunes in war turned, these guidelines became even more specific, such as 'what should be written in a letter to home'. Addressing letter-writers on the home front, one announcement explained, 'It is a heavy burden for the men who have to read letters full of complaints, which cause them worry, rather than relieving it'.[32] Alongside criticism of the Army and the government, the spreading of rumours and above all, corruption of the army was forbidden. From 1938 it was National Socialist policy to punish such criticism with imprisonment or even the death penalty. Approximately thirty to forty thousand people were prosecuted on this basis. A tenth of these cases were found through the government censorship of mail.[33]

Feldpostbriefe were read randomly by censors and were also subject to chemical testing for invisible ink, before being resealed with an adhesive strip and stamped 'opened by the field letter-screening services' (*Geöffnet Feldpostprüfstelle*).[34] Private letters also had to be composed in a language that the censor could understand. The use of codes of whatever style, letters, numbers, signs, symbols or formulae were forbidden.[35] Incidentally, censorship was not just limited to totalitarian powers in war. The British and US governments also monitored what people wrote during the war, with the upkeep of morale being their primary concern.[36] Censorship was also a matter of security – certain information should not be imparted in letters in case the mail should fall into enemy hands. As a result, soldiers could or should have written only very vaguely about where they were and exactly what they were doing. As one soldier explained in a letter to his wife, 'You would really like to know where we are now, but I am not allowed to tell you via letter. Our letters are not only now screened in random samples by the official Field Post organization, but also by the battalion commander.'[37] But not only were letters censored, from time to time they were also deliberately withheld by the government. Fearing that the truth about the conditions on the Eastern Front would badly damage morale at home and concerned that mail from the East might contain Soviet propaganda, the Reich Security Head Office arranged that all mail from Germans held PoW in Soviet camps should be kept from its intended recipients. By October 1943 it had 7000 such letters. Over the course of the war it withheld an estimated 20,000 letters.[38]

Alongside governmental attempts to control the content of wartime mail, individuals sometimes invoked self-censorship to spare their loved ones the horrible realities of their wartime experience. Some soldiers and their relatives were reticent when it came to expressing their most personal feelings. This was partly an overhang from the days of more formal relationships within German families. People could be reluctant to share feelings and experiences from the most intimate sphere in letters. In this context, it is interesting to note that use of the name of one's partner was sometimes shunned in favour of the less personal 'my dear wife'.[39] An awareness that letters were being read by censors also on occasion stopped people expressing their feelings freely on paper, as some soldiers mentioned. Corporal Hubert S. wrote to his wife that, 'I can always see through your letters how much you care for me. You ask if I still care for you. Oh my dear girl, you know that to be true, but I just cannot always write my letters so as to convey this, because of the censor. But I do care for you just as much as ever, if not more so.'[40]

For obvious reasons, soldiers' letters only very rarely mention visiting brothels, sexual relations with local women or homosexual experiences. Similarly, the desire to wound oneself so as to be out of action was simply not an issue that soldiers raised in letters to loved ones. But it was not that soldiers did not experience or feel these things. Not including any unregulated activity, the German Army alone opened at least 500 brothels for its soldiers. Furthermore there were approximately 1700 convictions yearly of homosexual activity after 1941 and 10,000 soldiers were punished for self-inflicted wounds – half of them with death.[41]

Soldiers commonly wrote selectively of their experiences in combat. However given the variety of places, people and experiences, it is remarkable how similar letters from all different fronts were. In many letters the war is not present at all. Military action was seldom described, and if so, it was very rarely described in great detail – this was partly due to the censor and partly also to avoid facing up to reality. There are hardly any descriptions of wounds, illnesses or freezing – though these do increase during the conflicts at Moscow and Stalingrad. Even when wounds or illnesses are described, they are downplayed as harmless, even when their seriousness is obvious for the reader to see.[42]

What soldiers wrote in letters home often depended on what they felt their families at home would be able to understand, for example, discussions of plans for the house, for work and more generally for the time 'afterwards' (*danach*). Letters also talked of the battle with mud and dirt, with midges, mosquitoes and lice, suffering from cold, boring and unnerving periods of quiet, and the exhaustion from standing on duty. They spoke of hunger and the constant worry about whether letters had found their way between the Front and home – all of which was bound up with the enormous joy that people experienced on receiving post. All these things were very much separate from the immediate realities of war: the struggle with the enemy, the huge casualty figures, the pain and suffering of the wounded.[43] As soldiers they fought against an enemy, yet letters home talked of love and faithfulness with far greater frequency than any expressions of hostility against the enemy or ideological motivations for fighting. These were subjects, which, interestingly, were rarely mentioned in such correspondence.[44] Soldiers generally did not mention either their own action directly or death. Instead, instruments of war such as machine-guns and bombs were presented as the primary actors in the fighting, as if they operated by themselves. And when referring to death, this was normally done obliquely using the impersonal pronoun 'it' to describe people, and instead of talking about death and killing, letters would say that 'it affected, 'it caught' or 'it cost'. In this way, soldiers distanced themselves from their involvement in the killing.[45]

Letters home also tended to try to reassure rather than worry relatives. One soldier recorded his dilemma as to whether to be honest or reassuring when writing home: 'Mummy writes how much she is agonizing over the knowledge of our suffering. Would it be better if I described nothing, but rather sent greetings and news that I was keeping well?'[46] Heinrich Böll, who later became a famous author among the so-called 'Rubble Literature' (*Trümmerliteratur*) group, further described how letters home invariably did not always share the full story of the horrors of war with relatives: 'What does the German soldier write home? That he feels unspeakably happy to be part of this big master plan, which will change the face of Europe. That morale is fabulous, the food tasty and plentiful and the pay captivating. This is what the German soldier writes home.'[47] As one father later explained to his daughter,

> I could not describe to her [his wife] how it was to be lying in a shelter when all of a sudden there's a terrifying rumbling noise and the soldier next to me is killed, his chest ripped open and his beating heart still visible. Or should I have described how we had positioned our guns and took cover behind a barn? And how this one time there was an enormous bang and the soldier next to me had his head blown off by one small quick shot, which had penetrated through the barn.[48]

These factors were rarely mentioned and if they were, then in very diluted form. And this most likely had nothing to do with official rules but rather was based on a more personal judgement of what one should share with those back home and what one should withhold. The level of self-censorship, as well as the subjects covered, also undoubtedly varied according to whom the letter was directed.[49]

Separation was made all the more difficult due to the small amount of leave to which soldiers were entitled. As one soldier joked, in reference to the long gaps between holidays or leave from the Front (*Fronturlaube*), 'Already one week down! Already a week closer to the next holiday!'[50] But as the military situation got worse and men could not be spared from the field, holidays from the Front were frequently cancelled. In this sense, it was a war of two halves: in the first half of the war, soldiers fought short and successful campaigns, which allowed them the possibility of returning home for short periods, but after June 1941, when Germany was fighting war on two fronts, against the Soviet Union in the East and the Western Allies in the West, holidays from the Front became less and less frequent.[51]

In many senses, staying in touch after the war was no easier. Extensive bomb damage, combined with the havoc wreaked by the Allied armies invading on the ground in early 1945, meant that Germany's economic and social infrastructure was all but broken down at the end of the war. These conditions simply exacerbated existing communication difficulties. Gustav Stolper, an Austrian economist, journalist and politician, captured the scene at the end of the war: 'Railroad trains ceased to run, roads were blocked, bridges wrecked, vehicles that could be used for road traffic had largely broken down or disappeared.' He went on to observe further indications that societal order had been turned on its head:

> Since there was no coal, there was no gas or electric light, no food supply. Along with the authorities, civilian order dissolved. Prisons

were opened and along with the innocent political victims, criminal elements escaped, never to be apprehended again. Banks were closed. Since there was no regular employment, normal sources of income dried up. Few factories could afford to continue to pay wages to employees who had nothing to work on. Most plants, even the intact ones, depended on regular payments from a government that had vanished.[52]

With the train, post and telegram services all in chaos, it is no wonder that people complained about the lack of news from their spouses.[53] In the summer of 1945, for example, one wartime wife recorded in her diary the frustration at not having heard from or about her husband: 'The post is still not working! Only this dreadful waiting and waiting. When will we finally be able to learn something about our loved ones? Where on earth is he hiding? Perhaps I'll just give up entirely – Christoph often reproached me for doing that. But I don't think I can stand much more.'[54] Though families tried to retain contact with each other, communication had become nigh on impossible. Helmut B., for example, an 11-year-old child living in Mannheim at the end of the war, later described how he and his mother had no way to contact any of their relatives immediately after the war: 'My mother knew nothing about the whereabouts of my grandparents, her siblings or friends and nothing about where my father was. We had received no word from him since his departure.'[55] Keeping in touch was further hindered by the occupiers who initially requisitioned all radios, telephones and typewriters. Ursula von Kardorff, a 34-year-old journalist from Berlin described the resulting isolation in her diary on 5 June 1945: 'The days pass monotonously. Everything that goes on around us seems so dim and nebulous that one hardly feels that one is really experiencing it. No letters, no telephone, no news.'[56] In these conditions, it is no wonder that one contemporary said she may as well have been living on the moon, given how little communication with her family was possible.[57]

Further complicating communication between spouses was the fact that 11 million German soldiers were held in English, French, American and Soviet PoW camps at the end of the war.[58] Most couples had already been apart for several years during the war, so the detainment of these troops further prolonged the period of separation. Writing from a French camp in Toulon, 39-year-old husband and father Eugen N. expressed how he yearned to communicate with his wife face-to-face: 'I would be happy if I didn't need to write to you anymore but could rather hold you in my arms and say everything to you face-to-face.' Further inhibiting communication between couples were the difficult conditions in these camps. Eugen apologized if his PoW camp experience made him seem cold in his letters: 'If you don't like my letters as much as before, it is not entirely my fault. I care about you just as much as before. But think about my situation and you won't be able to imagine what it is like here. So you must be forgiving if my letters appear somewhat colder than they were before.' He felt his emotions to be stunted since he had not expressed affection for such a long time: 'I haven't been with you for such a long time. I can't remember what it is like to hold a woman in my arms.'[59]

The limited number of letters that PoWs were allowed to send (2 letters and 4 postcards per month) further hampered communication between husbands and wives. Prisoners of War frequently complained that they could not keep in touch properly because of this limited communication. Forty-nine-year-old Rolf M. was from a middle-class family in Gotha. A Field Officer in Soviet captivity, he wrote to his wife on 3 September 1954: 'Unfortunately I can't write the children an individual card this year, because the next cards have to go to my parents and Hilde, in order to explain to my parents my opinion about Gerold's visit to them, and to Hilde to offer my condolences for Karl's death.'[60] In a letter dated 7 July 1946, another PoW, 24-year-old Ernst K. from Emmendingen, explained how much he wished he could write more often: 'Irmgard, I'm really sorry that there been this gap in our communication. It is not my fault. I know you will be understanding. Of the two letters I can write every month, sometimes I have to send a letter to my parents too.'[61] Therefore not only did the conditions in these camps make letter-writing more difficult than normal, mail restrictions hampered the regularity of such communication.

Information about Soviet PoWs was particularly limited. Since Russia had not signed the Geneva Convention in 1929, she was not obliged to give the details of German prisoners to the International Red Cross. And Russia did not supply this information voluntarily. This meant that there was a great deal of uncertainty about who had fallen in the East and who had been taken Prisoner of War.[62] Twenty-three-year-old Beate K., a working-class housewife and mother of one from Königsberg, had not heard from her husband since January 1945. In a letter dated 16 August 1945, she explained how her worry concerning the ongoing lack of news from her husband had been fuelled by rumours about the treatment of Prisoners of War in Soviet hands:

> Gusti, where are you? Are you suffering from hunger or cold in your prisoner of war camp? Perhaps they've made you ill? I have already

heard such horrible things about the Russian area – I'd rather not think about what might be happening to you. They shouldn't do anything to you. They must finally let you come home to me.[63]

Her letter even went on to confess that she was jealous of other wives who had got their husbands back and wished that her husband had come back instead of them. A woman interviewed for *Sie*, Berlin's largest women's magazine, in April 1946 expressed similar feelings of frustration with this uncertainty: 'My husband is in captivity as a PoW. People say that the prisoners are now allowed to write. But I haven't heard anything from him. If only I knew whether he was alive or whether he is at rest forever.' The reporter further added 'You can read this uncertainty about life or death in the shadows in their eyes – this uncertainty about whether people are waiting for news of life or of death can be seen in so many people's eyes.'[64] For waiting wives the worry about their husbands never let up. One wife reported that 'The uncertainty gnaws at the heart like hunger gnaws at the stomach'.[65] Helmut B. from Mannheim later recalled how the first Christmas after the war was completely overshadowed by the fact that so many families were still waiting for the return of the men:

> Our host and her remaining children hoped for a message or a sign of life from her missing son Peter. Herrman Repelowsky hoped for a message which would give him information about the fate of his family who had fled from Danzig. We hoped for the imminent return of our father. The difficulties of the time weighed upon us all. There was an atmosphere of quiet melancholy throughout the evening.[66]

The uncertainty regarding the whereabouts and well-being of relatives could thus be very wearing for families after the war.

As some men got sent home from PoW camps, information trickled back to families who were still waiting.[67] Even so, a *Brigitte* reporter talked to a woman at Friedland pre-release camp in 1955, who was still waiting and hoping for news of her husband:

> She stands there day and night long amid the stream of returnees with her 'search placard'. Thousands go past her. The dearly longed for sentence 'I know something about your husband' never comes...'My husband isn't coming back' she says. 'He's not alive anymore, I know that'. The pale, slender woman has never received an official notification, and thus she can never achieve closure on her first life. Every time soldiers arrive at Friedland, she simply has to be there. She will

wait until the last transport arrives ... And then? What happens then? 'It is very simple,' she says quietly, 'either I will know by then, or I'll continue to wait.'[68]

This waiting was really only brought to an end in January 1956, when the last remaining Soviet Prisoners of War were released.

Husbands were often in a similar state of uncertainty about the fate of their wives. Whereas women could find out news about their husbands from men who returned earlier, men commonly had to wait for the post to be up and running before they heard the news. In PoW camps men often had little idea of how long they would be held and consequently when they could resume family life once more. As one man confessed in his diary on 1 August 1945, 'We hear nothing about transportation. Nerviness increases everyday with this terrible waiting.'[69] Given the considerable hardships facing both those men in PoW camp and those women at home after the war, prolonged uncertainty about the well-being of a spouse was an emotional burden to bear. As frustrating as communication by letter could be, a complete absence of communication between couples meant that neither partner could be reassured about the feelings of the other and in no way could their relationship be kept alive in the present.

As we have seen, letters came to be of great importance to separated couples. They were the principal way in which husbands and wives could stay in touch with each other. Many of the circumstances caused by war and its aftermath, be it stressed, worried or rushed individuals, the haphazard delivery of mail, or the restricted number of letters PoWs could write, made this medium far from unproblematic as the sole means of communication at this time.

On the move

Another practical obstacle to families trying to stay in touch was the fact that Germany was a country 'on the move' at the end of the war. Twelve million ethnic German 'expellees' were forced to leave their homes in Czechoslovakia, Hungary, Romania and other Southern European states because they lived on land that had been granted to Russia and Poland as part of the Yalta and Potsdam conferences in 1945.[70] A further group, numbered at 1.3 million, were the so-called 'Eastern zone refugees', who had fled the Russian-occupied Zone of Germany for personal or political reasons. There were also 10 million refugees from bombed out towns. On top of these three groups, there were also a further 325,000 homeless people in West Germany, a group that was made up of those left behind from the foreign forced labourers drafted in by the Nazis, and of course, Jews.[71]

After the war many people were trying to locate relatives with whom they had lost touch due to the unreliable postal service and the fact that huge numbers were on the move in the transition from war to post-war. No wonder then that every fourth German was searching for news of someone else in the immediate aftermath of the war.[72] Searching for relatives became part of everyday life after the war. This was particularly the case during the time that the post did not work. Since postal connections could take a long time, many people went to train stations whenever a train with returning PoWs was expected. Numerous pictures at the time show women holding placards saying 'Who knows this soldier?'[73] Furthermore, many men returning from PoW camp did not know where to look for their families. Not infrequently their relatives were refugees themselves, had been expelled from their homes, or even lived in Polish or Russian-occupied territories.[74]

Both the Protestant and Catholic churches and many other large societal organizations got involved in searching for missing people. The most famous of these was the German Red Cross Search Service in Munich. It worked together with the German Society for the Care of War Graves (*Volksbund Deutsche Kriegsgräberfürsorge*) and the German Search Service of the former Army Information Office (*Wehrmachtauskunftsstelle*), which had housed all the rules relating to human rights in war and the rights of relatives of deceased soldiers, as well as information about enemy PoW camps in Germany. The different search services gave individuals hope that they would be reunited with their loved ones at some point in the future.[75] In December 1946 the Missing Persons Bureau reported that in October and November of that year it received an average of 250 inquiries per day initiated by civilians and former PoWs. As of 1 January 1947, its cumulative totals showed 351,897 inquiries received, 191,881 inquiries answered by mail, 21,327 persons interviewed; 506,102 cards filed, and 7393 persons found.[76]

Symptomatic of the chaos caused by war is the case of husband and wife Erich and Anna Modrzinski, who lost touch with each other after Anna and her children fled Gut Zippnow towards the end of the war. Only in 1951 by complete coincidence when a man mentioned that he knew someone who shared her last name, did they discover that for years they had been living only 6 kilometres apart from each other.[77] Also indicative of the confusion caused by the war was one newspaper headline which read '500 who were declared dead have come back to life!', referring to the fact that 500 men and women who had been declared officially dead in wartime actually returned home to West Germany.[78] In one particular case of mistaken identity, a man found his own tombstone after the war when he went to the cemetery to pay his respects to a former comrade – a mistake that had been made since some of his possessions had been found by his friend's body.[79] Gaining reliable information about the fates of friends and relatives was thus far from easy. The path to reunion was often long and emotional, riddled with uncertainty.

Many children were lost in the chaos of the bombing and the mass population movements of refugees and expellees at the end of the war. At the very least 300,000 children were separated from their parents in this period. And an estimated 10,000 children roamed alone after the war, surviving by begging and stealing.[80] The Red Cross Child Search Service (*Kindersuchdienst*) in Hamburg received approximately 300,000 inquiries at this time, half of which related to children who had been born between 1940 and 1945. Many of these children did not know their own name, could not talk and had no official papers with them. For children who fell into this category, the Red Cross created its own file for each child, known as a 'wanted' file, (*Steckbrief*), in which the age, height, weight, hair and eye colour were recorded alongside other distinguishing features such as clothing, toys and where the child was found. Where they could talk, children were asked about their memories of siblings, pets and of their home. These files were used to narrow down the searches of parents for their children.

Similar problems faced the International Refugee Organization. Nearly a quarter of the displaced persons in their care were under 17 years of age, with the majority of them being under five. They too had difficulties identifying young children, particularly those brought in with no papers. Difficult cases were passed on to the International Tracing Service. Requisitioned German documents and police records were examined, and the services of German local authorities, welfare workers and heads of institutions for children were called upon to help. The spectacular success story of one little boy stands out. The Tracing Service had three pieces of information about him: that his father called him 'Chou-chou', that he spoke French and that he had a gold tooth. By checking his details against those of all the French-speaking parents looking for boys of his age, 'Chou-chou' was reunited with his parents. This was far from the norm, however. Four thousand and thirty children who were receiving care and maintenance as displaced persons in the western zones of Germany were still unidentified in July 1948.

A contemporary report from 1951 recorded that 'the number of boys and girls who can tell all about themselves and their families and where they are from, yet for whom no living relative can be traced, is tragically large'.[81]

Initiatives to help reunite missing children with their families included the *Kinder-Bildplakat*. Started in February 1946, it was a poster showing the faces of 20 girls and 20 boys, which was hung in social service offices, hospitals, rectories, in stations and in all search service centres. A year after this initiative, half of the children shown on the poster had been reunited with their parents. This success prompted the Hamburg Red Cross to bring out more *Kinder-Bildplakaten*. Despite these successes, the search services faced some pretty serious obstacles, in that many people had been forced by the war to move away from their former homes, making the reunion of estranged relatives particularly difficult.[82] In the ten years following the war the Red Cross *Kindersuchdienst* reunited 95,800 children with their parents or close relatives. But a further 7000 children still had not located their parents in 1955.[83]

Some children had been orphaned as a result of the war. Estimates vary between 30,000 and 50,000.[84] These children could obviously not be reunited with their parents. The Youth Authorities received 8000 applications for adoptions between 1955 and 1960, but in the majority of cases, orphans were placed in care homes.[85] And just as lost children could sometimes not find their parents because they were no longer alive, searching parents could face the same problem. This was particularly the case for Jewish parents, because in 90 per cent of such cases recorded by the International Tracing Service, the Jewish children were known to be dead.[86]

Alongside the stream of refugees and expellees 'on the move', thousands of German soldiers were trying to return home from war or captivity. After months if not years of communication with their families only by letter, these men were often nervous about reunion. 'When I think of arriving back home I feel trepidation and joy at the same time', wrote one released PoW in his diary on the journey home in March 1946. He continued to record his emotional experience:

> Fear of the shock of reunion. I don't know how it will be or how we will endure it. These were all processes which we hadn't thought of when we were in the camp. It is all much harder... I have ill-definable feelings of worry in my heart: What will I come across at home? What kind of surprises are waiting? Who is still alive?... Exhausted and breathless I stood in front of our iron garden gate.[87]

Wilhelm B., returning in September 1947 recorded similar feelings of nervousness: 'On the way home all sorts of thoughts ran through my head. Among them, was the fact that I hadn't seen my wife for nearly four years. I had also not yet seen my daughter.'[88] Returning was particularly worrying and stressful for those men who had not heard from their wives in a long time – they had no idea whether they would find their families alive.[89]

Waiting for returning men was also emotionally tense. The excitement and anticipation regarding the return of a husband from Prisoner of War camp could be intense, as one waiting wife noted in her diary on 3 July 1945:

> I can barely describe the nervous state that I've been waiting in since Saturday evening. Every car horn, every banging door, every bicycle bell, even the tiniest noise outside the door, every male voice or cough, makes my heart race at the thought that Christoph has come home at last.[90]

Twenty-nine-year-old Charlotte Reck from Jüterbog had been married for nearly two years when the war came to an end. She described existing in a constant state of anxiety and hope regarding her husband's potential return: 'I waited. I slept very lightly, thinking every noise could be him. If I went anywhere I would always leave a note to say when I would be back, I was determined to be there for that moment when, at long last, he would come back.'[91] Like Charlotte Reck, many women left notes when they went out, just in case their husband returned in their absence. After long periods of time apart, it is hardly surprising that the prospect of reunion was a nerve-wracking one. Spouses had become unfamiliar with each other and had no control over what they would find upon reunion. Uncertainty about how things would turn out when the couple were reunited commonly concerned both partners.

Letter-writing

Many factors stood in the way of separated family members who were trying to keep in touch. But censorship, for example, could not be all-pervasive since so many letters were sent daily.[92] Indeed more critical post got through than the existence of censorship would suggest. The hopeless military situation and the catastrophic living conditions were aspects of the wartime reality that were frequently mentioned in a number of letters, which openly talked of the exhaustion and low morale of the troops. Letters with forbidden content were occasionally treated with leniency, whereby the censor merely made the handwriting illegible. This was particularly the case with so-called 'farewell letters', (*Abschiedsbriefe*), sent from the increasingly hopeless military situation in Stalingrad, which were reportedly dealt with 'very generously by the censors'.[93]

It was also possible to circumvent censorship. Letters between family members used cover names. A dash at the end of a sentence conveyed that the author meant the opposite to what was written. Censors were also not able to detect or interpret in-jokes or private codes. More evasive hints were those such as Heinz Heppermann used in letters to his wife in which he would vaguely write 'I must explain this to you sometime later.'[94] In one case an Army officer from Berlin described how his wife cleverly wrote uncensored letters to him hidden inside the tooth-powder she sent him:

> My wife had a better idea. She cut loo paper into long strips, wrote on them with a feather pen, rolled the strips up together tightly and hid them in a bottle of toothpaste powder, which was filled right to the top. Then she carefully attached the aluminium cap and screwed the lid on top. One day when I was cleaning my teeth I came across this strange item in the bottle. To my amazement I found this long uncensored letter. Until I came home, this system worked a few times and meant that I was fully in the picture as to what was happening at home, both in my private life and more generally.'[95]

Censorship could also be avoided by giving mail to soldiers going home on leave.[96]

No doubt letter-writers did tailor their accounts of daily life from time to time according to what would be palatable for the recipient. Yet it is not as if spouses at the time were unaware of this possibility.[97] As Hans Georg T., a former judicial officer from Schwerin, serving in his third year as a Lieutenant, wrote to his wife, 'I am particularly pleased to hear that you are all well. I don't want to think that you are writing that just to reassure me.'[98] Indeed husbands like Fritz S., a former university professor from Würzburg, often exhorted their wives to write honestly about their day to day lives: 'I don't want you to conceal any of your worries from me. I will also withhold nothing.'[99] Upbeat accounts from bomb-destroyed cities or retreating regiments thus did not necessarily pull wool over the eyes of recipients.

Whilst some letters to and from the Front sometimes reflected a picture of what the author wanted the recipient to see, even if this was far from the reality, not all authors gave their letters a rose-tinted spin.

Josefa S., a housewife from Telgte, explained how she thought of leaving out bomb-raid descriptions in her letters, but that this was integral to her daily life: 'I often mean to leave out the word "Alarm" from my letters, but our day's work and our nights are so intertwined with the unrest caused by the raids, that I just can't leave it out.'[100] Equally one husband, Heinz R., who had been in the army as a lieutenant since 1939, found it impossible to write to his wife without sharing some of the realities of his experience with her: 'My dear, now I've described far too much to you about the war. Perhaps this isn't right, but I am such that I can only write you an accurate report of my experiences.'[101] Fear of defying the censorship rules certainly appears to have decreased as the war dragged on. This certainly comes across in Bruno's letter to his wife from Stalingrad:

> Everything is senseless and futile. When and how will deliverance from this take place? Maybe by death from a bomb or grenade? Perhaps through sickness or infirmity? All these questions nag at us without abating. On top of this is the constant longing for home, so much so that homesickness is becoming an illness. How can a person cope with this all? My loved ones, I shouldn't be writing all this to you, but my sense of humour escapes me – laughter is totally a thing of the past. We're all just bundles of quivering nerves. The heart and the brain are seriously overstrained and we shake all over as if in a fever. If I'm hauled before a war court for writing this letter and subsequently shot, it would be a relief.[102]

In the final stages of Stalingrad, men like Bruno knew that defeat in Russia had become unavoidable. Soldiers who feared that their number was up wrote farewell letters to their families giving their honest opinions of the situation. 'I was horrified when I saw the map' wrote one man. 'We're quite alone', he went on, 'without any help from outside. Hitler has left us in the lurch.'[103] Another described how futile the fighting had become: 'We are told that we are fighting this battle for Germany, but only very few of us believe that our senseless sacrifice can be of any avail to the homeland.'[104] It thus becomes clear that many soldiers wrote astoundingly honest letters, expressing their opinions undeterred by the censors.[105]

Overall, though contact between couples was essentially reduced to letter-writing, this was actually a very effective means of communication for many spouses. Some people were exceptionally good at letter-writing and hence were able to convey very vividly to their spouse a sense of their separate experiences. Jochen H. praised his wife Inge for doing just this in her letters:

> I sat on my bed and opened all your letters – I was so happy and relived everything that you've been doing in the first days after our parting, as if you had explained it yourself in person and as if I wasn't far away in Russia, but rather sitting next to you and listening to you. Your writing is so wonderfully animated and comes directly from the heart.[106]

Soldiers gained untold comfort from their wives' letters, as soldier Siegbert Stehmann described in a letter on 28 October 1944: 'Your last two letters were utterly wonderful and spread a warm light in the bunker around me – a feeling that I haven't had for a long time. So much comfort and strength can come from good words. Words are the only things that are left for us.'[107] Sergeant Heppermann, stationed in Russia, explained on 28 November 1941 that a letter from home could soothe the harshest of conditions at the Front:

> I often have the symptoms of something, sometimes a cold, then many headaches or stomach upsets, here and there also a torn ligament; but soldiers mostly don't pay attention to such things! All of this disappears when a letter from home arrives for us, with caring words, words of faithfulness and of affiliation.[108]

One man called his wife's letters 'the nicest and best source of strength'; another explained that on receiving a letter from his wife, 'I was as happy as a small child who had just received a present'. One soldier referred to letters as 'the only gleam of hope'; another to parcels as 'little brown darlings'.[109] Even where men found support from like-minded comrades at the Front, on whom they could rely, and with whom they could form a makeshift family, contact with men's real families back home always remained central to morale.[110]

In many ways, wartime circumstances actually opened up the channels of communication between couples. There was a new intensity and honesty in letters prompted by the threat of death that would not have been expressed, at least not so forcefully, in peacetime. Helma H. from Lötheringen was 25 when the war broke out. Shortly before the birth of her first child she received several such letters from her husband in Russia: 'My dear you! ... I would like to fly towards you; I would like to

Figure 2.1   A soldier on the Eastern Front reads a letter from home

embrace you and cuddle you to my heart's content; I would like to make all the pain and worry around me go away and I would like to soothe your longing. My H, I care about you from the bottom of my heart.' He went on to explain his conviction that the separation had brought them closer emotionally:

> I already feel that enduring all this has increased our love for one another – I even feel that through this separation we've become closer to each other, that our desire to be together has grown, and that the letters, written in so many different moods and places, have played an important role in creating a full, clear picture of each other.[111]

She echoed his confidence in response, adding that because they both valued their relationship highly, it would work: 'You are absolutely right: We don't want to worry or feel depressed. We want to strive to build a good true marriage and to create a happy family.'[112] Hans O., a Corporal stationed in Russia, was also positive in his assessment of how his marriage had been affected by war: 'From all your letters that I have received and read up until now, it seems to me that nothing has changed between us.'[113]

Even if one concedes that emotional intensity in letters was not inevitably transferred to relations in the flesh, where couples had successfully kept their relationship alive on the page they would have had good reason to feel optimistic and committed to working on their marriage post-reunion. The problems with communication by letter during the war can be overly emphasized by making much of the fact that letters could be censored and also be used to reassure loved ones rather than reflecting reality.[114] However, the power of the letter should not be underrated. Many people were able to have frequent and relatively constant communication, which helped enormously with the process of readjustment upon reunion. Couples who had had plenty of communication via letter during their time apart were, at least to a certain extent, informed about what was going on in the life of their partner, and hence the potential for terrible shocks upon reunion was significantly decreased. Therefore, though communication by letter was clearly nowhere near as satisfactory for couples as communication in person, correspondences could be particularly effective at helping to bridge the gap that had been enforced by separation in wartime.

Radio

Radio provided another link between home and the Front in wartime. People tuned in to light music to soothe the pain of separation from relatives. Since only a short war was expected, singers on the radio such as Rudi Schuricke sang songs entitled 'Come back!' or 'You'll be back with me soon'. As the war got more serious songs focused on the link between the Front and home. Lyrics such as 'Brave little soldier's wife' and 'I am waiting for you' were meant to provide consolation. Hits such as 'Near You' served to encourage separated couples to maintain their bond and loyalty to one another. Songs like 'It'll soon be over/It'll end one day', and 'Lili Marlene' were extremely popular and had texts full of anxiety about whether couples would ever see one another again.[115]

> *Lili Marlene* (Selected verses)
>
> Outside the barracks | When we are marching
> By the corner light | In the mud and cold
> I'll always stand | And when my pack
> And wait for you at night | Seems more than I could hold
> We will create a world for two | My love for you
> I'll wait for you | Inures my might
> The whole night through | I'm warm again, my pack is light
> For you Lili Marlene... | It's you Lili Marlene.[116]

On 1 January 1941 approximately 15 million people in Germany had a registered radio set and this did not include the numerous army radios, so millions and millions of people listened to the 'Request Concert', which was by far the most popular wartime radio program. This program was deliberately scheduled late on Sunday afternoons, in order to catch as wide an audience as possible for the mixture of propaganda, entertainment and sentimentality. Radio announcer Heinz Goedecke would take requests from soldiers and relay personal messages in return for donations to charity. Through these live broadcasts, listeners throughout the Reich experienced a sense of connection with those they were separated from. In wartime people had had to learn how to deal with highly emotional events like birth and death suddenly being taken out of their social context by war-related separation. The radio program offered a step towards the necessary support by reconstituting a sense of family and community with their familiar rituals. For example, frontline soldiers first learnt of their child's birth from Goedecke via the ether. In short, the radio was an emotional community-building medium.[117]

Two of the most popular wartime films in Germany, each selling more than 20 million tickets, were *Die Grosse Liebe* and *Wunschkonzert*, both of which dealt with lovers separated by the war. Like all home-front films, *Die Grosse Liebe*, released in 1942, highlighted the bond between civilians and servicemen. It was popular because it dealt with many of the emotional problems created by war, specifically, how people wavered between hope and desperation, dealt with feelings of abandonment, endured loneliness, and successfully adapted to a curtailed domestic life. In the wartime film made about the radio program *Wunschkonzert*, while a children's choir sings the lullaby 'Fall Asleep, My Little Prince', the camera turns to a grandmother in an armchair reading to a little boy and girl, to an elderly woman adorned with the Mothers Cross sewing at the radio, to a soldier who learns he is the father of a baby boy, to his radiant wife holding the child, and finally to a group of soldiers who add their deep voices to establish the nuclear family acoustically. Motion pictures such as this as well as the *Wunschkonzert* itself helped to create a sense of togetherness for German families even during separation. They provided an imaginary bridge between the Front and the home.[118]

Although wartime and post-war circumstances presented many practical obstacles to effective communication between separated family members, for the most part there continued to be ways which allowed people to stay in touch. This was crucial to family cohesion, for as we shall see, the link between home and the Front constituted an important emotional connection for families whose interactions had been confined to letter-exchanges.

3
Staying in Love

'For me it is a necessity to share with you what I think and feel, because I know you completely understand me, which is not something which I can take for granted in my environment here', wrote First Lieutenant Heinz R. to his wife Ursula from Russia two years after his call-up in September 1939. Vouching for the fact that their connection to each other was just as strong in spite of the long separation, he continued 'You yourself will have noticed, that when I have experienced something in particular or something has depressed me, I always send you a really long letter. It is the same for me as it is for you – I have to come to you with anything that deeply affects me.'[1] Yet not all partnerships were as resilient. The circumstances presented by war often made it difficult for couples to stay in love: husbands and wives were ripped apart by the call-up of men, had dramatically different experiences of the war, and often possessed limited means to communicate these to one another.[2] Overall then, how well did marital relationships fare in light of these challenging conditions?

Separation

On 1 December 1940 William L. Shirer wrote that 'there is no popular enthusiasm for the war. There never was.' This was true, yet Germans were able to tolerate the war so long as Germany was winning and their lives were not affected too much. While casualties remained low and those on the home front did not have to tighten their belts significantly, Shirer observed that people across Germany 'approvingly gazed at the maps in which little red pins showed the victorious advance of the German troops'.[3] But morale changed as the tide turned against Germany's fortunes in war. After a string of early victories, German defeats soon began to pile up: the failure to take Moscow in late autumn 1941 was followed by defeat at Stalingrad at the end of January 1943; then the defeat in North Africa and the Allied invasion of Italy in July 1943 soon followed, before the D-Day landings in France in June 1944.[4] On 19 July 1944 Nazi propaganda declared that 'our faith in victory has hardened into unshakeable certainty' but the myth of German invincibility had been shattered by defeat in so many theatres of war.[5] Soldiers' letters from the front only underlined the disparity between government reports and the reality. 'Men are dying like flies' wrote one man in the final stages of Stalingrad. 'No one even takes the trouble to bury them' he went on. 'They are lying all around us, some without arms, legs or eyes and others with their bellies torn open.'[6] More German troops died on the Eastern Front than in any other place during the Second World War. In the days and weeks after the fall of Stalingrad page after page in German newspapers was filled with little black crosses, each denoting the death of a soldier.[7] With these developments the harsh realities of war became all too apparent to Germans at home.

As the war became more serious and life-threatening, this was emotionally draining for couples. A large part of this was the worry derived from uncertainty about the whereabouts and well-being of loved ones. This was particularly the case as the war in the East turned against Germany and the bombing on the home front intensified. A Nazi Security Service report from 20 April 1944 noted that the constant worry about men in the East was taking its toll on the mood of the German population.

> The reports from the south of the Eastern Front and in particular from the Crimea have seriously startled the population...Many people seem to be tired out by the constant pressure, by the worry about the developments in the East, and again and again the dashed hopes of a miracle solution. Above all the women are particularly worried about their relatives at the Front.[8]

Thus even Security Service reports, which had tended to take a rather Panglossian view of events in earlier stages of the war, reported this strain. As the defeat of the Third Reich became increasingly apparent, people joked 'my how time flies! A thousand years have gone by already', making reference to Hitler's talk of a thousand year long Reich.[9] But the reality of these circumstances was no joke for separated families. The deterioration of Germany's military position in Russia hampered communication between home and front, just as families at home were desperate to be reassured that their relatives were alive. On 17 October 1944, Anne K., a 33-year-old housewife and mother of three, learned that her husband had been declared missing. She penned a diary entry on 17 December 1944 which gives an insight into her anxiety: 'If I received a greeting from Daddy [her husband], the sun would shine again for me. Where is my sweetheart? Have the Russians taken him prisoner? Or??? I can't think any further. Hopefully a miracle will happen and I will get a message soon.'[10] With mounting casualties at the Front which no amount of government propaganda could fully conceal, the day-to-day lives of many women like Anne K. were plagued with unease about their men in combat.

The Nazi government was keen to keep up morale among the German population, fearing that poor spirits would be damaging to the war effort. This was far from easy in the face of military disasters and mounting casualties. With the constant worry about men at the Front, alongside increasing difficulties simply negotiating daily life, the government's attempt to rally support for the Nazi war increasingly fell on deaf ears. Women were exhausted and, above all else, they wanted their husbands and sons to return home safe and sound. Flying in the face of reality, the Nazi regime was still intent on victory at all costs. To this end it sought to hush up the growing desire for peace. But as the war wore on, and the population grew wearier, even radical measures which sought to terrorize people into outward support of the war, could not stem the tide of defeatist remarks. No amount of Nazi terror could stop family members being wracked with worry about their relatives, even if such measures made it wiser for people not to express these feelings so freely.[11]

Alongside combat at the Front, Allied air raids at home were also the cause of much worry about the well-being of loved ones. And there was good cause for this worry, for by the end of the war 305,000 Germans had been killed, 780,000 injured and two million made homeless.[12] The attack on Germany by air, which started in earnest with a major raid on Lübeck in northern Germany on the night of 28–29 March 1942, brought the full reality of war into civilian life. Frequent air raid alerts meant that everyone at home, as well as at the Front, was vulnerable to the threat of death through an enemy attack. Authors from the Front were thirsty for details of the air raid attacks. Letters asked after bomb damage; whether the home still stood and whether the recipient, friends and relatives had survived the attacks unscathed. 'Always update me as to what's happening with the bombers; it is a little alarming when we hear swarms humming over us, but we don't know what they are going to destroy in Germany' wrote Heinrich Böll to his family, expressing both curiosity and worry about the bombing. 'I can only hope that the Tommys don't get it in their heads to visit you.'[13]

When the postal service broke down, soldiers were wracked with worry about their families on the home front.[14] One man wrote frustratedly to his wife, 'If we only received post... On top of this comes uncertainty, because we keep hearing on the radio about the bombing of West Germany. Indeed at this very moment everything could be being turned to rubble at home and we know nothing about it.'[15] At least in theory, women were able to send especially quick 'bomb cards', (*Bombenkarten*), also known as 'express messages', (*Eilnachrichten*), to their worrying relatives in the Armed Forces to report that they had survived an air raid.[16] However many soldiers obviously did not receive these, as they wrote home worriedly, anxious for news. In December 1943, Captain Orgel, the dutiful husband we met in Chapter 2, who had continued to write to his wife in spite of the halted postal service, wrote again to his wife Lieselotte from the Eastern Front after hearing of an air raid attack in his home town of Rügen: 'Dearest, how are you? And how are the parents? No, I've had no post today and there won't be any tomorrow. Perhaps the day after tomorrow! I don't taste the food anymore. All I do is think about you. If you were in trouble, I wouldn't be able to help you. No, it shouldn't be like this.'[17] Like Captain Orgel, many soldiers wanted to find out how their families were faring. In light of the bombing of Germany and the intermittent functioning of the postal system, men were plagued by their unanswered questions: How are you all? Have you got enough to eat? Are you being forced to freeze? What else are you missing? Are you well?[18] All of this worry and uncertainty about loved ones conspired to put relationships under strain.

Long separations and intermittent communication gave people time both to doubt their partner's fidelity and also to stray themselves. Soldiers made comments in letters home casting doubt on their wives' fidelity. Authors could be quite blunt when casting such aspersions: 'Were you well-behaved with him?' 24-year-old Private First Class Martin M. asked his wife. 'Do you also have to write to someone else?' asked 33-year-old Heinz R. of the same rank. Twenty-six-year-old Reinhold L. had been a fish farmer in Göttingen before the war broke out. Less than a year after his call-up in August 1939 he expressed anger at the insensitivity and thoughtlessness of his wife's letter whilst he was risking all at the Front: 'My dear, as far as I'm concerned you can do what you like, as long as you are clear with yourself that you are married and that you know where the line is. Are you trying to make me jealous?

You won't have any luck if that is your intention as I have many other things on my mind aside from jealousy.' Further admonishing his wife, he continued 'It would be very sad if I was here, staring death in the eye, and yet I couldn't trust my wife, for whom I lie here, and if I had to wonder "is she being faithful to me?" But I am completely calmed, if I know you as well as I think I do.' First Lieutenant Heinz M. was a former dentist from a middle-class Protestant family in Güstrow. He was alert to the possibility that his wife might go off with another man. Making an oblique reference to the dangers and temptations posed by separation, he ended one letter to his wife as follows: 'In the hope that you will always stay my best sweet little honeybunny.'[19] Full of doubt about their partners' love, such letters suggest that partnerships could be seriously undermined by prolonged separation.

Individuals were understandably hurt by their spouse's lack of faith in them. Gerhard Udke, the Berlin school teacher from Chapter 2 who was hard-pressed to find time to write home, was accused of cheating by his wife Dorothea. Hurt by his wife's accusations, he sought to allay her doubts in a letter on Easter Day 1943:

> Since we've known each other and in particular since I've been in a relationship with you, I have never done anything that I have had to hide from you, or done anything of which I am ashamed. For my part I've often had the feeling that women and respectively girls find me to be likeable. [20]

Like Udke, 25-year-old Gerda M. faced allegations of infidelity from her spouse. On 1 April 1941 she sought to quash her husband's fears, writing 'Don't write to me that you fear you're going to lose me. How can you think such a thing? At the registry office and again in the church I publicly promised to be faithful to you. There's no one else for me in this world.' Spouses in this position were keen to reassure their doubting partners of their continued loyalty. Gerda M.'s correspondence frequently made reference to this, saying things like 'Mummy is very well behaved and only cares for you'.[21] Otto Gasse was also keen to assure his wife that he was not visiting brothels like many of the other men. He explained that his comrades mocked him for going to the cinema instead of seeking out the company of local women and girls. Aware of his wife's suspicions, he wrote 'My dear wife, you can trust me. Although you have already expressed your doubts, I don't touch other women ... I know that at home I have a faithful loving wife and a doting daughter.'[22] Whether such statements should be taken at face value is *uncertain, but what is significant here is that spouses were keen to pay lip-service at the very least to the stability of their relationship, to reassure both their partner and themselves that there would be a strong relationship to return to after the war.

Some people were able to rationalize their jealousy and as such were able to discuss their feelings in letters to their spouse without assuming an accusatory tone. On 4 May 1941, 27-year-old Helma H. received a letter from her husband Günter admitting that he had written only one reply to her recent five letters due to his feelings of jealousy. However in contrast to other authors struggling with such emotions, he emphasized that the fault or irrationality lay with him, not his wife:

> Really I know that all your thoughts are of me, my H.;…It is just a stupid thing, this jealousy – something which I have to battle with from time to time. I never thought that I would have to do so. How nice that you had such a good time in Berlin and that you unexpectedly made some acquaintances, with whom you spent some lovely hours.[23]

Martin M. apologized in a letter to his wife for the irrational worries about her fidelity that he had expressed in a previous letter. He advised his wife not to take his words on this matter to heart, but to understand that it resulted from the depressing situation in Russia, further asking her to dismiss similar jealous comments that he might make in the future as the words of a stranger, which would only be caused by his enormous longing to be reunited with her.[24]

In all likelihood there was a greater level of infidelity by both sexes during the war compared to peacetime.[25] As the war went on, the behaviour of some war wives changed. In view of the separation, isolation, the daily worries and the intensification of the bombing, many sought out human contact and found an escape in dancing and other public events. Here of course women met men and new relationships formed while husbands were away. Sexual relationships also developed between German women and the many young male prisoners of war and foreign workers. This occurred most frequently in the countryside, where prisoners of war were often billeted on the farms where they worked.[26]

The Nazi regime objected to the forming of such relationships on several grounds: firstly, it argued, relations between German women and enemy men were an insult to the nation, and in particular to German soldiers; secondly, the regime had racial objections to these sexual relations, because they believed that any resulting progeny would pollute the Aryan gene-pool with inferior blood; thirdly, they claimed, women's

extra-marital affairs would destabilize the family and in so doing potentially undermine the war effort both at home and at the Front. With this
in mind, propaganda posters were put up in many public places to urge
women to refrain from entering into relations with these foreigners.
And women were threatened with imprisonment for such behaviour.
In spite of all these measures, many women still had extra-marital relations. Indicative of this are illegitimacy figures. In 1945, 20 per cent of
German births were estimated to be illegitimate. This stood in contrast
to illegitimacy rates in 1930 which were 4 per cent of all births.[27]

German soldiers also strayed, visiting both the official brothels set up
by the *Wehrmacht* where they had been stationed, or simply striking up
relations with foreign women whilst on active service.[28] One woman
recounted how on two visits to her soldier husband who was stationed
in Poland during the war, she found him in the arms of a Polish woman.[29] In some cases wartime infidelity led to the breakdown of a marriage, either because the woman had decided to abandon her marriage
for her new relationship or perhaps because the husband returned home
to find his wife with another man's child. How common this was, is difficult to say – but it was not rare. Interestingly though, a series of interviews conducted with women who were wives during this time found
that in conversations about infidelity no wife mentioned her husband
having visited a brothel, and none seemed aware of quite how many
brothels had been set up for men at this time. This would suggest that
male infidelity may well have been less often the cause of marital breakdown in this period.[30] Overall though, infidelity on the part of both
husbands and wives came hand in hand with long separations under
the stressful conditions of wartime. When faced with the close proxim-
ity to death, 'war aphrodisia' set in as people seized the moment and
grabbed what happiness they could find.[31] This did not bode well for
couples as they reunited after the war.

Wartime letters often described future life in colourful prose match-
ing the rose-tinted memories of the past. One soldier wrote, 'One day the
day will come where we'll be able to live in each other's arms forever and
we will be happy and devoted to each other for the rest of our lives.'[32]
Another reassured his girlfriend that 'There will be much better times
when this will all seem like a bad dream'. These positive statements
about the future that were made in *Feldpostbriefe* during the war played
an important function in reassuring spouses and the authors themselves
that there would be a nurturing home life to resume after the war. But
had people idealized their pre-war home life? Were people's memories
of their family life 'the product of fantasy', 'a concrete utopia', which
would then be hard to realize under the circumstances of the immediate

post-war years? Had separated couples in fact built up unrealistic expectations which could only lead to disappointment in reality?[33] A post-war issue of the women's monthly magazine *Das Blatt der Hausfrau* talked of 'the experience of a deep, often unscaleable chasm, between what people expected and then what the reality really was' and how reunion was 'over and over again so "very different" ...!'[34]

After the war, family members often did not meet the unrealistically perfect image that had been formed, as no one had been preserved in a vacuum from the effects of war. Many men felt that they had not found the woman they were expecting – the woman had changed. Many had been aged by war. One man released from Soviet captivity said in 1949, 'I could see one or two traces of the woman I had left behind, but the hardships of living in Berlin after the war had taken their toll. She was no longer the young, cheeky girl that I had dreamt of so often. She looked starved and her skin was grey.'[35] As a governmental report from after the war observed, in cases where couples had married just before or during the war, 'There has been hardly time for the young people to get to know each other. After a long period of separation they often find themselves faced with a complete stranger, not in the least suitable as a partner for life. The delirium of a short honeymoon subsides quickly under the daily grind.' The report further noted that 'Often enough the girl in love failed to see anything of her fiancé's personality when he appeared disguised in the attractive garb of a uniform, and now she looks in vain for the object of her love when [he] returns to her.'[36]

The problem page of *Das Blatt der Hausfrau* offered comforting words to Ilse Marlene who was disappointed by her returning husband: 'We can understand that you are sad about the fact that your fiancé, who has finally returned from Prisoner of War camp and to whom you have remained faithful the whole time, no longer measures up to the image that you had held close to your heart.'[37] Although husbands and wives were glad to be reunited, reunions often brought disappointment with them. Women did not live up to the idealized images that their husbands had created of them; and husbands were often very different from their pre-war selves. In some cases they were wounded, but in nearly all they were exhausted and at least initially not able to provide women with the active support they were expecting.[38]

Material shortages

Alongside the emotional challenges posed by separation and reunion, families also encountered material difficulties. While Nazi officials did not want to undermine the morale of the population by squeezing the consumer economy too hard, by 18 February 1943, with the announcement of 'total war', supplies of food, fuel and clothing became ever more restricted. The situation deteriorated further in the final months of the war, with worse to come in the early post-war years. 'Enjoy the war; the peace will be terrible' was a common phrase at the time, acknowledging the hardship that was to follow defeat. Did 8 May 1945 represent a significant change or 'Zero Hour' between war and peace? The end of the war may have been a psychological caesura. However in material terms, the period between Germany's defeat at Stalingrad on 31 January 1943 and the West German currency reform on 20 June 1948 was one of continuous hardship and difficulty. Only after the currency reform, when shop windows were once again full of a range of consumer goods and enough building materials were available to begin reconstructing homes, was there a sense that daily life could return to normal.[39] The following section focuses on the problems posed by food and housing shortages in this period, examining the implications of the difficulties for family relations.

(i) Food shortages

Short food rations were a factor that loomed large in the day-to-day reality of life in Germany during and after the war. Food rationing began on 28 August 1939. With their obsession about maintaining civilian morale and avoiding a repetition of the collapse of the home front in 1918/19, the Nazis were determined that, in the words of a popular slogan, there should be 'as much normality as possible, as much war as necessary'. With this in mind, Goebbels noted in his diary on 26 February 1942 that 'It's important for the war to keep our people in a good mood. We failed to do that during the [First] World War, and we had to pay for it with a terrible catastrophe. This example must under no circumstances be repeated.'[40] In practice though, as the war went on many goods became either completely unobtainable or only erratically available.[41] Nazi propaganda optimistically declared that 'community welfare comes before self interest' in the Third Reich. But as Christabel Bielenberg, a housewife in Berlin, noted, 'such pious slogans...made no impression whatsoever on the agile Hausfrau hellbent on a fruitful scavenge'.[42] Else Wendel, a wartime housewife and mother of two from Berlin, recorded how food shortages impacted life in the private sphere:

> Heiner and I spent hours that winter (1944/45) sorting out potatoes in the cellar. They had sent us a full winter's supply, and most of

them, part-frozen on arrival, had now thawed out and gone rotten in the heat of the cellar. But rotten or not we had got to eat them, as they were now our staple diet. Wolfgang and Klaus refused theirs, and started to cry because there was nothing else to eat.[43]

Housewives were forced to alter their recipes according to what food was available. And just like Else Wendel, they were faced with the challenge of trying to persuade their families to adjust their eating habits.[44] Symptomatic of the scarcity of food was the reaction of some wartime children from Bremerhaven on receiving chocolate bars in a parcel from their father, as mother of four Augusta Lühr explained: 'When it came to sharing them out, the two eldest could still remember what it was. But the two youngest were puzzled by it. When I asked them why they weren't eating it, they said, "Mum, it's just wood." '[45]

Compounding this was the further deterioration of food supplies after the war. In response to the question, 'How are you making out with food?' posed by American public opinion poll in May 1946, no Berliners (in the US and British sectors) responded 'well', 21 per cent said that they 'make out', while 79 per cent replied 'not well, badly'.[46] Shortages, and how to limit or alleviate them, were the overriding concern of the time. 'I can't afford to work – I have to feed my family', went a popular contemporary joke.[47] Families became survival units in the most basic sense. Mere survival necessarily preoccupied an inordinate amount of family life – be it through standing in queues for rations, going on foraging expeditions to the country, or through exchanging money or possessions for food on the Black Market. The 'law of wolves' prevailed and normal rules no longer seemed to apply in the struggle for survival.[48] One diarist living in Berlin at the end of the war observed the lengths to which hungry Berliners would go to find their next feed:

> During this time often ownerless and mostly wounded horses rest throughout the area. Men capture them and kill them, against all regulations. Hungry people stand and watch and cannot wait until the poor animal perishes. Each person saws off a piece, but it usually ends up in a knife fight between the scavengers. Then a butcher from Köpernick takes pity on the poor animal and the hungry people. He's always called when a horse has been captured. Afterwards he oversees a fair division of the spoils.[49]

Approximately 6000 Berliners had suffered from mushroom poisoning in August 1947 as a result of their efforts to supplement their ration allocations with mushrooms from the forest. This high number is indicative of the hordes of Germans who took to nature to search for extra food. Magazines and newspapers offered their readers advice on what to collect and how to make their gatherings edible. In June 1945 the *Deutsche Völkszeitung* advertised the opportunity to go on a guided tour of the Botanical Gardens in Berlin where one could learn about 'wild vegetables' (*Wildgemüse*).[50] Such measures indicate just how difficult it was to find enough to eat in this period.

The food situation was characterized by the following 'People's joke' (*Volkswitz*):

> Husband: What is there to eat today?
> Wife: Potatoes!
> Husband: And what else?
> Wife: Forks![51]

But in reality, the acute shortages were far from a laughing matter. Mothers described the terrible pressure of trying to provide enough for their children to eat, for whether a family had enough to eat often depended on the resourcefulness of the mother alone. Some children cried with hunger; others said that their dearest wish was to have more to eat. No wonder that some people expressed that they had 'had it better' under Hitler.[52]

Relations within families sometimes became strained as a result of the shortages. In some families sharing out the rations fairly became such a contentious issue that so-called *Brot-Separatismus*, whereby the bread ration was divided between family members and each person looked after his or her own share, became more common. Sociologist Hilde Thurnwald observed in her survey of 498 families in 1947 Berlin that often 'a man's ability to love was dictated by his stomach'. In the case of one family, arguments about food were a daily occurrence. It was only after the arrival of the first CARE parcel, a package of food and clothes donated by citizens in the United States, that the father stopped being so argumentative. Thurnwald learned from the wife how this man's good mood and tendencies towards his wife returned, so that their relationship was suddenly like it had been on their honeymoon.[53] Quite obviously then, limited supplies could have serious implications for marital harmony.

(ii) Housing shortage

Destruction caused by the bombing had a very tangible impact on the private sphere. Some of Germany had been a battleground during the war,

Figure 3.1 A 9-year-old girl licks cabbage soup from the edge of a pot in Berlin

other parts had been heavily bombed. In her diary Gabriele Vallentin, a wartime mother from Berlin, evoked a sense of the scene in Berlin in the aftermath of the Red Army's entry: 'Panzers had ripped down all the fences and devastated the gardens. It looked like the Panzers had driven straight through the middle of the little houses – some of which only had side walls remaining.'[54] The number of inhabitable rooms in Berlin had fallen by nearly 40 per cent between January 1943 and April 1946.[55] Overall in the Western zones, 45 per cent of the pre-war housing stock had been destroyed or severely damaged. Add to this the fact that German housing was already in short supply pre-1939, German society had a very serious housing problem after the war – a problem that persisted into the 1950s with an estimated housing deficit of 4.72 million homes in the Federal Republic.[56] On account of this, many families lived in one room, others lived in cellars and some even in bowling alleys. In Hamburg alone 20,000 people were reported to be living in cellars after the war.[57] 'Coal cellars, abors, shacks with leaking roofs are all inhabited', according to a report by the Relief Organisation of the Evangelical Churches in 1947. 'Several large families often have but one hearth between them and share the same crockery. Rows of rooms are in permanent semi-darkness because windowpanes have been replaced by bricks, cardboard, or wood.' Such places, they concluded, 'can no longer be called dwellings but, if anything, burrows'.[58]

Whilst the housing supply had been dramatically decreased by the severe bombing, the number of people in Germany seeking accommodation vastly increased after the war, because of the influx of refugees and expellees. Altogether, in the British, American and French zones of occupation the population rose by 49 per cent between 1939 and 1948. In the British Zone alone, the population rose to 113.5 per cent of the pre-war figure and in Bavaria to 127 per cent.[59] This had an enormous effect on German society after the war, both for the refugees and expellees, and for the rest of the population, which had to accommodate them.[60] In the context of such enormous destruction, the home should have provided families with some respite from the chaos outside. Practical shortages, such as cramped housing, meant that this was not always possible.

Much like the inadequate food supplies, cramped housing conditions could also have a detrimental effect on family relations. An article in *Für Euch*, a magazine focused on family concerns, discussed how the shortage of housing after the war had changed family life. Families commonly had less space and often had very few furnishings or personal belongings. In many cases children could not have their own personal corner, let alone their own room. Often only hoisted blankets acted as partitions between each family's own space.[61] In one case, where a Berlin family of five was living in one room, Thurnwald noted how the couple's relationship was affected by the shortage of accommodation:

The husband has become irritable as a result of the lack of room and the mother feels hampered in her work. In winter the parents cannot sit in their unheated bedroom, nor can they talk in the sitting room, because it would disturb the sleeping children, so they are forced to go to bed, which the husband prefers, because it avoids building up further hunger.[62]

Many couples thus had to live under circumstances totally different from what they were used to. Elaborating on the impact of the housing shortage, a government report from after the war noted that

Lack of accommodation, absence of comforts, living under the same roof with relations, the impossibility of ever being alone together, all this accounts for many discords and scenes that might otherwise not occur. Partners are advised that, even under the conditions as they are, they should try to arrange their days so that, for a while at least, they can be alone.[63]

Living in such crowded dwellings had implications for the intimacy and sex lives of couples, since their privacy was so limited. These practical limitations added another layer of difficulty to the psychological problems that affected couples' sex lives. These were just some of the factors that contributed to the shake-up of family life after the war.[64] Of course the extent to which these living conditions were new varied from class to class. Working-class families in urban areas were more accustomed to cramped housing conditions than middle-class families, so for the latter group this experience after the war was a particularly rude shock. Even so, conditions after the war considerably worsened across the board. Regardless of how much money or how many important contacts one had, some of the difficulties facing people at this time could not be avoided. As former signs of social class, such as houses and other possessions, were destroyed, and as people from all sectors of society lost close friends and relatives in the war, class no longer defined an individual's experience as much as it had done pre-war.[65] Families of all classes then, though most notably in urban settings, experienced a decline in living standards.

Marriage guidance centres sprung up after the war in a response to these circumstances. They provided free expert advice on medical and social problems and hoped, through their work, to assist families with the problems they faced and in doing so to help hold families together.[66] The centres in towns were visited more often than those in the country. This may have been because 'urban' couples had easier access to such centres. Nevertheless it suggests that the poor conditions in towns posed particular challenges for couples.[67] Divorce rates corroborate this conclusion, since the divorce rates in Hamburg and Berlin, where the destruction was some of the severest in Germany, were considerably higher than the average number of divorces in West Germany as a whole (Graph 3.1). In Baden-Württemberg by contrast there were only 0.8 divorces per 1000 people in 1947, which is a contrast with the higher figures for Hamburg and Berlin. This is partly explicable through religion, as more Catholics lived in this area than in Hamburg or Berlin, and Catholics were more reluctant to seek divorce than others. But these figures also reflect the harder conditions in the towns which contributed to the higher divorce rates in towns and cities.[68]

By 1948, many of the material difficulties that plagued daily life in the early post-war years had ameliorated significantly. Addressing the people of Berlin in a New Year Speech on 31 December 1947, the

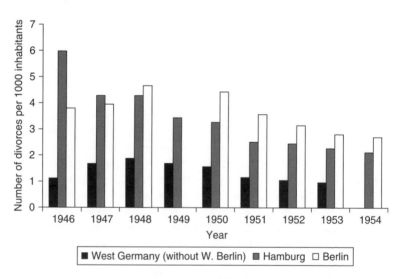

Graph 3.1   Number of divorces per 1000 inhabitants, in West Germany (without W. Berlin), Hamburg and Berlin[a]

Note: [a]DZI 20117, *Berliner Statistik. Monatsschrift 1955*, 8 (Amt für Statistik Berlin-Brandenburg, 1955) pp.237–8. The figures for Berlin in 1949 and West Germany in 1954 were not available, hence the gaps on the graph.

Director of OMGUS, Berlin Sector, Colonel Frank L. Howley, charted the improvements in living conditions since the end of the war:

> In Berlin the past year has witnessed considerable improvement: transportation facilities have been greatly increased, school feeding programs have been stabilized, telephone services have been tripled, the general health of the people has been improved ... No longer does the mother, anticipating the birth of a child, find herself confronted with the fact that her child will have only one chance in ten of living, as was true in the summer of 1945. The infant mortality rate today is so low that it approaches pre-war standards ... I wish the people of Berlin an optimistic point of view for 1948, an optimism based upon reality.[69]

A year later, there were signs that living conditions were becoming even more stable. In December 1948, six months after the introduction of a new currency, the Deutschmark, in West Germany, the US military governor reported that 'the German people have enough to eat'.[70] A few months later, in April 1949, *Das Blatt der Hausfrau* reported on the improved availability of groceries, noting that it was much easier to cook now than it had been in the early post-war years because many goods were available without coupons.[71] And by the end of 1949 the US occupation authorities reported that rationing measures where food was concerned had become pretty meaningless, because the supply of food for West Berlin was no longer a problem.[72] The housing shortage took longer to improve due to a lack of building materials and the damaged transport system at the end of the war. New housing construction only began in the late 1940s. By the mid 1950s, however, the last groups of expellees in West Germany had been resettled in new apartments and many bomb-damaged homes had been repaired. A decade on therefore, both the food and housing shortages caused by the war were largely at an end.[73] The material conditions of the immediate post-war era certainly posed a challenge for couples as they struggled to hold a family together, often with very limited means. As couples negotiated these difficulties, partnerships were put to the test.

Endurance

Numerous factors made it difficult for couples to maintain their relationships in the war and post-war circumstances. For many in wartime however, the family acted as a centripetal force holding individuals together, mentally if not physically, even from afar. In the period after the war also, the family became an important survival group. In fact at the end of the war the family acted as a magnet. In the most difficult conditions family members sought to find their families again. Soldiers who were able, always tried to 'go home'.[74] Far from this being a default decision borne of the fact that their options were curtailed by the post-war circumstances, these men were emotionally motivated to search for their families.

Enforced separation and the very real possibility of losing one's spouse made individuals keenly aware of, and grateful for what they had and what they might lose.[75] One wartime wife described how her 'heart goes into spasms whenever [she] thinks about loved ones who are far away'.[76] Another wife expressed her all-consuming worry regarding her husband's well-being: 'The days fly by and always with this same waiting. Waiting for you, my Hein, waiting upon fate... I am still not feeling much better. I'm sure that it is emotional worries that are draining my energy. Worry about you never leaves me, and it makes it impossible to relax... If only I had news from you!'[77]

Letters from both husbands and wives, of different ages and class backgrounds, written from different places in the war, expressed how important their partner was to their lives. Twenty-three-year-old Heinrich Böll did just this in a letter to his future wife Annemarie Cech on 29 October 1940: 'It would be impossible for me to bear this alone. Thank you very much.'[78] Filled with anxiety, 43-year-old mother of two Luise S.'s letter of 23 January 1944 demonstrates her keen awareness of the possibility she might lose her husband Paul, who had been declared missing on 25 November 1943: 'Even when I summon all my energy together, your uncertain fate eats away at me constantly.'[79] Soldiers longed for home, as 41-year-old Wilhelm K. expressed on 16 August 1942: 'My mind is at home. Love is there; my longing is for there.'[80] Thoughts of loved ones and the desire to be reunited with them gave individuals courage to continue in hard conditions.[81]

Because 'traditional' family values were more difficult to fulfil in wartime, they were treasured all the more. As Nikolaus Gross, held as a Soviet PoW, observed first-hand,

The importance of the family has been powerfully reinforced by the period of separation from it. In the times of worry and danger it has grown closer to our hearts... Habit had previously covered up a lot about home. So we came to notice things that were previously left unappreciated. From the letters of our wives we sensed a person who was deeply emotionally connected to us. From the children's clumsy letters we discovered a love, which they had hardly ever shown us before.[82]

The chaotic and often life-threatening unpalatable reality highlighted the desirability of the private sphere, and consequently family values.

Danger prompted people to reaffirm the importance of those close to them. 'I am thinking of you and our little son', wrote an unknown German soldier at Stalingrad in a letter which never reached his wife. 'The only thing I have left is to think of you. I am indifferent to everything else. Thinking about you breaks my heart.'[83] Many soldiers like Günter H. wrote of the sustaining power of their wife's love. On 13 May 1941 Günter wrote from Russia to his wife Helma: 'In the past few days I've been really tired ... Your dear, dear words really refreshed my heart again ... Outside it is grey and stormy, but in my heart it is warm and bright.'[84] One soldier nostalgically recalled happier pre-war days in a letter to his wife from Stalingrad: 'Once again I have held your picture in my hand. As I gazed at it my mind was filled with the memory of what we shared together.'[85] Letters and diaries looked back on happy family times as the difficulties of war brought into relief how much pleasure could be derived from family life in peacetime.[86]

When war forced couples apart, even those who were not normally openly affectionate expressed their feelings more freely. 'My darling Henny! I want to tell you something lovely: You were the only woman I've ever loved' declared one German infantryman.[87] 'I want to sit hand in hand with you this evening and explain everything about the past days' wrote Eugen N. from PoW camp in Toulon, France. He continued 'You'll probably laugh about the sitting hand in hand bit, but right now I can't think of anything nicer.'[88] Men may well have given voice to their emotions more easily on the page than in the flesh. One man wrote to his girlfriend from the Front that

> I cannot describe to you how it all affects me. I have been looking at your picture and the tears began streaming down from my eyes. I feared that my heart would break ... if I should be shot ... all I can say is that I am sure that you will never find another man who loves you as much as I do.[89]

Helma H. echoed these sentiments in a letter to her husband, expressing her impatience for the end of the war so that they could be together again:

> I am sitting cosily in my dear room with your picture, your letters and some blackcurrants. Sometimes a real impatience with this war and the separation wells up within me, because there seem to be no signs

of it ending. But don't worry; I'm completely calm again now. I take your picture in my hand and lovingly look at it for a long time.[90]

The possibility of losing one's loved ones made people valued all the more. On 29 December 1942 Sergeant Heinz Heppermann wrote home from Stalingrad. He explained: 'Separation and worry about loved ones really makes clear the love for one another that exists. I badly want to be back with you again; to cuddle you and stroke your hair; to be quiet and happy with you.'[91] Separation from loved ones and the threat of death certainly contributed to nostalgic romanticization about pre-war lives. Looking back on happy memories from before the war reminded family members that they had had good times together. It also offered them some hope for the future.[92]

Through letters family structures were preserved during long periods of separation. Though couples could be nostalgic about the past and optimistic about the future, these sentiments should not be dismissed out of hand as far from reality. As we saw earlier, letters were not censored of all negative emotions – wartime correspondences also included the instances when a spouse was annoyed with the other. Letters thus displayed more than superficial lip-service to what their partner (or indeed they themselves) wished to hear or wanted to be true. Whilst a recognition of the importance of loved ones and a nostalgia for pre-war family life could not in itself overcome the very real problems of estrangement brought about by long separation or the tensions caused by cramped living conditions and inadequate food and heating after the war, overall many couples endured this because they held onto the prospect of family life in better times ahead.[93]

Did husbands and wives expect to face serious problems of adjustment upon reunion? Or had the war had lowered the bar of what made people content and brought into relief just how important loved ones and home life were? On 1 July 1945 Beate K., the wartime wife and mother who was fretting about the lack of news from her husband in Chapter 2, recognized that it was her family that she treasured above all else: 'I am so lucky, in spite of the fact that I have lost all the earthly goods that I could call my own. As long as I can only hold onto you, and our little one stays healthy, I will be overjoyed.'[94] The war had made families grateful for simple things. Reflecting on what made her content, another mother described what made her happy in a diary entry on 13 July 1945: 'In the evenings, I'm simply happy if we've got our daily bread again and that the family is reasonably full, and if everyone's healthy and not too sad or despondent, but rather more often fresh and happy.'[95]

Historians have suggested that with focus on the hope of family reunion, potential problems in the family were not thought of. Marital problems after the war, they contend, stemmed from an expectation that pre-war married life would resume as if without interruption after the war.[96] Letters between husbands and wives during the war, however, show that couples were aware of the challenges they faced ahead. Heinrich Böll, writing to his wife from the Western Front, expressed how he anticipated difficulty readjusting to normal life: 'If I come back from the war, you'll have to be very very patient with me at first; I will be difficult, lazy and fidgety, and I probably won't see the point in working.'[97] Others too voiced their recognition that reunion would not be seamless and perfect. 'Of course I knew that it was going to be difficult' recalled one wife who had been separated from her husband by the war. 'We had never really lived together properly. After we'd been married half a year, the war broke out. So it was not really a proper marriage.'[98] There was, then, a real awareness that relationships would not resume as if uninterrupted after the war.

People did not expect things to be normal straight away upon reunion as Dr Rolf M.'s letter to his wife from Soviet Prisoner of War camp demonstrates: 'We've both certainly changed a great deal. Everyone can recognise this in themselves and can guess it about others, without knowing really how much they themselves or the others have changed.'[99] Even Helma H., whose correspondence with her husband Günter conveys the strength of their marital bond, also showed an awareness that marital relations might be tricky at first and as such she was steeled to make an effort: 'My dear husband, I am also thinking about whether this struggle and hardship has changed you – about whether it will take a while before we fully know each other again. I've also probably changed in this time.'[100] Realizing that separate experiences in the war might make spouses feel estranged from one another, some wives, like farmer's wife Cläre S. from Quallnitz, who had been unable to send letters to their husbands, wrote them unsent letters: 'My dear Hans! Even though I don't know your address yet, I am going to start explaining to you how we have fared.'[101] The idea behind this was that returning soldiers could read their wives' letters later and have an insight into what she had experienced. The women's magazine *Sie* also gave advice preparing couples for reunion, acknowledging that it was not necessarily going to be easy:

> People want to 'find' each other again. This will most easily be achieved if, as quickly as possible, a new basis for the relationship

can be created on the basis of shared experiences. There are better ways than to spend the first few weeks after reunion desperately trying to explain in great detail what each had experienced during their time apart. Such stories serve to reinforce the link with things and people which are unknown to the partner...It is of primary importance not to look backwards, but rather to deal with the future ahead together...Every hour of joint activity creates the basis of a new togetherness. If you can start by saying 'You know how yesterday, we...' or 'do you remember how, three days ago we...' then you've already accomplished a lot.[102]

Many people displayed a sense of realism about the challenges that would face their marriage after reunion. Not all spouses had unrealistic expectations of their partner which were impossible to meet. Given the numerous threats and challenges which both partners had faced in wartime, many were simply looking forward to acting as a team once more.

Did marital problems after the war stem from a failure to understand or acknowledge the different but equally challenging role of their spouse in wartime?[103] In July 1948 *Constanze* reported on 'Men's lack of understanding', (*Unverständlichkeit der Männer*), elaborating: 'Men always forget what women went through during the war and the capitulation; how they had to develop and harness their strength, in order to pull through the difficult times alone.'[104] Did men underestimate what women had been through on the home front, sitting in air raid shelters as bombs rained down on them night after night?[105] Some men may have been so wrapped up in their own experiences of suffering that they failed to acknowledge or empathize with what their wives had been through. But letters from husbands in war often express recognition of the tough conditions on the home front that their wives faced. Eugen N., for example, understood his wife's difficulties and wanted to share them: 'I think it is harder for you than it is for me. You have more worries at home than we have here. You look after the children, the bread, the clothing and the fire. I wish I could come home to share your worries.'[106] It was far from the case that soldiers felt that they had the monopoly on suffering during the war. As another husband wrote regarding his wife's experience of the war at home, 'You have it at least as tough at home as I do far away.'[107] Many husbands showed an understanding of their wives' burdens in letters home and often expressed the wish that they could be there to share them.[108] Husbands thus could and did relate to what their wives had been through on the home front.

Husbands' letters frequently cautioned their wives not to overdo it, which is indicative of the fact husbands were aware of the challenges facing their wives on the home front. One husband implored 'Don't wear yourself out...Let all superfluous things slide.'[109] Another told his wife that she should not feel obliged to write him long letters, because he could imagine how tiring and chaotic the constant air raids must have been for her.[110] Eugen N. sympathized with how hard it must have been for his wife Ursula to lose their family home in an air raid attack: 'I know how hard it must have been for you. You lost everything. Particularly as the home is the world of the woman and as you always looked after it and made everything look so clean.'[111] Soldiers were therefore not ignorant or indifferent to what went on at home and the hardships involved.

The war and its aftermath did of course hugely affect families during this period. It did leave widows and fatherless children, and it did increase the number of divorces.[112] However the many different permutations of the family model that war prompted actually demonstrate its strength and ability to adapt to change and endure these challenging circumstances.[113] Helmut Schelsky was a pioneer in the field of German sociology. Interested in German families after the war as a crystallization point for all the social changes that took place following on from the war, his sociological study of families in northern Germany found that the family was the 'remaining source of stability in our societal crisis'.[114] *Sie* magazine ran an article in 1946 which concurred with his findings: 'the family fragment dominates the hour but the idea of the family as a basic formation – that is, as an imaginary space which one can restore and fill – seems to have remained alive.'[115] Married life after reunion varied according to how long couples had been married. There were numerous couples who got married in a hurry during the war, many of whom had not lived together until after the war.[116] In fact the highest divorce rates after the war were among couples that had got married between 1939 and 1944.[117] In view of the difficult conditions of the war and its aftermath though, it is astounding how many wartime marriages actually survived.

Many people who were keen to re-establish the conventions of family life in peacetime were barred from doing so. Imprisonment and missing status of so many men after the war also stopped numerous couples from picking up married life as soon as the war was over.[118] Writing to her husband, from whom she had not heard since January 1945, Beate K. described her desire to be together as a family in July 1945: 'What a life that would be! Gusti, I imagine it to be so lovely and more and more I am looking forward to the time when once again you will be sitting with me at the table.'[119] From Soviet PoW camp after the war Eugen N. wrote encouragingly to his wife about the good family life that they would rebuild in the future once it was possible: 'Don't be sad and weary of life just because I am not with you now. Things will get better and we will build a nest where camaraderie and love prevails.'[120] Home life in the future was deemed desirable because it represented a secure haven offering emotional comfort in contrast to the constant stresses and strains of wartime.[121]

Over 5 million men did not return from the war. And thus many wives had to face the unwelcome news that their husband had been killed. Heinrich Böll's story 'Breaking the news' captures a sense of the impact such news would have:

> 'Don't be alarmed', I said, my voice tense, and instantly I knew that was the worst way I could possibly have chosen to begin, but before I could go on she said, in a strangely composed voice: 'I know all about it, he's dead...dead.' I could only nod. I reached into my pocket to hand over his few belongings...I slowly placed the wedding ring, the watch, the pay book with the well-thumbed photographs on the green plush tablecloth. Suddenly she started to sob, terrible cries like an animal's...She collapsed onto the sofa, leaning on the table with her right hand while with her left she fingered the pathetic little objects.[122]

The official number of war widows was never declared precisely. However in 1950 there were 890,000 war widows with children who were entitled to their husband's pension, out of 2.8 million widows in total in West Germany. Incomplete family units became known as 'two-eyed half families', (*Zwei-Augen-Halb-Familien*), as opposed to the normal 'complete four-eyed family', (*Voll-Vier-Augen-Familie*), since only one parent ran the household. As well as the death of husbands in war, increased numbers of divorces after the war played a role here. In West Germany 12 per cent of all adult females were widowed and 1.5 per cent of all adult women were divorced.[123] In many senses the adjustment process was similar for newly single women, be it through the death of a husband or through a divorce. In both cases, there were fewer shoulders on which to spread the burdens of the era and as such the difficult phase of rebuilding the home was generally much more difficult for those who were struggling alone. In general, where the war caused a reformation of the family unit without a father, this had a huge practical and emotional impact after the war. Jobs that once were in the domain of the father, which mothers took on temporarily during the war, became her responsibility permanently. In families where the wife was used to leaving all the administrative matters and decisions concerning the family to the husband, his death could lead to the wife having severe difficulties in taking over the running of family life on a long-term basis. Most often, however, the loss of a husband often meant that women had to get a job to support her family.[124] For these women, circumstances prevented them from resuming their marriages after the war was over. It is 'full families' however, which are the prime focus of this book, since even in 1946 before most of the German PoWs had returned home, three-quarters of all West German families were 'complete' ones.[125]

Pointing to the sudden jump in divorce and illegitimacy after the war, many contemporary writers and then later historians assumed that the war only had negative consequences for family life.[126] This has led to a rather disproportionate sense of families being 'in crisis' at this time. Sixteen in every 100 marriages in 1950 did break down, but turn this around and 84 in 100 marriages did not.[127] So many marriages survived in spite of the circumstances. In the post-war press, happy marriages got less attention than divorces but there were many more of them than unhappy marriages. In a survey of married couples, *Brigitte* found that between 62 and 85 per cent of these couples considered themselves happily or very happily married. And of marriages longer than ten years, 85 per cent of husbands and even more wives said that given the choice again, they would remarry their spouses.[128] Of course these figures could reflect the fact that people wanted to have happy marriages. But even if we acknowledge that the large numbers of people who identified themselves with the highly nebulous category 'happily married' cannot necessarily be taken as indicative of reality, their desire to fulfil this image is significant in showing that the concept of the family was strong and considered worth fighting for, in spite of the inimical circumstances.

Happy unions were largely overlooked in this whirlwind of negative press surrounding the institution of marriage after the war, as two women's magazines in 1949 noted. One of these, *Der Regenbogen*, ran an article in its eighth issue of the year entitled 'There are also happy marriages'. It explained that

> People are always talking about unhappy marriages, divorces and crises. But there's very little talk about happy marriages. Today we want to make a start. Even from some provisional enquiries, our

assumption has been confirmed: there are many more happy marriages than one is led to believe in the face of the general gloomy predictions surrounding the doubtful future of marriage as an institution.[129]

The women's magazine *Constanze* was criticized by its readership for its negative reporting on marriage. One reader wrote, '*Constanze*'s articles on the subject of marriage only ever seem to report on marriages being in crisis or divorce, as if there are no longer any happy marriages. Would it not be better to emphasize these happy marriages instead?'[130] Why then did magazines like *Constanze* project such a negative picture of the private sphere when its readers were suggesting the contrary? This disparity may have some basis in new groups in society that were created by war, such as *Mischlingskinder*, mixed race children born of black occupation soldiers and German women, who had high visibility in the press at the time, but represented a small fraction of the babies born in Germany after the war.[131] The magazine may also have derived its stance from the many speeches made by the West German Family Minister Franz-Josef Würmeling, who, through his rhetoric on the crisis of the family, ultimately hoped to reinforce the stability of the traditional bourgeois family. Given that wartime letters show how much people's experiences had reinforced the desirability of family life, it seems surprising that Würmeling was so worried about the state of the family.

Since historians of this period have often based their findings on public sphere discourse, it is unsurprising that they have bought into this picture of the 'fragmented' family in 'deep crisis'.[132] Until recently, historians have assumed that the post-war dynamic between couples was problematic, spotlighting the difficulties outlined in the source material, rather than setting these issues in the context of many easily resumed unions.[133] After the initial excitement surrounding reunion calmed down, problems arose both in families that made a good final adjustment to living together again and in families that did not. However some families resumed family life as if it had never been interrupted. Waltraud S. recounted the ease with which her marital life continued after the wartime separation. Recalling how she and her husband had initially spent a few quiet hours alone together, she remembered how happy they were to see each other. She felt that they could not have wished for a more harmonious or happy marriage.[134] 'Everything was a little bit easier for me' recalled Elisabeth Rendel, describing the period after her husband's return from Russia in March 1946. Her husband got work quickly and his earnings greatly eased the household's finances.[135] Children of the post-war era also remembered their parents' joyous reunions. 'Look! There is somebody outside the window', whispered young Helmut B. to his mother. 'As she turned around' he recalled, 'time seemed to stop for a moment. Then, with a scream she jumped out of the window and hugged her husband for several minutes. My father had just returned home from Russian Prisoner of War camp. The joyful emotion and the excitement that caught hold of the four of us caused us all to cry. We were all crying with relief.'[136] Like Helmut B. in Mannheim, 7-year-old Renate Dziemba recalled her mother's delight that her father had finally returned to Berlin:

> Mummy ripped open the door. She was completely out of breath and was laughing and crying at the same time. When she was at the milk shop someone told her that a soldier asked after a family with our name in the chemist's shop at the station. Mummy then ran all the way home. She was so happy. Now we were a real family again![137]

From this day onwards, 5 December became an important day in the Dziemba household. Every year the family celebrated being together again by exchanging small presents.

Far from it being the case that marriages after the war were 'fragmented and split, unable to withstand the shock of reunion', these accounts of happy reunions suggest a positive basis upon which the rebuilding of family life could take place.[138] In families where the father did return home, the end of the war represented an opportunity for a fresh start.[139]

'The teamwork required to counter material shortages brought spouses closer together' concluded Helmut Schelsky's study of German families after the war.[140] Within the context of challenging circumstances after the war, difficult times could be bonding for couples. The years of material shortages following the war decreased the social distance between parents and their offspring, partly because the war and its aftermath had undermined traditional roles within the family, which parents had previously used as a benchmark for their own families, and partly because children had grown used to the situation in which they took on more, formerly adult responsibilities.[141] In light of the difficult material conditions caused by expulsion, bomb damage and general shortages, many modified their expectations of life. People focused on trying to achieve personal happiness, and in so doing solidarity within the family emerged as having a new importance in life.[142] For the family members who remained together in this era, the difficult conditions

Figure 3.2 A wife portrays the reunion with her husband in a picture diary on 20 June 1945

often led to more time spent together. During the Allied bombing campaign, mothers sat for hours with their children in shelters. Also after the war, when there was often no electrical light and limited heating capacity due to coal shortages, families would sit by candlelight in their one heated room.[143] Historians of the period have thus far focused on the negative impact of these shortages on family relations.[144] However, though limited space could be a problem for families, it was a far from insurmountable issue. Renate Dziemba, for example, recalled how with some simple rearrangement, her family made room for her father: 'We removed the piano from the room and replaced it with a chaise-longue. Mummy slept on it from then on, and Daddy had the top bunk.'[145] All of this suggests that the detrimental impact of these material shortages on family relations has been exaggerated.

Desperation could knit families together emotionally and thus conditions may have actually fostered good relations. 'Where the struggle against hunger and cold has prompted families to join forces, the hardship of the time shows a positive side alongside the horrors', Thurnwald noted. Parents and children worked together to collect enough food and fuel for the family's survival. Going on foraging trips to the country together or refurbishing a bomb-damaged home created a sense of unity in families which had previously not existed.[146] Though the inimical conditions after the war did put families under strain, most showed themselves able to work together which further enhanced intra-familial bonds. 'Far from the difficult social conditions and the poverty of the time undermining family life, its cohesion actually increased and was strengthened', Schelsky declared in his study. He further added that

> Personal tensions, which had previously threatened marriages, or the indifference of husbands and wives or parents and children to each other, were replaced by increased and recaptured feelings of belonging together. With the collapse of the governmental and economic order...marriage and the family was found to be a natural foothold and point of protection, and the last place where safety could be had.[147]

Families could thus be strengthened by joint struggle.

A major talking point after the war was the concept of *Fluchtburg Familie*, that is to say the family as a place of refuge from the outside world. Good marriages and family networks were 'oases in the generally fateful disruption and destruction to which we are subjected'.[148] In 1953 the newspaper *Frankfurter Illustrierte* called this 'retreat into the smallest social circle' a 'sign of the times' and succinctly concluded that 'much of our society has collapsed in the last decades, but the family has held together'.[149] Nowhere was this clearer than in families who were refugees, expellees or bombed out, because they, far more than other families, had to function independently of other institutional support, necessitating an increased importance of family members in daily life.[150]

After the war, general expectations seem to have lowered and people appeared content with less than before. Signs of happiness meant no more than reconstructing and constructing family, home life and career, settling down around children, and having enough to eat.[151] It is clear from wartime letters and diaries that war made people appreciative of what they did have. People were just simply grateful to be alive. Quoting from Schiller's 'Ode to Joy', Berlin-based journalist Ursula von Kardorff expressed such sentiments in a diary entry on 17 December 1943: 'After every raid I get the same feeling of bubbling vitality. I feel like "throwing my arms round the whole world", because it has been given back to me again.'[152] In Leipzig wartime wife and mother Hildegard R. explained the impact of the war on her mindset on 4 May 1945: 'All brooding and thinking doesn't help at all – only getting on with the daily grind, and being thankful for all the food and other commodities, for the nature outside that we still have, and for the fact that the three of us are still together.'[153] The simple fact of being alive after the close threat of death gave people a new perspective, as *Das Blatt der Hausfrau* observed in September 1949: 'People's hearts still beat somewhat anxiously and fearfully, but inside feelings of immense joy build up at every instance of success – a joy that can only be felt when compared with the recent depths experienced by the human spirit.'[154]

The experience of war often made people appreciate their family all the more; they were grateful that they had a family at all, particularly when they contrasted their situations with those who had lost their relatives. 'It is the happiest day of my life!' rejoiced Anne K. on 13 November 1945. She had just found out that her husband would soon be released from PoW camp. Thrilled by the news, she penned the following diary entry:

> Daddy [her husband] is alive! He's alive! I want to tell the whole world. His release is imminent and so he should be home with us by Christmas. So everything is looking bright and sunny for us…Who can grasp how happy I am? The whole house was full of laughing and singing today. When Daddy's name came up, Christel kissed my hand and Bärbele danced round and round. We can't wait to see him again.[155]

And, in Leipzig 9-year-old Gisela Wolff welcomed her father home. She and her family felt very grateful to be together again. In other families, she recalled, fathers were missing or dead, which made her family feel particularly lucky.[156] Many others described feeling similarly relieved and thankful that their families had made it through the war, giving them another chance at life together. Above all they were simply happy to have survived and to still have a roof over their heads.[157] Overall, separation made family members appreciate each other all the more. It made relationships between spouses 'firmer and more heartfelt', Schelsky concluded, adding 'The senseless separation in war has actually had a favourable impact on relationships in the family in the present, because all family members are desperate to be together and to be able to live together'. Tough times had made people realize how important their spouse was.[158]

People quickly adjusted their conceptions of what constituted 'good' in the context of war and its aftermath, as a letter from one family to the father on 18 March 1945 showed: 'This week went well for us again. We were in the cellar a lot, but we were not harmed. Only light and water are often cut off.'[159] In 1950 *Für Euch* magazine ran the story of one particular couple who, since the war, had found that smaller achievements made them happier. After they were bombed out, the pair had to rebuild their lives from scratch. To start with they only had a few boxes. But gradually they procured more possessions – a stool and then a table. By 1950 they had two fully furnished rooms, of which they were very proud.[160] Little signs of improved living conditions could boost people's happiness after the war. Material goods were in even shorter supply than in the war years, but as goods gradually became more readily available, from 1948 onwards, each little improvement was a sign of progress, be it getting water out of the tap instead of collecting it in buckets from the street, receiving an extra allowance, or being able to use gas central heating instead of just the oven. Straightened times had, it seems, tempered expectations.[161]

Some families were just so pleased that the father had come home, that the post-war hardships were easier to bear. They worked together as a family and the prospect of a brighter future lay ahead.[162] Wartime experiences thus prompted individuals to reassess their priorities. In light of the large numbers of soldiers and civilians who had lost their lives during the war, those families who could come back together were usually grateful that they could do so. War had highlighted to people what was most important to them, and this was most often their family.

Wartime correspondence between husbands and wives gives us a wonderful insight into the intimate world of individual marriages. It shows how couples were able to keep their relationships alive via letter.

Furthermore, it demonstrates that the context of war, with the threat of death close by, brought into relief how important family members were. Sceptics have argued that the rosy descriptions of past and future lives, which were penned in wartime letters, could not be matched in reality after the war, and reunion, they claim, was commonly a bitter disappointment for all concerned.[163] In fact, however, many letters demonstrated a perceptive realism and anticipated that reunion would be a process of adjustment rather than an unproblematic transition.[164] The crisis in relationships was therefore neither as widespread nor as serious as current perceptions suggest.[165] As people learned to cope with less, they adjusted their outlooks accordingly. This meant that couples were more consciously grateful to be together after the war. The experience of war and the chaos of the post-war thus encouraged cohesion between husbands and wives, rather than undermining it. Many couples, in fact, expressed, like Helma H., that 'our love has only grown in this hard period of separation'.[166]

4
Empowerment or Endurance?

'Despite men's admiration for their working wives, husbands don't want to come home to a secretary, a teacher, a politician, a governess or a shop keeper – he wants to come home to nothing other than his wife.'[1] This was the advice given to women in *Das Blatt der Hausfrau* magazine in July 1949. As men were conscripted into the Armed Forces, more and more wives were left to manage their families alone. At the same time more wives than ever were taking up paid employment to fill the gaps in the market left by their soldier-husbands. Magazine articles like this one encouraged women to stick to traditional conceptions of gender roles, with women being above all wives and mothers. This, they suggested, would be best for marital harmony upon reunion. But had women's wartime experiences changed their views on being consigned to the home?[2] And if so, what would this mean when husbands returned from war or captivity expecting to resume familial authority? Were families reunited after wartime separation battlegrounds between partners? Overall then, we are looking to understand how, if at all, the Second World War changed a wife's role. And what did this mean for the balance of power between husbands and wives?

The Hour of the Woman

Women played a pivotal role in holding families together when men were away during and immediately after the war. Their contribution in the post-war period was crucial to German society, yet their input has often been overlooked, feminist historians argue.[3] They focus on 'The Hour of the Woman', (1942–48), emphasizing the image of the strong woman as epitomized by the so-called Women of the Rubble, *Trümmerfrauen*, who cleared the rubble from Germany's streets after the war. The *Trümmerfrau*, who became a symbol of the strong woman, featured frequently in newspapers of the early post-war years. 'Looking at the achievements of women today working on the reconstruction of Berlin, and in particular on the work removing the rubble', a magistrate's report from August 1946 noted, 'we notice that women have already come to be a symbol of the time, with the way that they have willingly and bravely adapted to the difficult conditions.'[4] Alfred Schumann, from the Prenzlauer Berg district of Berlin, was in his first year of school at the end of the war. He too noticed the impressive work of the *Trümmerfrauen* in Berlin: 'They earned admiration in every way... They looked after their family, stood in queues outside shops, they went foraging... they were tireless in finding new and tasty recipes to make from substitute ingredients. In short they were a force.' Alongside this, he later noted, they achieved 'the most positive reconstruction work as women of the rubble. On every corner you could hear the hammers at work, which they used to clean up the bricks. The stones were passed from hand to hand and then were stacked up in layers on the roadside.'[5]

Work undertaken by women ensured the initial rebuilding of German society after the war. Contemporary commentary in magazines from after the war drew attention to this 'Strong Woman', capable of simultaneously running the household and maintaining full-time paid employment. 'All women have a hard training in being and acting alone behind them,' observed one journalist writing for *Constanze*, a national women's magazine in May 1948. Stressing women's achievement in coping alone, he continued:

> They have had to live through night air raids with their children, evacuation, and the loss of a home or possessions. Often they have rebuilt a life for themselves under the most difficult of conditions. They combined the male role of protector and provider with the female role of educator and child-minder. So they literally did the work of two people, no, in fact the work of four or six people – because they had it two or three times harder than a married couple with children living in peacetime.[6]

Women also played an important role in restarting German society after the war: 'After the collapse it was the women who first regained their mental equipoise and did all they could to re-establish some order in the general chaos' observed a governmental report looking back on the early post-war years. It continued 'Even where all economic security had disappeared, the women, left entirely to their own resources, started to support their families.'[7] Day after day women took care of their families. They stood in queues for hours to get food, took long trips to the countryside to forage for extra supplies, and somehow prepared meals out of meagre food supplies. At home they got to work clearing the debris left by the Allied air raids. Frequently too, these women sacrificed their own rations so that their children would not go hungry.[8]

Further enhancing the perception of 'The Strong Woman' was the difficulty encountered by many men seeking to get work after the war. Nearly 1.5 million men were registered as unemployed in the western zones of Germany in 1946.[9] Even for those men who did find work, many found it hard to get a job of the same standing as their pre-war posts. The Allied occupation forces soon set about removing all traces of National Socialism from Germany. Part of these so-called denazification procedures were assessments of how involved individuals had been with the party. These measures were not entirely rigorous and were applied in a very haphazard manner. Nonetheless they made it especially difficult for former members of the NSDAP to find employment.[10]

Moreover some jobs people simply could not return to, and that went for the non-Nazis as well. The whole nature of employment and industry had changed: Whereas the majority of the industrial economy had been devoted to war production in 1944, in 1946 none of it was. Also, offices and factories had been destroyed in the air raids and thus jobs there no longer existed.[11] And in some cases war and imprisonment had taken its toll on the bodies of these former soldiers, so that they could no longer keep up with the demands of heavy physical labour. Particularly for manual labourers who had relied on their muscles to work in industry, physical ruin seriously undermined their ability to work. In one case, a man's career as a pianist was brought to an end by his exposure to the extreme cold in Russia. 'My hands are done for' he explained to his wife. 'The little finger of my left hand is missing and – what's even worse – the three middle fingers of my right one are frozen. I can only hold my mug with my thumb and little finger. I'm pretty helpless; only when a man has lost any fingers does he see how much he needs them for the very smallest of jobs.'[12] For many men like this one, long-term physical repercussions from their time in combat made it difficult to find work again after the war. In contrast to the more visible presence of women in the workplace at this time, the problem of male unemployment only served to reinforce the image of 'The Strong Woman'.

More women entered the workplace as a result of the war. Given that female employment potentially offered women a chance to change embedded structural inequalities, women's position with regard to their husbands appeared to be strengthened. A *Constanze* article argued that the relationship between the sexes had fundamentally changed as a result of women working in traditionally 'male' jobs (*Männerberufe*). In doing men's jobs, women discovered that on average, men's jobs 'were really quite boring, but equally not as demanding as the snarling and exhausted husband had implied on his return from work'. These women, by contrast, could not afford to be snarly and exhausted after they finished work because they had to look after their families.[13]

Women appeared to be self-confident and independent, made strong by their experience of war. What role did this leave for husbands returning to wives who had grown used to running family life alone? And what about these wives, who had managed for years on their own? How did they feel about the prospect of placing themselves once more under orders from their husbands?[14] Contemporaries suspected the worst. Fears that war and its aftermath had caused an upset to traditional gender relations were prevalent. In light of the high visibility of lone females immediately after the war, be it working the Black Market or in more formal employment, strong independent women appeared to be so common that the status of the patriarchal society in which gender roles were defined by the public/private sphere divide, seemed to have been severely undermined.[15] Magazines wrote articles under the headlines 'Recipes for good marriages', 'Schools for Happy Marriages', 'The End of the Family', confirming a definite sense of marriage crisis. In essence, 'The Strong Woman' became defined as a threat to societal values.[16]

The position of women vis-à-vis their male counterparts became of great interest to politicians after the war. Politicians in West Germany worried that traditional gender roles had been seriously undermined by the independence and employment opportunities afforded to women while their husbands were away. Franz-Josef Würmeling, Family Minister for the Christian Democratic Union, referred to a state of crisis in the family at this time, fearing the end to 'traditional' families in the long term.[17] The West German Family Ministry, which was founded in 1953 in light of the perceived threat to family values, sought to take vigorous counter-action to promote and reinstate sex-specific roles within the traditional family model.[18] Such action was required because in their plans for rebuilding Germany, women, in their role as housewives and mothers, were to be the rock on which post-war stability would rest.

In 1949 Konrad Adenauer was elected as West Germany's first chancellor under the slogan 'no experiments'. This mantra extended to family policy as well. The Basic Law of 1949, for example, acknowledged women's equality with men, but simultaneously declared that women needed protecting and that women could best serve German reconstruction in their roles within the home.[19] To this end, Family Ministry rhetoric focused on the belief that the woman should fulfil her traditional role as housewife and mother, and argued that female employment was incompatible with the requirements of the female in the home. In a campaign to promote the 'traditional' family, the ministry introduced child benefits to enable mothers to be 'freed' from the necessity of work. Furthermore, in the family law reform of 1957, patriarchal authority within families was enshrined in the law, underlining contemporary fears that the nuclear family unit was fragile and needed reinforcing.

In part, fears about the state of the family were provoked because the experience of war had proved that many women were capable of doing men's work. They were also a reaction against the Communist government in the East, which expected women to work. In the eyes of the Communists, a female's activity in the private sphere prevented her from fulfilling her potential in the workforce. Moreover they saw family life as being self-serving, and at the root of class and political differences, and thus sought to undermine its strength. As with pre-war Nazi policies, Communist intentions regarding 'the family' and their impact in this sphere were two different things. Although their rhetoric implied a wish to eradicate the nuclear family model, in reality the SED operated on the basis that pre-war family structures would remain, the only difference being that mothers would work. In the propaganda wars between East and West Germany, West German politicians seized on such rhetoric and used the potential threat of Communism to the family unit as a political tool. This rather exaggerated the impact of Communism on East German families. As much as the SED may have wished it, it was not actually that straightforward to incorporate mothers into the East German workforce. Ingrained gender roles could not be washed away overnight and women continued to prioritize the private needs of their families over their jobs; men too resisted the wider employment of women, fearing that it could adversely affect their employment chances.[20]

Whether or not fears for the long-term future of the family were valid, in West Germany, conservative politicians clearly felt that 'traditional' gender roles were under attack and that in the face of the perceived 'Strong Woman' an energetic and defensive campaign to promote traditional 'norms' was required.[21] In their view, reimposing the traditional nuclear family model 'from above' was crucial to societal stability in the young democracy.

What remained

The image of the strong woman dominating the public sphere is not the whole story, however. Highly politicized images of *Trümmerfrauen* implied a far greater participation by women after the war than was actually the case. Indeed they only constituted 5 to 10 per cent of employed women in Berlin post-war. Overall, for every one woman working in West Germany there were two men working in 1946. And only one in three women worked. Even in this post-war phase of a surplus of women (*Frauenüberschuss*) and a shortage of men (*Männermangel*), where women outnumbered men at a ratio of seven to one, men still convincingly dominated the work place.[22]

The most common scenario for married couples was in line with the traditional gender-differentiated public/private sphere, since the majority of women in the workplace were single women without children.[23] Of course many women, notably those from humble backgrounds, had worked prior to the war out of financial necessity. In 1933, for example 29.1 per cent of married women were employed.[24] But only a fifth of married women were employed in Munich in 1946, which hardly constituted a massive threat to the husband's role as main breadwinner, especially since it was not a big change from the number of married women who worked pre-war.[25]

Overall the number of women in the German workforce increased from 3.4 million in 1938 to 4.5 million in 1951.[26] What the numbers do not show, however, is that this merely constituted a stronger representation of women in traditionally female spheres of employment. Even though more women entered the workplace as a result of the war and post-war circumstance, the type of work that these new entrees to the labour market were most commonly engaged in were predominantly jobs that women had done pre-war, for example secretarial work, nursing, and working in the textile industry. Thus the war did not prompt a big change surrounding the genre of work that women did.[27]

Contemporary fears that traditional gender roles, and, more specifically, the institution of marriage, were under threat from women's allegedly new competence, were ill-founded. The proportion of women marrying in West Germany after the war was very similar to the number in the decades preceding the war, with 9.4 marriages per 1000 adults in 1938 in comparison to 10.6 per 1000 in 1948.[28] Though 2.4 per cent fewer women were recorded as being of married status in 1946 as compared to 1939, this can be explained by several factors: firstly economic hardship in the wake of the war encouraged couples to delay marriage;

and secondly an increased number of women were widowed as a result of the war. Overall these figures challenge the argument that women were increasingly choosing to be without men, as several articles in women's magazines suggested. One piece, for instance, from *Das Blatt der Hausfrau* in January 1949, entitled *Frauenüberschuss – anders gesehen*, (the surplus of women seen from a new perspective), argued that women were increasingly opting to remain single. The article concluded that, 'Women have become very, very different. It is no longer about waiting for a husband and a life confined to the family.'[29]

The number of marriages did not increase as dramatically after the Second World War as after the first. But this was not necessarily because newly independent women were rejecting marriage and opting for the single life. More likely, this was because soldiers returned home much more during the Second World War, allowing them the opportunity to marry during the war, in contrast to the First World War, where most couples had to wait until after the war to marry. Moreover in spite of the relative scarcity of men in Germany immediately after the war, because many men had died and because those who had survived did not return home immediately after the defeat, the marriage rate still did not decrease. The officially 'single' category of females also included women in so-called Uncle Marriages, *Onkel-Ehen*. These were war widows who lived with a new partner but remained unmarried in order to retain the war pension from their dead husband. Such women were not choosing to be without men, but their unofficial partnerships may well have contributed to fears that societal values were under threat, since they were not adhering to 'traditional' norms where relationships were concerned. Furthermore, since the marriage rate in the decade after the Second World War was on average slightly higher than the average rate in the decade before the war, hovering at around ten marriages per 1000 German inhabitants, this further brings into question the notion that women increasingly chose to live alone after the war.

High divorce rates after the war prompted the view that a dislocation of traditional gender roles posed a threat to the institution of marriage in the long term.[30] The assumption was that men were not prepared to give up the last vestiges of masculinity to fit in with the new status quo they found at home, and that women, having ruled the roost alone, were no longer willing to defer to their husband.[31] There is no doubt that instances of divorce did increase during this period. The divorce rate reached a high of double the pre-war rate in 1948 at 88,374 divorces, with 24 divorces per day in Hamburg, in comparison to 13 in 1938. And the divorce rate rose after the war despite the fact that the

Allies reinstated legislation from the Civil Code of 1900, which made divorce far harder than it had been under National Socialist law.[32]

Yet the vastly increased number of divorces in the immediate post-war years is misleading. The high divorce rates before 1950 were largely symptomatic of the divorces which had not taken place due to the war: From 1943 the activity of the divorce courts was increasingly scaled down; and they only resumed normal services in 1946. The overhang of outstanding divorces explains the particularly high divorce figures between 1946 and 1948. So actually there was less of a boom in divorce rates than the raw data would lead us to believe.[33] And in comparing the divorce rates with the World War One, it is important to remember that in the First World War men did not really come back on leave as much, and there were not *Ferntrauungen,* long-distance marriages, which allowed couples to get married without being in the same place. The lower divorce rate after the First World War reflects this fact. Above all, though divorce rates soared in the immediate post-war years, they dropped considerably by the mid-fifties (Table 4.1).The rate of divorce in

Table 4.1   Divorce, 1910–53

Year[a]	Divorce per 1000 inhabitants	Divorce per 1000 existing marriages
1910	2.3	1.4
1924	5.8	*
1937	6.9	3.0
1939	8.91	3.8
1946	11.21	5.2
1947	16.80	*
1948	18.77	*
1949	16.85	*
1950	15.66	7.0[b]
1951	11.61	*
1952	10.48	4.7[c]
1953	9.67	*

Notes:
[a]1939 Reichsgebiet: Area as it stood on 31.12.1937; from 1946 West Germany.
[b]Not including married women whose husbands had gone missing.
[c]Estimated.
*Of course we would like to know the figures for these intervening years; however, they are missing in the Statistisches Jahrbuch records.

Sources: *Statistisches Jahrbuch für die Bundesrepublik Deutschlands 1955* (Wiesbaden, 1955) p.63; *Statistisches Jahrbuch 1957* quoted in Lehmann, *Gefangenschaft und Heimkehr*, p.147; DZI 22729, Information für die Frau, 3 (1954) p.2.

the early years after the war was not therefore indicative of a breakdown of families in the long-term, but was rather circumstance-specific.[34]

Which sex filed for divorce more commonly is informative about the power balance between the sexes after the war. Between 1945 and 1955, half of the applications for divorce came from men. Pre-war, by contrast, two-thirds of the applicants for divorce were women. These figures, also mirrored in East Germany, suggest that woman who had coped and could cope without men did not necessarily want to do so. Indeed they show that the wartime conditions had made wives more hesitant to abandon their marriage, be it for emotional or economic reasons, indicating that they in fact valued their partnership more, having experienced what it was like to have to cope alone.

After the war Christian publications urged returnees to forgive their wives for any possible 'missteps', particularly as between 50 and 80 per cent of men had also committed adultery during the war.[35] In spite of this, men were slower and less inclined to forgive infidelity, as a survey conducted by *Das Blatt der Hausfrau* in 1950 shows. Asked 'What would you do if your spouse had been unfaithful?', 36 per cent of male respondents declared that they would seek divorce, in contrast to only 13 per cent of female respondents.[36] The survey results demonstrated very clearly that men would be quicker to seek divorce at this time. The reason so many more men filed for divorce in the post-war period may have been due to the surplus of women, *Frauenüberschuss*, and the fact that as a result men had more chance of finding a new wife in the remarriage market (*Wiederverheiratungsmarkt*). Viewed in terms of the balance of power between the sexes after the war, far from women being dominant in this period, divorce cases would suggest that men were in a much more powerful position.[37]

Exhaustion

Contemporary fears and imagery of 'The Strong Woman' were far more advanced than the reality of women's attitudes to their 'new' independent position. In most cases the reality of running a household alone was not a desirable one, it was a double burden. Women's increased involvement in the workplace was due to the practical reality created by the shortage of men, *Männermangel*. Women worked out of financial necessity because men were still away or dead. And even when men did return after the war, circumstances forced many women to keep working. When a woman was employed this was usually because she was either standing alone or because her husband's income was insufficient to support them both.[38] And in some cases this was because couples had lost their house and possessions and had to rebuild their lives from scratch. Need rather than personal motivations often brought women into the workplace, as a *Brigitte* article from December 1955 emphasized: 'The word "must" is of primary importance... Millions of women work for this reason – even when they absolutely do not want to work.' Pointing out some of the less desirable realities facing women with the double burden of looking after a family and holding down a job, the article continued

> Does anyone think that it is fun for women to get up at six, take their children to playschool and then hurry on to the factory or office? And then in the evenings shop, cook and afterwards wash up? At the weekend, washing, ironing, darning and patching, and general cleaning of the home are on the to-do list. It is energy draining and undermining of one's health.[39]

Given the choice, most women would have relinquished their extra tasks.[40] The National Socialists' focus on women as predominantly wives and mothers in the private sphere may also have influenced women's perceptions of their role. This would further contribute to the idea that women worked out of necessity not emancipatory desire.[41] Given that the circumstances after the war made holding down a job and running the household even harder than it would have been under normal peacetime conditions, the post-war situation was hardly an ideal time for women to enter the workplace for the first time.

World War Two did not bring a radical change in mindset regarding gender roles. Women's independence, in terms of coping without men both emotionally and financially, was viewed as a temporary change enforced by practicalities.[42] There are several hints of this unchanged outlook in *Constanze*. One reporter asked a widowed female factory worker whether or not her situation would improve if she found a new husband to provide for her instead of working, and she said yes. Another woman wrote into *Constanze's* problem page, explaining that 'My husband lost his job through the denazification process. I was thus forced to earn to support us and our three children.'[43] The use of the word 'forced' (*gezwungen*) is very telling of how traditional gender roles were firmly ingrained in her mind. Similarly, 23-year-old Beate K., mother of eight-month-old Peter, whose letters in Chapters 2 and 3 showed her longing to hear from or see her husband soon, reluctantly acknowledged on 1 August 1945 that she would have to take up a job if her husband did not return imminently, but added hopefully 'But you're coming soon, aren't you? You are probably already somewhere on your journey back to me.'[44] Her hope was of course partly derived from a simple desire for reunion, but there is also a sense that she would put off getting a job until it was absolutely essential. The majority of women's attitudes to their own position had evidently not changed.

Suggestions that women were toughened by war neglect to mention how difficult conditions for mere survival were. These conditions wore down women's strength and endurance rather than the opposite. Rather than 'surprising themselves with their capabilities', evidence indicates that women did know their limits and the circumstances after the war came very close to this boundary.[45] During the war there was a severe shortage of labour in Germany caused by the conscription of so many men into the Armed Forces. In Western Württemberg, one wife, who had been trying to run the family farm while her husband was away, died in childbirth in March 1943. The doctor who treated her diagnosed the cause of death as severe overwork. 'In particular mothers and wives suffered from being overburdened by work' noted sociologist Helmut Schelsky in his survey of German families after the war. After the war housewives only received the basic ration allocation, even though their levels of activity were often the equivalent of an engine driver or a miner, who received more food.[46] Indeed women were responsible for procuring, dividing up and controlling food supplies in the home – tasks which could be both physically and emotionally demanding. 'If you put everything together, the result of this state of emergency is often serious mental exhaustion' a contemporary report on the social conditions in the Berlin district Zehlendorf concluded on 28 March 1947. Commenting on the wearing impact of the difficult conditions, it went on: 'The ability to withstand nervous and emotional difficulties has disappeared. What's left is fatigue, apathy or despair.'[47] Maxi-Lore E., a diarist in Leipzig, echoed the findings of this report: 'I feel weary and lack energy. In the last few days I simply couldn't summon up the energy to write my diary. The bitterness and hopelessness of this time weighs upon people and takes away any initiative from them.'[48] Doctors and social workers pointed out that housewives were particularly prone to chronic exhaustion and this could only be alleviated by better nourishment. Instead, however, many women were doing without a part of their own ration and giving it to their husbands and children.[49] This state of exhaustion was not new to the period after the war. Security Service reports had reported the war-weariness of women in 1943.[50]

Females who had to support a family on their own often struggled financially. One such case was Hermine P., who had to support herself and her child alone after her husband was declared missing in 1943. When her war pension stopped in 1945, and her money ran out, she took up a job in a magistrate's court. The money was terrible so she supplemented it by working in the evenings on her typewriter.[51] Another wartime mother, Irene B., waited for the return of her husband at the end of the war. She explained how the financial support from social services provided less than half the money necessary to support her family.[52] For middle-class women, many of whom were undertaking paid employment for the first time, the double burden was more of a shock than for working-class women, many of whom had worked pre-war. Nevertheless the inimical circumstances of the time were worse than usual for all, regardless of class. In 1948 *Constanze* conducted a survey of women standing alone. It revealed widespread difficulties as women coped with working and caring for a family on a single and frequently insufficient wage. One participant in the survey explained that she could not sleep because she was so worried about holding everything together.[53] It is not, therefore, as if women found their new responsibilities so easy that the role of the male as breadwinner was ever seriously threatened.

For all that circumstances had opened up the world of work and offered women a chance to be independent from men, the reality was much less desirable. Wartime mother Elisabeth L. described her difficulties in managing the demands made of her. On 18 February 1944 she wrote to her husband Max: 'I haven't been able to sleep for a long time. It feels like I would receive an admonition from you: Don't let the children want for love. Don't forget the little darlings amid the enormous amount of work. But it is so difficult to do everything and also to be a good mother to the children.'[54] Forty-three-year-old Luise S. was a mother of two who had taken over the family-run garden centre in Fellbach since her husband was called up. She also described being at the end of her tether in a diary entry from 18 August 1944: 'Oh, I'm so tired of struggling' she wrote. 'How long will I have to put up with this misery?' she asked, nine months after her husband Paul had been declared missing. She went on

Why aren't I just lying beneath the rubble? There are always so many difficulties to negotiate and it is really not in my nature to be a battler. I'm in despair...I don't know if you are ever coming back or if you've been dead for a long time. And I would so like to be able to relax again. I am at the end of my tether. With all the worry and concern about you, on top of the general situation, it is as if a great weight is pressing down upon me.[55]

Figure 4.1   A woman records her sadness at her husband's return to the Front in a picture diary on 10 April 1944

Children of these overburdened mothers later remembered how difficult their mothers found it coping alone during this time. 'When I think of my mother back then, I can only picture her working. During the war I saw my mother cry a lot' recalled one daughter. Another explained, 'She used up her last reserves of energy. I could see that as a child.'[56] Wives thus had a hard time struggling alone in wartime.

'We noticed how much women missed their husbands and his significant help with this or that heavy work, both in the home and also with the bomb damage', wrote Nikolaus Gross, noting how the everyday difficulties posed by war were so much more difficult for wives to bear because they lacked their husbands' support:

> And even more difficult than everything else was the fact that women were without the love and companionship of their husbands. They were lonely and had to cope with everything by themselves, when they really craved companionship. For the children's sake, they had to show a happy face, yet they themselves were often in desperate need for comfort.[57]

Husbands also knew that they were needed by their wives and families back home, as Wilhelm B. noted in his diary: 'It is hard to go off to war when you know how much you are needed at home.'[58] These statements by men, which emphasize how much wives missed the support of their husbands, possibly served to reassure the authors themselves that there would be a role for them in the home upon their return. But in light of the desperate female voices we have heard, it seems plausible that their views were not exaggerated and reflect the fact that many wives genuinely struggled without their husbands.

Revealing of a general attitude to the double burden enforced on women is an article in *Das Blatt der Hausfrau* in March 1949, entitled 'Work and Home', which automatically presumed that women had too much to deal with and it offered coping strategies to its readers. 'Above all' it told weary mothers, 'you should not demand too much of yourself. Try to simplify the running of your home as much as possible. Content yourself with the fact that you have done the most important things.' The article went on to offer mothers time-saving tips:

> It is important that your children get used to saving you work, so for example that they don't bring dirt into the home, that they don't throw anything on the floor and that they tidy up their belongings. Also make meals simpler. During the cold time of year, do cooking for two days at the same time...Just try to create as little work for yourself as possible.[59]

The journalist warned these women not to burn out. She told them to be wary of getting too tired and stressed by all the burdens: 'Those who are stuck on the conveyor belt of everyday life today, are pushed from early morning to late at night, often without leaving time to breathe... Alone, the relentless diligence of such people, with their never ending thread of productive activity, risk the danger of total collapse.'[60] On 19 December 1945 housewife Beate K. found time once more to update her husband on her daily life. Describing the principal ways in which the shortages made her life difficult, she wrote

> There are new regulations everywhere for every piece of bread or meat and we have to read the paper carefully to find out what is available on the ration card. When I go shopping, people in the shops talk about nothing apart from food, foraging and where goods can be obtained off the ration card, or when one should be able to get this or that again. This everyday palaver is getting increasingly on my nerves. At home there is the constant worry about what we are going

to cook... We lack so many of the ingredients that we need. So Gusti, housewives are certainly not having it easy at the moment.[61]

Family separations placed a heavy burden on mothers. They alone were responsible for their children's welfare and education. With material goods being in such short supply after the war, mothers struggled to give their growing children much-needed clothing and food.[62] Inside the home there was the struggle against the cold; windows were commonly only papered over; water supplies were often unusable for months. Washing and particularly the drying of clothes was difficult because of the cold. Some mothers tried to help with hot water bottles and heated stones. Others kept their children in bed to contain their hunger.[63] Exhaustion and despair threatened these struggling mothers.

Son of German-Jewish émigré Alexander Gollancz, Victor Gollancz was a left-wing journalist and publisher who lived in England. He described a case from his time as the British Welfare officer for Düsseldorf in October 1946, which offers an insight into how burdensome the conditions were for mothers trying to provide for their children after the war: 'A haggard and yellow-faced woman came in and you could barely hear what she said for her sobbing. Her two children had no shoes: she had been applying to the *Wirtschaftsamt für Bezugsmarken* since February, and had just been told to apply again next year. One of her children had died of malnourishment in 1943.'[64] Similarly, Charles Bray, an English journalist writing from Berlin for the *Daily Herald* on 24 August 1946, found that women were struggling with the burden of coping alone: 'One woman, emaciated, with dark rings under her eyes and sores breaking out all over her face, could only mutter self-condemnation because she was unable to feed her two whimpering babies. I watched her trying desperately to force milk from her milkless breasts – a pitiful effort that only left her crying at her failure.'[65] No doubt compounding the strain was the fact that these difficulties had not started with the end of the war, but rather with its outbreak six years before.

Many women yearned for the return of their husbands, for reunion represented the chance to share their responsibilities and heralded, at least in their minds, a return to a more stable form of existence. Although women coped (and this was hard) this did not make them tough or convince them that they could do without men – they ideally wanted their husband to come back and help. In July 1948 *Constanze* reported that many women were keen to give up the extra burdens created by their expanded role: 'There are a large number of women who, with a sigh of relief, would gladly hand back the heavy burden of responsibility to the strong shoulders of their husbands.'[66] So when one woman wrote to her husband on 28 April 1945 saying 'hopefully you will be back with us soon. I care about you so much and cannot get used to being alone,'[67] she spoke not only for herself but also for many others in similar situations.

Through all the difficulties women held onto the prospect of reunion. Many women expected that their difficulties would be lessened once their husbands returned to share the daily tasks. Women hoped for help and support from their husbands in the difficult, chaotic everyday. Women were holding everything together with their last reserves of strength and banking on the imminent return of their husband to relieve them of the wearisome burdens of responsibility. It was the thought of their imminently returning husband that spurred these women on to hold everything together.[68] One boy from Karlsruhe, who was four when the war ended, later described the impact of his father's long absence after the war on his mother: 'Worrying about the whereabouts of my father really tired out my mother' he remembered. Nothing was harder than the uncertainty:

> Was he in PoW camp? Had he survived? He had been reported missing after Stalingrad, but we still held onto the hope that he would return. As ever my mother got on with the struggles of daily life, and looking after us two children alone...Life was exhausting and energy-draining. But we worked most definitely on the basis that my father would be returning home soon.[69]

'If only Daddy was here, everything would be a lot easier to cope with,' was a common refrain in the diaries and letters of wartime and post-war mothers who were standing alone.[70]

In numerous diary entries across the war and post-war period, Elisabeth L. described her sense of vulnerability. Her descriptions of life after the war stand in stark contrast to the all-powerful, all-competent *Trümmerfrauen* portrayed in magazines after the war. On 20 November 1944 she wrote to her husband 'In your lovely letters you call me your brave little wife, but so often I'm not that.' In no sense had these changes been liberating for her. On 25 January 1946 she further complained: 'It would do me so much good to be able to breathe freely again, without the incessant worry about you, the children, the shop, the future. How wonderful it would be to have you back by my side and to be able to deal with everything with you.' She was relying on her husband to return, as her letter from 18 November 1945 explicitly expressed: 'Come! Oh come soon. I keep working, always with the thought that you will be able to take over from me when you return. Please write just once so that I know for sure that you are still alive.'[71]

Wives across Germany agreed that their husbands were indispensable to family life. In Fellbach Luise S. wrote 'I am living in the hope of our reunion. What will become of the children if you don't come back? They could so desperately do with a father. Come back! Come soon! I am so tired!'[72] Wracked with worry at the possibility of facing the future without her husband 34-year-old housewife Anne K. from Berlin confessed: 'I can't imagine my life just with the children...Daddy must come back to us. I want to and have to believe he will, otherwise I simply won't be able to bear this life anymore.'[73] Another woman wrote to her imprisoned husband about how she was struggling to cope alone: 'I am at the end of my tether...How am I meant to do everything by myself? I can't do any more, I'm not up to it. I'm so weary of life that I just say yes to whatever the children say. Your absence is notable everywhere. You are right that it is a hard time for us, but I must say it is the worst for me.'[74] So even though wives probably did not want to make their husbands worry while they were away, they still wrote explicitly about the strain they were under, indicative of how seriously this affected them. Such letters do not really suggest that 'these women learned to act in a way less subservient to men'.[75]

Women were desperate for support, as the significant number who got involved with occupation soldiers indicates. Sometimes this was for practical reasons, hoping that their lover might be a source of extra food supplies or serve as a protector against the advances of other occupation troops.[76] But many women were simply desperate to have someone around to help them negotiate the difficulties of the initial stages after the war. American troops often performed this role: 'The essential kindness of the American soldier was in evidence' recorded an early American Intelligence report from Aachen. It went on: 'Soldiers helped German housewives with their chores, played with the children and through other small acts of friendship made living more tolerable through the creation of a friendly atmosphere.'[77] If their husbands were not there, then substitutes were clearly necessary for some struggling mothers.

Ultimately women wanted to return to a sense of normality. This was most obviously represented by pre-war gender roles in the context of the post-war, in which mere survival rather than speculation about potentially improved models of the family set-up were paramount. Most women expected to overcome the poverty with a return to the old familiar track. They were hoping for normalization, not only in the public sphere in the sense of a flourishing economy, but also in the private sphere with the return of the men and a resumption of the old role divisions. The increase in tasks that women had to undertake as a result of the absence of men and the crisis situation could in no way be described as liberating, but was rather experienced as burdensome, and meant that single woman had to cope with all the work, all the responsibility and all the worries about the future alone. Most women thought their situation would be made easier not by a change in gender roles, but rather by the reinstatement of old ones.[78]

Women were both physically and mentally worn out by the experience of holding the family together during the war, and were, at least in their letters, demonstrably keen to hand over their responsibilities to the husband. Theoretically of course, a woman could be both emancipated by her experiences of independence and also miss her husband simultaneously. But women's voices from the time do not suggest that this was the case. On the whole women viewed their enlarged sphere of responsibility as a temporary arrangement that was enforced by the war, not a milestone for their own personal development. Women were extremely exhausted after the war, and not poised to lead a revolution in gender roles.[79]

There is no sense in Elisabeth L.'s letters that the independence enforced on her by circumstance had rendered her husband redundant, or that the experience of coping alone made her question the man's role in the home or in society. She stressed on many occasions that she wanted to return to the pre-war norm, in which her husband was there to assume the commanding role in the home. On 23 December 1945 she addressed her husband, demanding: 'Come home soon. I so want to be rid of all the responsibility ... It is all so difficult and so hopeless.' She later observed:

> Oh how easy it all was before, when you had all the responsibility. I only needed to act out what you had come up with, so I didn't have to make decisions for myself. When all was said and done you took charge of everything. I've only realised this since I've had to make decisions for myself. And even then, when I've made a decision, I am so unsure and I often worry if it was the right one. It is not in my nature to act independently, but I am nonetheless forced to do so.[80]

According to the statistical research sample, 8 per cent more wives than husbands expressed that they were looking forward to reunion in the final year of the war, further undermining the notion that women's

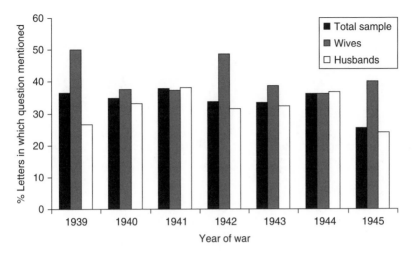

Graph 4.1 Does the author mention looking forward to reunion?

wartime experience had rendered men redundant to them.[81] In every year bar 1941 and 1944, where the difference in mentions between husbands and wives was 1 per cent more from husbands, wives consistently expressed looking forward to reunion with greater frequency (Graph 4.1). This suggests that women were keen to share the double burden of home and work life.

While women were waiting for news from their husbands, they pinned pictures of their captured or missing soldiers to the notice-boards of railway stations in the hope that, seeing one, a returning comrade might bring them news. When they had exhausted the avenues provided by the Red Cross, Protestant and Catholic welfare organizations, they turned to the newspaper advertisements of dubious firms, who offered search services.[82] For at least 15 years after the end of the war, West German women placed advertisements in veterans' newspapers, hoping that their husbands' former comrades would contact them.[83] Fortune telling also became much more popular. In 1951 the magazine *Der-Die-Das* reported that the practices of clairvoyants had become more scrupulous. No longer did customers pay 10 Pfennig to see their future via a letter which a parrot or budgerigar would pull out of a box. After the war, fortune tellers studied the horoscopes of each customer to learn about their future, and these services no longer cost only 10 Pfennig.[84] All these measures were simply indicative of the fact that women were longing for the return of their husbands.

Figure 4.2 Women go to the Friedland 'arrivals' camp to try and find out the fates of their husbands from Prisoners of War returning from Russia

For women standing alone, mere survival was a burdensome struggle. Rather than these years being 'the heyday of women',[85] they constituted a decade of struggle and difficulty which many wives wished would end.[86] For many women it was the prospect of relinquishing these tasks in the imminent future that gave them the strength to continue. Women had successfully filled the gap in the workforce created by the *Männermangel*. Fearing that traditional gender roles had been eroded by this, Family Minister Würmeling declared himself to be the 'Protective Patron of the Family' in the post-war period, using his position within the Cabinet to advocate the traditional nuclear family with clearly defined gender roles for men and women within it. As it turned out, women were not pressured back into resuming traditional roles within the home. As men returned, convalesced and then entered the workforce once more, women were predominantly glad, where this was materially possibly, to return to the security of their roles in the home and the private sphere. Just as fears and imagery of the 'New Woman' in the interwar years were far more advanced than the reality for most women, so too was this the case with the 'Strong Woman' of the post-war era. Many women were only too happy to return to their traditional role as 'only' wives and mothers.[87]

Injured masculinity

Soldiers too longed for the resumption of 'normal' home life after the war. Home and family life were poles apart from what men experienced in combat. The familiarity and comfort of home stood in stark contrast to the strict routines and unfamiliar places that characterized daily life in the Armed Forces. Thinking of life at home offered soldiers some escape from the harsh reality of battle. Thus husbands reciprocated their wives' desire to be back together: 'In every one of your letters', wrote one soldier writing from Russia in early 1943, 'I sense your wish to have me back with you soon. It is not surprising that you should long for this: I too look forward – quite passionately – to being back with you.'[88] Soldiers' letters often emphasized how far away from home they felt, signing off with phrases like 'from far away' or 'from far away in the east'. Just like their wives, husbands wrote of their longing to be back with their families and to get on with normal life once more.[89]

With Germany's loss in war however, men's return could be neither triumphant nor victorious. Men were not greeted as heroes on their return, as only victors could really be heroes.[90] Feelings of failure and humiliation were compounded by the fact that men's status had been considerably inflated during the Hitler regime. The importance of the German soldier and fighter was at the heart of National Socialist imagery. Indicative of this was Hitler's speech at the Nuremberg Rally on 14 September 1935. Here he explained that the ideal Nazi man possessed qualities which equipped him to fight in war:

> The ideal of manhood [is] ... the young man who can stand all weathers, the hardened young man. Because what matters is not how many glasses of beer he can drink, but how many blows he can stand; not how many nights he can spend on the spree, but how many kilometres he can march.[91]

The effect of this, and numerous other propaganda efforts to encourage men to fight for the Nazi cause, was limited. Symptomatic of this was the fact that soldiers' letters to their wives only very rarely mentioned political motivations for the war.[92] Some talked about their belief in Hitler as a leader who would see them through difficult times. But the idea that these soldiers would draw deep from their well of National

Socialist convictions to remind themselves why they were fighting, as Hitler suggested in 1943, seems improbable. For in spite of governmental efforts to spiritually mobilize the population for war from 1933, the outbreak of war itself had sparked a muted response at best. And this was before private lives had been ripped apart and in some cases destroyed in the service of the state. Without a doubt many men felt duty-bound to serve their country irrespective of their attitude towards the Nazis.[93] As infantryman Dreher wrote home on 15 November 1940, 'My dear, I would come straight to you without a moment's thought, but some magic force keeps me here in Bann – a sense of my duty as a man to protect our homeland.'[94] For the majority, protecting loved ones at home was the most compelling reason to endure numerous hardships in combat.

Returning home was all the more difficult for soldiers because they had justified their actions in the war in the name of protecting and defending their families from the ravages of the enemy.[95] Contrary to the perception that most soldiers were fighting for *Führer* and Fatherland, (a perception that was most likely derived from death announcements and gravestones, which often said that soldiers had sacrificed themselves for *Führer* and Fatherland), these were rarely mentioned as motivating factors in letters, with more soldiers seeming to share the view expounded in a wartime letter by dentist Heinz M.-B. serving on the West Wall that 'soldiers are here so that those at home have it better'.[96] Like Heinz M.-B., Paul Fischer was motivated to fight by a desire to shield his family from war and its consequences. Snatching a moment to write home from combat, he explained 'I am a soldier to help protect you, my loved ones'.[97] However, since the war had massively invaded the private sphere, soldiers' sacrifices had been for nothing.

Affairs between occupation soldiers and German women also enhanced the German male's sense of defeat, especially as these troops appeared so strong, healthy, and hence manly, in comparison to German men, physically and often psychologically weakened by war and captivity. Women, who became known as chocolate girls (*Schokoladenmädchen*) in the British Zone, may have got involved with occupation soldiers to receive material benefits. Using euphemistic phrases to allude to the method by which their goods had been procured, they joked about the 'major's sugar' and 'violation shoes' that these relationships had brought them.[98] But returning German soldiers felt betrayed by these women, for all their suffering and hardship had been endured in order to protect those on the home front. And even though their efforts had concluded in defeat and, ultimately failure, the fraternization with enemy troops was insulting to all that they had tried to achieve. A common sentiment that was expressed at the time was that the German soldier fought for five years, whereas his wife had not even fought for five minutes.[99]

Rape was also a by-product of defeat and this had serious impact on relationships between the sexes in the private sphere. Between January and March 1945 Russian troops carried out multiple rapes of women when they occupied towns and villages in East Prussia. And then in the final stages prior to capitulation, many women were raped by occupation soldiers in Berlin. Figures for the number of women raped vary enormously, but most realistic totals are in the 100,000s.[100] Particularly in Berlin as men returned from PoW camps and gradually resumed their positions as *Paterfamilias*, there was very little discussion regarding the mass rapes, for the very fact that they had happened only served to highlight that men had failed to protect their women on the home front. The victorious power's sexual 'occupation of the body' compounded the sense and reality of defeat in Germany, and with it the humiliation of German men.[101] On the rare occasions that husbands were present when Russian occupation soldiers tried to rape their wives, it was often the case that they could not actually prevent it. One woman in this situation, who had just been raped by two Russian soldiers recalled, 'I had to console my husband and help restore his courage'.[102] Men certainly experienced this as a failure, which put their sense of masculinity under threat. And apparently some women were disdainful of German men who had been unsuccessful in protecting them from the violators. But it was not just the husband's position that had been undermined by his wife's rape. Wives who had been raped were also in a difficult position in their relationship as a consequence. Though most survived being raped, this was traumatizing, and far from being able to talk about it with their husbands, wives were forced to repress any resulting feelings for fear of wounding their husbands' sense of masculinity or potentially facing the rejection of a husband who, with the existence of a far greater number of adult women after the war, could at least theoretically choose a new partner quite easily.[103]

Rape, alongside other factors, played into the sexual difficulties that couples faced after reunion. Social workers reported that wives often refused to have sex with husbands whom they no longer found attractive, be that because of wartime injuries or otherwise, and husbands did not want to touch wives who had been raped. Doctors in general expressed concern that men were having difficulties 'finding their way back to women'. Premature ejaculation and impotence were both problems which were reported to plague the sex lives of returning soldiers. And of course many returnees suffered from malnutrition resulting from long periods with insufficient nourishment in PoW camps. This also stood in the way of resuming couples' pre-war sex lives, as it significantly decreased their sex drive. In such cases, men were reported to have a 'eunuch-like absence of sexual desire' when they returned to their wives. Returnees' desexualization was then another factor hindering men's successful resumption of their roles as husbands within recently reunited families.[104]

Exposure to the horrors of war left some men emotionally stunted after the war, which also contributed to difficulties in resuming relationships. Dr Jessel from the Research Institute for *Heimkehrer* (Returnees) reported to the social authorities in Hamburg on 28 February 1950 about the problems that *Heimkehrer* experienced on their return: 'Relatives of the *Heimkehrer* found their husband, son or father considerably changed by their experiences, whether he had become deadened and apathetic or inexplicably irritable with sudden outbreaks of anger.' In one case a man who had returned from PoW camp several months previously visited the Institute for Returnees, accompanied by his wife. His wife explained that her husband hardly spoke and despite all her efforts and encouragement he showed no interest in rebuilding a new life. After about half an hour, Dr Jessel managed to get the man to speak. From comrades, Jessel found out that the man had said pretty much nothing during the return journey to Germany, but had cried constantly. Only after months of therapy was Jessel able to report that his patient had something approaching a normal healthy mental state. In another case, a returnee, who had been brought to the advice centre by his wife, tried to escape. When he finally talked to the advisor he explained that he had a constant feeling that someone was standing behind him waiting to catch him. Many returnees, who were not otherwise psychologically damaged by their experiences, admitted to similar feelings.[105]

For nearly all returnees the various types of psychological damage caused by their experiences, captured in the umbrella term 'dystrophy' at the time, prevented an immediate resumption of 'normal' family life. Symptoms frequently included depression, inability to concentrate, sudden outbursts of anger, and the feeling of being constantly pursued by enemies. Though there are no statistics to tell us how widespread 'dystrophy' was, extensive discussions in medical and psychological literature suggest that it was relatively common.[106] This was particularly the case for Soviet *Heimkehrer*. People talked of their 'Russification', whereby their character and facial expressions had become Russian as a result of their experiences. War and captivity left a long-term mark on Rudolf G., for example. After five years serving in the army and four years in Soviet captivity, Rudolf G. tried to reopen his business. But, his patient record noted, he began to notice odd changes in his mood and behaviour. He became extremely timid and often wanted to go outside only at night. Preferring to be alone or with his wife, he did not even want to see his brothers and sisters. He was often bad-tempered and angry, yet also frequently broke into tears for no good reason.[107] Many wives struggled to overcome the emotionally distant behaviour of their returnee husband. Like many others in her position, one wife explained 'I constantly tried to figure out what I could do to find him again'.[108]

For veterans, adjusting to life at home after the war could be difficult. The contrast between life in the army and life at home was particularly stark. Wolfgang Borchert was a soldier on the Eastern Front during the war. He later became famous for his play *Draussen vor der Tür*, which depicted the despair of soldiers returning from war. In his play, he used the metaphor of a puppet to describe the absolute reduction of the individual man in the battle of the masses. After the war ends, the former soldiers are torn from the strings that had controlled them, giving rise to the paralysing experience of sudden functionlessness and uselessness. The individual soldier returning home from war had not learned to re-establish an identity for himself. The very fact that men's identity had become so bound up with their role as soldiers, meant that the period after the war was necessarily a time of a reshaping of male identity according to new criteria. In the army members' personalities were deliberately subordinated, privacy was undermined and individual differences were repressed. The family by contrast generally encourages the development of individual personality, it gives people privacy and it is sensitive to the needs of individual members.[109] Prolonged periods of incarceration as Prisoners of War also contributed to problems of reintegration into family life. Prison camp life was very institutionalized and regimented. The change from being known as a number to being known as a person on returning to life in Germany could often be a disorientating experience. Transition to life at home thus involved a series of adjustments. *Brigitte* reported that men who had been deprived of basics like shaving cream and razors behaved like children in a fantasy world when reacquainted with such items. One daughter said that her father would spend hours in the bath after having lived so long without one. And a returnee later recalled that for the first few nights at home he slept on the floor because after doing so for so long, he had to get used to sleeping in a bed again.[110]

Figure 4.3   A Prisoner of War returns to Berlin, *circa* 1950

Where men had been disabled in war, and this accounted for 1.3 million men in West Germany, this did make them less able to engage in protecting and providing for their families. The census of 1950 showed that of the 1.3 million people permanently injured by war (*Kriegsbeschädigte*)

635,000 were unable to work. Even those who were not *kriegsbeschädigt* in the official sense of the term often had physical problems which prevented them from resuming employment immediately. Indeed 95 per cent of returning prisoners of war needed medical attention and 30 per cent were not able to resume their former professions. And of the 45,000 men who returned to the American zone from Russia in 1946/47, 90 per cent were described by the registration authorities as 'human wrecks'.[111] The physical state of PoWs as they arrived back in Berlin was later recalled by an eyewitness: 'Tattered, demoralized, tired and miserable. Some of them had bags on their back, which they tossed in front of themselves out of weakness.'[112] Circulation problems and malnutrition were the most common illnesses in returning PoWs. Overall though, 92 per cent of these men were able to take up their position as breadwinner for the family again.[113]

In contrast to the majority of these men, who were deemed to be in reasonable health and fit for work, war-wounded men were liable to feel 'superfluous and shoved to the side' and 'redundant'.[114] Where being *kriegsbeschädigt* permanently prevented men from being the breadwinner, this did alter gender relations significantly, since the wife had to

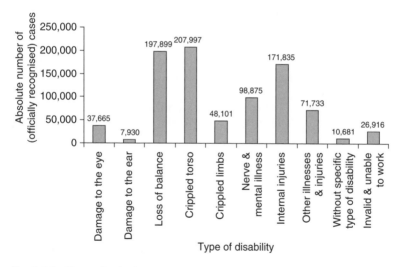

Graph 4.2   Physically disabled men* with at least 50% reduced working capacity, 13 September 1950

Note: *Not including the physically disabled over 65.

Source: *Statistisches Jahrbuch für die Bundesrepublik Deutschland 1955* (Wiesbaden, 1955) p.78.

take over this role. It should be made clear though that this group was a minority. Nonetheless, during the period in which they had managed alone, many women had held onto the idea that life would be easier upon their husbands' return. This could lead to bitter disappointment if this did not work out in reality. Soon after her husband's return, Helene Karwentel, a mother of one from Berlin, became frustrated that he just seemed to sit around at home while she was struggling to make ends meet for their family.[115] Charlotte Wagner, also a mother from Berlin, became increasingly impatient with her lethargic husband, who appeared to lounge about the house while she went out to work. Resentful that her husband's return had merely created more work, she saw no reason why she should wash his dirty underwear while he contributed nothing to the household, and eventually filed for divorce.[116] Returning men could thus be the source of new problems rather than heralding the relief of old ones. Even so, many wives performed a crucial role in nurturing their husbands back to physical and emotional health. The wife of one war-blinded man described her experience:

> Just as well that my husband cannot see me. He is so sensitive to every sign of depression and fatigue in me and I am sometimes ashamed of myself that I become irritable and unable to have the patience due to him, a blind man. But I have now found a way to become patient again. I just put a black cloth round my head for a while; then I know what it must be like to be blind and I regain the love and patience which I had almost lost.[117]

Alongside efforts within individual families to reintegrate returning soldiers, the *Sozialamt* in Berlin organized meetings in different districts to aid the transition from PoW to civilian life. A common format for such meetings was a musical or literary programme and speeches of welcome, after which the various problems and opportunities for former PoWs were discussed. Experts from the central administration were usually present to give advice to the men about things like training and employment.[118]

The polarized discourse about weak men and strong women masks a more complex reality. Though women were superior to men returning from war and Prisoner of War camps in their understanding of how life after the war, and in particular how the bureaucracy surrounding the procurement of food, functioned, this hardly constituted an enormous power that they held over men.[119] That women were running the household after the war was no radical change from the pre-war – this was

Table 4.2 'Do you get the impression that German PoWs who have been released from Russian captivity since 1949 still have problems with fitting into normal life today?'

September 1955	All (%)	Male (%)	Female (%)
Still had difficulties	30	30	30
Had no difficulties	42	47	38
Difficulties dependent on conditions	5	5	6
Undecided	23	18	26

Source: Elisabeth Noelle and Erich Peter Neumann, *Jahrbuch der öffentlichen Meinung* (Allensbach am Bodensee, 1957) p.209.

their traditional sphere. And even if returning men had wanted to have a greater understanding of the changes in this sphere, these would not have been difficult to grasp. Life at home after the war was, in effect, no different in this sense from pre-war, when women were also fundamentally in charge of running the home.

The initial health problems of returnees did not make them stick out as particularly dispensable members of society as the response to the survey conducted in September 1955 shows (Table 4.2). Given that the survey asked a leading question, implying that returning PoWs from Russia would still be facing problems of reintegration, the number of respondents believing that these PoWs had no particular difficulties in 1949 would most likely have been even higher had the question been a neutral one.

The mental and physical weakness of returning soldiers did not mean that women were automatically the stronger sex post-reunion. This would underestimate the level of suffering and exhaustion incurred on the home front. The challenge of readjusting to life as a couple in very changed circumstances was made all the greater by the fact *both* partners were mentally and physically exhausted.[120] Neither one sex nor the other alone was dramatically weakened, rather in fact both sexes faced challenges resulting from the war. Notions of a gender power reversal in the wake of World War Two were thus not nearly as clear-cut as current scholarship suggests.

Though the legacy of war in Germany may have damaged male pride in several aspects, women's self-worth was not correspondingly greater. The period after the war did not usher in the fight over power in the private sphere.[121] In spite of the disruptive impact of war in terms of the fulfilment of traditional gender roles, after the war men and women alike held onto the ingrained role structures.[122] This was by no means because people felt that these ingrained structures were ideal, but rather because in the emotional and practical chaos of the time, which did not lend itself to reflection about revising embedded structures, traditional gender models were the most obvious representations of peacetime normality, for which both sexes so keenly craved. Therefore, not only did conservative politicians wish to preserve pre-war structures within the home, so too did husbands and wives. The re-emergence of the traditional family model in the wake of the Second World War was thus as much the result of popular aspirations 'from below' as of government policies imposed 'from above'.[123]

Some contemporary observers maintained that as a result of wartime experiences, the relationship between spouses had increasingly changed from having the man being the dominant force in decision-making to a more equal partnership.[124] However a public opinion poll from 1949 found that in fact the majority of couples had not actually adopted this model of equal ranking, but had instead 'resumed their old authority patterns'.[125] In spite of the enforced independence that had been thrust upon women in their husbands' absence, many of the difficulties surrounding the marital power-dynamic after the war were not permanent ones and found private resolution in the transition from the period of adjustment to normalization. Of course from our perspective today, we can see that this enforced period of female independence may well have affected the process of women's emancipation in the long term, even if it was a hard and painful process, which women at the time viewed as a burden. Nonetheless, it was because these German war wives clearly retained traditional attitudes regarding their role within the family that some feminist historians write of women's missed opportunities (*Verpasste Chancen*) in this period.[126]

5
Parents and Children

'I try to be a stand-in father for Mummy, because I'm practical like you and Mummy's not good at that sort of thing' wrote 11-year-old Ulli Fromann on 3 December 1945 to her father who she had not seen since she was five. Like many other children, Ulli had taken on responsibilities at an early age to help her mother counter the challenging conditions of the era. Yet even with this help, her mother Christiane described the difficulties they faced making ends meet in bombed-out Berlin. The shortages of food were particularly tough, she told her husband Hans, especially when confronted with the constant pleas for more to eat from her children Ulli and Jutta. The best she could offer, she said, was to let them take it in turns to scrape out the saucepans after supper. The Fromann's were typical of many families across Germany who were negotiating inimical circumstances at the end of the war.[1]

Children growing up at this time experienced their impressionable formative years in a period of immense emotional and physical vulnerability. Helpless before events beyond their control, in many respects parents became every bit as vulnerable as their children in the war and post-war period. As enemy air raid attacks on Germany increased in intensity, death threatened both those at home and those in combat alike. After the war, many German families were homeless. Some had had their homes destroyed by Allied bombs. Others were expelled from their homes because they had lived on land that had been granted to Russia and Poland as part of the peace terms agreed at the Yalta and Potsdam conferences in 1945. On top of this, material goods were scarce. In this context, many parents were not able to provide adequate food or shelter for their children.[2] How, then, did the political events outside the control of the family condition relations between parents and children? Irrespective of the war and its legacy, in all likelihood some parent–child relationships were bound to be terrible, others bound to be excellent, and a large number bound to be somewhere between the two extremes. But how did the circumstances of war and its aftermath affect the interaction between the two generations?

Motherhood on the home front

When fathers were called up to war this changed the family dynamic within the home. Mothers frequently alluded to how much they missed the support of their husband in raising the children. 'If only Daddy were here with us, everything would be a lot easier to cope with', confessed 34-year-old housewife Anne K., whose diary entries in Chapters 3 and 4 also conveyed how keenly she felt her husband's absence.[3] Twenty-three-year-old mother of baby Peter, Beate K. from Königsberg, expressed similar sentiments in several diary entries (which she addressed to her child): 'It would be so lovely if only your father were here...Sometimes it is horribly difficult to keep going.'[4] Since most fathers did not return immediately after the war, and thus mothers had to continue caring for their children alone, the transition from war to peace did not, at least in this sense, bring an enormous change to life at home. Shortly after the war's end, mother of two, Diana-Ilse J., wrote to her husband Heinrich that she lacked his authority for disciplining the children: 'I had a sleepless night...Ilske was so difficult to subdue – she was constantly running away and disobeying me. She is missing the strong hand of a father.' Elaborating on the difficulties of single parenthood, she wrote: 'The children are sleeping. Time and again it is a relief for me when they're lying there so peacefully like angels.'[5]

From the mother's perspective, the experience of being solely responsible for the care and upbringing of her children was no light undertaking, particularly when one factors in the wartime considerations of rationing, air raid alerts and worry regarding relatives at the Front, not to mention the worsened living conditions at the end of the war. A wartime mother from Berlin-Grunewald described the relentlessness of her task in a letter to a friend on 2 March 1945:

> The alarm goes day and night now and in between we have power-cuts, no telephone and are very hungry. Thank goodness that I've been able to keep the little ones well fed up to now, even if I have to go to great lengths to fill their mouths...After we've eaten they always ask what else there is to eat.[6]

Looking after children single-handedly could thus put mothers under strain as they negotiated the difficulties of wartime on the home front.

Evacuation was another element of the wartime experience that mothers and small children went through without the father. Even where the father had not been called away to war therefore, families could be ripped apart. Relocated for their own safety to areas less threatened by the bombing, approximately half a million children and their mothers had to get to grips with their new life, be it with relatives or total strangers, and often in conditions which were considerably worse than they were used to. Warm welcomes, it seems, were rare for these evacuees, who were more often than not an unwanted presence in the homes they had been sent to. Quite apart from this, tensions arose with host families because of the differences in lifestyle between the town and the countryside. While farmer's wives sometimes looked upon evacuated women as lazy because they tended to look after their children rather than work, women evacuated from the towns encountered country bumpkins who seemed to have very blinkered horizons. In contrast to children, and in particular girls, who enjoyed spending this period of time with their mother, mothers often found this adjustment difficult. Christabel Bielenberg was one such mother. With bomb raids becoming a constant threat, she left her family home in Berlin with her three young boys. Looking back to the autumn of 1943, she recalled how wearing the experience of evacuation had been:

> I knew that I should be overflowing with gratitude for my lot, which was so much better than most, but I was tired of living in spare bedrooms, in easily spared bedrooms, of scrounging for my children, and apologizing for my children, of trying to resist the temptation to return home.[7]

On top of getting used to an unwelcoming and unfamiliar place, many women felt the separation from their husbands and older children very keenly.[8]

Separation from their older offspring, who were evacuated unaccompanied during the war, presented mothers with a different kind of challenge. This happened most commonly in the last two years of the war as part of the Extended Children's Evacuation to the Countryside (*erweiterte Kinderlandverschickung*). After the air raid attack on Hamburg of 25 July 1943 around 1.7 million children aged 6 to 14 were evacuated from areas across Germany threatened by bombing.[9] Emotions ran high amongst mothers and children alike as they were separated. As one girl later recalled of her departure: 'On the afternoon of 14 February, I was loaded onto a bus. Then my mother went crazy. She cried like mad and said, "I cannot leave my daughter alone, don't you see..." '[10] Not just mothers, but all family members were affected by the evacuation. One wartime child, Herbert Weber, later recalled the farewell scene with his mother prior to his departure for Rügenwalde:

> The big farewells began. Us boys, who were as hard as Krupp-manufactured steel, showed no emotion. Our mothers' tears apparently had no impact upon us. But I remember holding back the feelings that overcame me as my mother took me into her arms. I could have wailed. But who wanted to be that sissy in front of all one's peers?[11]

Evacuation disrupted family relationships and could lead to estrangement between parents and children, as Hermann D. from Hamburg explained, recalling the awkwardness of his mother's visit to his evacuation home in Bavaria:

> My mother was standing in the doorway. The only thing I could think of to say was 'Mummy'. I remember thinking, should I stay sitting down or should I stand up? I didn't know. In my bafflement all I could hear was Frau Groll, saying: 'Come on Hermann! Aren't you going to give your mother a kiss?' I was rigid, both internally and outwardly... Stiffly I shook my mother's hand and had none of it as she tried to pull me into an embrace. My greeting was a bitter disappointment to her. She had expected a very different welcome from her once cuddly son.[12]

A government Security Service report monitoring public opinion further illustrates the damaging effect of evacuation on morale: 'The longing of parents and children for each other is wearing everyone out. Visiting is rarely possible or allowed, so in some cases the process of estrangement is already underway. The fear is that with long separations this could become the norm.'[13] In many cases, children actually got over their initial homesickness and adjusted well to life in their new homes, though of course this was dependent on the family to whom they were evacuated. As the war dragged on however, more and more parents brought their children back home from their evacuation placements.[14]

The regime had an ulterior motive for encouraging parents to send their children away in addition to protecting children's lives. As ever, intent on bringing children round to the Nazi way of thinking, evacuation camps provided the opportunity to remove children from the influence of their families and to push the National Socialist agenda. While one boy from north Germany was reported to have picked up such a thick Bavarian accent that his parents had difficulty understanding him only months after he had been evacuated to the south, the extent to which these Nazi evacuation camps eroded parental influence in a more meaningful sense is less certain. In any case, when children heard that their hometowns had been subject to air raids, many went home of their own accord.[15]

Even so, as ever increasing numbers of boys were recruited into the war effort, and in particular, the so-called *Volkssturm*, a national militia established on Hitler's orders in October 1944, more young people were removed from the family unit.[16] And some evacuees did not return immediately to their families after the war, further adding to the prolonged period of separation. *Der Berliner* reported in October 1945 that between 13,000 and 15,000 Berlin school children were still where they had been evacuated to during the war.[17] Especially as young children tend to grow and develop so quickly, this further separation only increased the gap between the generations that had to be bridged after the war.

Where mothers and children stayed together during the war however, children could be a help and comfort for lonely wives as they forged an independent path. Herta S. was a sales assistant in Rosswein. On 30 August 1941 she explained to her husband that their child was an enormous source of strength when all else appeared bleak and hopeless: 'Dear Ernst, you mustn't think that I am completely bewildered and that I am letting myself go. Our little boy ensures that I don't do that... When I'm with the little one it is easy to forget all my worries.'[18] In the early post-war months, Beate K. expressed similar sentiments: 'When I'm feeling really down, I look at our little boy and I pull myself together for his sake.' A few months later, she again wrote of the source of strength she found in her child: 'Sometimes I think that I can't endure it anymore, but then I look at Peter and realize I must bear it. I can't cave in – Peter needs me.'[19] Children were a comfort to mothers while their husbands were away, as Mathilde W., 30-year-old business woman and mother of one from Stuttgart explained to her PoW husband on 29 June 1946: 'He [their son] comforted me so tenderly while I was crying with longing for you. I'm so pleased that I have him. He bridges the gap to you and with him I am not so lonely.'[20] Their children gave these women a focus, a sense of purpose, and importantly, an incentive not to fall apart when daily life became a struggle.

Some children's unawareness of the seriousness of the situation could be a calming influence on mothers, who were understandably often fraught with worry about the whereabouts and well-being of their husband, not to mention basic survival. One mother described the pleasure she derived from her daughter at a time when the war was reaching a feverish intensity on the home front:

> Fränzi is particularly sweet at the moment...'power-cuts' is one of her most recent words. She can tell the exact difference between the tones for the pre-alarm and the full alert. She always sits on my lap in the air raid shelter, nestles her head in my chest and goes to sleep.[21]

Margarete Onken, a wartime mother of three from Bremerhaven, also found that her daughter brought her relief in these hard times:

> I remember an occasion when my next-door-neighbour shouted, 'you'd better go and see to your little girl. She's over there playing in the bombed house.' I ran straight down, and what I saw was certainly dangerous, there was no denying it. But it was such a scene of childhood happiness that I didn't have the heart to disturb it...'Wheee!' My Ute shrieked in joyful chorus with the other children as, with gleaming eyes, they slid down a heap of rubble, just as if it were a children's slide. All around them was destruction, but the children's sheer joy showed that for them at least the world was not at an end...She looked at me with sheer delight in her eyes...I could only laugh with them.[22]

Children could be a source of great joy, and, in the context of the war and post-war, they enabled mothers to forget, at least momentarily, the pressures and stresses of the time. This certainly comes across in the post-war diaries of Hildegard R., a mother of three from Leipzig: 'Dieter plays so beautifully for many hours every day; it is exhilarating and often a pleasure to watch or join in his games.' In an entry a few months later, she again referred to how much she enjoyed watching her child playing: 'He often plays wonderfully for hours totally immersed in his child's world.'[23]

Many young children inhabited their own small world. As such they often remained oblivious to the dangers posed by war until these were threateningly close. Indeed children were drawn to watching wild fires burning in the distance after the enemy had dropped its bombs. The sight of American planes flying overhead in formation entranced Sabine

Kaufmann. She thought they looked like 'silver birds beneath the blue sky'. She recalled that 'My childish nature was so receptive to this spectacle that a feeling of happiness streamed through me. I had only one wish: to fly with them.'[24] Another wartime child later recalled that she remained unaware that the air raids could have been life-threatening: 'Although my first six years of life were during the war, I don't remember much about it, other than the fact that father was away. When the sirens wailed we had to go into the cellar, but I don't have any bad memories of this.'[25] For many wartime children, the seriousness of war and its potential consequences passed them by. They were not aware that anyone could be hurt, nor did they necessarily know to be afraid.[26]

There is a long tradition of children, but in particular boys, playing warlike games in peacetime. Symptomatic of the fact that children did not grasp the full seriousness of war was the fact that they continued to play war games, even when the real and immediate danger of war was so close by. One wartime child later described a much loved game called *Bombenwerfen*, whereby a pretend air raid shelter got targeted by things that were thrown at it. Heaps of rubble created by the bombings also made for exciting adventure playgrounds. Unaware or unconcerned by the dangers, children could climb up the mountains of rubble and have a great game of hide and seek. Collecting shrapnel from grenades, bombs or landmines, and then negotiating swaps of several small pieces for one large piece was another popular pastime.[27]

Younger children had nothing with which to compare their existence. The wartime and post-war years were the only reality they had known. The absence of their father and all the paraphernalia that accompanied living in a war zone were simply the norm. On 18 January 1945 one mother described her daughter's obliviousness to the goings-on in a letter to a friend: 'Sweet little Fränzi hardly notices anything about it all – she plays happily amid the chaos.'[28] Since younger children had no benchmark for comparison, they accepted the wartime and post-war situation as the norm. This meant that their observations were often rather matter-of-fact and without emotion. Writing to her husband on 23 December 1944, housewife Anne K. described their child's practical solution to his absence: 'Bärbela calls all the soldiers "Daddy", explaining "If our Daddy's not coming back, I'll need to find another father." '[29] Eleven-year-old Ulli Fromann's letter to her father after the war also effectively captures this detachment, which was typical of children:

Dear Daddy, I'm going to jump from the top bunkbed directly into your arms [when you come home] ... Yesterday we found a soldier's boot in a heap of rubble. There was still a bit of bone in it. We buried it next to the soldier's grave opposite the front garden. At school we sit on our files because we don't have desks. But we get school meals included in our ration allowance. Come home soon. With best wishes, Ulli.[30]

Ulli's younger sister Jutta also described her daily life to her father:

To my dear dear Daddy, when you come back home we are going to bake a cake. We will save all the ingredients beforehand, so that it won't be too dry. This week we got seven grams of yeast. We had to queue up for two hours for it. But when you've got yeast, you can cook a cake without fat. It tastes wonderful. We are always pleased when school is cancelled because there's no heating there. And we don't do any homework because we haven't got any books. When you come we are all going to do an enormous jig. Kisses from your daughter Jutta.[31]

Young children's limited experience of the world made them, in some senses, oblivious to its dangers. And this provided mothers with welcome relief from their own horror at the harsh realities they faced.

Older children could give other types of comfort to their mothers. In lieu of the absent husband, older offspring, who could be as young as seven or eight years old, sometimes took on the role of the father. A girl might act as a confidante by listening to her mother's hopes and fears. 'After my father went off to war, my mother said to me "You are my big one. I can rely on you. You are my helper"', one daughter later recalled. She described how the relationship with her mother became closer during the absence of her father at war. Since there were no adults around, her mother appointed her, the eldest child, as her helper. 'She would put her hand gently on my shoulder' the girl recalled, 'and say: "Look! What do you think?" Whenever she was there, she wanted me by her side...I was obviously very proud of being the eldest. And when she said "you are just like your father," I was ecstatic.'[32] Ingrid S. from East Prussia recalled how the dynamic of her relationship with her mother similarly changed after father had been called up: 'Mother totally changed...I was the eldest...She involved me in lots of things, and spoke to me about lots of things. We got on well. I even looked after the baby.'[33] Many children like Ingrid S. shared the mother's daily tasks in a sort of stand-in partnership (*Ersatzpartnerschaft*). After the war in particular, when material conditions had severely deteriorated, children took on practical as well as emotional responsibilities. 'I do a lot because my mother is so timid' wrote ten-year-old Theodor G. in his diary in February 1946. He had a finely attuned sense of what his mother found acceptable and was at great pains to conceal the source of his money from her scrupulous eye:

> I don't tell her when I do things on my own... I've already stolen stuff... Then I sell my booty. Mother can go shopping when there's lots of money. Each week I get between 12 and 15 Marks, mostly from the Americans. I bargain with them for 20 or 30 Marks. I don't show it all to my mother though, or else she takes it away from me.[34]

Through such tasks, children made significant contributions to the family income.

Children were often proud to help their mothers. Being able to contribute made them feel grown up and rightly important. Helga, who was ten when the war ended, played an important role in procuring food for the family after the war. Using English that she had learnt at school, she went to the nearby barracks of the occupying American troops, and negotiated deals to wash and iron their clothes in return for food.[35] Many children of the post-war era developed cunning methods of getting food for their families. Since she looked so malnourished, one little girl used her distressing appearance to her advantage on foraging trips, pulling at the heartstrings of better-fed farmer's wives. 'With me playing the role of the starving child', she later remembered, 'this foraging trip with my siblings was a great success. We surprised our mother with a bag of flour, three eggs and a few potatoes. And she was overjoyed.'[36]

In many cases therefore, children became key to the household's survival in this era. Pre-war, only a few children of primary school age from lower class and rural families made material contributions to the family, but after the war even children from middle-class families became involved with such tasks.[37] As such they assumed an importance within the family far greater than would have been the case in peacetime with the father at home. And thus, although wartime and post-war circumstances had forced mothers to cope with their children alone, offspring could be a source of comfort, strength, and crucially a provider of material goods in these difficult times.

Fatherhood from afar

The war prevented many fathers from building close relationships with their offspring. Günter H., the soldier and father-to-be we met in Chapters 2 and 3 who had preserved a sense of togetherness with his wife

Helma through regular letter-writing, was nonetheless forced to discuss potential children's names with his wife via letter, since they were separated during her pregnancy: 'My dear Helma, ...I am in total agreement with you that a simple one syllable name fits best with our surname. I think that all the names that you mentioned are very nice.'[38] And many men received news of the birth of their child via *Feldpostbrief* or even the radio programme *Wunschkonzert*. From Leipzig Irene B. sent word to her husband at the Front on 1 May 1943: 'Your May Day child has arrived and is called Holger. He weighs seven pounds and is healthy.'[39]

Fathers were all too aware that precious moments of fatherhood and family life were passing them by. Acknowledging this, one father wrote to his daughter: 'You were a little girl when I left, but now you are a grown up young lady. Oh, I've missed the most special stages.'[40] On 4 February 1945 mother of two Luise S. from Fellbach, who we heard from in Chapter 4, wrote to her husband Paul about how their two children had changed a lot since he was last at home: 'Did you receive the pictures I sent? The children have grown a lot since your last visit and have really changed. In fact you would barely recognise them now.'[41] Over the course of his long imprisonment in Russia, Field Officer Dr Rolf M. received several photographs from home. Like so many other fathers who were away from home for years, his letters home expressed amazement at how much his children had grown and changed:

4.2.51: How happy I was to find a picture of you all tucked in the letter. As far as I can tell from the photograph you all look well. I was only struck by how big the children are. Gerold looks very similar to a picture that was taken of me in the summer of 1917. Ute is almost a fully-fledged teenager with those thick plaits.[42]

6.6.54: My dear Thea! I received the picture of Ute's confirmation with your note. How lovely! ...I certainly wouldn't have recognised our two youngsters if I had met them.[43]

Away from home, fathers missed out on watching their children grow up, so much so that on receiving photographs, many men declared that they would not have recognized their own children in the street.

Though this paints a bleak picture of how the war affected the relationship between fathers and children, fathers eagerly tried to bridge the gap with their children. And their efforts often met with success in maintaining a relationship with their children from afar. Husbands desperately asked their wives to fill them in on the development of their

Figure 5.1 A mother records her son taking his first steps in her picture diary on Christmas day 1944

children. Albert S., a former sales agent from Westfalen, was serving as a midshipman in Finland. He expressed great sadness that he was missing out on his children growing up: 'I find it hard to believe that Michael is so big. It is such a shame that I wasn't able to see him in these early stages at all. You've always had to describe him in your letters.' He later elaborated on these feelings: 'I think I've read all your letters a good six times. Time and again I enjoy reading every little detail you write about the children.'[44] Former tradesman and wartime Lance Corporal Heinz R., who, as we saw in Chapter 2, was keen to know his wife's inner thoughts and feelings, was also eager to hear whether or not his daughter had started walking: 'Can she walk yet? Be sure to write when she takes her first steps.'[45] Like Albert S. and Heinz R., Rolf M. was also eager to learn more about his children. Writing from Soviet PoW camp after the war, Rolf M. asked his wife about the personalities and interests of his two children:

> Please tell me all about the children and how they have developed. Is Gerold learning to play the violin? Did he get the instrument from Uncle Ernst? Does Ute show any signs of having musical talent? Do the children do gymnastics?...What are their views on drawing and painting, and on weaving and handicrafts? And what has become of Gerold's love for horses and animals in general? After so many years I find it hard to picture how the children have grown and changed.[46]

Of course not all fathers asked after their children's progress with musical instruments, weaving and handicrafts, for these activities were largely the preserve of well-to-do middle-class children. Nonetheless, fathers of all classes demonstrated curiosity and interest in the development of their children. Indeed a sample of 1266 fathers' letters from the *Feldpostbriefarchiv* in Berlin, which were sent from husbands to wives during the war, demonstrates that fathers grew increasingly keen for news of their children.[47]

Eager to ensure that their children were thriving in their absence, soldiers sometimes gave parenting advice to their wives via letter, as did infantryman Josef B. to his wife Helene: 'Make sure Friedhelm [their son] always does his homework, so that he won't have to stay down a year at school. Help him as much as possible.'[48] Offering guidance to wives was a way of remaining involved in their children's upbringing and affecting their socialization. Gerhard Udke, the teacher from Berlin who found it difficult to write home from his noisy barracks, was nonetheless keen to oversee the rearing of his five children from the field. In a letter to his wife Dorothea, he stressed how important it was that his children established a good relationship with God, which amounted to more than simply repeating empty phrases. He told her not to let the children get away with little lies and to sing with them in the holidays. He also said that it was important to him that they spoke freely and without embarrassment, but properly. For his eldest son's behaviour, he outlined specific instructions to his wife:

> Gunnar should learn to do his homework on his own as soon as possible; sit with him at first, and guide him, and then leave him alone to work. Preferably stay in the room so that you can make sure he does his bits of work one after the other and is not distracted. And demand impeccable neatness and organization. He should never be

allowed to go to bed until he has tidied up all his things. He must be made to be responsible for himself. And if he doesn't manage this, you must deprive him of something nice every now and then.[49]

Fathers were thus able to remain involved in their families' lives, even if they were not physically there.

Many children regularly wrote and received letters from their fathers. Young children had time allocated in class to write to their fathers. In Dortmund 11-year-old Edith wrote to her father, explaining 'I am sitting here with my classmates. Everyone is writing to their fathers in the field. So that's why I am also writing.'[50] In some classes, letters to fathers were dictated.[51] In November 1944 the National Socialist Leadership Staff of the Armed Forces commanded soldiers to write directly to their children to explain (in appropriate terms) about life at the Front.[52] *Das Blatt der Hausfrau* also encouraged fathers to write to their children:

Sometimes write the little ones a letter of their own. A letter that they, rather than their mother, can open themselves! And if the child can't read yet, draw him something – perhaps the house you're staying in; the field kitchen; the horse you ride, or something like that. And then you can be sure of receiving a reply from the proud recipient of your letter.[53]

Many soldiers serving at the front were not able to meet their newborn children. 'You are now a whole week old and your father still does not know what his little darling looks like' wrote Klaus B. to his baby daughter Ulrike. He continued 'Your father only knows that you, the little bundle, were nine pounds, are called Ulrike and that you and your dear mummy are in good health. With all his heart he longs to hear more about you, because he wants to have a picture in his mind of you darling little creature…So I wait on post from one day to the next.'[54] Werner L., a First Lieutenant from Krefeld, also wrote to his two-year-old daughter:

I have your picture in front of me, in which you are looking at the camera attentively with child-like seriousness. It reinforces to me the fact that I haven't seen you in a long time, and how much you've changed in the time since I was last at home. You and your mother are going through all the wonderful early stages of child- and motherhood without me. I am still amongst soldiers, as I was two years ago when we knew that you were on the way.[55]

Letters kept the dialogue open between fathers and their children. Six-year-old Lorle, for example, received a letter from her father in Russia in 1943, expressing how much he missed her: 'I keep on seeing you before me, as you cried the night I had to leave again. Believe me, my child, I found it heart-wrenching. But I had no choice and had to go back, although I would have far rather stayed with you all.'[56] For fathers, letters offered a way of being part of their children's lives. Though they missed out on being with their children in person, through letters fathers could ask and hear about important landmark days in their child's life, such as their birthdays and their first days at school. A reserve officer from Thüringen, for example, told his daughter Liese, 'I would have loved to have eaten your first pancakes with you.'[57] Eugen N., the French PoW who longed to sit hand in hand with his wife in Chapter 3, expressed similar regret: 'It is a shame that I won't be able to hear Fred when he's doing a sing along on the radio. I would love to see the group.'[58] But though fathers like Eugen N. were sorry to miss out on being with their children, through effective communication they were kept abreast of their children's activities. Indeed these letters demonstrate a detailed knowledge on the part of fathers about the everyday lives of their children.

Fathers remained actively involved in the socialization and education of their offspring through letters. Children's schoolwork, for example, was the topic of many discussions in wartime correspondence. Gerhard Udke discussed his children's reports with his wife by letter, offering his opinions: 'Ulli's report is great. And justifiably so. Ernst is simply too lazy; without a doubt he could and must work hard and methodically. Udo has improved; Hanspeter appears to be a hopeless case. Klaus's mark for English has gone down due to laziness. He is lacking the disciplining influence of a father.'[59] In another correspondence, nine-year-old Richard sent his schoolwork to his father, who was very impressed by his son's efforts and frequently answered queries relating to his homework. Richard's father wrote, 'I am sending you your exercise book back. Carry on so diligently and you'll make your parents very proud. Your essay on local history is very good.'[60] One son, rather amusingly, wrote to his father in English to demonstrate his progress with the language:

Father! We come *grade* out the school. It was *Fliegeralarm. Ungefähr nach* one hour was again *Entwarnung*. One *Zeichenstunde* is *ausgefallen*. In English we have a *Lied* and a proverb learn must. That *Lied heisst* 'school is over'. The proverb *heisst*: 'Early to bed and early to rise, makes a man healthy, wealthy and wise. No gains without pains. *Uns go it all together good. Herzliche Grüsse,* Your Pet B..[61]

His father wrote back, proud to see that his son was doing well at school:

I was thrilled to receive your letter from 15.11.44. Thank you so much! I fear that in two or three years time I won't have enough knowledge of English to be able to read your letters... Mother writes that you are doing really well at school. I'm pleased to hear it and I expect that you keep up the good work.[62]

Far from wartime separation preventing meaningful communication between family members, through letters fathers could be involved in serious discussions with their wives and children. Fathers continued to give paternal advice during this period, if only by letter. One father advised his daughter to learn English, as it was so widely spoken worldwide;[63] another suggested his daughter learn to type as a way to earn money;[64] and another urged his son to darn his socks, assuring him that he was himself 'doing it here as well and it's good if you can do it too.'[65] One father offered his son advice about women: 'Above all, guard against bad girls. Keep in mind the proverb: "Act in haste, repent at leisure". Also don't be led astray by politics. Hopefully my well-meant advice won't come to you too late, in spite of my years of absence, and will be of much use to you.'[66] In spite of the war-enforced separation, therefore, fathers were still able to offer guidance to their offspring.

Many fathers' letters asked children to help their mothers. 'So you've just had three weeks of holiday, have you? Did you help your dear mother diligently? Did you do the drying-up well? I'll be so pleased if you are helping Mummy!' wrote Richard's father, imploring him to help his mother. On 4 July 1943 he further added: 'Give your mother lots of help. You are the eldest and thus must show her greater understanding.'[67] Another father asked his eldest, 12-year-old daughter, not to antagonize her younger siblings:

I sometimes worry when I think that Ulrich and Liesel, who are both younger than you, are not very kind and obedient. Do you think you can always set a good example to them? And can you not treat them too harshly?... You can make me very happy, if Mummy is able to write that you are just as nice to Ulrich and Liesel as to Lottie [the baby].[68]

Appealing to his eldest child to behave well and support his mother, Albert S. wrote to his son as follows:

> Help your mother when she is working in the garden or cleaning out the hen-house, so that she doesn't have too much to do…At the moment Tommy will be coming often with many planes, wanting to drop bombs. You must always go to the cellar very quickly, so that they can't harm you. Can you all put your own gas masks on? You are the eldest, and must be sure to know how to do this yourself…I hope that mother will always be able to write to me that you've been a good boy, so that I can be very proud of my eldest son.[69]

Some fathers used this correspondence to reprimand their children for unacceptable behaviour. When the father of 15-year-old Egbert found out that his son had been missing confirmation classes deliberately, he expressed his fury at his son in no uncertain terms via letter. On another note he wrote to Egbert imploring him to look after his appearance.[70] So fathers made a big effort to stay involved with and engaged in their children's lives. Though the circumstances of war, with separation, poor communication possibilities and many other pressures, were far from ideal for forging close relationships between fathers and children, fathers could still play an active role in the lives of their children, albeit via letter.

For some children, their absent father was still very much kept alive and part of family life in ways other than letters. On numerous occasions the picture of the absent father took on a life of its own for young children, as one wife reported to her husband in November 1942: 'Today Günter pointed at your picture and said "the other Daddy must also come home soon Mummy." '[71] In May 1945 Heinrich J. learned from his wife Diana-Ilse that she and the children had sat in bed with his picture talking about him: 'This morning I had both children in my bed and we thought about Daddy, who we miss so much. Ilske sometimes has long imaginary conversations with him and gesticulates in front of his picture.'[72] When she asked her children what Daddy would say to one of their demands, one wife reported to her husband, her son Bernd would run straight to the father's photograph in the bedroom and then return beaming, explaining that Daddy had allowed whatever it was![73] For many children, their absent fathers still made a powerful impression on their daily lives. Even in 1946, three years after the family last saw the father, Luise S. wrote in her diary that her children mentioned him daily: 'Your children haven't forgotten you. In fact, quite the reverse is true. We talk about you lots. Not a single day goes by in which Daddy doesn't crop up as we go about our daily business.'[74] Ten-year-old Edith kept her father's involvement alive in more literal terms. In a letter to her father who was at the Front on 6 April 1943, she explained 'When we eat supper in the evening there's someone missing. That someone is you. I always pretend that you are sitting there and I say "Daddy, are you making another sandwich?" and then Mummy is forced to laugh.'[75] In many respects then, though fathers were sometimes away from home for years on end, they did not become distant figures, but were rather very much part of day-to-day reality in the private sphere.

Many children longed for their father's return, as the observations of their mothers in letters and diaries testify. Annegret K. was one of many children who would go down to the station just in case their fathers arrived. Her mother Anne recorded this in her diary: 'Annegret often comes home with tear-stains on her face, saying "Daddy didn't come back on the train today either. So many soldiers got off the train Mummy, but he wasn't one of them." '[76] Like Annegret K., Ilske J. did this too, as her mother Diana-Ilse noted in her diary: 'Ilske plays outside with the other children. I often don't see her for over an hour...Recently she explained that she was merely looking to see if Daddy was coming.'[77] On 10 December 1945, one daughter wrote to her father: 'Oh Daddy, if only we were together. I don't want St. Nicholas to bring me anything but you.'[78] Across the country children got excited when they saw that a letter from their father had come, and this prompted them to ask expectantly when he was to return. All of this suggests that children may well have paid attention to the advice given by their fathers via letter, and thus, the desire to keep the relationship alive on both sides could go at least some way in bridging the gap caused by separation.

Through the efforts of both mothers and fathers, children did not forget their fathers in the periods of separation in war. With limited means, fathers often did a remarkable job at maintaining a presence in the lives of their offspring. Mothers in turn played their part in keeping fathers alive in the active imagination of their children. And of their own accord, children were keen to learn more about their fathers. All of these factors helped to overcome the conditions inimical to building family relationships.

Reunion

As fathers gradually trickled back from war and post-war internment as Prisoners of War, family members were confronted with the emotionally charged experience of reunion as a family, often after years apart. Everyone had questions racing through their minds: Is she here? Is he on the train today? Will she recognize me? What will she look like? Will my boy recognize me? Will I recognize him or will he have grown too much?[79]

Children like Irene Anhalt from Berlin sometimes expressed reservations about the return of their father:

> The news of your imminent return struck me quite differently from the way I had pictured it all those years. Anxiety, nervousness, the fearful question of how you might be – all this I experienced more clearly than my joy … I was uncertain – did I really still want you? Did I actually still need you? My relationship to you consisted of waiting for you. If you came back now, I would have to give up my longing and give you a place in my life, not just in my imagination. The memory of the grey, careworn men, the returnees of the first postwar years, came back to me: would you too look like that – perhaps even worse. I made an effort to suppress my doubts; I wanted to be happy about your return.[80]

Paul Z. from the Warthegau also awaited his father's return with trepidation. His father had been missing for years. This uncertainty had a conflicting effect on him. He recalled experiencing varying emotions from hope to fear, to worry about how it would be when his father returned. He had been told that his father was excellent at sport, but Paul by contrast was not so physically fit and was rather a mummy's boy. Paul worried that his father might boss him around and take away his privileges.[81] 'I had mixed feelings about the return of my father' said Falko Berg from Hebel, Nordhessen, who, like Irene Anhalt and Paul Z., recalled feeling apprehensive at the prospect of his father's return in the summer of 1946:

> Naturally I was pleased that the family would be complete again and I was particularly pleased that my mother was so happy. But I had never personally missed my father. I hardly knew him and my grandfather had always been the man of the house.[82]

Upon reunion some fathers found themselves openly rejected by their children, who shrank from them with fear. One returnee remembered his daughter saying 'that's not my father!' when introduced; another recalled being scratched in the face by his daughter; and another

Figure 5.2   A father and daughter meet again at a train station after years of wartime separation

remembered how his daughter asked his wife to send him away because they didn't need him.[83] Children of the post-war era often complained to their mother 'you described to me what father was like. He isn't like that at all.' As the father returned dirty and unshaven, he did not live up to the clean father as pictured in photos.[84] One father recalled, 'My little daughter, who was seeing me for the first time, passed her eyes distrustfully over my picture on the beside table as a security check, before greeting me hesitantly.'[85] Maria Thiel observed a similar experience as her husband and her daughter met for the first time:

> My husband stood in the doorway. Due to illness he had been released after a short period in PoW camp. Our youngest was sitting on the potty at the time. He introduced himself, beaming, presented himself and said over and over again 'I am Daddy'. But the little one shook her head vigorously, pointing to his picture, which was on the bedside table, and said 'Daddy's there'. She had not seen him before.[86]

In another case a father returned home to his family on Christmas Eve. His daughter, aged seven at the time, did not know how to behave around him. To her, he was a complete stranger. So when, amid the festivities, she refused to sit on his lap as her mother had asked, she was sent from the room in disgrace.[87] Many other families encountered similar situations. One young boy, Rolf, reacted very badly to his father's return. Used to climbing into his mother's bed every morning, he was extremely put out when one day his father returned home from war and sat on the end of the bed. Perhaps fearful that his close relationship with his mother would be threatened by his father's return, he shouted at his father 'Go away! Go away! Can't you see that this space is taken?'[88] Anna Falk too later described the distance between her husband and her son, who returned from nine years in Prisoner of War camp: 'It took over half a year until the boy got used to the fact that this man belonged to the family and that this picture or this word "Daddy", (*Vati*), was a person, who lived with us.'[89] For children who were used to living without their fathers, returning soldiers felt more like intruders than members of the family. 'For a long time it was like having a stranger in the family,' one daughter remembered about her father's return:

> This man was my father; he was called it and had been introduced to me as 'Father'. That much was clear. But I couldn't match my associations with the word father with this man...I understood and accepted that he was my mother's husband...[but] I remember saying to my mother, 'I see that this is your husband now. But where is our father?' Inside, I still waited for my father.[90]

Children's simplistic understanding of the ordeal of war did not aid their relationships with their war-weary fathers after the war. In contrast to the efforts made by husbands and wives to understand what their spouses had been through, young children did not empathize with their fathers' experiences. Even those who had the imagination to do so could not even begin to understand what their fathers had been through. For children, war was somewhere or something that required fathers to go and keep watch, to keep the evil enemy out of the country. Children prayed to God and to Hitler, asking that their father would not die. Sometimes fathers had leave from the war and came home. They wore scratchy uniforms and wanted to hold their children's hands when they went for walks. There were always letters to be sent and parcels to wrap. At the post office they had to wait in long queues to send the parcels because everyone wanted to send their fathers packages. The enemy took fathers Prisoners of War and removed them to far away places where it was always cold and they got nothing to eat. In practice for children this meant that fathers returned 'unable to work but demanding the lion's share of the rations'.[91] Whilst young children's lack of awareness of the seriousness of war could be helpful to mothers in wartime as an escape from the seriousness of the situation, so too could this be a hindrance to family interaction upon reunion.

Men too sometimes found reunion with their children awkward. In one story, a father marvelled at how much his children had grown up in his absence – so much so that they were really strangers to him:

> The eldest of the two children, a boy, dared to pull at the returnee's coat-tails and to ask: 'Are you really our father?' Franz disentangled himself from Agnes and turned to the children, who had no memories of him. So much time had passed. The once funny little things had become school children, who were now standing slightly awkwardly in front of him. Their faces were marked with new traits that he didn't recognise, but which he must get used to. The little creatures from his last holiday were now young people.[92]

Observing a father's behaviour at reunion, one onlooker noted: 'The man also didn't dare to hug his daughter. She was a stranger to him. He had never seen her before...It took a long time before the man could speak. And then he said "you're cute"...A totally banal sentence.'[93] Fathers sometimes found it difficult to respond to the affection shown by their children. Their exposure to death and suffering in war had stunted their interpersonal emotions, and they had become closed. Some children took such behaviour as rejection, particularly if they had had a much closer relationship with their fathers pre-war. Monika, born in 1943, recalled how war damaged her relationship with her father: 'I personally only have one really deep long-term loss from the war – the relationship with my father – because he was a stranger to me when he returned, and he remained one.'[94] In some cases the father–child relationship was a lot more distant as a result of the prolonged separation. As one wartime child later explained, her father's absence made her relationship with him more remote:

> When I was really little my father often used to pick me up in his arms and carry me around...Everything changed when the war broke out and my father had to become a soldier. I don't know what happened, but when he came home on leave I suddenly respected and even feared him. I can still see him as he came through the

door in his uniform, with tall boots and his soldier's cap. I always recognised him, but he seemed enormous in the door frame and somehow...different. He no longer showed much interest in us children.[95]

As fathers gradually returned home from war, readjustment was the order of the day. Whether it was the father feeling left out by his wife's close relationship with the children or the children feeling left out with the father now claiming the mother's attention, or even the mother feeling torn in her affections, war on a small scale, (*der Krieg in Kleinen*), referred to this emotional power play between family members which took place after the cessation of hostilities. Fathers and children often jealously competed for the mother's attention. Falko Berg, who was six when the war ended, remembered:

> Full of jealousy, I noticed that I had to take second place to my father in my mother's affections. This, and the fact that my annoying sister had become my father's favourite, infuriated me even more. The little changes also irritated me, as I have to give up my bed for my father, and from then on sleep on the sofa.[96]

Like Falko Berg, Ingrid S., expressed feelings of jealousy towards her father when he returned from Prisoner of War camp in 1947: 'I had to share my mother with him. I found this really difficult. We belonged together – it was great doing everything as a unit. And then my father came and it didn't suit me at all.'[97] Another daughter also felt resentful that she had to share her mother's attention on her father's return: 'He took my mother away from me. She then had him and didn't need me anymore. That's how I felt when my father came home.'[98] This could only add another layer to the inter-generational tension, which, to a degree could be expected when adolescents went through puberty.

Fathers sometimes felt intimidated by this mother–child bond, as one explained: 'They were really intimate with each other, and I came as a stranger to it all.'[99] Though by no means in all cases, some men 'felt left out of the close-knit family circle'.[100] Fathers who felt this way commonly sought to carve out a role for themselves in the home. This sometimes took the form of taking on the disciplining of the children. Fathers often wanted to make a proper man out of their son believing in the virtues of 'toughening up' or *abhärten*. Prior to this, sons would have picked up their behaviour from their grandmothers, grandfathers and mothers.[101] One 'helpless wife' (*ratlose Frau*) wrote in to the problem page of *Das Blatt der Hausfrau* in February 1949, complaining of how her husband had become much stricter with their son since returning from war:

> When my husband came home from PoW camp, he was pleased to see that everything had been kept in good order. Then the trouble began. First of all because of the boy. The child was reserved towards the father. He was estranged from his father. The boy resisted being treated roughly and wouldn't stop screaming. Even when he learnt not to do this, there was always friction. He was a nervous child. But my husband thought he could solve this by being heavy-handed.[102]

In some cases therefore, sons may have had a harder time adjusting to their father's return than daughters. But in many ways the father's behaviour in the home had less to do with the gender of his offspring than a more general desire to restore his former position, as one daughter described: 'For father, part of returning meant re-establishing the ancient division of labour: the man of the house vis-à-vis the womenfolk; the protector vis-à-vis the protected.'[103]

Where fathers sought to assert authority over their children by virtue of their traditional position as head of the household, this rarely went well. Either children rejected this authority, deferring instead to the instructions of their mother, to whom they were used to obeying. Or, children submitted to their father's authority, with the concurrent effect of worsening their relations through resentment. Mothers commonly felt that it was their job to hold their families together and smooth over tension between husbands and children. The question of authority was by no means always problematic, but it was nonetheless an additional concern on top of the generally difficult conditions after the war.[104] Ingrid S. remembered that her father tried and failed to reassert his authority after returning:

> The situation was so alien to him. He observed that everyone always had something to say, and how us children were also allowed to contribute. This is what we'd done when it was just mother and us children...I was eight when my father was called-up and twelve when he came home. The war had changed him a lot. Before the war he was strict, and he tried to re-establish this heavy-handedness after the war. But us children and also my mother no longer accepted it.[105]

Since fathers had not played a regular part in the child's home life, this sometimes made for a problematic relationship in the flesh post-war.[106] What role then did the father occupy within the home upon his return?

Did family life revolve around the figure of the father after the war, with him being the source of all authority, security and wisdom for the children?[107] Or had the experience of mothers coping alone in wartime provoked a trend towards greater equality and the sharing of ideals by husbands and wives?[108] Sociologist Hilde Thurnwald's study of Berlin families showed that both in rural and urban areas, the authoritarian family type was atypical. Overall, it seems that in most families the influence of the mother on education was more important than paternal authority.[109] Given the tendency of spouses to return to traditional roles within marriage after the war, it might seem logical that this return would apply to parenting too. However it seems more plausible that the war, and with it the occasion for mothers to interact with their children alone on a regular basis, altered the dynamic between parents and their children more significantly than the dynamic between husbands and wives, who, for all their different experiences, had been separated from each other and then reunited.[110]

While the initial impulse of returning fathers may have been to resume their pre-war parenting style, the family had become more central emotionally to men's lives than it had been before the war. Accordingly, in the decades following the war new styles of fatherhood emerged. All the Family Ministry's rhetoric in the early 1950s about the virtues of traditional roles within the family could not halt the move towards new ideals of fatherhood no longer based on orders and obedience but rather founded on children's trust for their fathers which had been earned. This shift did not occur suddenly or comprehensively, but took place in rather an indistinct, organic manner over the course of the 1950s and 60s.[111]

During the early post-war years, the transition from father–child reunion to the establishment of a new normality at home took place without a dramatic and negative impact on familial relations in many cases. Some children's initial reservation towards their father would quickly melt away. 'The little one, who initially stared at him like a stranger, will suddenly climb onto his lap, undo the right clasp on the father's rucksack where he keeps his sweeties, and push him to his customary place, saying "You must sit here!"' predicted an article in *Das Blatt der Hausfrau*, which tried to reassure mothers prior to reunion. It continued, 'he is like a once loved toy that has been put to one side and hasn't been played with in some time'.[112] After overcoming initial nervousness, some children, like seven-year-old Renate Dziemba from Berlin reacted excitedly at the arrival of their long-absent father: 'Slowly I opened the door. Before me stood a soldier. I could not believe what I saw. I still recognised my father and he said my name, but it sounded very strange to me. "Mummy isn't here" were my first words.' Then she recalled, 'suddenly I realised that my Daddy was standing in front of me. The Daddy that I'd waited for for so long. I embraced him and pulled him into the room.'[113] Another daughter recalled how she immediately warmed to the unpatronizing way in which her father interacted with her:

> All of a sudden there was a man at the garden gate. My grandmother called out 'Children! Children, your father is here!'...I went up behind Grandmother with a half full bowl of peas in my hand. The stranger came in, turned around to shut the garden gate, took a few steps forward, but did not come too close to me. I looked at him, and he said none of the avuncular phrases such as 'My, how big you are!' or 'You'll soon be going to school, won't you?' And at that moment I hoped that he was my father. He looked in my bowl and asked, 'Did you do all that?' I replied 'Yes father!' and jumped into his arms.[114]

It was actually quite common for children to accept their returning fathers. Finally in September 1947 it was Wilhelm B.'s turn to go home. On the way home to Wilhelmshaven, all sorts of thoughts passed through the head of the 34-year-old returning PoW. Among them was the fact that he'd never met his daughter. When he arrived his daughter was waiting for him. He knelt down and opened his arms. Though she was a little bit shy, she moved towards him and shouted 'Papa'.[115] Daughters like Wilhelm B.'s could enjoy the limelight that came with the return of their father. Suddenly such children would become the centre of attention at school, in the playground and in the neighbourhood in general.[116]

In some cases children were able to resume close relationships with their fathers after the war. 'After the war I became a real Daddy's girl' recalled one girl who grew up in the post-war era. 'I was constantly climbing onto his lap and playing with him. If ever I had a problem or something wasn't going well at school, I would always go to my father and he helped me. He always had time for me. It was a great feeling to have such a close-knit relationship with my father.'[117] Eleanore S. from Saxony also found that she and her father were able to pick up from where they had left off pre-war without any hiccups: 'Because I was born in 1933, I had already had the first six years of my life with my father around, which meant that my closeness to him was easily recaptured on his periods of leave during the war.'[118] Thus in spite of the wartime and post-war circumstances which had militated against the development of strong father–children bonds, parents and children were still able to maintain close relationships in this period. Likewise, when Christian Schwarz-Schilling's father returned from American PoW camp in autumn 1945, this marked the start of a wonderful time for the Schwarz-Schilling family. Christian recalled the sense of camaraderie that developed between him and his father as they set about doing tasks like chopping wood together to ensure the family's survival.[119] In Augsburg, ten-year-old Liselotte Miller and her family were thrilled to have their father back home at the end of the war: 'Daddy was home again! We felt safe and secure again after all those years of being fatherless. He hugged us in turn and we no longer felt the cold ground beneath the paper-thin soles of our shoes. Life had begun again!'[120] Reunions between fathers and their offspring were, without a doubt, sometimes difficult. However in many cases, given the lengthy periods of separation they were surprisingly good, and formed the basis of long-term emotional bonds between family members.

In the years that followed after reunion as a family, young people's experience of war during childhood, with the threat of death in bombing raids, separation from parents in evacuation, and loss of relatives, sometimes had long-term repercussions: For decades afterwards children who had experienced air raid attacks complained of nightmares about the bombings; in a practical sense, war had disrupted schooling, which, combined with the material devastation wreaked by war, meant that many of this generation, though particularly girls aged between 14 and 16 when the war ended, sought paid employment rather than pursuing vocational training or higher education. Naturally these experiences did not affect all German children, and the extent to which those who found them traumatic varied hugely according to factors such as age and the level of family support available. 'Trauma' sometimes manifested itself among this child generation only later, when, as adults, they could understand the enormity of what they had been through, not to mention coming to terms with their parents' actions during this period.[121]

There can be no definitive answers to the question of how the relationships between parents and children were affected by World War Two and its aftermath. The answer is that it could vary massively from one family to another. The difficulties posed by the circumstances of this era have been well documented, and rightly so, as mothers did have to bring up their children alone during the war years, fathers were not physically present in the formative years of their offspring, and reintegration of the father into the family was a process of adjustment.

Yet within this context, children did perform a beneficial role for mothers during the wartime years, both in an emotional and in a practical sense; with and without the help of their mothers children did keep the image of their father alive in their imaginations during his absence; fathers were able to fulfil much of their paternal role, albeit via letter; and given how long families had been separated for, the fact that some fathers slotted back into family life so seamlessly is quite remarkable.

Conclusion

Families, as we have seen, were at the very heart of most people's experience of the war. The fates of and interactions with other family members should be central to our understanding of what it meant to live through this period. Indeed it was family life that was broken up by the call-up of men and the evacuation of children; it was family life that husbands, wives and children alike longed for during long periods of separation; and again, it was family life that would provide the site for emotional, physical and material reconstruction after the war.[1] But far from all German families being thrown into crises by the challenges that World War II presented, the experience of war, and the transition in attitudes and expectations that it effected, in many cases actually proved to enhance family cohesion.

The outbreak of war forced the private sphere into the public one. The Nazis had already attempted to do this in peacetime, with policies intent on preparing the nation for war, but, as Chapter 1 showed, there were limits to Nazi power. Families were not always easy to penetrate and, as cohesive private units with their own values, they were certainly far from passive pawns at the disposal of the regime's will. Pre-war, the Nazi government may have tried to erode the privacy of the family, but many families retained considerable agency in their private lives. The war changed all of this.

With the outbreak of war families were ripped apart, sometimes permanently, more often for a number of years, as men were mobilized and children evacuated. The human consequences of war thus threatened to undermine the family. Ironically however, for individual families it actually reinforced the value of the private sphere. During the war, when demands were made on the individual in the service of the state, the home represented a haven in which the family's own private world was at the heart of his or her concerns. And in the wake of defeat, when most public institutions and services had ceased to function, families were a support unit, without which individuals struggled badly.[2] A source of emotional comfort during the war, the family of the early post-war years was a practical survival unit. Yet it was not just this. The deep invasion of family life during the war had brought into sharp relief the importance of loved ones, which then strengthened the private sphere as people retreated there after the war.[3]

The higher visibility of women and the new permutations of the family model, all of which were a consequence of the war, encouraged contemporaries in the public sphere and historians of the period to draw two conclusions: Firstly, that the experience of war had made women stronger,[4] more independent, and, by implication less desirous of male support. And secondly, that the experience of war threw families into a state of crisis.[5] After the war, the first West German government was seriously concerned that the experience of war had drastically altered pre-war conceptions of gender roles to the extent that traditional 'bourgeois' families, even if they never actually represented the majority in reality, would no longer be the prevailing ideal type of family. Women, who crucially were far more visibly present in employment in the public sphere, and more present generally, due to the large numbers of men who were dead, missing, or held in PoW camps, were seen by CDU politicians such as Family Minister Würmeling as a threat to established norms where gender roles were concerned.[6]

Magazine journalists fuelled further speculation that traditional conceptions of the family were under threat, featuring articles on the diverse permutations of the 'normal' family model which had been created by war – the *Onkel-Ehe*, whereby widowed women lived with a new partner outside marriage to retain their dead husband's pension; the *Farbige Besatzungskinder,* illegitimate offspring of German women and Black American occupation troops; or more general articles about women coping alone so well, the implication being that women no longer needed the support of a man.[7]

Further contributing to this picture of families being in crisis at the end of the war has been the view that letters were a poor way to communicate during wartime separation. The extent to which the channels of communication remained open has often been down-played, with the problems and shortfalls of letter-writing becoming the main focus.[8] Post did become intermittent in some theatres of war, particularly in Russia after Stalingrad; letters could lead to misunderstandings; and some authors may have been selective in what they wrote, perhaps to protect the recipient from the unpalatable truth. However, as Chapter 2 showed, in many ways letters were a very effective way to communicate. Couples sent hundreds of letters to each other – in this way they were able to gain an understanding of the issues that their spouse had faced.[9] So in many cases, when couples came to be reunited, they were not totally ignorant of the experiences of their partner. The channels of communication were even sometimes more open than in peacetime, because letters could act as an emotional compensation for the toughness of war, whereby people used letter-writing as an opportunity to pour out all their feelings because they had no choice but to cope and get on with their situation the rest of the time.[10]

Focusing on emotions in sources from the private sphere, such as letters, diaries, oral histories, and eyewitness reports, has shown that attitudes and responses to the experience of war and its aftermath often contrast sharply with the prevailing view of the impact of war on family life. By looking at the consequences of war for the private sphere through the experiences of contemporaries rather than through the policies that followed from the social disruption of warfare,[11] we have seen how people themselves reacted to the changes brought by war. And it is through this perspective that we see that although many wives were necessarily made more independent by the absence of their husband, they most commonly looked upon this independence as an undesirable burden, faced difficulties bridging the roles of father and mother for their children, and frequently expressed the wish that their husbands should come home to relieve them of these tasks.[12] Such a finding brings the common trope about strong women versus weak men after the war into question. Men were certainly often physically and emotionally weakened by their experiences in war and post-war internment. However it does not follow from this that women were therefore automatically stronger. Chapter 4 revealed that women too were emotionally and physically exhausted by their experiences. And just like the concern in 1920s Weimar, that the 'New Woman' was threatening to overturn traditional gender roles, contemporaries' fears about 'The Strong Woman' of the post-war years far outpaced the reality.

In spite of the difficult circumstances presented by wartime separation, relations between partners could be strengthened by this experience. *Feldpostbriefe* sent between husbands and wives during the war tell us a great deal about how marital relations were affected by war. They give us a fascinating insight into couples' most private thoughts and feelings in wartime. In particular they show two important factors: that spouses missed each other and longed to be reunited; and that the experience of war and the threat of losing loved ones made people value their families all the more. Sceptics have argued that the rosy descriptions of past and future lives together, which were penned in such letters, could not be matched in reality after the war, and reunion, they claim, was commonly a bitter disappointment for all concerned.[13] In fact, however, as we saw in Chapter 3, many letters demonstrated a perceptive realism and anticipated that reunion would be a process of adjustment rather than an unproblematic transition.[14]

War, it seems, had modified people's expectations. For many the experience of war, which made death and destruction commonplace, made people be more appreciative of what they did have, for example each other and a roof over their heads, since plenty of people, to whom they compared themselves, had neither a family nor a home left after the war was over.[15] In this book we have seen many cases where families reunited happily and adjusted to life together again. This does not necessarily mean that family life itself was better or happier after the war, for the practical conditions for survival were very tough. However, since individuals had learned to cope with less, had adjusted their expectations accordingly, and were more consciously grateful to have a family at all, this all comes together to explain why families remained intact and expressed their thankfulness at being able to do so. We should not, of course, forget the 7 million Germans who died in the war leaving many more bereft relatives behind. But this research has shown that families who were given the chance to reunite demonstrated a very real willingness to persevere through the difficult post-war situation.

For fathers who had been away at war for long periods and thus absent from the home and their children who were rapidly changing and developing, correspondence with and about their offspring was often an extremely effective way of bridging the gap. Not only could mothers share the latest stories about the children with the father via letter, and send him recent photographs, as soon as children could write, they too could communicate with their absent father. Chapter 5 showed the numerous and varied ways in which fathers retained a role in their children's lives and imaginations. And thus, in spite of (particularly young) children's obliviousness and thus lack of empathy for what their father had been through in war, the father's presence in the home, even in his absence, undoubtedly eased the transition of the father back into the home. The numerous exchanges of letters between family members help us to understand why families were often able to adjust with relative ease to life together again.

Narratives that focus on families in crisis at the end of the war form part of a wider account of this era with Germans as victims of the war. These narratives imply that ordinary Germans were passive in their acceptance, endurance and experience of circumstances beyond their control. Such understandings rely on the notion that the events of history were happening to them, rather than that they themselves were making history. By bringing individual agency into the analysis, this history has shown how the initiative and action of individual family members made the unit as a whole far more resilient than has previously been believed, in spite of the difficult conditions that they faced.

This book has asked how relationships within German nuclear families were affected by the experience of World War II. Writing an emotional history of this genre, it quickly became clear that seeking definitive, quantifiable conclusions would be problematic, for unlike other aspects of the past, emotions cannot be pinned down and categorized so rigidly. As we have seen, even families from the same place in the same period could respond differently to similar experiences. Such variations from one family to another could be as much dependent on the dynamics between the personalities in that particular group, as to do with what class or geographical location the family was situated in. The findings in this book can therefore claim to be representative of the people cited here only. However, analysis of the *Feldpostbriefe* sample has demonstrated a sense of scale regarding how common certain concerns were and how this varied over the course of the war. Furthermore, given that this research has drawn on the personal experiences of well over a thousand individuals, from a cross-section of different classes, regions and backgrounds, it is a solid basis from which conclusions about family life both during and after the war can validly be drawn.

After the war, factors such as the higher visibility of women in the workplace and the rise in the number of households headed by women stirred up debate among politicians about a re-definition of female equality. Family Minister Würmeling, a staunch advocate of the traditional family model, feared the decline of the family if liberal-inspired notions of equality were enshrined in the law. His mission was thus to defend and protect the family by reimposing his vision of it 'from above'.[16] Würmeling's fears did not, however reflect a widespread desire on the part of women for change, because war had disrupted rather than transformed their role in society.[17] As Leila Rupp argues, 'the idea that wars "liberate" women, that wars bring about social revolution, overlooks the fact that societies in time of war accept changes normally considered undesirable on a permanent basis.'[18] Most women, it seems, held onto the traditional concept of the family, for in the harsh and uncertain times of the post-war era, the appeal of the traditional – what was safe and secure – was understandably considerable.

The idea that the family was a place of refuge after the war is not a new one.[19] Indeed Peukert concluded that 'the quest for introspection, private harmony and harmless normality' arose from the 'shock of the collapse of 1945'.[20] However by considering the situation from the perspective of family members themselves, this book reveals a more nuanced understanding of the family life after the war. It was not just the 'shock of the collapse' that motivated the return to the private sphere. It was also a positive affirmation of the importance of the family, prompted by the difficulties that families had faced in war, which had actually brought into relief how important this unit was.[21] 'If only you would come home soon. I've imagined our reunion a thousand times over',[22] wrote one waiting wife Diana Ilse J., who, like so many others, longed for the return of her husband. 'Spouses have grown closer to each other as a result of the difficult war years', Schelsky observed in 1949, 'because each experienced how they missed their spouse as they went through misery and worries.'[23] The war and its aftermath did, then, bring about some change – if change of a rather indistinct, emotionally felt variety – to the family relationships of Germans, within a general framework of continuity. By approaching the topic 'from below', this book demonstrates that the well-known primacy of the family in 1950s West Germany can be understood in a new way, as the product of popular aspirations, of women as well as men.

Appendices

The statistical research sample

I have carried out a statistical research sample, in which I read every tenth letter of correspondence between husbands and wives, asking a specific set of questions of each letter. From this collection I read 1,595 letters out of a sample of 15,950 letters written between 1939 and 1945. Letters were selected on the basis that the author was either a husband or wife during the war, and that they had left behind a series of letters. Letter-writers who did not survive the war were also included, since their letters could still be informative about marital relations during wartime separation. Individual letters or series with fewer than ten letters were not included. And letter series that fulfilled these criteria were picked at random. The rationale behind reading one letter in every ten was to include a range of authors and to widen the scope of the sample. In total, the sample included 88 authors; 28 were wives, and 60 were husbands. And of the 1,595 letters read, wives wrote 369 and husbands wrote 1,226. The biggest number of letters from one author was 82 and the smallest number of letters from a single author was 1 (read from a series of 10 letters). There were six authors who only had one letter each in the sample.

Since the letters were chosen at random (by the archivist, on the basis that they met the stated criteria), there are unequal numbers of letters for each year of the war and an unequal number of letters written by men and women. However, the results have been converted to percentages to ensure that the findings do not give undue weight to years where there were the most letters in the sample. The sample thus gives an indication of how common certain concerns were to correspondents. Although far more letters remain from soldiers to home than the other way around (because it was generally easier to keep these letters at home than it was in combat), this sample represents both perspectives, and is analysed accordingly so that the abundance of letters from men does not give undue weight to the male perspective in the conclusions drawn. This sample includes letters originating from all over Germany and from all fronts so as to encompass the breadth of experiences during the war. It deliberately does not pick soldiers' letters from a particular rank. Instead the letter-writers come from a wide range of professional, regional and ideological backgrounds.

Before embarking on the statistical research sample, I read many wartime letters, which brought to the fore the kinds of topics that people wrote about most frequently. The majority of letters talk about the relationship with the recipient and family, and with it the separation and longing, as well as the practical impact of the war wherever the author happened to be. And it was on this basis that the questions for the sample were chosen. By systematically reading the selected letters with specific questions in mind, the sample gives quantitative results showing how common these concerns were, and whether their import changed over time during the course of the war, or whether they varied in import for husbands and wives along a gender divide.

156

Questions for the Feldpostbriefe sample:

- Does the author mention looking forward to reunion?
- Does the [male] author ask about his children?
- Does the author mention bombing?
- Does the author mention food shortages?
- Does the author express frustration at the poor postal service in wartime?

Note: In the appendices, the term *Mittlere Reife* refers to the German equivalent of GCSEs.

Appendix 1 Distribution of letters in the sample according to the year in which they were written.

Year	No. of letters
1939	52
1940	255
1941	277
1942	318
1943	294
1944	340
1945	59
Total	1595

Appendix 2   SRS: Social backgrounds of male authors

Reference number	Name	Year of birth	Home town	Marital status by 1945	Confession	Children by 1945
3.2002.0215	Waldemar A.	1908	Berlin	Married	Protestant	Yes
3.2002.0224	Klaus B.	1902	Unknown	Married	Protestant	Yes
3.2002.0238	Wolf M.	Unknown	Unknown	Unknown	Unknown	Unknown
3.2002.0279	Kurt O.	1909	Zingst/Rügen	Married	Unknown	None
3.2002.0301	Kurt B.	1914	Wuppertal	Married	Unknown	Unknown
3.2002.0349	Emst G.	1916	Unknown	Married	Protestant	None
3.2002.0837	Hans K.	1912	Stuttgart	Married	Protestant	None
3.2002.0844	Franz K.	1903	Vienna	Married	No confession	Unknown
3.2002.0861	Karl K.	1907	Neubrandenburg	Married	Protestant	Unknown
3.2002.0866	Wolfgang K.	1923	Nowawes (bei Potsdam)	Married	Protestant	Unknown
3.2002.0888	Peter D.	1897	Aachen	Married	Catholic	Yes
3.2002.0898	Heinz M.	1909	Güstrow/Meckl.	Married	Protestant	Unknown
3.2002.0904	Martin M.	1917	Berlin	Married	Protestant	None
3.2002.0921	Leopold H.	1907	Weiler	Married	Catholic	Unknown
3.2002.0933	Horst M-W.	1918	Unknown	Married	Protestant	Unknown
3.2002.0942	Thomas N.	1912	Unknown	Married	Catholic	Unknown
3.2002.0985	Heinz R.	1912	Heiligendorf/ b. Wolfsburg	Married	Protestant	None
3.2002.1218	Alois S.	1909	St. Ingbert/Saar	Married	Catholic	Yes
3.2002.1241	Albert S.	1910	Telgte /Westf	Married	Catholic	Yes
3.2002.1246	Walter K.	1907	Gronau bei Hannover	Married	Protestant	Yes
3.2002.1286	Georg N.	1914	Unknown	Married	No confession	Yes
3 .2002.1295	Georg S.	1908	Unknown	Married	Protestant	None

Education and job details	Call-up date	Branch of the Armed Forces	Last known rank	Place of service	Number of letters by the author in the sample
Plumber	1942	Army	Private First Class	Russia	14
A-levels, university degree in law	10.1940	Airforce	Midshipman	Russia	35
Labourer	Unknown	Unknown	Unknown	Unknown	23
A-levels, university degree in law, lawyer	Unknown	Army	Captain	France, Russia	9
Pharmacist	Unknown	Army	Private First Class	Russia	7
Mittlere Reife, career soldier	1938	Army	Staff Sergeant	Poland, France, Ukraine, Russia	27
A-levels, university degree in law, lawyer	29.01.1942	Army	Lieutenant at Sea	Russia	1
Elementary school, commercial apprenticeship, book keeper	Unknown	Navy	Private First Class	Norway	18
University degree, secondary school teacher	15.9.1940	Airforce	Sergeant	German territory, Crete	2
A-levels, university degree	Unknown	Airforce	Lieutenant at Sea	Holland	6
Commercial apprenticeship, confidential clerk	01.09.1939	Army	Sergeant Major	Belgium, France	7
A-levels, university degree, dentist	1939	Army	First Lieutenant	German territory, Russia	45
Mittlere Reife, banker	20.08.1939	Airforce	Corporal	France, Russia, Belarus	82
A-levels, tax collector, tax advisor	1942	Army	Private First Class	France	2
A-levels, industrial businessman	1938	Army	Staff Sergeant	France, Russia	19
Mittlere Reife, commercial sector employee	01.12.1940	Army	Corporal	Czechoslovakia, Poland, German territory	1
A-levels, university degree, military service, curate	09.1939	Army	First Lieutenant	Rumania, Russia, France	80
Elementary school, office assistant	Unknown	Army	Soldier	Poland, Holland, Russia	16
Mittlere Reife, selling agent	1940	Airforce	Midshipman	Norway, Finland	35
Commercial sector employee	16.10.1944	SS-Polizei	Soldier	France	7
A-levels, university degree in law, trainee lawyer	01.1940	Army	Second Lieutenant	Belgium, Poland, Africa, Russia	18
Post office clerk, telegraph-related construction work	1942	Army	Private/ Infantry Man	France, Russia	3

Continued

Appendix 2 Continued

Reference number	Name	Year of birth	Home town	Marital status by 1945	Confession	Children by 1945
3.2002.1317	Paul S.	1905	Berlin	Married	Protestant	Yes
3.2002.1323	Hans-gunter T.	1908	Schwerin	Married	Protestant	Yes
3.2002.1351	Alois S.	1905	Westborken	Married	Catholic	Yes
3.2002.1359	Will W.	1907	Mannheim	Married	Protestant	Yes
3.2002.1382	Kurtz Z.	1909	Berlin	Married	Protestant	Yes
3.2002.7115	Heinz R.	1911	Unknown	Married	Unknown	Unknown
3.2002.7127	Michael B.	1914	Saarbrücken	Married	Catholic	Yes
3.2002.7128	Franz-Xaver P.	1913	Oberpfalz	Married	Catholic	Yes
3.2002.7139 (AK56)	Hellmuth H.	1904	Cologne	Married	Protestant	Yes
3.2002.7161	Hans K.	1900	Unknown	Married	Unknown	Yes
3.2002.7130	Adalbert H.	1906	Munich	Married	Catholic	Yes
3.2002.7135	Feriedrich S.	1897	Würsburg	Married	Protestant	Yes
3.2002.7159	Reinhold L.	1914	Göttingen	Married	Unknown	Yes
3.2002.7163	Otto M.	1907	Berlin	Married	Catholic	None
3.2002.7198	Richard P.	1911	Großschönau/Sachsen	Married	Protestant	Yes
3.2002.7214	Josef B.	1911	Gelsenkirchen	Married	Unknown	Yes
3.2002.7236	Rudolf D.	1912	Dortmund	Married (10.10. 1944)	Catholic	None
3.2002.7247	Werner L.	1909	Krefeld	Married	Mennonitisch	Yes

Education and job details	Call-up date	Branch of the Armed Forces	Last known rank	Place of service	Number of letters by the author in the sample
Locksmith	09.1940	Airforce	Sergeant	Poland,Silesia,Russia, German territory	27
A-levels, university degree in law; judicial officer	1941	Army	Second Lieutenant	Italy, France, Russia	63
Business man	1944	Army	Private	Poland, Russia, East Prussia	15
Lathe operator, cast iron related supervisor	02.1942	Army	Corporal	Russia	22
Independent business man	12.1942	Army	Private/ Infantry Man	Russia	7
Commercial sector employee	Unknown	Army	Private First Class	Unknown	12
Elementry school, vocational school, electrician	20.10.1936	Army	Corporal/ Sergeant	German territory, Russia, Ukraine	18
Elementry school, moulder	27.1.1943	Army	Private First Class	Russia	12
A-levels, university degree, post-doctoral study, grammar school teacher	Unknown	Army	Staff Sergeant	France, Greece, Rumania, Russia	22
Unknown	Unknown	Unknown	Unknown	German territory, Italy	19
University degree, architecht	1940	Army	Corporal	German territory, Russia, Ukraine, Yugoslavia; Italy	40
A-levels, university degree, high school teacher	27.8.1939	Army	Captain	Poland, France, Russia	18
Fish farmer	27.8.1939	Army	Corporal	Poland, France, Russia,German territory	12
Elementrary school, apprenticeship for book printing, assistantship exams	Unknown	Army	Corporal	Germany, Russia	53
Business school, conveyence business man	26.02.1943	Waffen-SS	Private First Class	France, Russia	53
Unknown	17.06.1942	Army	Private/ Infantry Man	Belgium, Russia	8
Mittlere Reife, bakery apprenticeship, baker	Unknown	Army	Private/ Leader of the private First Class	Russia, Italy	16
A-levels, university degree, political economist, postdoctoral work	31.08.1939	Army	First Lieutenant	Poland, France, Russia, German territory	13

Continued

Appendix 2 Continued

Reference number	Name	Year of birth	Home town	Marital status by 1945	Confession	Children by 1945
3.2002.7261	Jochen H.	Unknown	Unknown	Married	Unknown	Unknown
3.2002.7264	Reinhold R.	Unknown	Unknown	Married	Unknown	Unknown
3.2002.7265	Erwin M.	1897	Belgard/ Pommen	Married	Protestant	Yes
3.2002.7327	Johannes S.	1909	Rietberg/ Wiedenbrück	Married	Catholic	Yes
3.2002.7401	Peter W.	1916	Herzogenrath Merkstein	Married	Catholic	Yes
3.2002.7505	Emst S.	1906	Plauen	Married	Protestant	Yes
3.2002.2002	Heinz E.	1916	Hamburg	Married	Unknown	None
3.2002.1283	Paul S.	1910	Berlin	Married	Unknown	None
3.2002.0828	Wemer B.	1912	Berlin	Married	Protestant	Unknown
3.2002.0860	Konrad R.	1902	Potsdam	Married	Protestant	Yes
3.2002.0924	Paul W.	1907	Berlin	Married	Catholic	Unknown
3.2002.1260	Walter S.	Unknown	Unknown	Married	Unknown	Yes
3.2002.7163	Vinzenz Deuk	Unknown	Unknown	Unknown	Unknown	Unknown
3.2002.0826	Hubert S.	1909	Düsseldorf	Married	Catholic	Yes
3.2002.1214	Hans-Joachim S.	1908	Berlin	Married	Protestant	Yes
3.2002.7208	Alfred A.	1909	Hagen	Married	Unknown	Yes
3.2002.7184	Johannes H.	1902	Berlin	Married	Protestant	Yes
3.2002.7227	Reinhard B.	1920	Osnabrück	Married	Protestant	Yes
3.2002.1376	Wilhelm B.	1899	Eisleben	Married	Protestant	Yes
3.2002.7341	Günther H.	1922	Lipperland	Unknown	Unknown	None

Education and job details	Call-up date	Branch of the Armed Forces	Last known rank	Place of service	Number of letters by the author in the sample
Unknown	Unknown	Unknown	Unknown	Unknown	37
Unknown	Unknown	Unknown	Unknown	Russia	1
Secondary school, business apprentice ship, commercial sector employee, independent businessman	1939	Army	Unknown	Poland, German territory	1
Elementary school, vocational school, butcher	1942	Army	Private First Class	Bohemia, German territory	22
A-levels, university degree	Unknown	Airforce	Unknown	German territory, Russia Lithuania, Estland, Lettland, WeißRussia	41
Elementary school, travel agent	Unknown	Airforce	Private First Class	German territory, Russia	35
A-levels, university degree, doctor	1937	Army	Unknown	Czechoslovakia, Belgium, Poland, France, Russia	10
Unknown	1939	Army	Private First Class	German territory, Norway, Belarus	11
Ambassador	Unknown	Army	Unknown	Russia	2
Secondary school, locksmith	01.06.1943	Army	Unknown	German territory, Russia	3
Bookseller and publisher	01.03.1943	Army	Unknown	German territory	3
Unknown	Unknown	Navy	Unknown	German territory	7
Unknown	Unknown	Unknown	Unknown	Unknown	3
Secondary school, clerk	23.10.1940	Airforce	Private First Class	France, Russia	74
A-levels, businessman	1940	Army	Second Lieutenant	Poland, France, Russia	29
Warehouse worker	2.1943	Waffen-SS	Unknown	Poland, Ukraine	13
A-levels, university degree, lawyer	5.1939	Army	First Lieutenant	Poland, France, Russia	33
University degree, architect	1940	Army	Midshipman	Poland, Russia, Italy	3
A-levels, university degree, lawyer	09.1939	Army	Major	France, Russia	4
Unknown	Unknown	Unknown	Unknown	Unknown	7

Appendix 3 SRS: Social backgrounds of female authors

Reference number	First name	Surname	Year of birth	Place of birth	Place of residence in wartime	Marital status until 1945	Confession	Children by 1945	Education and job details	No. of letters written by author in SRS
MKB 3.2002.7327	Anne	S.	1915	Echterhoff	Verensell	Married	Catholic	Yes	Elementary school, vocational training school	23
MKB 3.2002.1241	Jo	S.	1912	Teglte	Teglte	Married	Catholic	Yes	Basic schooling, housewife	10
MKB 3.2002.7247	Liselotte	L.	1918	Cologne	Unknown	Married	Protestant	Yes	A-levels, fashion advisor	20
MKB 3.2002.0904	Gerda	M.	1917	Unknown	Unknown	Married	Protestant	None	Unknown	64
MKB 3.2002.0224	Suse	B.	Unknown	Unknown	Bad Segeberg	Married	Unknown	Yes	Unknown	11
MKB 3.2002.1286	Greta	N.	1914	Unknown	Berlin	Married	Protestant	Yes	University graduate in biology	7
MKB 3.2.7128	Elisabeth	P.	1914	Neuötting/ Oberbayern	Unknown	Married	Unknown	Yes	Elementary school, housewife	1
MKB 3.2002.1211	Erika	P.	1916	Berlin-Weissensee	Panzig/ Oberlausitz	Married	Protestant	Unknown	Domestic service, shop assistant, business woman	5
MKB 3.2002.1359	Karola	W.	1912	Unknown	Unknown	Married	Catholic	Yes	Milliner	6

MKB 3.2002.837.0	Lore	K.	1911	Stuttgart	Unknown	Married	Protestant	None	Secondary modern, shop window decorator, housewife	2
MKB 3.2002.7163	Cilly	M.	1911	Unknown	Unknown	Married	Catholic	None	Dressmaker's assistant, shop-keeper selling colonial goods	2
MKB 3.2002.0844	Margarethe	K.	1915	Unknown	Unknown	Married	Unknown	Unknown	Unknown	2
MKB 3.2002.0238	Frau	M.-P.	Unknown	Unknown	Unknown	Married	Unknown	Unknown	Unknown	1
MKB 3.2002.7505	Herta	S.	1911	Rosswein	Unknown	Married	Unknown	Yes	Elementary school, shop assistant	19
MKB 3.2002.0826	Gertrud	S.	Unknown	Unknown	Berlin	Married	Unknown	Yes	Unknown	56
MKB 3.2002.1246	Erika	K.	Unknown	Unknown	Berlin	Married	Unknown	Yes	Unknown	1
MKB 3.2002.0349	Irene	G.	Unknown	Unknown	Unknown	Married	Unknown	None	Unknown	56
MKB 3.2002.0861	Hilde	K.	1905	Osnabrück	Unknown	Married	Protestant	Unknown	University degree, PhD, sport teacher, housewife	4
MKB 3.2002.0942	Paula	N.	Unknown	Unknown	Unknown	Married	Unknown	Unknown	Unknown	1
MKB 3.2002.7130	Trudl	H.	Unknown	Unknown	Unknown	Married	Unknown	Yes	Unknown	8
MKB 3.2002.7181	Inge	H.	Unknown	Unknown	Unknown	Married	Unknown	Unknown	Unknown	6
MKB 3.2002.0279	Liselotte	O.	1914	Strasbourg	Berlin	Married	Unknown	None	Unknown	6
MKB 3.2002.200.2	Ursel	E.	Unknown	Unknown	Unknown	Married	Unknown	Unknown	Unknown	11
MKB 3.2002.7401	Gertrud	W.	1912	Unknown	Unknown	Married	Unknown	Yes	Unknown	4
MKB 3.2002.7198	Frau	P.	Unknown	Unknown	Oldenburg	Married	Unknown	Yes	Unknown	8
MKB 3.2002.7135	Elisabeth	S.	1897	Unknown	Unknown	Married	Protestant	Yes	Unknown	20
MKB 3.2002.0367	Hildegard	Unknown	Unknown	Unknown	Unknown	Married	Unknown	Unknown	Unknown	4
MKB 3.2002.0828	Herta	B.	Unknown	Unknown	Unknown	Married	Unknown	Unknown	Unknown	2

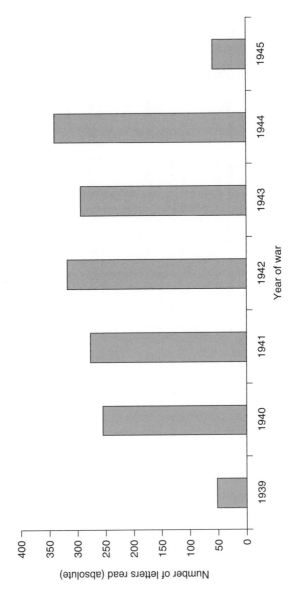

Appendix 4 SRS: Number of letters read per year

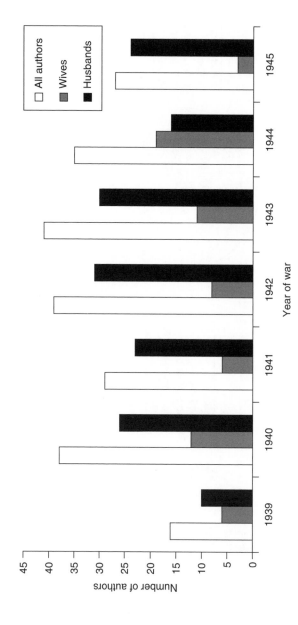

Appendix 5   SRS: Number of authors per year

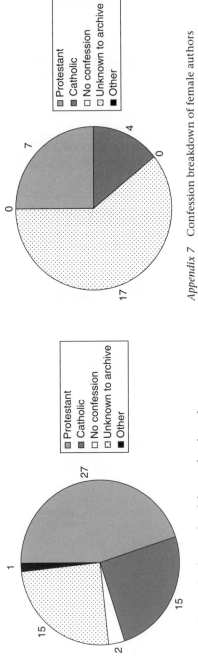

Appendix 6 Confession breakdown of male authors

Appendix 7 Confession breakdown of female authors

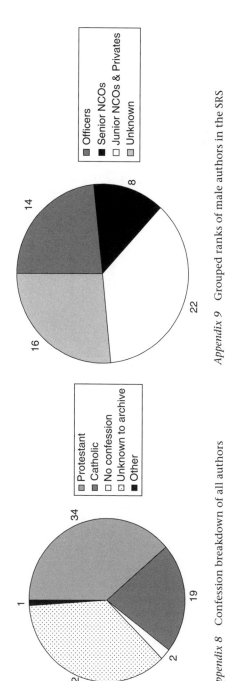

Appendix 8 Confession breakdown of all authors

Appendix 9 Grouped ranks of male authors in the SRS

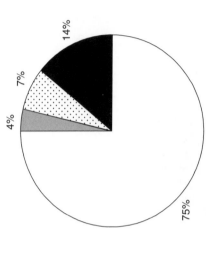

Appendix 10 Education levels of all males in the SRS

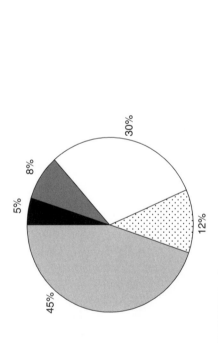

Appendix 11 Education levels of all females in the SRS

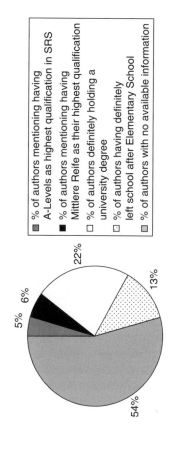

22%

5% 6%

54%

13%

% of authors mentioning having A-Levels as highest qualification in SRS

% of authors mentioning having Mittlere Reife as their highest qualification

% of authors definitely holding a university degree

% of authors having definitely left school after Elementary School

% of authors with no available information

Appendix 12 Education levels of all authors in the SRS

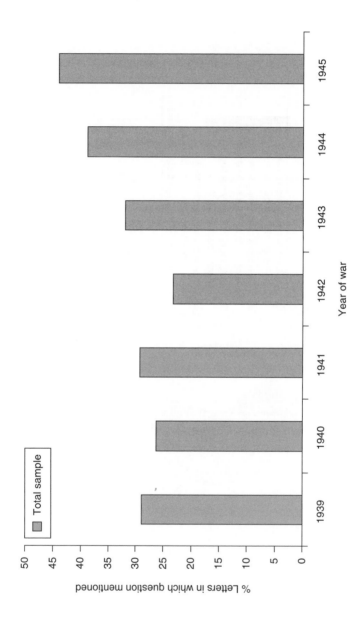

Appendix 13 Does the author express frustration at the poor postal service in wartime?

Note: In 1945 every second to third letter in a sample of letters mentioned the poor postal service in contrast to the earlier years when every fourth to fifth letter mentioned this subject.[1]

172

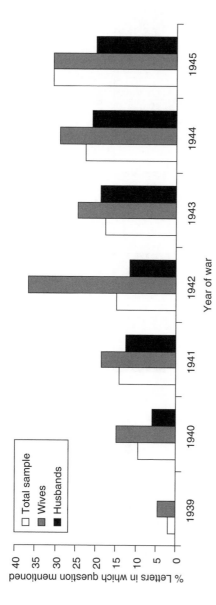

Appendix 14 Does the author mention bombing?

Note: As this graph shows, the number of letters which mention the bombing was higher during the later war years, reflecting the shift between the threat of bombs over Germany to the experience of intensive Allied air raids.[2] Whereas approximately 1 of the 10 letters mentioned bombing in 1940, in 1945 7 out of 10 letters mentioned this subject – representing a significant jump in mentions from the first to the last year of the war. Bombing, therefore, became a particularly significant concern of letter-writers in the later war years. Wives consistently mentioned bombing throughout the war more than men. The bombing was mentioned most by women in 1942, when the first major attacks on German cities took place. It is not surprising that women mentioned the bombing more – they were predominantly on the Home Front and hence more directly affected than men by the air raids. The number of letters in which husbands mentioned the bombings was significantly higher in the last 3 years of the war as their homeland came increasingly under attack from the air.

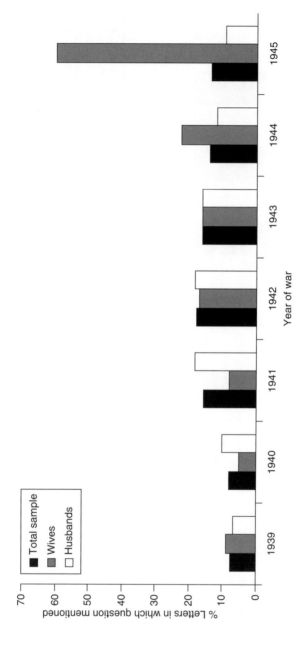

Appendix 15   Does the author mention food shortages?

Note: Less than 1 in 10 ten letters sent by women at home in 1939 mentioned food shortages.[3] By 1945 6 out of every 10 letters written by wives in the sample brought up this issue. This corresponds to the worsening food situation as the war dragged on. Whereas in 1940, 1941 and 1942, husbands at the Front complained more about food shortages than wives, in 1943, 1944 and 1945 more wives mentioned the shortage of food. The timing corresponds with the shift to total war and the squeeze on the domestic economy. Particularly in the final months of the war the average German diet became increasingly restricted both in size and variety. The large jump in mentions of food shortages by wives in 1945 reflects this fact.[4]

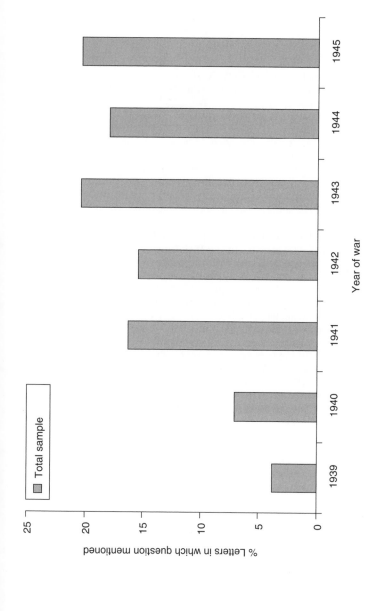

Appendix 16   Does the author ask about his children?
Note: Fathers grew increasingly keen for news of their children.[5]

Notes

Introduction

1. Elsbeth Emmerich, *My Childhood in Nazi Germany* (Hove, 1991) p.11.
2. Ute Frevert, *A Nation in Barracks. Military Conscription and Civil Society* (Oxford, 2004) p.255.
3. Elizabeth Heineman, *What Difference Does a Husband Make? Women and Marital Status in Nazi and Postwar Germany* (London, 1999); Eva Schulze and Sibylle Meyer, *Wie wir das alles geschafft haben. Alleinstehende Frauen berichten über ihr Leben nach 1945* (Munich, 1984).
4. Albrecht Lehmann, 'Die Kriegsgefangenen' *Aus Politik und Zeitgeschichte*, Vol. 7–8 (1995) p.17; Robert G. Moeller, *Protecting Motherhood. Women and the Family in the Politics of Postwar West Germany* (Oxford, 1993); Frank Biess, *Homecomings. Returning Prisoners of War and the Legacies of Defeat in Postwar Germany* (Oxford, 2006).
5. Eva Schulze and Sibylle Meyer, *Von Liebe Sprach Damals Keine. Familienalltag in der Nachkriegszeit* (Munich, 1985) p.188; Annette Kaminsky, ed., *Heimkehr 1948. Geschichte und Schicksale deutscher Kriegsgefangener* (Munich, 1998) p.17; Heineman, *What Difference Does a Husband Make?* pp.120–1.
6. Lisa Pine, *Nazi Family Policy, 1933–1945* (Oxford, 1997).
7. Heineman, *What Difference Does a Husband Make?* p.73; Lisa Pine, 'Women and the Family' in Sheilagh Ogilvie and Richard Overy, eds, *Germany. A New Social and Economic History. Volume 3 since 1800* (London, 2003) pp.373, 378; Adelheid von Saldern, 'Victims or Perpetrators? Controversies about the Role of Women in the Nazi State' in David F. Crew, ed., *Nazism and German Society, 1933–1945* (New York, 1994) pp.145–8.
8. Leila Rupp, *Mobilizing Women for War; German and American Propaganda 1939–45* (Princeton, 1978) pp.38–9.
9. Claudia Koonz, *Mothers in the Fatherland. Women, the Family and Nazi Politics* (London, 1986) p.388.
10. Brian R. Mitchell, *European Historical Statistics 1750–1975* (2nd edition, London, 1981) p.30; Statistisches Bundesamt, ed., *Statistische Berichte, Arb. Nr. VII/8/25* (Wiesbaden, 1953).
11. Heineman, *What Difference Does a Husband Make?* p.117; Atina Grossmann, *Jews, Germans, and Allies. Close Encounters in Occupied Germany* (Princeton, 2007) p.76.
12. Merith Niehuss, *Familie, Frau und Gesellschaft. Studien zur Strukturgeschichte der Familie in Westdeutschland 1945–1950* (Göttingen, 2001); Moeller, *Protecting Motherhood*; Astrid Joosten, *Die Frau, das 'segenspendende Herz der Familie.' Familienpolitik als Frauenpolitik in der Ära Adenauer* (Bamberg, 1990).
13. Niehuss, *Familie, Frau und Gesellschaft*.
14. *Wirtschaft und Statistik 1, 1949/1950* (Wiesbaden, 1950) p.385.
15. Moeller, *Protecting Motherhood*.

16. Margarete Dörr, ed., 'Wer die Zeit nicht miterlebt hat ...' Frauenerfahrungen im Zweiten Weltkrieg und in den Jahren danach. Vols. I–III (New York, 1998).

17. Schulze and Meyer, 'Von Liebe sprach damals Keiner'; Schulze and Meyer, Wie wir das alles geschafft haben; Heineman, What Difference Does a Husband Make?

18. Christian von Krockow, Stunde der Frauen. Bericht aus Pommern 1944 Bis 1947 (Munich, 1988).

19. Ute Frevert, Women in German History From Bourgeois Emancipation to Sexual Liberation (Oxford, 1989) p.263; Doris Schubert and Annette Kuhn, eds, Frauen in der deutschen Nachkriegszeit. Band 1. Frauenarbeit 1945–1949 (Düsseldorf, 1984) p.35; Karen Hagemann and Stefanie Schüler-Springorum, eds, Home/Front. The Military, War and Gender in Twentieth Century Germany (Oxford, 2002) p.29.

20. Robert G. Moeller, War Stories: The Search for a Useable Past in the Federal Republic of Germany (Berkeley, 2001) p.3; Bill Niven, ed., Germans as Victims. Remembering the Past in Contemporary Germany (London, 2006) p.22; Nicholas Stargardt, 'A German Trauma', Schweizerische Zeitschrift für Geschichte, Vol.57, No.1, 2007, pp.88–9.

21. Jörg Friedrich, Der Brand: Deutschland im Bombenkrieg, 1940–1945 (Munich, 2002); Nicholas Stargardt, Witnesses of War. Children's Lives under the Nazis (London, 2005) pp.7–8; Lothar Kettenacker, ed., Volk von Opfern? (Berlin, 2003).

22. Anthony Beevor, Berlin: The Downfall 1945 (London, 2002); Günter Grass, Im Krebsgang (Göttingen, 2002); Jane Caplan and Nicholas Stargardt, 'The Historikerstreit Twenty Years On', Germany History, Vol.24, No.4, 2006, pp.592; 597–8.

23. Anonymous, Eine Frau in Berlin. Tagebuchaufzeichnungen von 22. April zu 20. Juni 1945 (2nd edition, Frankfurt am Main, 2003).

24. Michelle Mouton, From Nurturing the Nation to Purifying the Volk. Weimar and Nazi Family Policy, 1918–1945 (Cambridge, 2007).

25. Alf Lüdtke, ed., The History of Everyday Life. Reconstructing Historical Experiences and Ways of Life (Princeton, 1995); Hans Medick and David W. Sabean, eds, Emotionen und materielle Interessen (Göttingen, 1984); Lutz Niethammer, Lebensgeschichte und Sozialkultur im Ruhrgebiet 1930 bis 1960 (Vol. I–III, Berlin, 1983–85); Detlev J.K. Peukert, Inside Nazi Germany. Conformity, Opposition and Racism in Everyday Life (London, 1989) pp.21–4; Barbara H. Rosenwein, Emotional Communities in the Early Middle Ages (Cornell, 2006) pp.1–2.

26. Geoff Eley, 'Foreword' in Lüdtke, ed., The History of Everyday Life, pp.vii–x; Geoff Eley, 'Labour History, Social History, Alltagsgeschichte', Journal of Modern History, 61 (1989) p.324; Charles E. Rosenberg., 'History and Experience' in Charles E. Rosenberg, ed., The Family in History (Pennsylvania, 1975) p.2; William M. Reddy, The Navigation of Feeling. A Framework for the History of Emotions (Cambridge, 2001) p.x.

27. Alf Lüdtke, 'What is The History of Everyday Life and Who Are Its Practitioners?' in Lüdtke, ed., The History of Everyday Life, p.6.

28. Konrad H. Jarausch, 'Towards a Social History of Experience: Postmodern Predicaments in Theory and Interdisciplinarity', Central European History, Vol. 22. No. 3/4, 1989, pp.429–32, 435, 441.

29. Peter Schöttler, 'Mentalities, Ideologies, Discourses on the "Third Level" as a Theme in Social-Historical Research' in Lüdtke, ed., *The History of Everyday Life*, p.72.

30. Hans Dollinger, 'Beitragen, den Krieg zu ächten' in Hans Dollinger, ed., *'Kain, wo ist dein Bruder?' Was der Mensch im Zweiten Weltkrieg erleiden musste – dokumentiert in Tagebüchern und Briefen* (Munich, 1983) p.391.

31. Ernest W. Burgess, Harvey J. Locke and Mary Margaret Thomes, *The Family. From Traditional to Companionship* (4th edition, New York, 1971) p.1.

32. Rayna Rapp, Ellen Ross and Renate Bridenthal, 'Examining Family History' in Judith Newton, Mary Ryan and Judith Walkowitz, eds, *Sex and Class in Women's History* (London, 1983) pp.239–40.

33. Philippe Ariès, *Centuries of Childhood* (New York, 1962).

34. Arthur W. Calhoun, *A Social History of the American Family from Colonial Times to the Present* (Cleveland, 1917–1919); Michael Mitterauer, 'The Family as an Historical Social Form' in Michael Mitterauer and Reinhard Sieder, eds, *The European Family* (Oxford, 1982) pp.1–2.

35. Tamara K. Hareven, 'The History of the Family as an Interdisciplinary Field' in Theodore K. Rabb and Robert I. Rotberg, eds, *The Family in History. Interdisciplinary Essays* (London, 1971) p.12.

36. Heidi Rosenbaum, *Familie als Gegenstruktur zur Gesellschaft. Kritik grundlegender theoretischer Ansätze der westdeutschen Familiensoziologie* (Stuttgart, 1978) pp.36, 151, 154–5; Heidi Rosenbaum, *Formen der Familie. Untersuchungen zum Zusammenhang von Familienverhältnissen, Sozialstruktur und sozialem Wandel in der deutschen Gesellschaft des 19. Jahrhunderts* (Frankfurt am Main, 1982) pp.45, 88–91, 97–8, 114–16, 188, 228, 457–62, 470–1; Richard J. Evans and William Robert Lee, eds, *The German Family, Essays on the Social History of the Family in Nineteenth and Twentieth Century Germany* (London, 1981) p.17; Nicholas Stargardt, 'German Childhoods: The Making of a Historiography', *German History*, Vol. 16, No.1, 1998, pp.1–2.

37. Rosenberg, 'History and Experience', p.6.

38. Judith R. Walkowitz, *City of Dreadful Delight. Narratives of Sexual Danger in Late-Victorian London* (London, 1992) p.9. Historians were influenced by the ideas in Jacques Derrida's *Of Grammatology* (Baltimore, 1967) and Michael Foucault's *Discipline and Punish* (New York, 1975) and *The Will to Knowledge* (New York, 1978 [1976]).

39. Joan W. Scott, 'Gender: A Useful Category of Historical Analysis', *The American Historical Review*, Vol. 91, No. 5, 1986, pp.1053–75.

40. Joan W. Scott, 'Experience' in Judith Butler and Joan W. Scott, eds, *Feminists Theorize the Political* (London, 1992) p.25.

41. Lila Abu-Lughod and Catherine A. Lutz, 'Introduction' in Catherine A. Lutz and Lila Abu-Lughod, eds, *Language and the Politics of Emotion* (Cambridge, 1990) p.2.

42. Peter and Carol Stearns, 'Emotionology: Clarifying the History of Emotions and Emotional Standards', *American Historical Review*, Vol. 90, No. 4, 1985, pp.813–36.

43. Peter and Carol Stearns, *Anger: The Struggle for Emotional Control in America's History* (New York, 1989); Ute Frevert, *Vertrauen: eine historische Annäherung* (Göttingen, 2003); Joanna Bourke, *Fear: A Cultural History* (London, 2005); For methodological debates about the history of emotion, see William

Reddy, *A Framework for the History of Emotions* (Cambridge, 2001); Barbara Rosenwein, *Emotional Communities in the Early Middle Ages* (London, 2006) pp.25, 27; Barbara Rosenwein, 'Worrying about Emotions in History', *American Historical Review*, Vol. 107, No. 3, June 2002, pp.30–1; Joanna Bourke, 'Fear and Anxiety: Writing about Emotion in Modern History', *History Workshop Journal*, Issue 5, 2003, p.119.

44. Biess, *Homecomings*. For similar methodological approaches, see Moeller, *Protecting Motherhood*, and contributions by Uta Poiger, Heide Fehrenbach, Robert Moeller and Frank Biess in Hanna Schissler, ed., *The Miracle Years. A Cultural History of West Germany, 1949–1968* (Princeton, 2001).

45. Laura Lee Downs, *Writing Gender History* (London, 2004) p.170.

46. Bourke, 'Fear and Anxiety', p.122.

47. Lyndal Roper, *Oedipus and the Devil. Witchcraft, Religion and Sexuality in Early Modern Europe* (London, 1994) p.26. See also, pp.10, 20.

48. Joan Hoff, 'Gender as a Postmodern Category of Paralysis', *Women's History Review*, Vol. 3, No. 2 (1994) pp.149–68; Catherine Hall, *White, Male and Middle-Class. Explorations in Feminism and History* (Oxford, 1992) p.24; Downs, *Writing Gender History*, p.96.

49. Laura Lee Downs, 'If "Woman" is Just an Empty Category, Then Why Am I Afraid to Walk Alone at Night? Identity Politics Meets the Postmodern Subject', *Comparative Studies in Society and History*, Vol. 35, No. 2 (April 1993) p.435; Richard J. Evans, *In Defence of History* (London, 1997) pp.185, 216–17.

50. Lüdtke, ed., *The History of Everyday Life*, p.13.

51. Ulla Roberts, *Starke Mütter – ferne Väter. Über Kriegs- und Nachkriegskindheit einer Töchtergeneration* (Frankfurt am Main, 1994); Ingeborg Bruns, *Als Vater aus dem Krieg heimkehrte* (Frankfurt, 1991); Jürgen Kleindienst, ed., *Hungern und hoffen. Jugend in Deutschland, 1945–1950* (Munich, 1993); Jürgen Kleindienst, ed., *Nachkriegs-Kinder. Kindheit in Deutschland, 1945–1950* (Berlin, 1998); Jürgen Kleindienst, ed., *Wir wollten leben. Jugend in Deutschland 1939–1945* (Berlin, 1998); Jürgen Kleindienst, ed., *Gebrannte Kinder. Zweiter Teil. Kindheit in Deutschland 1939–1945* (Berlin, 1999); Jürgen Kleindienst, ed., *Lebertran und Chewing Gum. Kindheit in Deutschland, 1945–1950* (Berlin, 2000).

52. Dörr, ed., *'Wer die Zeit nicht miterlebt hat…'*; Schulze and Meyer, *Von Liebe Sprach Damals Keine;* Schulze and Meyer, *Wie wir das alles geschafft haben*, p.95; Heineman, *What Difference Does a Husband Make?*

53. Stargardt, *Witnesses of War*, pp.373–6. Here, p.373; Lutz Niethammer, *Ego-Histoire? Und andere Erinnerungs-Versuche* (Cologne, 2002) pp.184–5, 188–91; Ben Highmore, *Everyday Life and Cultural Theory* (London, 2002) pp.66–7.

54. Rosenwein, *Emotional Communities*, pp.27, 196; Bourke, 'Fear and Anxiety', p.121.

55. Michael Roper, *Secret Battle: Emotional Survival in the Great War* (Manchester, 2009).

56. Stargardt, *Witnesses of War;* Roper, *Oedipus and the Devil*, pp.21, 26.

57. Stargardt, *Witnesses of War*, pp. 37–8, 217–18; Stargardt, 'German Childhoods', pp.13–14; Stargardt, 'Jeux de guerre sous le régime nazi', *Vingtième Siècle, Revue d'Histoire*, Vol. 89, No.1 (2006) pp.69–70.

58. Stargardt, *Witnesses of War*, pp.319, 242, 333–4.

59. Norman W. Bell and Ezra F. Vogel, 'Toward a Framework for Functional Analysis of Family Behaviour' in Norman W. Bell and Ezra F. Vogel, eds, *A Modern Introduction to The Family* (2nd edition, New York, 1968) p.6.

60. Angela Schwarz, 'Mit dem grösstmöglichen Anstand weitermachen'. Briefe britische Kriegsteilnehmer und ihrer Angehörigen im Zweiten Weltkrieg' in Wolfram Wette and Detlef Vogel eds, *Andere Helme – andere Menschen?* (Stuttgart, 1995) pp.206–10; Katrin Anja Kilian, *Das Medium Feldpost als Gegenstand interdisziplinärer Forschung. Archivlage, Forschungsstand und Aufbereitung der Quelle aus dem Zweiten Weltkrieg* (PhD Dissertation, Berlin, 2001) pp.21–2, 37.

61. Martin Humburg, *Das Gesicht des Krieges. Feldpostbriefe von Wehrmachtssoldaten aus der Sowjetunion 1941–1944* (Wiesbaden, 1998) pp.16–18; Benjamin Ziemann, 'Feldpostbriefe und ihre Zensur in den zwei Weltkriegen' in Klaus Beyer and Hans-Christian Täubrich, eds, *Der Brief. Eine Kulturgeschichte der schriftlichen Kommunikation* (Frankfurt, 1997) p.164; Angela Schwarz, '"Mit dem Grösstmöglichen Anstand weitermachen." Briefe britische Kriegsteilnehmer und ihrer Angehörigen im Zweiten Weltkrieg' in Wette and Vogel, eds, *Andere Helme – andere Menschen?* p.213.

62. Lutz Niethammer, 'Privat-Wirtschaft'. Erinnerungsfragmente einer anderen Umerziehung' in Lutz Niethammer, ed., *'Hinterher merkt man, dass es richtig war, dass es schiefgegangen ist': Nachkriegs-Erfahrungen im Ruhrgebiet* (Vol.II, Bonn, 1983) pp.46–8, 54, 93–4; See also Roberts, *Starke Mütter, Ferne Väter*, p.105; Detlef Vogel, '"...aber man muss halt gehen, und wenn es in den Tod ist" ' in Wette and Vogel, eds, *Andere Helme – andere Menschen?* p.38; Gerald Lamprecht, *Feldpost und Kriegserlebnis. Briefe als historisch-biographische Quelle* (Innsbruck, 2001) pp.34, 54–5; Humburg, 'Deutsche Feldpostbriefe im Zweiten Weltkrieg' in Wette and Vogel, eds, *Andere Helme – andere Menschen?*, pp.17–18; Humburg, *Das Gesicht des Krieges*, p.173.

63. Humburg, *Das Gesicht des Krieges*, pp.13, 250; Wolfram Wette, '"In Worte gefasst." Kriegskorrespondenz im internationalen Vergleich' in Wette and Vogel, eds, *Andere Helme – andere Menschen?* pp.329, 344; Klaus Latzel, 'Vom Kriegserlebnis zur Kriegserfahrung. Theoretische und methodische Überlegungen zur erfahrungsgeschichtlichen Untersuchung von Feldpostbriefen' in *Militärgeschichtliche Mitteilungen* Vol. 56 (1997) p.3; Herta Lange and Benedikt Burkard, eds, *'Abends wenn wir essen fehlt uns immer einer'. Kinder schreiben an die Väter, 1939–1945* (Tübingen, 2000).

64. Omer Bartov, *The Eastern Front, 1941–45. German Troops and the Barbarisation of Warfare* (2nd edition, London, 2001).

65. Thomas Kühne, *Kameradschaft: Die Soldaten des nationalsozialistischen Krieges und das 20. Jahrhundert* (Göttingen, 2006) pp.19, 137–8, 157–8, 160–4.

66. Peukert, *Inside Nazi Germany*, p.79; Jill Stephenson, *Hitler's Home Front. Württemberg under the Nazis* (London, 2006) p.172; Jörg Echternkamp, *Kriegsschauplatz Deutschland 1945* (Paderborn, 2006) p.8.

67. Jürgen Förster, 'Geistige Kriegsführung in Deutschland 1919 bis 1945' in Jörg Echternkamp, ed., *Das Deutsche Reich und Der Zweite Weltkrieg*, Vol.9/2, (Munich, 2005) p.633; Wette and Vogel, eds, *Andere Helme – andere Menschen?* p.8.

68. Gerard Minnaard and Werner Steinbrecher eds, *Eine Kiste im Keller. Das Schicksal eines 'guten' deutschen Soldaten im Zweiten Weltkrieg – eine künstlerische und theologische Verarbeitung* (Knesebeck, 2002) p.37.
69. See Appendix for detailed explanation of the statistical research sample.
70. Liselotte Orgel-Purper, *Willst Du meine Witwe werden? Eine deutsche Liebe im Krieg* (Berlin, 1995) pp.72–3. Liselotte to future husband Kurt Orgel, 3.4.43.
71. Susanne zur Nieden, *Alltag im Ausnahmezustand. Frauentagebücher im zerstörten Deutschland 1943 bis 1945* (Berlin, 1993) pp.73–7, 82.
72. Marlene A. Schiwy, *A Voice of Her Own. Women and the Journal Writing Journey* (New York, 1996) pp.11–12, 16, 18–19, 30, 43, 89, 115, 122–3, 126; Tristine Rainer, *The New Diary. How to use a Journal for Self-Guidance and Expanded Creativity* (London, 1980) pp.11, 115.
73. Hilde Thurnwald, *Gegenwartsprobleme Deutsche Familien. Eine soziologische Untersuchung an 498 Familien* (Berlin, 1948); Helmut Schelsky, *Wandlungen der Deutschen Familie in der Gegenwart* (Stuttgart, 1955).
74. Hartmann Tyrell, 'Helmut Schelsky's Familiensoziologie' in Horst Baier, ed., *Helmut Schelsky – ein Soziologe in der Bundesrepublik. Ein Gedächtnisschrift von Freunden, Kollegen und Schülern* (Stuttgart, 1986) pp.48, 51; Klaus-Jörg Ruhl, *Verordnete Unterordnung. Berufstätige Frauen zwischen Wirtschaftswachstum und konservativer Ideologie in der Nachkriegszeit, 1945–1963* (Munich, 1994) p.20.
75. LAB F. Rep. 240, Acc. 2651.
76. Kleindienst, ed., *Hungern und hoffen*; Kleindienst, ed., *Nachkriegs-Kinder;* Kleindienst, ed., *Wir wollten leben;* Kleindienst ed., *Gebrannte Kinder;* Kleindienst, ed., *Lebertran und Chewing Gum.*
77. Donna Harsch, *Revenge of the Domestic: Women, the Family and Communism in the German Democratic Republic* (Princeton, 2007) pp.1, 3–4, 6, 8, 44–5, 51, 198–9; Norman Naimark, *The Russians in Germany. A History of the Soviet Zone of Occupation, 1945–1949* (Harvard, 1995) pp.75, 79, 87, 89, 113, 127, 167.
78. Niehuss, *Familie, Frau und Gesellschaft,* pp. 38–41. See also pp.20, 36, 42; Stargardt, *Witnesses of War,* p.342; *Bayern in Zahlen 1* (1947) p.165; Thurnwald, *Gegenwartsprobleme Berliner Familien,* p.20.
79. Jennifer A. Loehlin, *From Rugs to Riches. Housework, Consumption and Modernity in Germany* (Oxford, 1999) p.24; Niehuss, *Familie, Frau und Gesellschaft,* p.356.
80. Carola Sachse, *Industrial Housewives: Women's Social Work in the Factories of Nazi Germany* (London, 1987) p.15.
81. Rosenbaum, *Familie als Gegenstruktur zur Gesellschaft,* pp.154–5, 267–9, 342–3; Karen Hagemann, *Frauenalltag und Männerpolitik. Alltagsleben und gesellschaftliches Handeln von Arbeiterfrauen in der Weimarer Republik* (Hamburg, 1990) pp.332–3, 343, 348–9; Josef Mooser, *Arbeiterleben in Deutschland 1900–1970, Klassenlagen, Kultur und Politik* (Frankfurt am Main, 1984) p.155; Heidi Rosenbaum, *Proletarische Familien. Arbeiterfamilien und Arbeiterväter im frühen 20. Jahrhundert zwischen traditioneller, sozialdemokratischer und kleinbürgerlicher Orientierung* (Frankfurt, 1992) pp.241–58; Gerhard Wilke and Kurt Wagner, 'Family and Household: Social Structures in a German Village Between the Two World Wars' in Evans and Lee, eds, *The German Family,* pp.129–30.

1   Family life under National Socialism

1. Jürgen Engert, *Heimatfront. Kriegsalltag im Deutschland 1939–1945* (Berlin, 1999) pp.14, 118–23; Richard J. Evans, *The Third Reich in Power* (London, 2005) pp.359, 705; Richard Bessel, *Nazism and War* (London, 2004).
2. Walther Hofer, ed., *Der Nationalsozialismus: Dokumente 1933–1945* (Frankfurt am Main, 1957) p.82.
3. Evans, *The Third Reich in Power*, p.108; Peukert, *Inside Nazi Germany*, p.105; Peter Fritzsche, *Life and Death in the Third Reich* (London, 2008) pp.20–1, 43.
4. Richard Grunberger, *A Social History of the Third Reich* (London, 1971) p.242; Norbert Franck, ed., *Heil Hitler, Herr Lehrer. Volksschule 1933–1945. Das Beispiel Berlin* (Hamburg, 1983) p.83.
5. *Reichsgesetzblatt* I (Berlin, 1933) p.135.
6. Klaus Behnken, ed., *Deutschland-Berichte der Sozialdemokratische Partei Deutschlands 1934–1940 (SOPADE)* Vol. 5 (Frankfurt am Main, 1979) pp.784–5.
7. Evans, *The Third Reich in Power*, pp.96, 104.
8. Jeremy Noakes and Geoffrey Pridham, eds, *Nazism 1919–1945 Volume II* (3rd edition, Exeter, 1997) p.180.
9. Michael Burleigh, *The Third Reich. A New History* (London, 2001) pp.176, 181; Robert Gellately, *Backing Hitler. Consent and Coercion in Nazi Germany* (Oxford, 2001) p.40; Evans, *The Third Reich in Power*, p.80.
10. Karl Dietrich Bracher, *The German Dictatorship. The Origins, Structure and Effects of National Socialism* (London, 1971) pp.451–2; Noakes and Pridham, eds, *Nazism: Volume II*, p.311; David Schoenbaum, *Hitler's Social Revolution: Class and Status in Nazi Germany 1933–1939* (New York, 1980) p.200.
11. Bracher, *The German Dictatorship*, p.450.
12. Noakes and Pridham, eds, *Nazism: Volume II*, p.382.
13. Robert Gellately, *The Gestapo and German Society. Enforcing Racial Policy 1933–1945* (Oxford, 1990) p.129; Heineman, *What Difference Does a Husband Make?* p.73; Lisa Pine, 'Women and the Family' pp.373, 378; Saldern, 'Victims or Perpetrators?', p.146; Jill Stephenson, *Women in Nazi Germany* (London, 2001) p.27; Mouton, *From Nurturing the Nation to Purifying the Volk*; Detlev Peukert, *Volksgenossen und Gemeinschaftsfremde. Anpassung, Ausmeize und Aufbegehren unter dem Nationalsozialismus* (Cologne, 1982).
14. Moeller, *Protecting Motherhood*, p.6; Heineman, *What Difference Does a Husband Make?* p.73; Rupp, *Mobilizing Women for War*, p.38; Kent Geiger, 'Changing Political Attitudes in Totalitarian Society: A Case Study of the Role of the Family' in Bell and Vogel, eds, *A Modern Introduction to The Family*, pp.174–6.
15. Evans, *The Third Reich in Power*, p.299.
16. Frevert, *A Nation in Barracks*, p.255.
17. Frevert, *A Nation in Barracks*, p.272; Bracher, *The German Dictatorship*, p.328; Detlev Peukert, 'Youth in the Third Reich' in Richard Bessel, ed., *Life in the Third Reich* (Oxford, 2001) p.27.
18. Grunberger, *A Social History of the Third Reich*, pp.240–1; Rupp, *Mobilizing Women for War*, p.38.
19. Burleigh, *The Third Reich*, p.234.

20. Pine, *Nazi Family Policy 1933–1945*, p.7.
21. Evans, *The Third Reich in Power*, p.271; Peukert, *Inside Nazi Germany*, p.151.
22. Noakes and Pridham, eds, *Nazism: Volume II*, p.223; See also Jürgen Reulecke, *Ich möchte so einer werden wie die…Männerbünde im 20. Jahrhundert* (Frankfurt, 2001) pp.226, 228, 233; Evans, *The Third Reich in Power*, p.274.
23. Noakes and Pridham, eds, *Nazism: Volume II*, p.223; Peukert, *Inside Nazi Germany*, p.145.
24. Evans, *The Third Reich in Power*, p. 264.
25. Arno Klönne, *Jugend im Dritten Reich. Die Hitler-Jugend und ihre Gegner* (Düsseldorf, 1982) pp.136–7; Peukert, *Inside Nazi Germany*, p.148; Kent Geiger, 'Changing Political Attitudes in Totalitarian Society', pp.174–6; Wilke and Wagner, 'Family and Household' in Evans and Lee, eds, *The German Family*, p.142; Franck, ed., *Heil Hitler, Herr Lehrer*, p.87.
26. Evans, *The Third Reich in Power*, pp.276, 262–3; Detlev Peukert, 'Youth in Nazi Germany', pp.27–31; Dagmar Reese, *Growing Up Female in Nazi Germany* (4th edition, Michigan, 2009) pp.40, 235, 250; Behnken, ed., *Deutschland-Berichte der Sozialdemokratischen Partei Deutschlands* Vol.5, pp.1378, 1391–2, 1379; Klönne, *Jugend im Dritten Reich*, pp.142–3.
27. Grunberger, *A Social History of the Third Reich*, p.275; Rolf Heberer, born 1927. Interview by Lutz Niethammer and Alexander von Plato, held in the Institut für Geschichte und Biographie, at the Fernuniversität Hagen; Peukert, 'Youth in Nazi Germany', p.28.
28. Evans, *The Third Reich in Power*, p.274.
29. Peter König, born 1919. Interview by Lutz Niethammer and Alexander von Plato, held in the Institut für Geschichte und Biographie, at the Fernuniversität Hagen; Franck, ed., *Heil Hitler, Herr Lehrer*, p.174; Reese, *Growing Up Female in Nazi Germany*, pp.59, 236.
30. Herr und Frau Arntzen, born 1918. Interview by Lutz Niethammer and Alexander von Plato, held in the Institut für Geschichte und Biographie, at the Fernuniversität Hagen; Evans, *The Third Reich in Power*, p.279; Reese, *Growing Up Female in Nazi Germany*, p.141.
31. Renate Finckh, *Mit uns zieht die neue Zeit* (Baden Baden, 1978); Koonz, *Mothers in the Fatherland*, p.195; Franck, ed., *Heil Hitler, Herr Lehrer*, pp.174–5; Evans, *The Third Reich in Power*, p.278.
32. Erik H. Erikson, *Childhood and Society* (2nd edition, London, 1965) p.333; Noakes and Pridham, eds, *Nazism: Volume II*, p.235; Grunberger, *A Social History of the Third Reich*, p.240; Reese, *Growing Up Female in Nazi Germany*, pp.154, 231.
33. See Mark Roseman, ed., *Generations in Conflict* (Cambridge, 2005).
34. Burleigh, *The Third Reich*, p.236; Reese, *Growing Up Female in Nazi Germany*, p.230.
35. Grunberger, *A Social History of the Third Reich*, p.240; Rupp, *Mobilizing Women for War*, p.38.
36. Christoph Klessmann, ed., *Nicht nur Hitlers Krieg. Der Zweite Weltkrieg und die Deutschen* (Düsseldorf, 1989) p.58.
37. Vandana Joshi, *Gender and Power in the Third Reich. Female Denouncers and the Gestapo (1933–45)* (London, 2003) pp.43–7, 81–2, 169–70, 194; Geiger, 'Changing Political Attitudes in Totalitarian Society', p.180; Carl J.

Friedrich and Zbigniev K. Brzezinski, *Totalitarian Dictatorship and Autocracy* (Cambridge, 1956) p.245.

38. Evans, *The Third Reich in Power*, pp.235–47.

39. Kleindienst, ed., *Wir wollten leben*, p.13; Reese, *Growing Up Female in Nazi Germany*, pp.222–4, 251; Sheila Fitzpatrick and Alf Lüdtke, 'Energizing the Everyday: On the Breaking and Making of Social Bonds in Nazism and Stalinism' in Sheila Fitzpatrick and Michael Geyer, eds, *Beyond Totalitarianism* (Cambridge, 2009) p.299; Christopher Lasch, *Haven in a Heartless World. The Family Besieged* (3rd edition, London, 1995) p.3.

40. 'Einfluss der HJ auf die Jugend' in Hitlerjugend memoranda, TS National Socialism Y67, Hoover Institute Archives. Quoted in Kimberly A. Redding, *Growing Up in Hitler's Shadow. Remembering Youth in Postwar Berlin* (London, 2004) pp.6–7.

41. Geiger, 'Changing Political Attitudes in Totalitarian Society', pp.174–7; Koonz, *Mothers in the Fatherland*, p.219.

42. Mouton, *From Nurturing the Nation to Purifying the Volk*, pp.152, 280–2.

43. Friedrich and Brzezinski, *Totalitarian Dictatorship and Autocracy*, pp.239, 244; Peukert, *Inside Nazi Germany*, pp.67–8.

44. Mouton, *From Nurturing the Nation to Purifying the Volk*, pp.18–19; Reese, *Growing Up Female in Nazi Germany*, pp.235, 243; Jane Caplan, 'Foreword' in Carola Sachse, *Industrial Housewives: Women's Social Work in the Factories of Nazi Germany* (London, 1987) p.7.

45. Ian Kershaw, *Popular Opinion and Political Dissent in the Third Reich, Bavaria 1933–1945* (2nd edition, Oxford, 1993) pp.378, xiv; See also George L. Mosse, *Nazi Culture* (London, 1966) pp.xxi, 26.

46. Jill Stephenson, *Women in Nazi Society* (London, 1975) p.40.

47. Friedrich and Brzezinski, *Totalitarian Dictatorship and Autocracy*, p.239; Pine, *Nazi Family Policy*, p.181; Clifford Kirkpatrick, *The Family as Process and Institution* (New York, 1955) p.638; Lewis A. Coser, 'Some Aspects of Soviet Family Policy' in Rose Laub Coser, ed., *The Family. Its Structures and Functions* (2nd edition, London, 1974) p.413.

48. Kirkpatrick, *The Family as Process and Institution*, p.638.

49. Peukert, *Volksgenossen und Gemeinschaftsfremde*, p.232; Noakes and Pridham, eds, *Nazism: Volume II*, p.273; Gloria Bird, and Keith Melville eds,, *Families and Intimate Relationships* (McGraw-Hill, 1994) p.277.

50. Lasch, *Haven in a Heartless World*, p.ix.

51. Peukert, *Inside Nazi Germany*, p.79; Reese, *Growing Up Female in Nazi Germany*, p.246; Sachse, *Industrial Housewives*, p.12.

52. Matthew Stibbe, *Women in the Third Reich* (Oxford, 2003) p.41; Rupp, *Mobilizing Women for War*, p.37; Peukert, *Inside Nazi Germany*, pp.23, 25; David L. Hoffmann and Annette F. Timm, 'Utopian Biopolitics. Reproductive Policies, Gender Roles, and Sexuality in Nazi Germany and the Soviet Union' in Fitzpatrick and Geyer, eds, *Beyond Totalitarianism*, pp. 104–5; SD report, 8 July 1943, quoted in Heinz Boberach, ed., *Meldungen aus dem Reich. Die geheimen Lageberichte des Sicherheitsdienstes der SS 1938–1945* (Band 14, Herrsching, 1984) p.5457; Mathilde Wolff-Mönckeberg, *On the Other Side. To My Children: From Germany 1940–1945*, Ruth Evans, ed., (London, 1979) pp.96–7.

53. *Reichsgesetzblatt* I, p.807; Mouton, *From Nurturing the Nation to Purifying the Volk*, pp.30–1, 70; Stibbe, *Women in the Third Reich*, pp.50–1; Helmut

Schelsky, 'The Family in Germany' in *Marriage and Family Living*, Vol.16, No.4 (November 1954) p.331.

54. Jeremy Noakes, ed., *Nazism. Volume IV. The German Home Front in World War II* (2nd edition, Exeter, 1998). pp.368–70; Evans, *The Third Reich in Power*, p.521; Ute Frevert, *Women in German History*, p.237; Dagmar Herzog, *Sex after Fascism. Memory and Morality in Twentieth Century Germany* (Oxford, 2005) pp.56, 59–61, 259.

55. Noakes and Pridham, eds, *Nazism: Volume II*, p.259; Hoffmann and Timm, 'Utopian Biopolitics', p.123.

56. Noakes, ed., *Nazism: Volume IV*, p.303.

57. The year 1939 was the first full year of the new divorce law's operation. The new law made divorce easier, which is reflected in the higher rate. This should not imply that people made use of the law purely prompted by Nazi ideological motivations about breeding. They did not. 50 per cent of these marriages had taken place 20 years before. These couples were divorced on the grounds of the irretrievable breakdown of the marriage and had nothing to do with fertility.

58. Noakes and Pridham, eds, *Nazism: Volume II*, pp.256, 265; Jill Stephenson, 'Women, Motherhood and the Family in the Third Reich' in Michael Burleigh, ed., *Confronting the Nazi Past. New Debates on Modern German History* (London, 1996) p.173; Hoffmann and Timm, 'Utopian Biopolitics', p.89.

59. Schelsky, 'The Family in Germany', p.331; Mouton, *From Nurturing the Nation to Purifying the Volk*, pp.30–1.

60. Statistischen Reichsamt, ed., *Statistisches Jahrbuch für das Deutsche Reich* (Berlin, 1940) pp.50–1.

61. Stibbe, *Women in the Third Reich*, p.53; Mouton, *From Nurturing the Nation to Purifying the Volk*, p.279.

62. Stephenson, *Women in Nazi Society*, p.40.

63. Stephenson, 'Women, Motherhood and the Family in the Third Reich', pp.181–2.

64. Moeller, *Protecting Motherhood*, pp.17–18; Mouton, *From Nurturing the Nation to Purifying the Volk*, p.279; Sachse, *Industrial Housewives*, p.61.

65. Sachse, *Industrial Housewives*, pp.63, 65, 68–9. More generally on female conscription see Richard J. Evans, *The Third Reich at War* (London, 2008) pp.358–61, 656; Noakes, ed., *Nazism: Volume IV*, pp.317–19, 322.

66. Noakes and Pridham, eds, *Nazism: Volume II*, pp.181–3, 327.

67. Noakes and Pridham, eds, *Nazism: Volume II*, p.183; Jeremy Noakes, 'Social Outcasts in the Third Reich' in Bessel, ed., *Life in the Third Reich*, pp.83–4; Burleigh, *The Third Reich*, p.165.

68. Gellately, *Backing Hitler*, pp.93–5; Uwe Lohalm, 'Für eine leistungsbereite und "erbgesunde" Volksgemeinschaft Selektive Erwerbslosen- und Familienpolitik' in Forschungsstelle für Zeitgeschichte in Hamburg, ed., *Hamburg im 'Dritten Reich'* (Göttingen, 2005) pp.418–26; Burleigh, *The Third Reich*, pp.354, 357, 358, 376; Noakes, 'Social Outcasts in the Third Reich', pp.86–7; Mouton, *From Nurturing the Nation to Purifying the Volk*, p.139; Stibbe, *Women in the Third Reich*, pp.71–2; Evans, *The Third Reich in Power*, pp.88–90.

69. William Carr, 'Nazi Policy against the Jews' in Bessel ed., *Life in the Third Reich*, pp.70–2; Noakes and Pridham, eds, *Nazism: Volume II*, pp. 338, 263–5, 336–46; Noakes, ed., *Nazism: Volume IV*, p.368; Evans, *The Third Reich in Power*, p. 537.

70. Martin Chalmers, ed., *I Shall Bear Witness. The Diaries of Victor Klemperer 1933–1941* (2nd edition, London, 1998) pp.306–7, 20 March 1938. For more detailed discussion on Jewish family life under the Nazis, see Marion Kaplan, *Between Dignity and Despair. Jewish Life in Nazi Germany* (Oxford, 1999) and Pine, *Nazi Family Policy*, pp.147–78.

71. Noakes and Pridham, eds, *Nazism: Volume III*, pp.1071–3, 1122, 1208.

72. Günter Grau, *Hidden Holocaust? Gay and Lesbian Persecution in Germany 1933–45* (London, 1995) p.5.

73. Noakes, 'Social Outcasts in the Third Reich', pp.89–91.

74. Koonz, *Mothers in the Fatherland*, p.180; Rupp, *Mobilizing Women for War*, p.38; Pine, *Nazi Family Policy*, p.182.

75. Rupp, *Mobilizing Women for War*, p.38.

76. Koonz, *Mothers in the Fatherland*, p.388.

77. Evans, *The Third Reich in Power*, pp.107–8; Marlis G. Steinert, *Hitlers Krieg und die Deutschen. Stimmung und Haltung der deutschen Bevölkerung im Zweiten Weltkrieg* (Düsseldorf, 1970) p.30.

78. Helmut Schelsky, 'The Family in Germany', p.331; Peukert, *Volksgenossen und Gemeinschaftsfremde*, p.232; Ulrich Herbert, 'Die guten und die schlechten Zeiten. Überlegungen zur diachronen Analyse lebensgeschichtliche Interviews' in Lutz Niethammer, ed., *'Die Jahre weiss man nicht, wo man die heute hinsetzen sol.' Lebensgeschichte und Sozialkultur im Ruhrgebiet 1930–1960 Vol I* (Berlin, 1983) p.88.

79. Gellately, *The Gestapo and German Society*, p.130; Fitzpatrick and Lüdtke, 'Energizing the Everyday', p.299; Mark Roseman, 'World War II and Social Change in Germany', in Arthur Marwick, Clive Emsley and Wendy Simpson, eds, *Total War and Historical Change: Europe 1914–1955* (Philadelphia, 2001) p.246; Herbert, 'Die guten und die schlechten Zeiten', p.88.

80. Behnken, ed., *Deutschland-Berichte der Sozialdemokratische Partei Deutschlands*, Vol. 5, pp.481–2.

81. Behnken, ed., *Deutschland-Berichte der Sozialdemokratische Partei Deutschlands*, Vol. 5, pp.683–4; Kershaw, *Popular Opinion and Political Dissent*, pp.xvi, xxi; Lasch, *Haven in a Heartless World*, p.187.

82. Peukert, *Inside Nazi Germany*, p.236; Fitzpatrick and Lüdtke, 'Energizing the Everyday', pp.267–8.

83. Mouton, *From Nurturing the Nation to Purifying the Volk*, pp.3–4, 174, 280–2; Kershaw, *Popular Opinion and Political Dissent*, p.xxi.

84. Moeller, *Protecting Motherhood*, p.6; See also Gellately, 'Die Gestapo und die deutsche Gesellschaft: Zur Entstehungsgeschichte einer selbstüberwachenden Gesellschaft' in Detlef Schmiechen-Ackermann, ed., *Anpassung, Verweigerung, Widerstand: Soziale Milieus, Politische Kultur und der Widerstand gegen den NS in Deutschland im regionalen Verleich* (Berlin, 1997) pp.109–21.

85. William L. Shirer, *Berlin Diary. The Journal of a Foreign Correspondent, 1934–1941* (New York, 1942) pp.153, 162.

86. Berndt Engelmann, *In Hitler's Germany: Everyday Life in the Third Reich* (New York, 1986) p.170.

87. Peukert, *Inside Nazi Germany*, pp.67–8; Kershaw, *Popular Opinion and Political Dissent*, p.378; Stephenson, *Hitler's Home Front*, p.12; Tamara K. Hareven, 'The History of the Family as an Interdisciplinary Field' in Rabb and Rotberg, eds,

The Family in History, p.223; Mouton, *From Nurturing the Nation to Purifying the Volk*, p.174.

2 Staying in touch

1. Boberach, *Meldungen aus dem Reich* 15, p.6025; see also Bessel, *Nazism and War*, p.87.
2. MKB 3.2002.0904, Gerda M. to husband Martin, 16 January 1940; DTA Reg. Nr. 230/II, Eugen N. to wife Ursula, 9 October 1946; MKB 3.2002.7177; Lamprecht, *Feldpost und Kriegserlebnis*, p.42.
3. Böll, *Briefe aus dem Krieg 1939–1945*, Jochen Schubert, ed., (Vol. II. Cologne, 2001) p.1071.
4. MKB 3.2002.0985, Heinz R. to wife, 14 September 1941. Throughout the book, the surnames of authors who wished to remain anonymous have been abbreviated.
5. MKB 3.2002.0224, Klaus B. to wife Suse, 18 July 1943.
6. Gerwin Udke, ed., *'Schreib so oft Du kannst'. Feldpostbriefe des Lehrers Gerhard Udke. 1940–1944* (Berlin, 2002) pp.14, 101, Gerhard Udke to wife Dorothea, 3 March 1940 and 12 December 1942.
7. MKB 3.2002.0985, Heinz R. to wife, 12 June 1942; Evans, *The Third Reich at War*, p.206.
8. Echternkamp, *Kriegsschauplatz Deutschland 1945*, p.55.
9. Stephenson, *Hitler's Home Front*, p.154.
10. Hans-Jochen Gamm, *Der Flüsterwitz im Dritten Reich* (Munich, 1963) p.157.
11. Mathilde Wolff-Mönckeberg, *Briefe, die sie nicht erreichten. Briefe einer Mutter an ihre fernen Kinder in den Jahren 1940–1946* (2nd edition, Hamburg, 1980) p.111, 25 March 1944.
12. LAB (STA) Rep. 134/13, Nr. 178, Bl.141–142, Ursula T.; LAB F. Rep. 240, Acc. 2421, Gabriele Vallentin, *Die Einnahme von Berlin*, 23 April 1945.
13. Jens Ebert, ed., *Stalingrad, – eine deutsche Legende. Zeugnisse einer verdrängten Niederlage* (Hamburg, 1992) pp.57–60; Echternkamp, *Kriegsschauplatz Deutschland 1945*, pp.55, 50; Ziemann, 'Feldpostbriefe und ihre Zensur in den zwei Weltkriegen', p.165; Humburg, *Das Gesicht des Krieges*, p.252; Dörr, ed., *'Wer die Zeit...' Vol. II*, p.199.
14. Echternkamp, *Kriegsschauplatz Deutschland 1945*, p.45; Richard Lakowski and Hans-Joachim Büll, *Ein Lebenszeichen 1945. Feldpost zwischen Oder und Elbe* (Berlin, unpublished) pp.21–2; Katrin Kilian, 'Funktionsweise der deutschen Feldpost 1939 bis 1945' in http://www.feldpost-archiv.de/09-arbeit-der-feldpost.html p.2.
15. See Appendix 13.
16. Echternkamp, *Kriegsschauplatz Deutschland 1945*, pp.53–5; Walther H. Bähr, *Kriegsbriefe Gefallener Studenten, 1939–1945* (Stuttgart, 1952) p.160.
17. Ebert, ed., *Stalingrad*, p.67, 29 December 1942.
18. MKB 3.2002.7208, Alfred to wife Marta, 5 December 1943.
19. MKB 3.2002.0933, Horst M. to partner Gisela, 22 August 1944.
20. Zentralverlag der NSDAP, ed., *'Darüber lache ich heute noch.' VB-Feldpost. Soldaten erzählen heitere Erlebnisse* (Berlin, 1943) pp.58–9.

21. Anatoly Golovchansky, *'Ich will raus aus diesem Wahnsinn.' Deutsche Briefe von der Ostfront 1941–1945 aus Sowjetischen Archiven* (Wuppertal, 1991) p.160.
22. Orgel-Purper, *Willst Du meine Witwe werden?* p.174. Husband Captain Kurt Orgel to wife Liselotte.
23. Lamprecht, *Feldpost und Kriegserlebnis*, p.42; Humburg, *Das Gesicht des Krieges*, p.251.
24. LAB F. Rep. 240, Acc. 2651, Nr. 6, Bericht 654, Gertrud Tenniger.
25. Böll, *Briefe aus dem Krieg 1939–1945*, Vol.II, p.842.
26. Ibid., p.838.
27. LAB (STA), Rep. 134/13, Nr. 182/1, Bl.273–274. Traute S.; Bärbel Wirrer, ed., *'Ich glaube an den Führer'. Eine Dokumentation zur Mentalitätsgeschichte im nationalsozialistischen Deutschland 1942–1945* (Bielefeld, 2003) p.37. Inge to Fred, 4 November 1942; John Costello, *Love Sex and War. Changing Values 1939–45* (London, 1985) p.25; Humburg, *Das Gesicht des Krieges*, pp.55, 251, 269.
28. MKB 3.2002.0904, Martin M. to wife Gerda, 12 September 1941.
29. Ingeborg T. quoted in Ingrid Hammer and Susanne zur Nieden eds, *Sehr selten habe ich geweint. Briefe und Tagebücher aus dem Zweiten Weltkrieg von Menschen aus Berlin* (Zürich, 1992) pp.157–8; See also MKB 3.2002.0349, Irene G. to husband Ernst, 17 March 1940.
30. MKB 3.2002.0904, Gerda M. to husband Martin, 13 July 1940.
31. MKB 3.2002.7247, Werner L. to wife, 18 July 1940.
32. Humburg, *Das Gesicht des Krieges*, pp.16–18.
33. Ziemann, 'Feldpostbriefe und ihre Zensur in den zwei Weltkriegen', p.164.
34. Humburg, *Das Gesicht des Krieges*, pp.16–18.
35. Schwarz, 'Mit dem grösstmöglichen Anstand weitermachen', p.213.
36. Margaretta Jolly, ' "Briefe, Moral und Geschlecht." Britische und amerikanische Diskurse über das Briefeschreiben im Zweiten Weltkrieg' in Wette and Vogel, *Andere Helme – andere Menschen?* p.174.
37. MKB 3.2002.0224, Klaus B. to his wife Suse.
38. Biess, *Homecomings*, pp.24–8.
39. Detlev Vogel, ' "…aber man muss halt gehen, und wenn es in den Tod ist" '. in Wette and Vogel, eds, *Andere Helme – andere Menschen?* p.43.
40. MKB 3.2002.0826, Hubert S. to wife Gerda, 2 December 1940.
41. Humburg, *Das Gesicht des Krieges*, pp.109–12; Christoph Rass, *'Menschenmaterial': Deutsche Soldaten an der Ostfront. Innenansichten einer Infanteriedivision 1939–1945* (Paderborn, 2003) pp.178–9; Birgit Beck, *Wehrmacht und sexuelle Gewalt* (Paderborn, 2004) pp.105–16.
42. Ebert, ed., *Stalingrad*, p.58.
43. Humburg, 'Deutsche Feldpostbriefe im Zweiten Weltkrieg', pp.17–18; Lamprecht, *Feldpost und Kriegserlebnis*, p.34.
44. Humburg, *Das Gesicht des Krieges*, p.173.
45. Klaus Latzel, 'Der "Krieg von unten" in Soldatenbriefen' in *Rhein-Reden. Texte aus der Melanchthon-Akademie Köln* (Vol.II, Cologne, 1999) p.47.
46. Harald Henry, 10 September 1941, quoted in Bähr, *Kriegsbriefe Gefallener Studenten*, p.76.
47. Heinrich Böll, *Briefe aus dem Krieg, 1939–45*, ed., Jochen Schubert (Vol.I, Cologne, 2001) p.32. A letter to parents and siblings, Osnabrück, 29 December 1939.
48. Dorothee Schmitz-Koster, *Der Krieg meines Vaters. Als deutscher Soldat in Norwegen* (Berlin, 2004) p.306.

49. Humburg, 'Deutsche Feldpostbriefe im Zweiten Weltkrieg', pp.17–18.
50. Udke, ed., *'Schreib so oft Du kannst'* p.201. Gerhard Udke to wife Dorothea, 28 May 1944.
51. *Die Junge Dame*, 5 (1941) p.1, quoted in Laura Wehr, *Kamerad Frau? Eine Frauenzeitschrift im Nationalsozialismus* (Regensburg, 2002) p.91.
52. Gustav Stolper, *German Realities*, quoted in Charles P. Kindleberger, *The German Economy, 1945–1947. Charles P. Kindleberger's Letters from the Field* (London, 1989) p.xi; Klaus-Jörg Rühl, ed., *Deutschland 1945. Alltag zwischen Krieg und Frieden in Berichten* (Darmstadt, 1984) pp.66, 146, 197; Nikolaus Wachsmann, *Hitler's Prisons. Legal Terror in Nazi Germany* (Yale, 2004) pp.324–31.
53. Paul Steege, *Black Market, Cold War. Everyday Life in Berlin, 1946–1949* (Cambridge, 2007) p.28; LAB F. Rep. 240, Acc. 2651, Nr. 6, Bericht 697, Gertrud Oppermann; Ruth Andreas-Friedrich, *Schauplatz Berlin. Tagebuchaufzeichnungen 1938–1948* (2nd edition, Frankfurt, 2000) pp.342, 13 June 1945; 7 July 1945.
54. DTA Reg. Nr. 228/I,1, Erika D., *Tagebuch 1945–51*, 22 May 1945–3 July 1945.
55. DTA Reg. Nr. 952,1, Helmut B.
56. Ursula von Kardorff, *Diary of a Nightmare. Berlin 1942–1945* (London, 1965) p.196; see also Anonymous, *Eine Frau in Berlin. Tagebuchaufzeichnungen vom 20. April bis 22. Juni 1945* (Frankfurt, 2003) pp.201, 16 May 1945.
57. DTA Reg. Nr. 340,1, Maxi-Lore E., 10 May 1945.
58. Brian R. Mitchell, *European Historical Statistics 1750–1975* (2nd edition, London, 1981) p.30.
59. DTA Reg. Nr. 230/II, Eugen N. to wife Ursula, 22 July 1946, 21 May 1946 and New Year 1947.
60. KA BIO 6176, Dr. Rolf M., *Letters from Russian POW camp 7150 to family.*
61. DTA Reg. Nr. 1108, Ernst K. to fiancée and later wife Irmgard.
62. Deutsches Rotes Kreuz-Suchdienst, ed., *Zur Geschichte der Kriegsgefangenen im Westen* (Bonn, 1962) p.13.
63. DTA Reg. Nr. 111,2, Beate K., 16 August 1945.
64. *Sie*, 21 (1946) p.5. 'Das Haus ohne Männer', Gerland Grindel.
65. Deutsches Rotes Kreuz-Suchdienst, ed., *Zur Geschichte der Kriegsgefangenen im Westen*, p.9.
66. DTA Reg. Nr. 952,1, Helmut B.
67. DTA Reg. Nr. 162/III,1, Will S.
68. *Brigitte*, 23 (1955) pp.4–5.
69. DTA Reg. Nr. 42,1, Walter M., 1 August 1945; Barbara Wilde, 'Das Interview mit Bettina S. Geschlechterdifferenz nach 1945: Keine Zeiten im Umbruch' in Joanna Meyer-Lenz, ed., *Die Ordnung des Paares ist unbehaglich. Irritationen am und im Geschlechterdiskurs nach 1945* (Hamburg, 2000) p.107.
70. Pertti Ahonen, *After the Expulsion. West Germany and Eastern Europe, 1945–1990* (Oxford, 2003) pp.17–24.
71. Pieter Jan Bouman, Gunther Beijer and Jan J. Oudegeest, *The Refugee Problem in Western Germany*, (The Hague, 1950) p.viii; Grossmann, *Jews, Germans, and Allies*, p.1. (Figures for Displaced Persons vary considerably. This is because different sets of statistics exclude or include particular groups that fall under this definition).
72. Deutsches Rotes Kreuz-Suchdienst, ed., *Zur Geschichte der Kriegsgefangenen im Westen*, p.20.

73. Rüdiger Overmans, *Soldaten Hinter Stacheldraht. Deutsche Kriegsgefangene des Zweiten Weltkrieges* (Munich, 2002) pp.298, 295.
74. Dörr, ed., *'Wer die Zeit...' Vol. II,* p.243.
75. DTA Reg. Nr. 228/I,1, Erich D.; DTA Reg. Nr. 111,2, Beate K.; See also Rüdiger Overmans, ed., *Deutsche Militärische Verluste im Zweiten Weltkrieg* (Munich, 1999) pp.68–93.
76. LAB B. Rep. 036, 4/18–3/1; LAB F. Rep. 280 LAZ Sammlung. Film Nr. 57, Sammlung Nr. 11863: *Bericht über die Heimkehrerfürsorge für den Monat Oktober 1949.*
77. *Constanze*, erstes Dezemberheft (1951) pp.60–1.
78. DZI 11763, Kurt Zentner, ed., *Aufstieg aus dem Nichts* (Vol. I Berlin, 1954) pp.81–2.
79. *Der Heimkehrer*, May (1952) p.5.
80. LAB B. Rep. 036, 4/18-3/6; Dorothy Macardle, *Children of Europe. A Study of the Children of Liberated Counties: Their War-time Experiences, their Reactions, and their Needs, with a Note on Germany* (London, 1949) p.285; Andreas-Friedrich, *Schauplatz Berlin*, p.396, 3 October 1945; Almut Leh and Alexander von Plato, *Ein unglaublicher Frühling. Erfahrene Geschichte im Nachkriegsdeutschland, 1945–48* (Bonn, 1997) p.47.
81. Macardle, *Children of Europe*, pp.295–6, 233–4, 292; Sabine Bode, *Die vergessene Generation. Die Kriegskinder brechen ihr Schweigen* (Munich, 2005) pp.131–43.
82. Deutsches Rotes Kreuz-Suchdienst, ed., *Zur Geschichte der Kriegsgefangenen im Westen*, p.20; *Soziale Arbeit*, 4 (1958) p.153.
83. DZI 385, *Anstalts Umschau* (1955).
84. DZI 22217, *Mitteilungen der Evangelischen Frauenarbeit in Deutschland*, 46 (1952) p.7; DZI B-0018, The Hilfswerk of the Evangelical Churches in Germany, ed., *Living Conditions in Germany. 1947*, p.66.
85. Niehuss, *Familie, Frau und Gesellschaft*, pp.126–7.
86. Macardle, *Children of Europe*, pp.233–4.
87. KA BIO 3168, Fröhlich, ed., *'Ich konnte einfach nichts sagen'*, March 1946.
88. KA BIO 3675, Wilhelm B., September 1947.
89. KA BIO 2657, Regina B., p.145; *Das Blatt der Hausfrau*, August (1949).
90. DTA Reg. Nr. 228/I,1, Erich D., 3 July 1945.
91. Colin Townsend and Eileen Townsend, *War Wives: A Second World War Anthology* (London, 1989) p.190.
92. Lange and Burkard, eds, *'Abends wenn wir essen fehlt uns immer einer'*, p.265.
93. Ziemann, 'Feldpostbriefe und ihre Zensur in den zwei Weltkriegen', p.170; Ortwin Buchbender and Reinhold Sterz, *Das Andere Gesicht des Krieges* (Munich, 1982), pp.19–20.
94. Humburg, *Das Gesicht des Krieges*, p.101, 18 September 1941; Kilian, *Das Medium Feldpost*, pp.21–2.
95. DTA Reg. Nr. 162/III,1, Will S.
96. Lamprecht, *Feldpost und Kriegserlebnis*, pp.46–7.
97. Vogel, ' "...aber man muss halt gehen, und wenn es in den Tod ist," 'p.38; See also Lamprecht, *Feldpost und Kriegserlebnis*, pp.54–5.
98. MKB 3.2002.1323, Hans Georg T. to wife Elisabeth, 5 July 1944.
99. MKB 3.2002.7135, Fritz S. to wife Elisabeth, 30 May 1940.
100. MKB 3.2002.1241, Josefa S. to husband, 14 April 1944.

101. MKB 3.2002.0985, Heinz R. to wife, 2 July 1941.
102. Ebert, ed., *Stalingrad*, pp.70–1, 31 December 1942, and p.54.
103. Anthony G. Powell, ed., *Last Letters from Stalingrad* (London, 1956) p.17.
104. Ibid., p.11.
105. Jürgen Kleindienst, 'Feldpost im Zweiten Weltkrieg' in Udke, ed., *'Schreib so oft Du kannst'* p.13; Klaus Latzel, 'Der "Krieg von unten" in Soldatenbriefen', p.39.
106. MKB 3.2002.7181. Jochen H. to wife Inge, 9 October 1942.
107. Siegbert Stehmann, quoted in Gerhard Sprenger, ed., *'Die Bitternis verschweigen wir.' Feldpostbriefe 1940–1945* (Hannover, 1992) pp.315, 28 October 1944.
108. Heinz Heppermann, 28 November 1941 quoted in Humburg, *Das Gesicht des Krieges*, p.252.
109. KA BIO 3742, Wilhelm K. to wife, 4 September 1942; DTA Reg. Nr. 1108, Ernst K. to his fiancée and later wife Irmgard, 7 April 1946; MKB 3.2002.7181, Jochen H. to wife Inge. 3 March 1943; Reuben Hill, *Families under Stress. Adjustment to the Crises of War Separation and Reunion* (New York, 1949) p.141.
110. Kühne, *Kameradschaft*, pp.134, 137–8, 157–8, 160–4, 489.
111. DTA Reg. Nr. Handbibliothek B Hack 1. Helma H., 19 May 1941, 30 July 1941.
112. Ibid., 30 July 1942.
113. MKB 3.2002.7186, Hans O. to wife Elsbeth, 25 October 1947.
114. Eva Schulze and Sybille Meyer, 'Krieg im Frieden. Veränderungen des Geschlechterverhältnisses untersucht am Beispiel familiärer Konflikte nach 1945' in Klaus Bergmann, Annette Kuhn, Jörn Rüsen and Gerhard Schneider eds, *Frauenmacht in der Geschichte. Beiträge des Historikerinnentreffens 1985 zur Frauengeschichtsforschung* (Düsseldorf, 1986) p.192.
115. Günter Grull, *Radio und Musik von und für Soldaten. Kriegs- und Nachkriegsjahre 1939–1960* (Cologne, 2000) pp.23, 138–9.
116. Ibid., pp.155–6.
117. Mary-Elizabeth O'Brian, 'The Celluloid War. Packaging War for Sale in Nazi Home-Front Films' in Richard A. Etlin, ed., *Art, Culture and Media under the Third Reich* (Chicago, 2002) pp.161–2; Aristotle A. Kallis, *Nazi Propaganda and the Second World War* (New York, 2005) pp.34–5; Alfred-Ingemar Berndt, 'Foreword' in Heinz Goedecke and Wilhelm Krug, *Wir beginnen das Wunschkonzert für die Wehrmacht* (Berlin, 1940) p.8.
118. O'Brian, 'The Celluloid War', pp.165–6; 169; Grull, *Radio und Musik von und für Soldaten*, p.142; Evans, *The Third Reich at War*, p.572.

3 Staying in love

1. MKB 3.2002.0985, Heinz R. to wife, 29 October 1941.
2. Pine, 'Women and the Family', p.372; Roberts, *Starke Mütter, Ferne Väter*, p.105; Niethammer, 'Privat-Wirtschaft', pp.46–8, 54, 93–4; Heineman, *What Difference Does a Husband Make?* pp.108–11.
3. Shirer, *Berlin Diary*, pp.176, 464, 20 September 1939 and 1 December 1940.
4. Stephenson, *Hitler's Home Front*, p.153.
5. Martin Chalmers, ed., *To the Bitter End. The Diaries of Victor Klemperer, 1942–1945* (London, 1999) p.409.

6. Powell, ed., trans., *Last Letters from Stalingrad*, p.24.
7. Noakes and Pridham, eds, *Nazism: Volume III*, p.874; Bielenberg, *When I Was A German*, p.110.
8. Report from 20 April 1944, in Boberach, ed., *Meldungen aus dem Reich 16*, pp.6498–9. And Report from May 1944, in Boberach, ed., *Meldungen aus dem Reich 17*, p.6535. For discussion about fluctuating morale, see Stargardt, 'A German Trauma', p.93.
9. Gamm, *Der Flüsterwitz im Dritten Reich*, p.159.
10. DTA Reg. Nr. 528. Anne K., 17 December 1944; See also Echternkamp, *Kriegsschauplatz Deutschland 1945*, p.172.
11. Stephenson, *Hitler's Home Front*, pp.187–8; Evans, *The Third Reich at War*, pp.686, 714–15.
12. Noakes, ed, *Nazism: Volume IV*, p.552. *Luftwaffe* raids on Britain led to a far smaller loss of life, with 60, 000 air-raid related deaths throughout the whole war. In London there were 30,000 deaths in comparison to 35,000 Germans who died in one night when the Allies bombed Dresden in 1945.
13. Böll, *Briefe aus dem Krieg, 1939–1945*, Vol.I, pp.333, 329; Bähr, *Kriegsbriefe Gefallener Studenten*, pp.123, 361, 365, 428.
14. See Appendix 13.
15. MKB 3.2002.0826, Hubert S. to wife Gertrud, 12 May 1942.
16. LAB F. Rep. 280, LAZ Sammlung. Film Nr. 1. Sammlung Nr. 1170, 'Gratis "Eilnachrichten" durch die Post': November 1944; Kilian, *Das Medium Feldpost*, p.52.
17. Orgel-Purper, *Willst Du meine Witwe werden?* p.118. Kurt Orgel to wife Liselotte, 2 December 1943; KA BIO 977/2.
18. KA BIO 3915, *Die Familie Bruche/Boehm. 1945–46*, 22 November 1945.
19. MKB 3.2002.0904, Martin M. to wife Gerda, 20 March 1941; MKB 3.2002.7115, Heinz R. to wife Melanie, 15 February 1944; MKB 3.2002.7159, Reinhold L. to wife Elisabeth, 2 June 1940; MKB 3.2002.0899, Heinz M. to wife Elli, 26 April 1940.
20. Udke, ed., *'Schreib so oft Du kannst'* p.127. Gerhard Udke to wife Dorothea, Easter Sunday 1943.
21. MKB 3.2002.0904, Gerda M. to husband Martin, 1 April 1941, 3 August 1940, 2 June 1941, 5 February 1942, 15 February 1942, 25 May 1941.
22. Otto Gasse to wife, 16 March 1941, quoted in Frank Schumann, ed., *'Zieh dich warm an! Soldatenpost und Heimatbriefe aus zwei Weltkriegen* (Berlin, 1989) p.170.
23. DTA Reg. Nr. Handbibliothek B Hack 1, Helma H., 4 May 1941.
24. MKB 3.2002.0904, Martin M. to wife Gerda, 12 September 1941.
25. Heineman, *What Difference Does a Husband Make?* pp.53–4, 95–6; Mouton, *From Nurturing the Nation to Purifying the Volk*, p.63; Heide Fehrenbach, *Race after Hitler. Black Occupation Children in Postwar Germany and America* (Oxford, 2005) p.9.
26. Uwe Lohalm, 'An der inneren Front. Fürsorge für die Soldatenfamilie und "rassenhygienische" Krankenpolitik' in Forschungsstelle für Zeitgeschichte in Hamburg, ed., *Hamburg im "Dritten Reich"* pp.453–4; Birthe Kundrus, 'Forbidden Company: Romantic Relationships between Germans and Foreigners, 1939 to 1945' in Damar Herzog, ed., *Sexuality and German Fascism* (Texas, 2005) pp.201, 219.

27. Costello, *Love Sex and War*, p.343; *Wirtschaft und Statistik*, 1 (Wiesbaden, 1950) p.6; Kundrus, 'Forbidden Company', pp.204, 207, 214.
28. Humburg, *Das Gesicht des Krieges*, pp.110–12; Letter to the editor of *Stern* quoted in Dagmar Herzog, 'Hubris and Hypocrisy, Incitement and Disavowal' in Herzog, ed., *Sexuality and German Fascism*, p.16.
29. Anneliese F., quoted in Dörr, ed., *'Wer die Zeit...' Vol. II*, p.161.
30. Dörr, ed., *'Wer die Zeit...' Vol. II*, p.170.
31. SD report from 3 April 1944, quoted in Noakes, ed., *Nazism: Vol. IV*, pp.385–90.
32. Albert Pretzel quoted in Klaus Latzel, *Deutsche Soldaten – Nationalsozialistischer Krieg? Kriegserlebnis, – Kriegserfahrung, 1939–1945* (Bielefeld, 1996), pp.332.
33. Niethammer, 'Privat-Wirtschaft', pp. 46–8, 54, 93–4; Roberts, *Starke Mütter, Ferne Väter*, p.105; Heineman, *What Difference Does a Husband Make?* pp.108–11.
34. *Das Blatt der Hausfrau*, 15 (1950) p.2.
35. Sieder, *Sozialgeschichte der Familie*, p.237.
36. LAB B. Rep. 012, Nr. 177.
37. *Das Blatt der Hausfrau*, September (1950) p.17.
38. Meyer and Schulze, 'Krieg im Frieden', p.188.
39. Werner Abelshauser, *Wirtschaftsgeschichte der Bundesrepublik Deutschland 1945–1980* (Frankfurt am Main, 1983) p.51; Michael Wildt, *Am Beginn der 'Konsumgesellschaft'. Mangelerfahrung, Lebenshaltung, Wohlstandshoffnung in Westdeutschland in den fünfziger Jahren* (Hamburg, 1994) pp.33–5; Geoffrey J. Giles, ed., *Stunde Null: The End and the Beginning Fifty Years Ago* (Washington, 1997) pp.13, 76, 105, 195.
40. Evans, *The Third Reich at War*, p.563.
41. See Appendix 15.
42. Bielenberg, *When I was a German*, p.61.
43. Else Wendel, *Hausfrau at War. A German Woman's Account of Life in Hitler's Reich* (London, 1957) p.203.
44. Noakes, ed., *Nazism: Volume IV*, p.519.
45. Auguste Lühr quoted in Colin and Eileen Townsend, *War Wives*, p.199.
46. Report on the Nutritional Status of Berlin Population (17 October 1947) quoted in Steege, *Black Market*, p.45.
47. Heineman, *What Difference Does a Husband Make?* p.86; Christine von Oertzen, *The Pleasure of a Surplus Income. Part-Time Work, Gender Politics, and Social Change in West Germany, 1955–1969* (London, 2007) p.16.
48. Konrad H. Jarausch, *After Hitler. Recivilizing Germany, 1945–1995* (Oxford, 2006), pp.80–1; Rainer Gries, *Die Rationen-Gesellschaft* (Münster, 1991) p.11.
49. LAB F. Rep. 240, Acc. 2421,Vallentin, *Die Einnahme von Berlin*, Early postwar days, p.15; Margret Boveri, *Tage des Überlebens: Berlin 1945* (Munich, 1968) pp.79–80.
50. LAB F. Rep. 240, Acc. 217 Nr. 10, *Deutsche Volkszeitung*, 26 June 1945, p.4; LAB F. Rep. 280 LAZ Sammlung. Film Nr. 33, Sammlung Nr. 7405.
51. Rottenberger, *Die Hungerjahre*, p.115.
52. Stargardt, *Witnesses of War*, pp.331–4; LAB F. Rep. 240, Acc. 2651. Nr. 4, Bericht 396, Gerda Hachmeister; Rottenberger, *Die Hungerjahre*, p.176; Wirrer, ed., *'Ich glaube an den Führer'*, p.322. Inge to Fred, 11 April 1945;

Anna J. Merritt and Richard L. Merritt, *Public Opinion in Occupied Germany. The OMGUS Surveys, 1945–1949* (Illinois, 1970) p.294.

53. Thurnward, *Gegenwartsprobleme Deutsche Familien*, pp.192, 217, 235, 274, 284.

54. LAB F. Rep. 240, Acc. 2421, Vallentin, *Die Einnahme von Berlin*, 24 April 1945.

55. LAB B. Rep. 010–02, Acc. 1888, Nr. 739.

56. Klaus-Jörg Rühl, *Frauen in der Nachkreigszeit, 1945–1963* (Munich, 1988) pp.11–15; DZI 9957, Hans Joachim von Merkate, Wolfgang Metzner, and A. Hillen Ziegfeld, eds, *Deutschland Taschenbuch. Tatsachen und Zahlen* (Frankfurt, 1954) p.89; DZI 5041, Institut zur Förderung öffentlicher Angelegenheiten, ed., *Sozialtaschenbuch 1952. Deutsche Sozialstatistik für die Praxis* (Frankfurt, 1952) p.13.

57. StaAH. 351-10 (II) Sozialbehörde II: 012.12-5; 230.02-2; 012.84-1; 129.89-9; 012.10-21.

58. DZI B-0018, The Hilfswerk of the Evangelical Churches in Germany, ed., *Living Conditions in Germany. 1947*, p.25.

59. DZI B-0018, The Hilfswerk of the Evangelical Churches in Germany, ed., *Living Conditions in Germany. 1947*, pp.26–7; DZI 5041, Institut zur Förderung öffentlicher Angelegenheiten, ed., *Sozialtaschenbuch 1952. Deutsche Sozialstatistik für die Praxis* (Frankfurt, 1952) p.13.

60. Victor Gollancz, *Our Threatened Values* (London, 1946) pp.95–7; Ahonen, *After the Expulsion*, pp.21–4; Bouman et al., *The Refugee Problem in Western Germany*, pp.2–3; Ian Connor, *Refugees and Expellees in Post-war Germany* (Manchester, 2007) pp.18, 29–38, 59–96.

61. StaAH. 351-10 (II) Sozialbehörde II 012.10–21.

62. Thurnward, *Gegenwartsprobleme Berliner Familien*, pp.270, 273; See also Schelsky, *Wandlungen*, pp.250–2.

63. LAB B. Rep. 012, Nr. 177. 64. *Für Euch*, 1 (1950) p.8.

65. Niehuss, *Familie, Frau und Gesellschaft*, p.380. For a more detailed discussion of why class was rendered less important, see William Sheridan Allen, *The Nazi Seizure of Power* (London, 1965) p.294; Werner Abelshauser, *Die langen Fünfziger Jahre* (Düsseldorf, 1987) pp.50–1; Martin Kitchen, *Germany at War* (London, 1995) p.101.

66. LAB B. Rep. 036, 4/2-1/16. PR/LJG 908; LAB B. Rep. 012, Nr. 177. DZI 82916, 'Eheberatung-Ehescheidung' *Soziale Arbeit*, 11 (1954).

67. LAB B. Rep. 012, Nr. 177.

68. Landesamt Baden Württemberg 1955, ed., *Statistisches Handbuch, Baden Württemberg*, 1 (1955) p.66..

69. LAB B. Rep. 036. 4/2-1/16/PR/LMH 817.

70. Karl Hardach, *The Political Economy of Germany in the Twentieth Century* (London, 1980) pp.98–100; Niehuss, *Familie, Frau und Gesellschaft*, p.13; Jennifer A. Loehlin, *From Rugs to Riches. Housework, Consumption and Modernity in Germany* (Oxford, 1999) pp.36, 39.

71. *Das Blatt der Hausfrau*, April 1949.

72. LAB B. Rep. 010–02, Nr. 309. B. Rep. 010–02, Acc. 1663, Nr. 309.

73. Axel Schildt and Arnold Sywottek, ' "Reconstruction" and "Modernization": West German Social History during the 1950s' in Robert Moeller, ed., *West Germany Under Construction* (Michigan, 2000) p.422; 427; Josef Mooser, *Arbeiterleben in Deutschland 1900–1970* (Frankfurt, 1984) p.73; Merith Niehuss, 'Kontinuität und Wandel der Familie in den 50er Jahren' in Axel

Schildt and Arnold Sywottek, *Modernisierung im Wiederaufbau* (Bonn, 1993) p.321; Richard Bessel, *Germany, 1945* (London, 2009).

74. Engert, *Heimatfront*, p.131; Nori Möding, 'Die Stunde der Frauen?' in Martin Broszat, Klaus-Dietmar Henke and Hans Woller, eds, *Von Stalingrad zur Währungsreform. Zur Sozialgeschichte des Umbruchs in Deutschland* (Munich, 1988) p.620.

75. Costello, *Love Sex and War*, p.25; See also Vogel, '...aber man muss halt gehen, und wenn es in den Tod ist', p.44.

76. DTA Reg. Nr. 856/II 5, Hildegard R., 27 May 1945.

77. KA BIO 1676, Diana-Ilse J., 6 June 1945.

78. Böll, *Briefe aus dem Krieg, 1939–45*, Vol.I, p.120.

79. DTA Reg. Nr. 1002, Luise S., 23 January 1944.

80. KA BIO 3742, Wilhelm K., 16 August 1942.

81. MKB 3.2002.7181, Jochen H. to wife Inge, 28 September 1942; See also MKB 3.2002.1286, Georg N. to wife, 1 January 1940; Horst Schleberger, ed., *Kriegesbriefe eines jungen Lehrers 1941–1945* (Pössneck, 2004) pp.129–30.

82. DZI 10662, Nikolaus Gross, *Rückkehr zur Familie* (Heidelberg, 1947) pp.7–14.

83. Beevor, *Stalingrad*, p.364.

84. DTA Reg. Nr. Handbibliothek B Hack 1, Helma H., 13 May 1941.

85. Carl Bertelsmann, ed., *Last Letters from Stalingrad* (London, 1956) p.11.

86. Biess, *Homecomings*, p.123; DTA Reg. Nr. 1108, Ernst K. to his fiancée and later wife Irmgard, 25 March 1945; Bähr, *Kriegsbriefe Gefallener Studenten*, p.115.

87. German Infantryman in 1939 quoted in Costello, *Love Sex and War*, p.19.

88. DTA Reg. Nr. 230/II, Eugen N. to wife Ursula, New Year 1947.

89. German soldier quoted in Costello, *Love Sex and War*, p.27.

90. DTA Reg. Nr. Handbibliothek B Hack 1, Helma H., June 1941.

91. Heinz Heppermann quoted in Humburg, *Das Gesicht des Krieges*, p.182; Böll, *Briefe aus dem Krieg 1939–1945*, Vol.II, p.950; Hill, *Families under Stress*, p.252.

92. Humburg, *Das Gesicht des Krieges*, p.174–6; Biess, *Homecomings*, p.123.

93. Thurward, *Gegenwartsprobleme Berliner Familien*, pp.220, 229, 280.

94. DTA Reg. Nr. 111,2, Beate K., 1 July 1945.

95. DTA Reg. Nr. 856/II 5, Hildegard R., 13 July 1945.

96. Heineman, *What Difference Does a Husband Make?* pp.108–11, 115; Heinz Bude, *Bilanz der Nachfolge. Die Bundesrepublik und der Nationalsozialismus* (Frankfurt, 1992) p.69.

97. Böll, *Briefe aus dem Krieg, 1939–1945*, Vol.I, p.395, 19 July 1942.

98. Bruns, *Als Vater aus dem Krieg heimkehrte*, p.11.

99. KA BIO 6176, Dr. Rolf M.; MKB 3.2002.7186.

100. DTA Reg. Nr. Handbibliothek B Hack 1, Helma H., 30 July 1941.

101. DTA Reg. Nr. 289, Cläre S., 24 March 1945.

102. F. 240. Acc. 863 Nr.20; *Sie*, 1 (December, 1945) p.1.

103. Bruns, *Als Vater aus dem Krieg heimkehrte*, p.105; Heineman, *What Difference Does a Husband Make?* p.115; Roberts, *Starke Mütter, Ferne Väter*, p.105; Meyer and Schulze, 'Krieg im Frieden', p.187.

104. *Constanze*, 9 (July, 1948) p.10.

105. Bude, *Bilanz der Nachfolge*, p.69.

106. DTA Reg. Nr. 230/II, Eugen N. to wife Ursula, 27 September 1946 and also 12 October 1946.

107. MKB 3.2002.0826, Hubert S. to wife Gertrud, 17 February 1941.

108. MKB 3.2002.888.0, Peter D. to wife, 25 May 1944; See also MKB 3.2002.0224, Klaus B. to his wife Suse, 5 November 1943; MKB 3.2002.7184, Hans H. to wife Käthe, 15 February 1945; MKB 3.2002.1241, Albert S. to his wife, 11 June 1941.

109. Drechsler, *Mamatschi schenk mir ein Pferdchen*, p.203. 22 September 1944.

110. MKB 3.2002.0826, Hubert S. to wife Gertrud, 31 March 1944.

111. DTA Reg. Nr. 230/II, Eugen N. to wife Ursula, 23 November 1946.

112. Klaus-Jörg, *Frauen in der Nachkreigszeit, 1945–1963*, p.123.

113. Niehuss, *Familie, Frau und Gesellschaft*, pp.384–5; Heineman, *What Difference Does a Husband Make?* p.108; *Brigitte*, 19 (1955) p.3.

114. Schelsky, *Wandlungen*, pp.13, 51.

115. *Sie* 1/15 (1946) p.6, quoted in Heineman, *What Difference Does a Husband Make?* p.108.

116. Overmans, *Soldaten Hinter Stacheldraht*, p.308.

117. DZI 20809, *Die Innere Mission*, 3 (1950).

118. Sibylle Meyer und Eva Schulze, ' "Alleine war's schwieriger und einfacher zugleich." Veränderung gesellschaftlicher Bewertung und individueller Erfahrung alleinstehenden Frauen in Berlin 1943–1955' in Annette Kuhn and Anna-Elisabeth Freier, eds, *Frauen in der Geschichte V* (Düsseldorf, 1984) pp.348–85.

119. DTA Reg. Nr. 111,2, Beate K., July 1945.

120. DTA Reg. Nr. 230/II, Eugen N. to wife Ursula, 31 March 1946.

121. Humburg, *Das Gesicht des Krieges*, p.176.

122. Heinrich Böll, *The Stories of Heinrich Böll* (Trans. by Leila Vennewitz, London, 1986), pp.4–5.

123. *Soziale Arbeit*, 3 (1955) p.177; *Caritasdienst*, 6 (1954) p.50; *Wirtschaft und Statistik*, 7, 1954 (Wiesbaden, 1956) p.328; DZI 14820, Alice and Robert Scherer, Julius Dorreich, eds, *Ehe und Familie. Grundsätze, Bestand und Fördernde Massnahmen* (Freiburg, 1956) pp.135–6; Niehuss, *Familie, Frau und Gesellschaft*, p.116; Frevert, *Women in German History*, p.263.

124. Rene König, *Die unvollständige Familie* (Zurich, 1951) p.31.

125. Niehuss, *Familie, Frau und Gesellschaft*, pp.40–2. In this context, Niehuss refers to families as being 'complete' where a married couple was living together with or without children.

126. Heineman, *What Difference Does a Husband Make?* p.119; Matschenz, 'Der Onkel da ist Dein Vater', in Annette Kaminsky, ed., *Heimkehr 1948*, p.17; Stargardt, *Witnesses of War*, p.329; DZI B-0018, *Living Conditions in Germany. 1947*, p.68; DZI 10065, Hans von Hattingberg, *Ehekrisen Entwicklungskrisen. Ein Problem unserer Zeit* (Munich, 1949), pp.9–10.

127. Ralf Rytlewski and Manfred Opp de Hipt, eds, *Die Bundesrepublik Deutschland in Zahlen 1945/9–1980* (Munich, 1987) p.46.

128. *Brigitte*, 19 (1955) p.3.

129. Angela Seeler, 'Ehe, Familie und andere Lebensformen in den Nachkriegsjahren' in Annette Kuhn and Anna-Elisabeth Freier, eds, *Frauen in der Geschichte V. 'Das Schicksal Deutschlands liegt in der Hand seiner Frauen.' Frauen in der deutschen Nachkriegsgeschichte* (Düsseldorf, 1984) p.99.

130. *Constanze*, 10 (1949) p.19.

131. Heide Fehrenbach, 'Of German Mothers and Negermischlingskinder. Race, Sex and the Postwar Nation' in Schissler, ed., *The Miracle Years*, p.164;

Til van Rahden, 'Demokratie und väterliche Autorität. Das Karlsruher "Stichentscheid" – Urteil von 1959 in der politischen Kultur der frühen Bundesrepublik' in *Zeithistorische Forschungen/Studies in Contemporary History* 2 (2005) p.162.

132. Heineman, *What Difference Does a Husband Make?* p.117; Hill, *Families under Stress*, pp.117, 252; Grossmann, *Jews, Germans, and Allies*, p. 76.
133. Bielenberg, *When I was a German*, p.252; Ingeborg Wells, *Enough, No More* (London, 1948) p.126; DTA Reg. Nr. 302/II, Waltraud S.; DTA Reg. Nr. 1103/ II, Anneliese P.; Roberts, *Starke Mütter, Ferne Väter*, p.51.
134. DTA Reg. Nr. 302/II, Waltraud S.
135. LAB F. Rep. 240, Acc. 2651, Nr. 5, Bericht 598, Elisabeth Rendel.
136. DTA Reg. Nr. 952,1, Helmut B., 25 August 1946.
137. Renate Dziemba in Kleindienst, ed., *Lebertran und Chewing Gum*, pp.125–6.
138. Grossmann, *Jews, Germans, and Allies*, p.76.
139. Roberts, *Starke Mütter, Ferne Väter*, p.51.
140. Schelsky, *Wandlungen*, p.64.
141. Barbara Willenbacher, 'Zerrütung und Bewährung der Nachkriegs-Familie' in Broszat, Henke and Woller, eds, *Von Stalingrad zur Währungsreform*, pp.613–14.
142. Schelsky, *Wandlungen*, pp.262–3.
143. Thurward, *Gegenwartsprobleme Berliner Familien*, pp.273, 217; KA BIO 3811, Elisabeth L.. 2 March 1945.
144. Roberts, *Starke Mütter, Ferne Väter*, p.106; Matschenz, 'Der Onkel da ist Dein Vater', p.132; Moeller, *Protecting Motherhood*, p.3; John Borneman, *Belonging in the Two Berlins* (Cambridge, 1992) p.213.
145. Renate Dziemba in Kleindienst, ed., *Lebertran und Chewing Gum*, pp.125–6.
146. Thurnwald, *Gegenwartsprobleme Berliner Familien*, p.189; Costello, *Love, Sex and War*, p.19; Moeller, *Protecting Motherhood*, p.33; Grunberger, *A Social History of the Third Reich*, p.319; Schelsky, 'The Family in Germany', pp.331–2; Eva Kolinsky, *Women in West Germany. Life, Work and Politics* (Oxford, 1989) p.29.
147. Schelsky, *Wandlungen*, pp.63, 66, 75, 91, 262; Rottenberger, *Die Hungerjahre*, p.175; Frevert, *Women in German History*, p.265.
148. DZI 10065, Hattingberg, *Ehekrisen Entwicklungskrisen.*, pp.9–10.
149. Frevert, *Women in German History*, p.265.
150. DZI 6828, *Familiengerechte Wohlfahrtspflege und Sozialpolitik* (Berfusverband Katholischen Fürsorgerinnen); Schelsky, *Wandlungen*, p.93; Elisabeth Pfeil, *Der Flüchtling* (Hamburg, 1949); Bouman et al., *The Refugee Problem in Western Germany*, p.8.
151. Dorothee Wierling, 'Mission to Happiness: The Cohort of 1949 and the Making of East and West Germans' in Schissler, ed., *The Miracle Years*, p.110; Hill, *Families under Stress*, p.87; Bruns, *Als Vater aus dem Krieg heimkehrte*, p.173.
152. Kardorff, *Diary of a Nightmare*, pp.76, 114.
153. DTA Reg. Nr. 856/II 5, Hildegard R., Tagebuchbrief, 25.4, 22 July 1945.
154. *Das Blatt der Hausfrau*, September (1949).
155. DTA Reg. Nr. 528, Anne K., 13 November 1945.
156. Gisela Wolff quoted in Kleindienst, ed., *Lebertran und Chewing Gum*, p. 107.

157. LAB F. Rep. 240, Acc. 2651, Nr. 3, Bericht 152, Herbert Wirsig; Gustav Trampe, ed., *Die Stunde Null* (Reinbek, 1986) p.66; 178; Wells, *Enough, No More*, p.126.
158. Schelsky, *Wandlungen*, pp.66, 73.
159. Echternkamp, *Kriegsschauplatz Deutschland 1945*, p.161.
160. *Für Euch*, 7 (1950) p.11.
161. KA BIO 2657, Herr K., quoted in Regina Bruss, *Mit Zuckersack und Heiße Getränk* (Bremen, 1988) p.207.
162. LAB F. Rep. 240, Acc. 2651, Nr. 5, Bericht 555, Hildegard Lietich.
163. Niethammer, 'Privat-Wirtschaft', pp.46–8; Heineman, *What Difference Does a Husband Make?* p.115.
164. Böll, *Briefe aus dem Krieg 1939–1945*, Vol. I, p.395, 19 July 1942; KA BIO 6176, Dr. Rolf M.; MKB 3.2002.7186, Hans O., 25 October 1947; DTA Reg. Nr. Handbibliothek B Hack 1, Helma H., 30 July 1941; Johannes Steinhoff, Peter Pechel and Dennis Showalter, eds, *Voices from the Third Reich. An Oral History* (London, 1991) pp.338–9; Wierling, 'Mission to Happiness', p.110; Bruns, *Als Vater aus dem Krieg heimkehrte*, p.173.
165. Pine, *Nazi Family Policy*, p.372; Roberts, *Starke Mütter, Ferne Väter*, p.105; Sieder, *Sozialgeschichte der Familie*, p.236; Niethammer, 'Privat-Wirtschaft', pp.46–8, 54, 93–4; Heineman, *What Difference Does a Husband Make?* pp.108–11.
166. DTA Reg. Nr. Handbibliothek B Hack 1, Helma H., 19 August 1941.

4   Empowerment or endurance?

1. *Das Blatt der Hausfrau* (July 1949).
2. Doris Schubert and Annette Kuhn, eds, *Frauen in der deutschen Nachkriegszeit. Band 1. Frauenarbeit 1945–1949* (Düsseldorf, 1984) pp.29, 35; Meyer and Schulze, 'Krieg im Frieden', pp.188, 190–1; Moeller, *Protecting Motherhood*, p.12; Hagemann and Schüler-Springerum, eds, *Home/Front*, p.35; Annette Kuhn, 'Power and Powerlessness: Women after 1945, or the Continuity of the Ideology of Femininity' *German History*, Vol. 7, No.1 (1989) pp.35–6.
3. Meyer and Schulze, *Wie wir das alles geschafft haben*, pp.179–80; Meyer and Schulze, 'Krieg im Frieden', p.188.
4. Meyer and Schulze, eds, *Wie wir das alles geschafft haben*, p.97.
5. LAB F Rep. 240, Acc. 2651, Nr. 3: Bericht 262, Alfred Schumann; LAB (STA) Rep. 134/13, Nr. 182/2, Bl.97. F.
6. *Constanze*, 6 (May 1948) p.6.
7. LAB B. Rep. 012, Nr. 177; Schubert and Kuhn, eds, *Frauen in der deutschen Nachkriegszeit. Band 1*, p.31; Harsch, *Revenge of the Domestic*, pp.21, 59.
8. Meyer and Schulze, eds, *Wie wir das alles geschafft haben*, p.8.
9. Statistisches Amt des Vereinigten Wirtschaftsgebietes, ed., *Wirtschaft und Statistik* (Stuttgart, 1950) p.1353.
10. Wendel, *Hausfrau at War*, p.21; Uwe Timm, *In My Brother's Shadow* (London, 2005) p.58.
11. LAB F. 240, Acc. 2651, Nr. 4, Bericht 331, Elisabeth Blau; Meyer and Schulze, 'Krieg im Frieden', p.188.
12. Powell, ed., *Last Letters from Stalingrad*, pp.12–13.
13. *Constanze*, 1 (March 1948) p.3; *Constanze*, 3 (April 1948) p.19.

14. Schubert and Kuhn, eds, *Frauen in der deutschen Nachkriegszeit. Band 1*, p.56; *Sie*, 2 (1945) p.8; Frevert, *Women in German History*, p.263; Schulze and Meyer, 'Von Liebe sprach damals Keiner', p.216.

15. See Franz-Josef Würmeling, *Familie -Gabe und Aufgabe* (Cologne, 1963); Möding, 'Die Stunde der Frauen?' p.623; Uta Poiger, 'Krise der Männlichkeit. Remaskulinisierung in beiden deutschen Nachkriegsgesellschaften' in Klaus Naumann, ed., *Nachkrieg in Deutschland* (Hamburg, 2001) pp.228–9.

16. *Constanze*, 10 (1954) p.100; DZI 22217, *Mitteilungen der Evangelische Frauenarbeit in Deutschland*, 47, (1952) p.6; DZI 20891, *Caritas*, 1/2 (1950) p.23; DZI 13532, Berufsverband Katholischer Sozialarbeiter Nordrhein-Westfalen, ed., *Familiennot und ihre Überwindung* (Bad Godesberg, 1955) p.3; DZI 22217, 'Das Ende der Familie', in *Mitteilungen der Evangelischen Frauenarbeit in Deutschland*, 47 (1952); Stanley Cohen, *Folk Devils and Moral Panics. The Creation of the Mods and the Rockers* (2nd edition, Oxford, 1980) pp.9, 17.

17. *Brigitte*, 5 (1954) pp.4–5; Joosten, *Die Frau, das 'segenspendende Herz der Familie'*, p.27; Willenbacher, 'Zerrütung und Bewährung der Nachkriegs-Familie', pp.604–5.

18. Moeller, *Protecting Motherhood*, pp.3, 148; Ruhl, *Verordnete Unterordnung*, p.13; *Brigitte*, 19 (1955) p.3.

19. Robert Moeller, 'Reconstructing the Family in Reconstruction Germany', in Moeller, ed., *West Germany under Construction*, p.112; Van Rahden, 'Demokratie und väterliche Autorität', p.162; Loehlin, *From Rugs to Riches*, p.1.

20. Harsch, *Revenge of the Domestic*, pp.1, 3–4, 45, 51, 198, 200; Naimark, *The Russians in Germany*, p.125; Oertzen, *The Pleasure of a Surplus Income*, pp.5–7; Gisela Helwig, 'Familienpolitik in der SBZ' in Ugo Wengst, ed., *Geschichte der Sozialpolitik in Deutschland seit 1945* (Vol. 2/1, Munich, 2001) p.664.

21. Ruhl, *Verordnete Unterordnung*, pp.11–13, 332, 334; Joosten, *Die Frau, das 'segenspendende Herz der Familie'*, p.42.

22. Heineman, *What Difference Does a Husband Make?* p.91; Meyer and Schulze, eds, *Wie wir das alles geschafft haben*, p.97; Harsch, *Revenge of the Domestic*, pp.44–5; DZI 5041, Institut zur Förderung öffentlicher Angelegenheiten, ed., *Sozialtaschenbuch 1952. Deutsche Sozialstatistik für die Praxis.*(Frankfurt, 1952) p.60; Niehuss, *Familie, Frau und Gesellschaft*, pp.34, 38.

23. Niehuss, *Familie, Frau und Gesellschaft*, p.227.

24. DZI 5041, Institut zur Förderung öffentlicher Angelegenheiten, ed., *Sozialtaschenbuch 1952. Deutsche Sozialstatistik für die Praxis* (Frankfurt, 1952) p.60. (The term 'employed' in this context is translated from the German word *berufstätig*).

25. 'Münchener Familienstatistik' in Statistischen Amt der Landeshauptstadt, ed., *Münchner Statistik*, 3 (1949) p.49.

26. *Statistisches Jahrbuch für die Bundesrepublik Deutschland 1952* (Wiesbaden, 1955) p.86; *Deutschland Taschenbuch. Tatsachen und Zahlen* (Frankfurt, 1954) p.138. Employees and workers for 1938 are according to workbook estimates of the civil service office in charge of paying employees in 1939; figures for 1948 and 1951 include employees and workers. Figures are in thousands. There is a question mark over whether or not casual and part-time employment was included in these statistics. The difficulty with such statistics is

confusion between the German terms *erwerbstätig*, which means economi-cally active, and *berufstätig*, which means employed. *Erwerbstätig* women could be those who ran their own shops or small business, usually as part of a family business.

27. Ruhl, *Verordnete Unterordnung*, p.50; Niehuss, *Familie, Frau und Gesellschaft*, p.81.
28. *Statistisches Jahrbuch für die Bundesrepublik Deutschland 1955* (Wiesbaden, 1955) p.54.
29. *Das Blatt der Hausfrau*, (January 1949).
30. Niehuss, *Familie, Frau und Gesellschaft*, p.105.
31. Schubert and Kuhn, eds, *Frauen in der deutschen Nachkriegszeit. Band 1*, p.56; See also *Sie*, 2 (1945) p.8; Meyer and Schulze, 'Krieg im Frieden', pp.188–9.
32. Lehmann, *Gefangenschaft und Heimkehr*, p.147; *Constanze*, 2 (January 1949) p.21; Noakes and Pridham, eds, *Nazism: Volume II*, p.273.
33. Niehuss, *Familie, Frau und Gesellschaft*, p.105; Biess, *Homecomings*, p.122.
34. Stibbe, *Women in the Third Reich*, p.155; LAB B. Rep. 012, Nr. 177, 'Deutschland in den fünfziger Jahren' in *Informationen zur politischen Bildung* 256 (1947) p.6.
35. Richtlinien für die Pastoration der Heimkehrer, ADCV, 372.025, Fasz.3 and ' "Ein Wort zum Ehebruch". Soll der Mann seiner Frau vergeben'? *Der Heimkehrer* 1 (1947); Biess, *Homecomings*, p.122; Harsch, *Revenge of the Domestic*, p.27; Naimark, *The Russians in Germany*, pp.125–6.
36. *Das Blatt der Hausfrau*, 12 (September 1950) p.8.
37. Willenbacher, 'Zerrütung und Bewährung der Nachkriegs-Familie', p.599; Harsch, *The Revenge of the Domestic*, p.34.
38. *Das Blatt der Hausfrau*, (November, 1948); Ruhl, *Verordnete Unterordnung*, pp.12, 331; Von Oertzen, *The Pleasure of a Surplus Income*, p.30.
39. *Brigitte*, 12 (1955) p.3; See also *Für Euch*, 2 (1950) p.11.
40. Meyer and Schulze, eds, *Wie wir das alles geschafft haben*, p.180.
41. Beate Hoecker and Renate Meyer-Braun, eds, *Bremerinnen bewältigen die Nachkriegszeit* (Bremen, 1988) p.194.
42. James M. Diehl, *The Thanks of the Fatherland. German Veterans after the Second World War* (North Carolina, 1993) p.70.
43. *Constanze*, 4 (1948) p.19; See also Dörr, ed., *'Wer die Zeit...'* Vol. III, p.89.
44. DTA Reg. Nr. 111,2, Beate K., 16 August 1945.
45. Heineman, *What Difference Does a Husband Make?* p.82.
46. Stephenson, *Hitler's Home Front*, pp.199, 346; Schelsky, *Wandlungen*, p.246; Mathilde W. quoted in Dörr, ed., *'Wer die Zeit...'* Vol. II, p.39; Thurnwald, *Gegenwartsprobleme Berliner Familien*, pp.37, 284, 85–6.
47. LAB F. Rep. 280, LAZ Sammlung. Film Nr. 39, Sammlung Nr. 8482: 28 March 1947, *Bericht über die soziale Lage im Verwaltungsbezirk Zehlendorf.*
48. DTA Reg. Nr. 340, 1 Maxi-Lore E., 15 May 1945.
49. Frevert, *Women in German History*, p.259; Schubert and Kuhn, eds, *Frauen in der deutschen Nachkriegszeit, Band. I*, pp.164–5.
50. SD report 18 November 1943, quoted in Wolfgang Michalka, *Das Dritte Reich. Dokumente zur Innen- und Aussenpolitik. Band 2. Weltmachtanspruch und nationaler Zusammenbruch 1939–1945* (Munich, 1985) pp.304–5.
51. *Constanze*, 9 (July 1948) p.10.
52. DTA Reg. Nr. 131, Irene B.
53. *Constanze*, 16 (October 1948) p.5.

54. DTA Reg. Nr. 454/III, Elisabeth L.
55. DTA Reg. Nr. 1002, Luise S.; KA BIO 1676, Diana-Ilse J., 31 July 1945.
56. Roberts, *Starke Mütter, Ferne Väter*, p.42.
57. DZI 10662, Gross, *Rückkehr zur Familie*, pp.15–16.
58. MKB 3.2002.1376.0, Wilhelm B., pp.6–7, 29 October 1939.
59. *Das Blatt der Hausfrau* (March 1949).
60. *Das Blatt der Hausfrau* (January 1949).
61. DTA Reg. Nr. 111, 2, Beate K., 19 December 1945.
62. DZI B-0018, The Hilfswerk of the Evangelical Churches in Germany, ed., *Living Conditions in Germany. 1947*, p.67–8.
63. Thurnwald, *Gegenwartsprobleme Berliner Familien*, p.59.
64. Victor Gollancz, *In Darkest Germany* (London, 1947) pp.57–8.
65. Charles Bray writing in the *Daily Herald*, 24 August 1946, quoted in Gollancz, *Our Threatened Values*, p.99.
66. *Constanze*, 9 (July 1948) p.10.
67. Echternkamp, *Kriegsschauplatz Deutschland 1945*, p.251.
68. Thurnwald, *Gegenwartsprobleme Berliner Familien*, pp.235, 284; Sieder, *Sozialgeschichte der Familie*, p.236.
69. Willi Volka quoted in Kleindienst, ed., *Lebertran und Chewing Gum*, pp.249–50.
70. DTA Reg. Nr. 528, Anne K., 7 January 1945; Wirrer, ed., *Ich glaube an den Führer*, p.324. Inge to Fred, 17 April 1945; KA BIO 1676, Diana-Itse J., 20–28 May 1945.
71. DTA Reg. Nr. 454/III, Elisabeth L., 20 November 1945, 25 January 1946, 18 November 1945.
72. DTA Reg. Nr. 1002, Luise S., 12 September 1944; See also Wendel, *Hausfrau at War*, p. 220.
73. DTA Reg. Nr. 528, Anne K., 4–25 January 1945.
74. DZI 23021, *Vinzenz-Blätter*, 4 (1955) p.80.
75. Meyer and Schulze, eds, *Wie wir das alles geschafft haben*, pp.179–80.
76. Niehuss, *Familie, Frau und Gesellschaft*, pp.107–8; Gabriele Jenk, *Steine gegen Brot: Trümmerfrauen schildern den Wiederaufbau in der Nachkriegszeit* (Bastei-Lübbe, 1988) p.30; Naimark, *The Russians in Germany*, pp.93, 98.
77. Costello, *Love Sex and War*, p.343; Maria Höhn, *GIs and Fräuleins* (North Carolina, 2002) p.74.
78. Schubert and Kuhn, eds, *Frauen in der deutschen Nachkriegszeit. Band 1*, pp.67–8.
79. Möding, 'Die Stunde der Frauen' p.621; Meyer-Lenz, ed., *Die Ordnung des Paares ist unbehaglich*, p.42.
80. DTA Reg. Nr. 454/III, Elisabeth L., 23 December 1945 and 16 January 1947; DTA Reg. Nr. 111,2. Beate K., 1 July 1945.
81. Typical ways in which looking forward to reunion was mentioned in the letters: MKB 3.2002.7505, Ernst S. to Herta his wife, 6 May 1942, 'I really hope that it works out like before, that I'll be able to come home soon so that we can get on with our life as a family of three again'; MKB 3.2002.0904, Martin M. to wife Gerda, 29 September 1941, 'I just want to come home on leave soon. Hopefully I won't be out here for too much longer'; MKB 3.2002.0904, Gerda to Martin M.,17 August 1941, 'If you come home on leave...'; MKB 3.2002.0826, Hubert S. to Gertrud,

17 February 1941, 'I'm just so looking forward to the day when we're together again'.
82. Stargardt, *Witnesses of War*, p.343; *Das Blatt der Hausfrau*, (February 1949) p.6; *Constanze*, 2 (February 1951) p.35.
83. Heineman, *What Difference Does a Husband Make?* p.111.
84. DZI XVE3 21755, *Der-Die-Das*, 1 (1951) p.13.
85. DZI XVE3 21755, *Der-Die-Das*, 1 (1951) p.8.
86. Frevert, *Women in German History*, p.266.
87. Niehuss, 'Kontinuität und Wandel der Familie in den 50er Jahren', p.334; Herzog, *Sex after Fascism*, p.104; Von Oertzen, *The Pleasure of a Surplus Income*, pp.5–7; Frevert, *Women in German History*, p.179; Hoecker and Meyer-Braun, eds, *Bremerinnen*, pp.9, 194.
88. Powell, ed., *Last Letters from Stalingrad*, p.12.
89. MKB 3.2002.7505, Ernst S. to Herta his wife, 6 May 1942; Hubert S. to Gertrud, 17 February 1941; Thomas A. Kohut and Jürgen Reulecke, ' "Sterben wie eine Ratte, die der Bauer ertappt". Letzte Briefe aus Stalingrad' in Jürgen Förster, ed., *Stalingrad. Ereignis, Wirkung, Symbol* (Munich, 1993) p.463.
90. Albrecht Lehmann, 'Die Kriegsgefangenen' *Aus Politik und Zeitgeschichte*, 7–8 (1995) p. 17; James M. Diehl, *The Thanks of the Fatherland. German Veterans after the Second World War* (North Carolina, 1993) p.70; Biess, *Homecomings*, p.12; Poiger, 'Krise der Männlichkeit', pp.228–9.
91. Noakes, ed., *Nazism: Volume IV*, p.222; Naimark, *The Russians in Germany*, p.125.
92. Kohut and Reulecke, ' "Sterben wie eine Ratte, die der Bauer ertappt"...', p.460.
93. Gellately, *Backing Hitler*, p.260.
94. Latzel, *Deutsche Soldaten*, p.285.
95. Humburg, *Das Gesicht des Krieges*, p.173; Echternkamp, *Kriegsschauplatz Deutschland 1945*, pp.63–4.
96. MKB 3.2002.0899. Heinz M.-B. to wife Elli, 21 October 1939.
97. Paul Fischer, quoted in Schumann, ed., *Zieh dich warm an*, p.170.
98. Stargardt, *Witnesses of War*, p.323; Doris Foitzik, ' "Sittlich verwahrlost". Disziplinierung und Diskriminierung geschlechtskranker Mädchen in der Nachkriegszeit am Beispiel Hamburg' in *Zeitschrift für Sozialgeschichte des 20. und 21. Jahrhunderts* 1/97, p.68; Höhn, *GIs and Fräuleins*, pp.126–8; Kundrus, 'Forbidden Company', p.219.
99. Grossmann, *Jews, Germans, and Allies*, p.77.
100. Harsch, *The Revenge of the Domestic*, pp.30–1; Wolff-Mönckeberg, *On the Other Side*, p.129; Grossmann, *Jews, Germans, and Allies*, p.49; For a more general discussion about rape in war, see Joanna Bourke, *Rape: A History from 1860 to the Present* (London, 2007) pp.359, 361.
101. Kundrus, 'Forbidden Company', p.204; Atina Grossmann, 'A Question of Silence: The Rape of German Women by Occupation Soldiers' in Moeller, ed., *West Germany under Construction*, pp.35–52.
102. Stibbe, *Women in the Third Reich*, p.168.
103. Dörr, ed., *'Wer die Zeit...' Vol. II*, p.420; Naimark, *The Russians in Germany*, pp.72, 74, 80, 126–7.
104. Harsch, *The Revenge of the Domestic*, p.34; Dagmar Herzog, 'Desperately Seeking Normality. Sex and Marriage in the Wake of the War' in Richard

Bessel and Dirk Schumann, eds, *Life After Death. Approaches to a Cultural and Social History of Europe during the 1940s and 1950s* (Cambridge, 2003) p.164; Frank Biess, ' "Men of Reconstruction." The Reconstruction of Men. Returning POWs in East and West Germany 1945–55' in Hagemann and Schüler-Springorum, eds, *Home/Front*, p.339; Biess, *Homecomings*, p.88.

105. StaAH. 351–10 (II) Sozialbehörde II: 136.50–2; *Neue Berliner Illustrierte* (2 October 1945) quoted in Grossmann, *Jews, Germans, and Allies*, p.78.
106. StaAH. 351–10 (II) Sozialbehörde II: 012.12–5; Bode, *Die vergessene Generation*, pp.48–9; Biess, *Homecomings*, p.73.
107. Biess, *Homecomings*, p.70; Biess, 'Men of Reconstruction', p.339.
108. Meyer and Schulze, '*Von Liebe sprach damals Keiner*', p.142.
109. Hans-Gerd Winter, 'Brutal Heroes, Human Marionettes, and Men with Bitter Knowledge' in Roy Jerome, ed., *Conceptions of Postwar German Masculinity* (New York, 2001) pp.197–8; Poiger, 'Krise der Männlichkeit', p.263; Burgess et al., *The Family*, p.577.
110. *Brigitte*, 23 (1955) pp.4–5; LAB F. Rep. 240, Acc. 2651, Nr. 3: Bericht 269: Hans Frielinghaus, Easter 1948.
111. Statistisches Bundesamt, ed., *Statistische Berichte, Arb. Nr. VII/8/25* (Wiesbaden, 1953); Leh and Plato, *Ein unglaublicher Frühling*, p.17; DZI 3949, Helmut Bohn, *Die Heimkehrer aus russischer Kriegsgefangenschaft* (Frankfurt, 1951) pp.30–1; Niehuss, *Familie, Frau und Gesellschaft*, p.108.
112. LAB F. Rep. 240, Acc. 2651, Nr. 3, Bericht 151, Elfriede von Witzleben.
113. LAB B. Rep. 012, Nr. 7.
114. *Das Blatt der Hausfrau* (February 1949) p.9; See also Sabine Kienitz, 'Body Damage. War Disability and Constructions of Masculinity in Weimar Germany' in Hagemann and Schüler-Springerum, eds, *Home/Front*, p.187.
115. Helene Karwentel quoted in Jenk, *Steine gegen Brot*, pp.46–7; Meyer and Schulze, 'Krieg im Frieden', p.190.
116. Charlotte Wagner quoted in Meyer and Schulze, eds, *Wie wir das alles geschafft haben*, pp.52–3.
117. LAB B. Rep. 012, Nr. 177.
118. LAB B. Rep. 036, 4/18–3/12.
119. DZI 3949, Bohn, *Die Heimkehrer aus russischer Kriegsgefangenschaft*, p.39; Frevert, *Women in German History*, p.262; Moeller, *Protecting Motherhood*, p.29; Niehuss, *Familie, Frau und Gesellschaft*, p.115.
120. DZI 3949, Bohn, *Die Heimkehrer aus russischer Kriegsgefangenschaft*, p.39; Mechthild Evers, 'Recht und Unrecht' in Zeitzeugenbörse, ed., *Jugend unter brauner Diktatur* (Berlin, 2003) p.56; Maria Höhn, 'Stunde Null der Frauen? Renegotiating Women's Place in Postwar West Germany' in Giles, ed., *Stunde Null*, pp.76–85; Katrin Kilian, 'Kriegsstimmungen' in Jörg Echternkamp, ed., *Die Deutsche Kriegsgesellschaft 1939 bis 1945* (Vol.II. Munich, 2005) pp.284–5.
121. Kolinsky, *Women in West Germany*, pp.30–1; Meyer and Schulze, 'Krieg im Frieden', pp.190–1; Borneman, *Belonging in the Two Berlins*, p.225; Andreas Matschenz, ' "Der Onkel ist dein Vater." Die Heimkehr der Kriegsgefangenen nach Berlin bis 1948', p.213. From the empirical studies, there is no evidence to suggest that social roles had moved away from their traditional grids. Wurzbacher's vision of a new family life, based on equal recognition of a vision of a new family life, and based on equal recognition of men and

women and paving the way forwards for an equal distribution of tasks did not correspond with a social reality, which reinstated traditional practices and expectations. The expectation that a woman should marry, raise a family and build her life around the private sphere remained in force.

122. Rita Polm, *'Neben dem Mann die andere Hälfte eines Ganzen zu sein?!' Frauen in der Nachkriegszeit* (Münster, 1990) p.185.
123. Benjamin Ziemann notes that couples during the First World War also held on tightly to pre-existing gender roles. See Ziemann, 'Geschlechterbeziehungen in deutschen Feldpostbriefen des Ersten Weltkrieges' in Christa Hämmerle and Edith Saurer, eds, *Briefkulturen und ihr Geschlecht. Zur Geschichte der privaten Korrespondenz vom 16. Jahrhundert bis heute* (Vienna, 2003) p.282.
124. Niehuss, *Familie, Frau und Gesellschaft*, p.288; Brigitte Löhr and Rita Meyhöfer, 'Wandel in Ehe und Familie' in Lutz Niethammer, ed., *Bürgerliche Gesellschaft in Deutschland. Historische Einblicke, Fragen, Perspektiven* (Frankfurt, 1990) p.601; Van Rahden, 'Demokratie und väterliche Autorität', pp.162, 172, 176, 178–9.
125. Willenbacher, 'Zerrütung und Bewährung der Nachkriegs-Familie', pp.612, 606; Wilke and Wagner, 'Family and Household' in Evans and Lee, eds, *The German Family* p.144; Noelle and Neumann eds, *Jahrbuch der öffentlichen Meinung*, p.207.
126. Kuhn, 'Power and Powerlessness', pp.35–6; Schubert and Kuhn, *Frauen in der Nachkriegszeit, Band I*, p.29.

5 Parents and children

1. LAB F. Rep. 240, Acc. 2651, Nr. 1. Christiane Fromann, p.11: Letter from 11-year-old Ulli, 3 December 1945.
2. Stargardt, *Witnesses of War*, p.319; Ute and Wolfgang Benz, *Sozialisation und Traumatisierung. Kinder in der Zeit des Nationalsozialismus* (Frankfurt, 1992) p.131; Echternkamp, *Kriegsschauplatz Deutschland 1945*, p.68.
3. DTA Reg. Nr. 528, Anne K., 27 January 1945.
4. DTA Reg. Nr. 111,1 and 2, Beate K., July 1945.
5. KA BIO 1676, Diana-Ilse J., 15 May 1945 and 20 May 1945.
6. KA BIO 3811, Elisabeth L., 2 May 1945; See also Charles Bray writing in the *Daily Herald*, 24 August 1946, quoted in Gollancz, *Our Threatened Values*, p.99; Meyer and Schulze, 'Krieg im Frieden', p.186.
7. Bielenberg, *When I Was A German*, p.119.
8. Dörr, ed., *'Wer die Zeit...' Vol. II*, pp.314–15, 321, 329, 337; Stargardt, *Witnesses of War*, p.54; Engert, *Heimatfront*, pp.127–30.
9. Noakes, ed., *Nazism: Volume IV*, pp.360, 421–40; Stargardt, *Witnesses of War*, p.257; Redding, *Growing Up in Hitler's Shadow*, p.11; Werner, *Through the Eyes of Innocents*, pp.48–59.
10. Alison Owings, *Frauen. German Women Recall the Third Reich* (New Brunswick, 1993) p.194; Dörr, ed., *'Wer die Zeit...' Vol. II*, p.325.
11. DTA Reg. Nr. 752, Herbert W., p.2; Anna Freud and Dorothy T. Burlingham, *War and Children* (New York, 1943) pp.37, 50, 84.
12. KA BIO 7255, Hermann D., p.126.
13. Heinz Boberach, *Meldungen aus dem Reich. Auswahl aus den geheimen Lageberichten des Sicherheitsdienstes der SS 1939–1944* (Munich, 1968) p.364.

14. Dörr, ed., *'Wer die Zeit...' Vol. II*, p.325; Carsten Kressel, *Evakuierungen und Erweiterte Kinderlandverschickung im Vergleich. Das Beispiel der Städte Liverpool und Hamburg* (Frankfurt am Main, 1996) pp.106, 134–5.

15. Stargardt, *Witnesses of War*, p.55; Noakes, ed., *Nazism: Volume IV*, p.430; Martin Rüther, ed., *'Zu Hause könnten sie es nicht schöner haben!' Kinderlandverschickung aus Köln und Umgebung 1941–1945* (Cologne, 2000) pp.28–31.

16. O. Jean Brandes, 'The Effect of War on the German Family', *Social Forces*, Vol. 2, No.2, pp.167–8; Redding, *Growing Up in Hitler's Shadow*, p.11; Werner, *Through the Eyes of Innocents*, pp.128–32.

17. LAB F. Rep. 280, LAZ Sammlung. Film Nr. 17. Sammlung Nr. 3657: *Der Berliner*, 16, October 1945; LAB F. Rep. 280, LAZ Sammlung. Film Nr. 15. Sammlung Nr. 3516.

18. MKB 3.2002.7505, Herta S. to husband Ernst, 30 August 1941.

19. DTA Reg. Nr. 111,2. Beate K., June 1945 and 16 August 1945.

20. Mathilde W., quoted in Dörr, ed., *'Wer die Zeit...' Vol. I*, p.129.

21. KA BIO 3811, Elisabeth L., 2 March 1945.

22. Margarete Onken quoted in Townsend and Townsend, *War Wives*, pp.144–6.

23. DTA. Reg Nr. 856/II 5, Hildegard R., 4 May 1945 and 13 July 1945.

24. Wilhem Rössler Archiv, Essen, OII. Sabine K, 20 January 1956, p.2, school essay, quoted in Stargardt, *Witnesses of War*, p.243.

25. Bruns, *Als Vater aus dem Krieg heimkehrte*, p.179.

26. Bruns, *Als Vater aus dem Krieg heimkehrte*, p.104; Echternkamp, *Kriegsschauplatz Deutschland 1945*, p.133.

27. Lotte Werner, 'Granatsplitter sammeln' in Kleindienst, ed., *Gebrannte Kinder II*, pp.86–7; Manfred Glashagen, 'Gefährliche Spiele' in Kleindienst, ed., *Gebrannte Kinder II*, p.90; Stargardt, *Witnesses of War*, pp.37–8, 217–18.

28. KA BIO 3811, Elisabeth L., 18 January 1945; Echternkamp, *Kriegsschauplatz Deutschland 1945*, pp.66–8, 133.

29. DTA Reg. Nr. 528, Anne K., 23 December 1944.

30. LAB F. Rep. 240, Acc. 2651, Nr. 1. Christiane Fromann, p.11. Letter from 11-year-old Ulli, 3 December 1945.

31. LAB F. Rep. 240, Acc. 2651, Nr. 1. Christiane Fromann, p.11. Letter from 9-year-old Jutta, 3 December 1945.

32. Bruns, *Als Vater aus dem Krieg heimkehrte*, p.57; Roberts, *Starke Mütter, Ferne Väter*, p.47; Matschenz, 'Der Onkel da ist Dein Vater', p.179.

33. Ingrid S., born 1936, quoted in Roberts, *Starke Mütter – ferne Väter*, p.76.

34. DTA Reg. Nr. 540,1-3, Theodor G., February 1946.

35. Helga Ansari, quoted in Kleindienst, ed., *Lebertran und Chewing Gum*, p.26.

36. Bruns, *Als Vater aus dem Krieg heimkehrte*, p.25.

37. Gerhard Baumert, 'Beobachtungen zur Wandlung der familialen Stellung des Kindes in Deutschland' in *Neue wissenschaftliche Bibliothek 5 Soziologie. Jugend in der modernen Gesellschaft* (Berlin, 1965) p.310.

38. DTA Reg. Nr. Handbibliothek B Hack 1, Helma H., 20 September 1941.

39. DTA Reg. Nr. 131, Irene B.,1 May 1943; MKB 3.2002.1376.0, Wilhelm B., p.21, 11 December 1939; Burckhard Garbe, quoted in Lipp, ed., *Kindheit und Krieg*, pp. 58–60.

40. Lange and Burkard, eds, *'Abends wenn wir essen fehlt uns immer einer'*, p.13; See also MKB 3.2002.7184, Hans H. to wife Käthe, 16 February 1942; Udke,

ed., *'Schreib so oft Du kannst'* p.38, Gerhard Udke to wife Dorothea, 24 September 1940; and Willy W., 4 August 1946, quoted in Dörr, ed., *'Wer die Zeit...' Vol. I,* p.131.

41. DTA Reg. Nr. 1002, Luise S., 4 February 1945.
42. KA BIO 6176, Dr. Rolf M., 4 February 1951.
43. KA BIO 6176, Dr. Rolf M., 6 June 1954; See also 10 July 1955.
44. MKB 3.2002.1241, Albert S. to his wife, 1 May 1941 and 20 November 1941.
45. MKB 3.2002.7115, Heinz R. to wife Melanie, 2 November 1944.
46. KA BIO 6176, Dr. Rolf M., 4 February 1951.
47. See Appendix 16.
48. MKB 3.2002.0238, Josef B. to wife Helene, 20 June 1942.
49. Udke, ed., *'Schreib so oft Du kannst.'* pp.76–7, Gerhard Udke to wife Dorothea, 6 April 1942.
50. Udke, ed., *'Schreib so oft Du kannst',* p.195.
51. Edith, born 1932, quoted in Lange and Burkard, eds, *'Abends wenn wir essen fehlt uns immer einer',* 24 August 1943; Stargardt, *Witnesses of War,* p.38.
52. 'Feldpostbrief an unsere Kinder?' in *Nationalsozialistische Führungsstab der Wehrmacht* (November, 1944) quoted in Echternkamp, *Kriegsschauplatz Deutschland 1945,* pp.67–8.
53. *Das Blatt der Hausfrau,* 16 (1940/41) p.25.
54. KA BIO 977/2, Klaus E. B., p.62, November 1944.
55. MKB 3.2002.7247, Werner L. to 2-year-old daughter, 7 July 1940.
56. Bruns, *Als Vater aus dem Krieg heimkehrte,* p.170.
57. Liese, born 1925, Thüringen. Extracts from letter exchange with her father, quoted in Lange and Burkard, eds, *'Abends wenn wir essen fehlt uns immer einer',* p.19, 10 September 1939.
58. DTA Reg. Nr. 230/II, Eugen N. to wife Ursula, 24 November 1946.
59. Udke, ed., *'Schreib so oft Du kannst'* p.73, Gerhard Udke to wife Dorothea, 3 April 1942. More generally, see Lamprecht, *Feldpost und Kriegserlebnis,* p.224.
60. Richard, born 1934. Letters exchanged with his father, quoted in Lange and Burkard, eds, *'Abends wenn wir essen fehlt uns immer einer',* p.240, 1 November 1943.
61. MKB 3.2002.0224, Peter B. to father Klaus, 9 November 1944.
62. MKB 3.2002.0224, Klaus B. to son Peter, 27 November 1944.
63. Rosemarie, born 1927. Extracts from letters exchanged with her father, quoted in Lange and Burkard, eds, *'Abends wenn wir essen fehlt uns immer einer',* p.35, 11 January 1940.
64. Liese, born 1925, Thüringen. Extracts from letters exchanged with her father, quoted in Lange and Burkard, eds, *'Abends wenn wir essen fehlt uns immer einer',* p.19, 10 September 1939.
65. Stargardt, *Witnesses of War,* p.36.
66. DTA Reg. Nr. 818, Viktor Richard S., 19 July 1949.
67. Richard, born 1934. Letters exchanged with his father, quoted in Lange and Burkard, eds, *'Abends wenn wir essen fehlt uns immer einer',* pp.230–1, 24 May 1943 and 4 July 1943.
68. Ingeborg, born 1932. Letter exchange with her father in Russia, quoted in Lange and Burkard, eds, *'Abends wenn wir essen fehlt uns immer einer',* p.214, 30 December 1944.

69. MKB 3.2002.1241, Albert S. to son, 18 November 1943.
70. Egbert, born 1929. Extracts from letter exchange with his father, quoted in Lange and Burkard, eds, *'Abends wenn wir essen fehlt uns immer einer'*, p.63, 26 January 1944.
71. MKB 3.2002.7505, Herta S. to husband, 26 November 1942.
72. KA BIO 1676, Diana-Ilse J., 13 May 1945.
73. MKB 3.2002.1246, Erika K. to husband Walter, 10 June 1946.
74. DTA Reg. Nr. 1002, Luise S., 17 January 1946.
75. Edith, born 1933, quoted in Lange and Burkard, eds, *'Abends wenn wir essen fehlt uns immer einer'*, p.189, 6 April 1943.
76. DTA Reg. Nr. 528, Anne K., 27 December 1944 and 25 January 1945.
77. KA BIO 1676, Diana-Ilse J., 20 May 1945.
78. KA BIO 3915, *Die Familie Bruche/Böhm*, 1945–46.
79. Hill, *Families under Stress*, p.50; Bielenberg, *When I was a German*, p.254; Hiltrud Häntzschel quoted in Lipp, ed., *Kindheit und Krieg*, p.75; Matschenz, ' "Der Onkel ist dein Vater" ', p.118.
80. Irene Anhalt, 'Farewell to My Father', in Barbara Heimannsberg and Christoph J. Schmidt, eds, *The Collective Silence. German Identity and the Legacy of Shame* (San Francisco, 1993) pp.38–40.
81. Paul Z., quoted in Dörte von Westernhagen, *Die Kinder der Täter. Das Dritte Reich und die Generation danach* (Munich, 1987) pp.97–8.
82. Anhalt, 'Farewell to My Father', p.39; Renate Neumann quoted in Lipp, ed., *Kindheit und Krieg*, pp.96–7.
83. Jenk, *Steine gegen Brot*, p.44; Inge S. in Roberts, *Starke Mütter – ferne Väter*, p.90; Fritz Sallman, born 1915, in Gabriele Rosenthal, ed., *'Als der Krieg kam, hatte ich mit Hitler nichts mehr zu tun.' Zur Gegenwärtigkeit des Dritten Reichs in Biographien* (Opladen, 1990) p.137.
84. Ute Benz, ' "Maikäfer, flieg! Dein Vater ist im Krieg". Aspekte der Heimkehr aus familiarier Sicht' in Kaminsky, ed., *Heimkehr 1948*, pp.180–1; Bruns, *Als Vater aus dem Krieg heimkehrte*, pp.27, 51, 100; Helm Stierlin, 'The Dialogue between the Generations about the Nazi Era' in Heimannsberg and Schmidt, eds, *The Collective Silence*, p.147; Roberts, *Starke Mütter – ferne Väter*, p.90.
85. LAB F. Rep. 240, Acc. 2651, Nr. 6, Bericht, 754, Siegfried Kettner.
86. LAB F. Rep. 240, Acc. 2651, Nr. 4, Bericht 414, Maria Thiel.
87. Bruns, *Als Vater aus dem Krieg heimkehrte*, p.28.
88. Sibylle Meyer and Eva Schulze, ' "Als wir wieder zusammen waren, ging der Krieg im Kleinen weiter": Frauen, Männer und Familien in Berlin der vierziger Jahre' in Lutz Niethammer and Alexander von Plato, eds, *'Wir kriegen jetzt andere Zeiten': Auf der Suche nach der Erfahrung des Volkes in nachfaschistischen Ländern* (Bonn, 1985) pp.316–19.
89. Sieder, *Sozialgeschichte der Familie*, p.238.
90. Bruns, *Als Vater aus dem Krieg heimkehrte*, p.53.
91. Heineman, *What Difference Does a Husband Make?* pp.120–1; See also Thurnwald, *Gegenwartsprobleme Berliner Familien*, p.150.
92. *Das Blatt der Hausfrau*, (September 1949).
93. *Brigitte*, 23 (1955) pp.4–5.
94. Monika G., quoted in Roberts, *Starke Mütter – ferne Väter*, p.81; See also Bruns, *Als Vater aus dem Krieg heimkehrte*, p.67.

95. Bruns, *Als Vater aus dem Krieg heimkehrte*, p.82; See also DTA Reg. Nr. 952,1, Helmut B.; Benz, '"Maikäfer, flieg! Dein Vater ist im Krieg"', p.180.
96. Falko Berg in Kleindienst, ed., *Nachkriegs-Kinder*, p.208.
97. Roberts, *Starke Mütter, Ferne Väter*, p.112.
98. Bruns, *Als Vater aus dem Krieg heimkehrte*, p.60; Baumert, 'Beobachtungen zur Wandlung der familialen Stellung des Kindes in Deutschland', p.310; Benz, '"Maikäfer, flieg! Dein Vater ist im Krieg"', p.179.
99. Heineman, *What Difference Does a Husband Make?* p.120.
100. Meyer and Schulze, '*Von Liebe sprach damals Keiner'*, pp.133, 147; See also Kaminsky, ed., *Heimkehr 1948*, p.17; Bruns, *Als Vater aus dem Krieg heimkehrte*, p.53.
101. Lehmann, *Gefangenschaft und Heimkehr*, p.145.
102. *Das Blatt der Hausfrau* (February 1949); Thurnwald, *Gegenwartsprobleme Berliner Familien*, p.97; Bruns, *Als Vater aus dem Krieg heimkehrte*, p.29.
103. Christian von Krockow, *Hour of the Woman* (London, 1991) p.205; Stargardt, *Witnesses of War*, p.328; Biess, *Homecomings*, pp.122, 124–5; Lucia K in Franck, ed., *Heil Hitler, Herr Lehrer*, p.226.
104. Ruhl, *Verordnete Unterordnung*, pp.133–4; Baumert, 'Beobachtungen zur Wandlung der familialen Stellung des Kindes in Deutschland' in *Neue wissenschaftliche Bibliothek 5 Soziologie. Jugend in der modernen Gesellschaft* (Berlin,1965) pp.310, 315–17; Pine, 'Women and the Family', p.373.
105. Roberts, *Starke Mütter, Ferne Väter*, p.112.
106. DTA Reg. Nr. 952,1, Helmut B.; See also LAB (STA), Rep. 134/13, Aufsatz Nr. XVII,13, Christa G., Jahrgang 1931; Niehuss, *Familie, Frau und Gesellschaft*, p.111.
107. Bertram Schaffner, *Fatherland: A Study of Authoritarianism in the German Family* (New York, 1948) p.15; Rene König, 'Family and Authority: The German Father in 1955' *The Sociological Review*, Vol.5 No. 1 (1957–58) p.113.
108. David Rodnick, *Postwar Germans* (Yale, 1948) p.9
109. Thurnwald, *Gegenwartsprobleme Berliner Familien*, p.97; Gerhard Baumert, *Jugend der Nachkriegszeit* (Darmstadt, 1952) p.79; Gerhard Baumert, *Deutsche Familien nach dem Krieg* (Darmstadt, 1954) p.127.
110. Kolinsky, *Women in West Germany*, p.31.
111. Van Rahden, 'Demokratie und väterliche Autorität', pp.153, 162, 172, 176.
112. *Das Blatt der Hausfrau*, 16 (1940/41) p.245.
113. Renate Dziemba in Kleindienst, ed., *Lebertran und Chewing Gum*, p.125.
114. Bruns, *Als Vater aus dem Krieg heimkehrte*, p.14.
115. KA BIO 3675, Wilhelm B., 10 September 1947.
116. *Brigitte*, 23 (1955) pp.4–5.
117. Bruns, *Als Vater aus dem Krieg heimkehrte*, p.72
118. Eleonore S. quoted in Roberts, *Starke Mütter, Ferne Väter*, p.113.
119. Dr. Christian Schwarz-Schilling quoted in Werner Filmer and Heribert Schwan, eds, *Besiegt, befreit … Zeitzeugen erinnern sich an das Kriegsende 1945* (Munich, 1995) p.324.
120. Liselotte Miller quoted in Kleindienst, ed., *Lebertran und Chewing Gum*, p.219.
121. Werner, *Through the Eyes of Innocents*, pp.215, 220–3; Freud and Burlingham, *War and Children*, p.18; Stargardt, *Witnesses of War*, pp.363, 371; Stargardt,

'Jeux de guerre sous le régime nazi', pp.69–70; Heimannsberg and Schmidt, eds, *The Collective Silence.*

Conclusion

1. Möding, 'Die Stunde der Frauen?' p.620; Böll, *Briefe aus dem Krieg, 1939–45,* Vol.I, p.120; MKB 3.2002.7181, Jochen H. to Inge, 28 September 1942; MKB 3.2002.1286, Georg N. to wife, 1 January 1940.
2. Irmgard Wilharm, 'Wiederaufbaudynamik und Wertewandel' in Niethammer, ed., *Bürgerliche Gesellschaft in Deutschland,* p.574.
3. Humburg, *Das Gesicht des Krieges,* p.176.
4. Meyer and Schulze, eds, *Wie wir das alles geschafft haben,* pp.179–80.
5. Heineman, *What Difference Does a Husband Make?* p.119.
6. DZI 13532, Bernard Karte, 'Über die Aufgaben der Jugend und Eheberatung' in Berufsverband Katholischer Sozialarbeiter Nordrhein-Westfalen, ed., *Familiennot und ihre Überwindung* (Bad Godesberg, 1955) p.3; Joosten, *Die Frau, das 'segenspendende Herz der Familie',* p.42.
7. *Constanze,* 3 (April 1948); *Der-Die-Das,* 1 (1952) p.2; DZI 20217, Dr. Walter Becker, 'Probleme der "faktischen" Ehe' in Landesjugendamt und den Verbänden der freien Wohlfahrtspflege in Baden-Württemberg, eds, *Blätter der Wohlfahrtspflege* (Baden Württemberg, 1952); Costello, *Love Sex and War,* p.343.
8. Echternkamp, *Kriegsschauplatz Deutschland 1945,* p.45; Kilian, 'Funktionsweise der deutschen Feldpost 1939 bis 1945' in http://www.feldpost-archiv.de/09-arbeit-der-feldpost.html p.2. Richard Lakowski and Hans-Joachim Büll, *Ein Lebenszeichen! 1945. Feldpost zwischen Oder und Elbe* (Berlin, unpublished) pp.21–2.
9. See Appendix 2 and 3.
10. DTA Reg. Nr. 230/II, Eugen N. to Ursula; DTA Reg. Nr. Handbibliothek B Hack 1, Helma H., June 1941; Humburg, *Das Gesicht des Krieges,* p.181.
11. Moeller, *Protecting Motherhood.*
12. Frau G., quoted in Echternkamp, *Kriegsschauplatz Deutschland 1945,* p.251; MKB 3.2002.0921, Erika H. to husband, 19 May 1946; MKB 3.2002.0826, Gertrud S. to husband Hubert, 31 March 1944.
13. Niethammer, 'Privat-Wirtschaft', pp.46–8; Heineman, *What Difference Does a Husband Make?* p.115.
14. Böll, *Briefe aus dem Krieg, 1939–1945,* Vol.I, p.395, 19 July 1942; KA BIO 6176, Dr. Rolf M., *Letters from Russian POW camp 7150 to family;* MKB 3.2002.7186, DTA Reg. Nr. Handbibliothek B Hack 1, Helma H., 30 July 1941.
15. Steinhoff et al., eds, *Voices from the Third Reich,* p.338; Wierling, 'Mission to Happiness', p.110; Hill, *Families under Stress,* p.87; Bruns, *Als Vater aus dem Krieg heimkehrte,* p.173.
16. Moeller, *Protecting Motherhood,* pp.72–3; 102–3; Heineman, *What Difference Does a Husband Make?* pp.147–8; Joosten, *Die Frau, das 'segenspendende Herz der Familie',* pp.29, 37.
17. Kolinsky, *Women in West Germany,* pp.31, 79.
18. Rupp, *Mobilizing Women for War,* p.176.

19. Peukert, *Inside Nazi Germany*, pp.190–1, 196, 238; Schubert and Kuhn, *Frauen in der Nachkriegszeit*, Band I, p.30; Frevert, *Women in German History*, p.265; Schelsky, *Wandlungen*, p.91; Irmgard Wilharm, 'Wiederaufbaudynamik und Wertewandel', p.574.
20. Peukert, *Inside Nazi Germany*, p.191.
21. DZI 10662, Nikolaus Gross, *Rückkehr zur Familie* (Heidelberg, 1947) pp.7–16; Filmer and Schwan, eds, *Besiegt, befreit*, p.128; Heinz Heppermann quoted in Humburg, *Das Gesicht des Krieges*, p.182; Böll, *Briefe aus dem Krieg 1939–1945*, Vol.II, p.950; Hill, *Families under Stress*, p.252.
22. KA BIO 1676, Diana-Ilse J., 28 May 1945.
23. Schelsky, *Wandlungen*, p.73. See also pp.63, 87.

Appendices

1. Typical ways in which this frustration was expressed are listed in the following examples: MKB 3.2002.1214, Hans-Joachim S., precise date unknown 1944. 'I've had no mail from home since December'; MKB 3.2002.7505, Ernst S. to Herta his wife, 10 February 1940, 'I've waited in vain for post from you'; MKB 3.2002.7505, Ernst S. to Herta his wife, 1 December 1941, 'I'm never sure whether I've received all your letters, or whether some are missing'; MKB 3.2002.0985, Heinz R. to wife, precise date unknown 1941, 'I haven't had any post from you for a long time.'; MKB 3.2002.0985, Heinz R. to wife, 17 November 1941, 'Hardly any post has come, except for delayed mail, which is now out of date.'
2. Typical ways in which the bombing was mentioned in letters: MKB 3.2002.0844, Margarethe to Franz K., 22 March 1944. 'I'm just writing to tell you that we have thus far remained unscathed in the daily bomb raids. But the attacks are getting ever more intensive.' MKB 3.2002.0904, Martin M. to wife Gerda, 13 August 1941. 'Have you written me a letter to explain what happened during the last English air-raid on Berlin? I'm wracked with worry about you.' MKB 3.2002.0224, Klaus Becker to his wife Suse, 20 August 1942. 'We're consumed with worry about the gutless night air-raids of the Brits on German towns.'
3. Typical ways in which food shortages were mentioned in the SRS: MKB 3.2002.7505, Ernst S. to Herta his wife, 12.3.42. 'Sorry to hear that food supplies are so short and that you can't afford to buy any extra.' MKB 3.2002.0844, Margarethe to Franz K., 7.4.44. 'Everyone's complaining that there are hardly any vegetables available.' MKB 3.2002.0828, Werner B. 13.2.45., 'From about three weeks ago we've just been living off our ration cards...I'm constantly hungry.' MKB 3.2002.0924, Paul W. to wife, 4.3.45. 'The bread situation's an absolute catastrophe. With this I'm sending 1000 grams to you. There's less and less available to eat here, so eat the bread sparingly.'
4. Noakes, *Nazism. Volume IV*, p.511; Engert, *Heimatfront*, pp.119–120. In Britain, by contrast, though the nation's diet became increasingly stodgy, reflecting the abundance of potatoes and the limited availability of fruits like oranges and bananas, the supply of food remained sufficient throughout the war. For more detail, see Angus Calder, *Britain at War* (London, 2002) pp.36–37.

5. Typical examples of what counted as a mention: MKB 3.2002.7184, Hans H. to wife Käthe, 16 February 1942. 'I'm really missing the children and would really love it if you could send me a picture of them soon.' MKB 3.2002.7247, Werner L. to 2-year-old daughter, 7 July 940. 'My dear little daughter...I've got a photograph of you in front of me. I can see your child-like seriousness – something that I haven't seen before.'

Bibliography

Unpublished sources

I. DZI (Deutsches Zentralinstitut für Soziale Fragen, Berlin)

DZI 10662, Nikolaus Gross, *Rückkehr zur Familie* (Heidelberg, 1947).

DZI 22509, *Nachrichten der Arbeitsgemeinschaft für Gesundheitswesen*, 3 (1953).

DZI B-0018, The Hilfswerk of the Evangelical Churches in Germany, ed., *Living Conditions in Germany.1947* (Stuttgart, June 1947).

DZI 14820, Alice and Robert Scherer and Julius Dorreich, eds, *Ehe und Familie. Grundsätze, Bestand und Fördernde Massnahmen* (Freiburg, 1956).

DZI 23105, *Mädchenbildung und Frauenschaffen*, 1 (1956).

DZI 10065, Hans von Hattingberg, *Ehekrisen Entwicklungskrisen. Ein Problem unserer Zeit* (Munich, 1949).

DZI B-6211, Edward Kaufman, *Kranke Ehen. Alltagsprobleme im Eheleben, die häufig zur Scheidung führen* (Basel, 1952).

DZI 3949, Helmut Bohn, *Die Heimkehrer aus russischer Kriegsgefangenschaft* (Frankfurt, 1951).

DZI 13532, Bernard Karte, 'Über die Aufgaben der Jugend und Eheberatung' in Berufsverband Katholischer Sozialarbeiter Nordrhein-Westfalen, ed., *Familiennot und ihre Überwindung* (Bad Godesberg, 1955).

DZI 23545, *Hand am Pflung*, 3 (1954).

DZI 20227, *Berliner Gesundheitsblatt*, 23 (1951).

DZI 00089, *Bundesversorgungsblatt*, 7 (1952).

DZI 22217, *Mitteilungen der Evangelische Frauenarbeit in Deutschland*, 47 (June 1952).

DZI 20807, *Die Innere Mission*, 3/4 (1948).

DZI 6828, *Familiengerechte Wohlfahrtspflege und Sozialpolitik. Bericht über die soziale Schulungstagung und Generalversammlung von 5. bis 8. September in München* (Berfusverband Katholischen Fürsorgerinnen, 1953).

DZI 5041, Institut zur Förderung öffentlichen Angelegeneheiten, ed., *Sozialtaschenbuch 1952. Deutsche Sozialstatistik für die Praxis* (Frankfurt, 1952).

DZI 5366, *Statistik des Gesundheitswesens in Niedersachsen 1947 bis 1949*.

DZI 11573, *Archiv für Bevölkerungswissenschaft und Bevölkerungspolitik* (Leipzig, 1939).

DZI 12639, Maria Pfister-Ammende, ed., *Geistige Hygiene. Forschung und Praxis* (Basel, 1955).

DZI. 10165, *Arbeitsbericht der Arbeitsgemeinschaft für Jugend und Eheberatung in Hannover 1953/1954*.

DZI 20809, *Die Innere Mission*, 3 (1950).

DZI 20701, *Nachrichtendienst des Deutschen Vereins für öffentliche und private Fürsorge*, 1 (1951).

DZI 22217, 'Scheidung bei Zerrüttung der Ehe', in *Mitteilungen der Evangelischen Frauenarbeit in Deutschland*, 51 (1952).

DZI 22729, *Information für die Frau*, 3 (1954).

DZI 20112, *Berliner Statistik* , 8 (1950).

DZI 503, *Die Christliche Frau*, 5 (1953).

DZI 226, *Gewerkschaftliche Monatshefte*, 1 (1954).

DZI 20217, Landesjugendamt und den Verbänden der freien Wohlfahrtspflege in Baden-Württemberg, eds, *Blätter der Wohlfahrtspflege* (Baden Württemberg, 1952).

DZI 22217, *Mitteilungen der Evangelischen Frauenarbeit in Deutschland*, 47 (1952).

DZI 21322, *Neues Beginnen*, 10 (1955).

DZI 8227, Arbeitsgemeinschaft der Katholischen Sozialen Woche, ed., *Die Familie, Ihre Krise und Deren Überwindung* (Munich, 1951).

DZI 18815, Franz Prinz, 'Die Familie als Gemeinschaft' in *Christilich-soziale Werkbriefe*, 18 (1955).

DZI 5992, 'Bericht über die Arbeitstagung für evangelische Eheberatung am 26./27. September 1951 in Bethel', veranstaltet vom Central-Ausschuss für die Innere Mission in Verbindung mit der Evang. Arbeitsgemeinschaft für sittliche Volkserziehung.

DZI 385, *Anstalts Umschau* (1955).

II.   LAB (Landesarchiv, Berlin)

LAB Rep. 134/13. School essays from Berlin, 1946.

LAB (STA) Rep. 134/13, Nr. 180/2, IV, 79.

LAB (STA) Rep. 134/13, Nr. 178, Bl.141–142. Ursula T.

LAB (STA) Rep. 134/13, Nr. 181/1, Bl.218, XII, 36. Irmgard T.

LAB (STA) Rep. 134/13, Nr. 181/1, Bl.12–13, XVII, 11. Sigrid I.

LAB (STA) Rep. 134/13, Nr. 181/1, Bl.17–19.5. Christa J.

LAB (STA) Rep. 134/13, Nr. 181/1, Bl.20–21, XVII, 21. Christel B.

LAB (STA) Rep. 134/13, Nr. 182/2, Bl.134–135. Ruth H.

LAB (STA) Rep. 134/13, Nr. 182/1, XXIV, 20. Rita B.

LAB (STA) Rep. 134/13, Nr. 183, Bl.165. Walter T.

LAB (STA) Rep. 134/13, Nr. 182/1, Bl.273–274. Traute S.

LAB (STA) Rep. 134/13, Nr. 182/2, Bl.97. F. (name abbr.).

LAB (STA) Rep. 134/13. Aufsatz Nr. XVII, 13. Christa G.

LAB F. Rep. 240. Die zeitgeschichtliche Sammlung.

LAB F. Rep. 240. Acc. 2651. Nr. 1. Erna Sänger.

LAB F. Rep. 240. Acc. 2651. Nr. 1. Brief. Christiane Fromann.

LAB F. Rep. 240. Acc. 2651. Nr. 2/85. H. Fleischmann.

LAB F. Rep. 240. Acc. 2651. Nr. 2/44. Willi Reckmann.

LAB F. Rep. 240. Acc. 2651. Nr. 2/67. Eva Stadermann.

LAB F. Rep. 240. Acc.2651. Nr. 2. Frida Kain.

LAB F. Rep. 240. Acc. 2651. Nr.2/22. Gertrud Herrmann.

LAB F. Rep. 240. Acc. 2651. Nr. 2/81. Hildegard Schwarz.

LAB F. Rep. 240. Acc. 2651. Nr. 2/126. Elsa Thomas.

LAB F. Rep. 240. Acc. 2651. Nr. 2/62. Liesbeth Krieg.

LAB F. Rep. 240. Acc. 2651. Nr. 2/98. H. Gnädig.

LAB F. Rep. 240. Acc. 2651. Nr. 2/103. Margarete Müller.

LAB F. Rep. 240. Acc. 2651. Nr. 2/116. Elsa Hellwig.
LAB F. Rep. 240. Acc. 2651. Nr. 2/81. Hildegard Schwarz.
LAB F. Rep. 240. Acc. 2651. Nr. 2/131. Gertrud Strubel.
LAB F. Rep. 240. Acc. 2651. Nr. 3/160. Werner H. Wäldchen.
LAB F. Rep. 240. Acc. 2651. Nr. 3/156. Else Golgath.
LAB F. Rep. 240. Acc. 2651. Nr. 3/237. Rudolf Gross.
LAB F. Rep. 240. Acc. 2651. Nr. 3/201. Elisabeth Taubert.
LAB F. Rep. 240. Acc. 2651. Nr. 3/247. Getrud Trox.
LAB. F. Rep. 240. Acc. 2651. Nr. 3/231. Liselotte Hohenschuh.
LAB F. Rep. 240. Acc. 2651. Nr. 3/152. Herbert Wirsig.
LAB F. Rep. 240. Acc. 2651. Nr. 3/151. Elfriede von Witzleben.
LAB F. Rep. 240. Acc. 2651. Nr. 3/293. Heinz Gorecki.
LAB F. Rep. 240. Acc. 2651. Nr. 3/269. Hans Frielinghaus.
LAB F. Rep. 240. Acc. 2651. Nr. 3/262. Alfred Schumann.
LAB F. Rep. 240. Acc. 2651. Nr. 3/272. Berta Hilinga.
LAB F. Rep. 240. Acc. 2651. Nr. 3/225. Karl Stötzer.
LAB F. Rep. 240. Acc. 2651. Nr. 3/170. Gerhardt Mondt.
LAB F. Rep. 240. Acc. 2651. Nr. 3/226. Frieda Altmann.
LAB F. Rep. 240. Acc. 2651. Nr. 3/221. Walter Jeske.
LAB F. Rep. 240. Acc. 2651. Nr. 3/205. Franziska Jessa.
LAB F. Rep. 240. Acc.2651. Nr. 3/156. Else Golgath.
LAB F. Rep. 240. Acc. 2651. Nr. 3/224. Johanna Karl.
LAB F. Rep. 240. Acc. 2651. Nr. 3/271. Fritz Feige.
LAB. F. Rep. 240. Acc. 2651. Nr. 4/329. Gertrud Philipps.
LAB F. Rep. 240. Acc. 2651. Nr. 4/318. Katharina Müller.
LAB F. Rep. 240. Acc. 2651. Nr. 4/499. Elisabeth Schulz.
LAB F. Rep. 240. Acc. 2651. Nr. 4/396. Gerda Hachmeister.
LAB F. Rep. 240. Acc. 2651. Nr. 4/351. Doris Berndt.
LAB F. Rep. 240. Acc. 2651. Nr. 4/359. Erhard Deter.
LAB F. Rep. 240. Acc. 2651. Nr. 4/331. Elisabeth Blau.
LAB F. Rep. 240. Acc. 2651. Nr. 4/414. Maria Thiel.
LAB F. Rep. 240. Acc. 2651. Nr. 4/348. Gustav Schneider.
LAB F. Rep. 240. Acc. 2651. Nr. 5/581 L. Kafka.
LAB F. Rep. 240. Acc. 2651. Nr. 5/540. Eva Reichmann.
LAB F. Rep. 240. Acc. 2651. Nr. 5/531. Ursula Schmidt.
LAB F. Rep. 240. Acc. 2651. Nr. 5/488. Franz Wimmer.
LAB F. Rep. 240. Acc. 2651. Nr. 5/487. Ilse Meyer.
LAB F. Rep. 240. Acc. 2651. Nr. 5/506. Charlotte Zech.
LAB F. Rep. 240. Acc. 2651. Nr. 5/592. Martin Mürben.
LAB F. Rep. 240. Acc. 2651. Nr. 5/598. Elisabeth Rendel.
LAB F. Rep. 240. Acc. 2651. Nr. 5/534. Kurt Zahn.
LAB F. Rep. 240. Acc. 2651. Nr. 5/561. Helene Sciuszko.
LAB F. Rep. 240. Acc. 2651. Nr. 5/554. Charlotte Meissner.
LAB F. Rep. 240. Acc. 2651. Nr. 5/555. Hildegard Lietich.
LAB F. Rep. 240. Acc. 2651. Nr. 5/595. Frieda Schneider.
LAB F. Rep. 240. Acc. 2651. Nr. 5/539. Rolf Schwanke.
LAB F. Rep. 240. Acc. 2651. Nr. 6/738. Hildegard Stephan.
LAB F. Rep. 240. Acc. 2651. Nr. 6/697. Gertrud Oppermann.
LAB F. Rep. 240. Acc. 2651. Nr. 6/604. Charlotte Damrosch.

LAB F. Rep. 240. Acc. 2651. Nr. 6/655. Erna Köhnte.
LAB F. Rep. 240. Acc. 2651. Nr. 6/713. Margarete Franke.
LAB F. Rep. 240. Acc. 2651. Nr. 6/694. Martha Janiak.
LAB F. Rep. 240. Acc. 2651. Nr. 6/675. Margarethe Siedschlag.
LAB F. Rep. 240. Acc. 2651. Nr. 6/745. Charlotte Reimann.
LAB F. Rep. 240. Acc. 2651. Nr. 6/665. Maria Lersow.
LAB F. Rep. 240. Acc. 2651. Nr. 6/697. Gertrud Oppermann.
LAB F. Rep. 240. Acc. 2651. Nr. 6/754. Siegfried Kettner.
LAB F. Rep. 240. Acc. 2651. Nr. 6/669. Walther Wolf.
LAB F. Rep. 240. Acc. 2651. Nr. 6/653. Rudolf Rückert.
LAB F. Rep. 240. Acc. 2651. Nr. 6/654. Gertrud Tenniger.
LAB F. Rep. 240. Acc. 217. Nr. 3.
LAB F. Rep. 240. Acc. 217. Nr. 10.
LAB F. Rep. 240. Acc. 834. Nr. 50.
LAB F. Rep. 240. Acc.834. Nr. 65.
LAB F. Rep. 240. Acc. 863. Nr. 7.
LAB F. Rep. 240. Acc. 863. Nr. 10.
LAB F. Rep. 240. Acc. 863. Nr. 20.
LAB F. Rep. 240. Acc. 1690. Nr. 5.
LAB F. Rep. 240. Acc. 1707. Nr. 1.
LAB F. Rep. 240. Acc. 1707. Nr. 6.
LAB F. Rep. 240. Acc. 2054. Nr. 49.
LAB F. Rep. 240. Acc. 2421.

LAB B. Rep. 010-02. Senatsverwaltung für Wirtschaft und Ernährung
LAB B. Rep. 010-02. Acc. 1888. Files: 309; 331; 554; 557; 673; 739.

LAB B. Rep. 012. Senatsverwaltung für Gesundheit
LAB B. Rep. 012. Files: 7; 8; 10; 11; 23; 41; 52; 148; 165; 177; 197.

LAB B Rep. 036-01. Office of Military Government, Berlin Sector
LAB. Ref. B. Rep. 036. PR/JWB 585.
LAB Ref. B. Rep. 036. 4/2-1/16. LG-PR/JWB 707.
LAB Ref. B. Rep. 036. PR JWB 622.
LAB Ref. B. Rep. 036. PR JWB 650.
LAB Ref. B. Rep. 036. Bd.1. 4/2-1/15. PR/JWB 621.
LAB Ref. B. Rep. 036. 4/2-1/16. LG/PR-JWB 716.
LAB Ref. B. Rep. 036. 4/2-1/16. PR/JWB 895.
LAB Ref. B. Rep. 036. PR/JWB 665.
LAB Ref. B. Rep. 036. 4/2-1/16/ PR/LMH 817.
LAB Ref. B. Rep. 036. PR/LHD 474.
LAB Ref. B. Rep. 036. PR/LHD 500.
LAB Ref. B. Rep. 036. 4/2-1/16. PR/EHM 741.
LAB Ref. B. Rep. 036. 4/2-1/16/ PR/LJO 874.
LAB Ref. B. Rep. 036. PR/LMH 555.
LAB Ref. B. Rep. 036. 4/2-1/16. PR/LJG 769.
LAB Ref. B. Rep. 036. 4/2-1/16. PR/LJG 763.
LAB Ref. B. Rep. 036. 4/2-1/16. PR/EHM 909.

LAB Ref. B. Rep. 036. 4/2-1/16. PR/LJG 923.
LAB Ref. B. Rep. 036. 4/2-1/16. PR/LJG 908.
LAB Ref. B. Rep. 036. 4/18-3/1.
LAB Ref. B. Rep. 036. 4/18-3/6.
LAB Ref. B. Rep. 036. 4/18-3/12
LAB Ref. B. Rep. 036. 4/18-2/1.
LAB Ref. B. Rep. 036. 4/18-3/11.
LAB Ref. B. Rep. 036. 4/20-1/16.
LAB Ref. B. Rep. 036. 4/21-1/18.
LAB Ref. B. Rep. 036. 4/21-2/10.
LAB Ref. B. Rep. 036. 4/23-3/24.
LAB Ref. B. Rep. 036. 4/24-1/4.
LAB Ref. B. Rep. 036. 4/24-2/7.
LAB Ref. B. Rep. 036. 4/25-3/13.
LAB Ref. B. Rep. 036. 4/26-1/27.

LAB F. Rep. 280 LAZ Filmsammlung

LAB F. Rep. 280. LAZ Film Nr.1. Sammlung Nr 1170.
LAB F. Rep. 280. LAZ Film Nr.2. Sammlung Nr. 1784.
LAB F. Rep. 280. LAZ Film Nr.9. Sammlung Nr.3122.
LAB F. Rep. 280. LAZ Film Nr.15. Sammlung Nr.3502.
LAB F. Rep. 280. LAZ Film Nr.15. Sammlung Nr. 3516.
LAB F. Rep. 280. LAZ Film Nr.17. Sammlung Nr. 3657.
LAB F. Rep. 280. LAZ Film Nr.33. Sammlung Nr. 7405.
LAB F. Rep. 280. LAZ Film Nr.39. Sammlung Nr. 8474.
LAB F. Rep. 280. LAZ Film Nr.39. Sammlung Nr. 8482.
LAB F. Rep. 280. LAZ Film Nr.41. Sammlung Nr. 8512.
LAB F. Rep. 280. LAZ Film Nr.41. Sammlung Nr. 8525.
LAB F. Rep. 280. LAZ Film Nr.43. Sammlung Nr. 8908.
LAB F. Rep. 280. LAZ Film Nr.43. Sammlung Nr. 90941.
LAB F. Rep. 280. LAZ Film Nr.46. Sammlung Nr. 9753.
LAB F. Rep. 280. LAZ Film Nr.57. Sammlung Nr. 11863.
LAB F. Rep. 280. LAZ Film Nr.57. Sammlung Nr. 11868.
LAB F. Rep. 280. LAZ Film Nr.64 Sammlung Nr. 12092.
LAB F. Rep. 280. LAZ Film Nr.439. Sammlung Nr. 8370.

III.   DTA (Deutsches Tagebucharchiv, Emmendingen)

DTA Reg. Nr. 131, Irene B.
DTA Reg. Nr. 454/III, Elisabeth L.
DTA Reg Nr. 1002, Luise S.
DTA Reg. Nr. 111,2, Beate K.
DTA Reg. Nr. 528, Anne K.
DTA Reg. Nr. 340,1, Maxi-Lore E.
DTA Reg. Nr. 302/II, Waltraud S.
DTA Reg. Nr. 1103/II, Anneliese P.
DTA Reg. Nr. 230/II, Ursula N.
DTA Reg. Nr. 228/I,1, Erich D.
DTA Reg. Nr. Handbibliothek B Hack 1, Helma H.

DTA Reg. Nr. 856/II 5, Hildegard R.
DTA Reg. Nr. 49, Marja B.
DTA Reg. Nr. 1108, Ernst K.
DTA Reg. Nr. 680, Martin S.
DTA Reg. Nr. 289, Cläre S.
DTA Reg. Nr. 42,1, Walter M.
DTA Reg. Nr. 540,1–3, Theodor G.
DTA Reg. Nr. 952,1, Helmut B.
DTA Reg. Nr. 752, Herbert W.
DTA Reg. Nr. 818, Viktor Richard S.
DTA Reg. Nr. 786, Richard and Margarete P.

IV. KA (Kempowskiarchiv, Akademie der Kunst, Berlin)

KA BIO 1676, Diana-Ilse J.
KA BIO 3168, Roswitha F.
KA BIO 37, Hildegard W.
KA BIO 3742, Wilhelm K.
KA BIO 6176, Dr. Rolf M.
KA BIO 3675, Wilhelm B.
KA BIO 2657, Regina B.
KA BIO 3811, Elisabeth L.
KA BIO 7255, Hermann D.
KA BIO 977/2, Klaus E. B.
KA BIO 6348, Albert B.
KA BIO 3915, Die Familie Bruche/Böhm.

V. MKB or AK (*Feldpostbriefarchiv* at the Musuem for Communication, Berlin)

MKB 3.2002.0904, Letter exchange between spouses Martin and Gerda M.
MKB 3.2002.0224, Letter exchange between spouses Suse and Klaus B.
MKB 3.2002.1286, Letter exchange between spouses Greta and Georg N.
MKB 3.2002.0844, Letter exchange between spouses Franz and Margarethe K.
MKB 3.2.7128, Letter exchange between spouses Franz Xavar and Elisabeth P.
MKB 3.2002.0826, Letter exchange between spouses Gertrud and Hubert S.
MKB 3.2002.1359, Letter exchange between spouses Karola and Willi W.
MKB 3.2002.1246, Letter exchange between spouses Erika and Walter K.
MKB 3.2002.837.0, Letter exchange between spouses Hans and Lore K.
MKB 3.2002.0329, Letter exchange between spouses Irene and Ernst G.
MKB 3.2002.0828, Letter exchange between spouses Herta and Werner B.
MKB 3.2002.0861, Letter exchange between spouses Karl and Hilde K.
MKB 3.2002.7130, Letter exchange between spouses Adelbert and T.
MKB 3.2002.0367, Letter from Heinrich to Hans H.
MKB 3.2002.7135, Letter exchange between spouses Elisabeth and Fritz S.
MKB 3.2002.7327, Letter exchange between spouses Anne and Johannes S.
MKB 3.2002.1241, Letter exchange between spouses Albert and Jo S.
MKB 3.2002.7181, Letter exchange between spouses Jochen and Inge H.
MKB 3.2002.0279, Letter exchange between spouses Liselotte and Kurt O.
MKB 3.2002.7163, Letter exchange between spouses Otto and Cilly M.

MKB 3.2002.0946, Letter exchange between spouses Ursel and Heinz E.
MKB 3.2002.7247, Letter exchange between spouses Lisalotte and Werner L.
MKB 3.2002.7505, Letter exchange between spouses Ernst and Herta S.
MKB 3.2002.7401, Letter exchange between spouses Trude and Peter W.
MKB 3.2002.1218, Letter exchange between spouses Alois and Frieda S.
MKB 3.2002.0238, Letter exchange between spouses Wolf and Frau M.-P.
MKB 3.2002.0985, Heinz R. to wife Ursula.
MKB 3.2002.0933, Horst M.-W. to wife Gisela.
MKB 3.2002.7161, Hans K. to wife Katharina.
MKB 3.2002.0238, Joseph B. to wife Helene.
MKB 3.2002.7115, Heinz R. to wife Melanie.
MKB 3.2002.7159, Reinhold L. to wife Elisabeth.
MKB 3.2002.7172, Michael B. to wife Martha.
MKB 3.2002.1382, Kurt Z. to wife.
MKB 3.2002.7184, Hans H. to wife Käthe.
MKB 3.2002.1351, Aloys S. to wife Anne.
MKB 3.2002.1357, Günter to wife Liselotte.
MKB 3.2002.1376, Wilhelm B. to wife Susanne.
MKB 3.2002.7186, Hans O. to wife Elsbeth.
MKB 3.2002.0888, Peter D. to wife.
MKB 3.2002.1283, Paul G. to wife Irmgard.
MKB 3.2002.215.0, Waldeman A. to wife Klara.
MKB 3.2002.0301, Kurt B. to wife Magdelene.
MKB 3.2002.1323, Hans-Georg T. to wife Elisabeth.
MKB 3.2002.0899, Heinz M.-B. to wife Ellie.
MKB 3.2002.0866.0, Wolfgang K. to wife Dorit.
MKB 3.2002.0860, Konrad R. to wife Friedl.
MKB 3.2002.0921, Leopold H. to wife Erika.
MKB 3.2002.0924, Paul W. to wife Herta.
MKB 3.2002.0942, Thomas N. to wife Herta.
MKB 3.2002.1260, Walter S. to wife Greta.
MKB 3.2002.7177, Rudi D. to wife Hilde.
MKB 3.2002.7179, Reinhold R. to wife Anne.
MKB 3.2002.7180, Erwin M. to wife.
MKB 3.2002.1295, Georg S. to wife Helga.
MKB 3.2002.1317, Paul S. to wife.
MKB 3.2002.1211, Erika P. to husband Herbert.
MKB 3.2002.7163, Vinzenz D. to girlfriend Franziska.
MKB 3.2002.7198, Richard to wife Martha and daughter Hella.
MKB 3.2002.0943, Karl Ludwig N.
MKB 3.2002.7136, Rudolf S.
MKB 3.2002.1211, Herbert.
MKB 3.2002.0367, Hans to wife Hildegard.
MKB 3.2002.7227, Reinhard.
MKB 3.2002.7139, Helmuth to wife Edith.
MKB 3.2002.7208, Alfred to wife Marta.
MKB 3.2002.1214, Hans Joachim S.
MKB 3.2002.0225, From Eberhard B. to his family.
MKB 3.2002.0821, Heinz M. to mother.

AK 96 ' "Wie schön ist die Treue der Wenigen im Leid mit uns sind."
*Auszüge aus Karten und Briefen der Gefangenen und ihrer Angehörigen',
Kriegsgefangenenlagern in der Sowjetunion, 3* (Munich, 1953).

VI. StaAH (Hamburg Staatsarchiv)

Allgemeines 1940–44. Familienunterhaltsberechtigung.
StaAH. 351-10 (I) Sozialbehörde I: AF 92.10.
Betreuungsstelle für Fronturlauber 1943–1944.
StaAH. 351-10 (I) Sozialbehörde I: VG 11.38.
Zuständigkeit für die Bearbeitung von Familienunterhaltssachen 1936–1945.
StaAH. 351-10 (I) Sozialbehörde I: VG 11.41.
Berichte und Beschwerden über Wohnungsfürsorgeamt 1941–1943.
StaAH. 351-10 (I) Sozialbehörde I: VG 26.53.
Form, Aufbau und Führung der Familien-Unterhalt-Akten. Allgemeines 1939–1944.
StaAH. 351-10 (I) Sozialbehörde I: VG 32.40.
Jährliche Arbeitsberichte des Amtes für Wohlfahrtsanstatten 1928–1946.
StaAH. 351-10 (I) Sozialbehörde I: VG 54.56.
Allgemeines 1941–1943 (Unterbringung Obdachloser nach Luftangriffen).
StaAH. 351-10 (I) Sozialbehörde I: EF 91.01.
*Verluste, Veruntreuung, Diebstähle, Plünderung u. a. bei der Sicherstellung des Hausrats
Fliegergeschädigen und von Bergungsgut 1941–1943.*
StaAH. 351-10 (I) Sozialbehörde I: EF 91.37.
*Beschaffung von Kochgelegenheiten und Eßgeschirren usw. für Obdachlose und
Massenspeisungen. Einzelfälle 1939–1945.*
StaAH. 351-10 (I) Sozialbehörde I: EF 91.58.
Sonderbetreuung der Bewohner von Behelfs- u. Notunterkünften.
StaAH. 351-10 (II) Sozialbehörde II: 129.89-9.
*Betreuung von durch Haus- bzw. Ruinensturz Betroffenen und durch Bombenglück
Verletzten.*
StaAH. 351-10 (II) Sozialbehörde II: 129.86-4.
Interessenverbände des Kriegs- und Besatzungsgeschädigten.
StaAH. 351-10 (II) Sozialbehörde II: 012.84-1.
Band I-III: Laufende Berichte an den Bürgermeister über die Tätigkeit.
StaAH. 351-10 (II) Sozialbehörde II: 012.12-5.
*'Mitteilungen' für die Verwaltung der Freien und Hansestadt Hamburg 1949 (Arbeits
u. Sozialbehörde).*
StaAH. 351-10 (II) Sozialbehörde II: 230.20-2.
Band I und II. Jahresberichte der Fürsorgekräfte der Wohnunterkünfte.
StaAH. 351-10 (II) Sozialbehörde II: 012.10-21.
*Berichte für die englische Militärregierung über die Aufgaben der Sozialbehörde und der
Verwaltung für Jugendertüchtigung und Jugendhilfe.*
StaAH. 351-10 (II) Sozialbehörde II: 012.12-3-1.
Einzelne Personengruppen.
StaAH. 351-10 (II) Sozialbehörde II: 231.02-1.
Gesundheitsbehörde (1946–).
StaAH 351-10 (II) Sozial Behörde II: 109.02-5.
Entlassenenhilfe. Band III. 1945–52.
StaAH. 351-10 (II) Sozial Behörde II: 136.50-2.

Allgemeine Speisung der Bevölkerung Hamburgs.
StaAH. 351-10 (II) Sozial Behörde II: 123.58-1.

VII. ADW (Archiv des Diakonischen Werkes – Innere Mission, Berlin)

ADW BA/HW 59.
ADW BA I 1 Nr. 144/5.
ADW CAW 141.

VIII. BA (Bundesarchiv, Koblenz)

B6-05/A.

Primary printed materials

Statistical collections

Bayern in Zahlen 1 (Bayern, 1947).
Berliner Statistik. Monatsschrift No.8 (1955).
Faust, Anselm, Dieter Petzina and Werner Abelshauser, eds, *Sozialgeschichtliches Arbeitsbuch III. Materialien zur Statistik des Deutschen Reiches 1914–1945* (Munich, 1978).
Merkate, Hans Joachim von, Wolfgang Metzner and A. Hillen Ziegfeld, eds, *Deutschland Taschenbuch. Tatsachen und Zahlen* (Frankfurt, 1954).
'Münchener Familienstatistik' in Statistischen Amt der Landeshauptstadt, ed., *Münchner Statistik*, 3 (1949), 45–50.
Rytlewski, Ralf and Manfred Opp de Hipt, eds, *Die Bundesrepublik Deutschland in Zahlen 1945/9-1980* (Munich, 1987).
Statistischen Reichsamt, ed., *Statistisches Jahrbuch für das Deutsche Reich 1926* (Berlin, 1926).
Statistischen Reichsamt, ed., *Statistisches Jahrbuch für das Deutsche Reich* (Berlin, 1940).
Statistisches Amt des Vereinigten Wirtschaftsgebietes, ed., *Wirtschaft und Statistik 1, 1949/1950* (Wiesbaden, 1950).
Statistisches Amt des Vereinigten Wirtschaftsgebietes, ed., *Wirtschaft und Statistik* (Stuttgart, 1950).
Statistisches Amt des Vereinigten Wirtschaftsgebietes, ed., *Die Frau im wirtschaftlichen und sozialen Leben der Bundesrepublik. Statistische Berichte* (Wiesbaden, 1952).
Statistisches Amt des Vereinigten Wirtschaftsgebietes, ed., *Wirtschaft und Statistik*, No.4 (Wiesbaden, 1952).
Statistisches Amt des Vereinigten Wirtschaftsgebietes, ed., *Statistisches Jahrbuch für die Bundesrepublik Deutschland 1952* (Wiesbaden, 1955).
Statistisches Bundesamt, ed., *Statistische Berichte, Arb. Nr. VII/8/25* (Wiesbaden, 1953).
Statistisches Jahrbuch für die Bundesrepublik Deutschland, 1955 (Wiesbaden, 1955).
Statistisches Landesamt Baden Württemberg, ed., *Statistisches Handbuch Baden Württemberg* (1955).

Magazines

Brigitte, 12 (1955).
Brigitte, 19 (1955).

Brigitte, 23 (1955).
Caritas, 1/2 (1952).
Caritas, 1/2 (1950).
Constanze, 3 (April 1948).
Constanze, 4 (April 1948).
Constanze, 6 (May, 1948).
Constanze, 9 (July, 1948).
Constanze, 11 (August,1948).
Constanze, 16 (October, 1948).
Constanze, 2 (January, 1949).
Constanze, 1 (January, 1950).
Constanze, 2 (February, 1951).
Constanze, 11 (November, 1953).
Constanze, 10 (October, 1954).
Das Blatt der Hausfrau, 9 (1940).
Das Blatt der Hausfrau, 16 (1940/41).
Das Blatt der Hausfrau, 4 (1942).
Das Blatt der Hausfrau, June (1942).
Das Blatt der Hausfrau, July (1943).
Das Blatt der Hausfrau, January (1944).
Das Blatt der Hausfrau, May (1944).
Das Blatt der Hausfrau, November (1948).
Das Blatt der Hausfrau, January (1949).
Das Blatt der Hausfrau, February (1949).
Das Blatt der Hausfrau, March (1949).
Das Blatt der Hausfrau, July (1949).
Das Blatt der Hausfrau, August (1949).
Das Blatt der Hausfrau, September (1949).
Das Blatt der Hausfrau, September (1950).
Das Blatt der Hausfrau, August (1950).
Der-Die-Das, 1 (June 1951).
Der Weg zur Seele, Monatschrift für Seelsorge, Psychotherapie und Erziehung (1952).
Deutsche Kinderhilfe, 4 (1953).
Die Antwort, 5 (1954).
Für Euch, 2 (1950).
Für Euch, 7 (1950).
Sie, 2 (December 1945).
Sie, 15 (March 1946).
Sie, 21 (April 1946).
Soziale Arbeit, 6 (1953).
Soziale Arbeit, 2 (1954).
Soziale Arbeit, 11 (1954).
Vinzenz-Blätter, 4 (1955).

Printed primary sources

Andreas-Friedrich, Ruth, *Berlin Underground 1939–1945* (Trans. Barrows Mussey, 3rd edition, London, 1989).

Andreas-Friedrich, Ruth, *Schauplatz Berlin. Tagebuchaufzeichnungen 1938–1948* (2nd edition, Frankfurt, 2000).

Anonymous, *Eine Frau in Berlin. Tagebuchaufzeichnungen vom 20. April bis 22. Juni 1945* (Frankfurt, 2003).

Bähr, Walther, ed., *Kriegsbriefe Gefallener Studenten, 1939–1945* (Stuttgart, 1952).

Bähr, Hans-Walther, ed., *Die Stimme des Menschen. Briefe und Aufzeichnungen aus der ganzen Welt, 1939–1945* (Munich, 1961).

Bertelsmann, Carl, ed., *Last Letters from Stalingrad* (London, 1956).

Boberach, Heinz, ed., *Meldungen aus dem Reich. Auswahl aus den geheimen Lageberichten des Sicherheitsdienstes der SS 1939–1944* (Munich, 1968).

Boberach, Heinz, ed., *Meldungen aus dem Reich. Die geheimen Lageberichte des Sicherheitsdienstes der SS 1938–1945* (Vol. I–XVII, Herrsching, 1984).

Bielenberg, Christabel, *When I was a German. An Englishwoman in Nazi Germany*, Klemens von Klemperer, ed. (Nebraska, 1998).

Böll, Heinrich, *Briefe aus dem Krieg, 1939–45*, Jochen Schubert, ed. (Vol. I, Cologne, 2001).

Böll, Heinrich, *Briefe aus dem Krieg, 1939–45*, Jochen Schubert, ed. (Vol. II, Cologne, 2001).

Boveri, Margret, *Tage des Überlebens: Berlin 1945* (Munich, 1968).

Deutschland-Berichte der Sozialdemokratische Partei Deutschlands 1934-1940 (SOPADE Berichte) (Frankfurt, 1979).

Finckh, Renate, *Mit uns zieht die neue Zeit* (Baden Baden, 1978).

Hofer, Walther, ed., *Der Nationalsozialismus: Dokumente 1933–1945* (Frankfurt am Main,1957).

Goebbels, Josef, *Michael. Ein deutsches Schicksal in Tagebuchblättern* (Munich, 1929).

Groscurth, Helmuth, *Tagebücher Eines Abwehr Offiziers*, Helmut Krausnick, ed. (Stuttgart, 1970).

Jacobson, Hans-Adolf and Werner Jochmann, eds, *Ausgewählte Dokumente zur Geschichte des Nationalsozialismus 1933–1945* (Bielefeld, 1961).

Kardorff, Ursula von, *Diary of a Nightmare. Berlin 1942–1945* (Trans. Ewan Butler, London, 1965).

Kleindienst, Jürgen, ed., *Hungern und hoffen. Jugend in Deutschland, 1945–1950* (Munich, 1993).

Kleindienst, Jürgen, ed., *Nachkriegs-Kinder. Kindheit in Deutschland, 1945–1950* (Berlin, 1998).

Kleindienst, Jürgen, ed., *Wir wollten leben. Jugend in Deutschland 1939-1945* (Berlin, 1998).

Kleindienst, Jürgen, ed., *Gebrannte Kinder. Zweiter Teil. Kindheit in Deutschland 1939–1945* (Berlin, 1999).

Kleindienst, Jürgen, ed., *Lebertran und Chewing Gum. Kindheit in Deutschland, 1945–1950* (Berlin, 2000).

Krockow, Christian Graf von, *Hour of the Woman* (London, 1991).

Langgässer, Elisabeth, *Briefe 1924–1950* (Düsseldorf, 1990).

Noakes, Jeremy and Geoffrey Pridham, eds, *Nazism 1919–1945. Volume III. Foreign Policy, War and Racial Extermination* (3rd edition, Exeter, l997).

Noakes, Jeremy, ed., *Nazism. Volume IV. The German Home Front in World War II* (2nd edition, Exeter, 1998).

Noakes, Jeremy and Geoffrey Pridham, eds, *Nazism. Volume II. State, Economy and Society. 1933–9* (5th edition, Exeter, 2000).

Nossack, Hans Erich, *Die Tagebücher 1943–1977*, Gabriele Söhling, ed. (Frankfurt, 1997).

Orgel-Purper, Liselotte, *Willst Du meine Witwe werden? Eine deutsche Liebe im Krieg* (Berlin, 1995).

Reichsgesetzblatt I (Berlin, 1933).

Timm, Uwe, *In My Brother's Shadow* (London, 2005).

Udke, Gerwin, ed., *'Schreib so oft Du kannst'. Feldpostbriefe des Lehrers Gerhard Udke. 1940–1944* (Berlin, 2002).

Vetter, Lilli, ed., *Briefe aus jener Zeit* (Berlin, 1948).

Wells, Ingeborg, *Enough, No More* (Trans. Lord Sudley, London, 1948).

Witkop, Philipp, ed., *German Students' War Letters* (Trans. A.F. Wedd, London, 1929).

Wolff-Mönckeberg, Mathilde, *On the Other Side. To My Children: From Germany 1940–1945*, Ruth Evans, ed. (Trans. R. Evans, London, 1979).

Wolff-Mönckeberg, Mathilde, *Briefe, die sie nicht erreichten. Briefe einer Mutter an ihre fernen Kinder in den Jahren 1940–1946*, Ruth Evans, ed. (2nd edition, Hamburg, 1980).

Würmeling, Franz-Josef, *Familie – Gabe und Aufgabe* (Cologne, 1963).

Secondary literature

Abelshauser, Werner, *Die Langen Fünfziger Jahre. Wirtschaft und Gesellschaft der Bundesrepublik Deutschland 1949–1966* (Düsseldorf, 1987).

Abercrombie, Barbara, *Writing Out the Storm. Reading and Writing Your Way Through Serious Illness or Injury* (New York, 2002).

Ahonen, Pertti, *After the Expulsion. West Germany and Eastern Europe 1945–1990* (Oxford, 2003).

Aly, Götz, *Hitlers Volksstaat, Raub, Rassenkrieg und nationaler Sozialismus* (Frankfurt, 2005).

Anhalt, Irene, 'Farewell to My Father' in Barbara Heimannsberg, Christoph J. Schmidt, *The Collective Silence. German Identity and the Legacy of Shame* (Trans. Cynthia Oudejans Harris and Gordon Wheeler, 2nd edition, San Francisco, 1993), 31–48.

Aries, Philippe, *Centuries of Childhood: A Social History of Family Life* (New York, 1962).

Baier, Horst, ed., *Helmut Schelsky – ein Soziologe in der Bundesrepublik. Ein Gedächtnisschrift von Freunden, Kollegen und Schülern* (Stuttgart, 1986).

Bartov, Omer, *Hitler's Army. Soldiers, Nazis and War in the Third Reich* (Oxford, 1991).

Bartov, Omer, 'Savage War' in Michael Burleigh, ed., *Confronting the Nazi Past. New Debates on Modern German History* (2nd edition, London, 1996), 125–139.

Bartov, Omer, *The Eastern Front, 1941–45. German Troops and the Barbarisation of Warfare* (2nd edition, London, 2001).

Baumert, Gerhard, *Jugend der Nachkriegszeit* (Darmstadt, 1952).

Baumert, Gerhard, *Deutsche Familien nach dem Krieg* (Darmstadt, 1954).

Baumert, Gerhard, 'Beobachtungen zur Wandlung der familialen Stellung des Kindes in Deutschland' in *Neue wissenschaftliche Bibliothek 5 Soziologie. Jugend in der modernen Gesellschaft* (Berlin,1965), 309–320.

Bänsch, Dieter, ed., *Die fünfziger Jahre. Beiträge zu Politik und Kultur* (Tübingen, 1985).

Beck, Birgit, *Wehrmacht und sexuelle Gewalt* (Paderborn, 2004).

Becker, Josef, Theo Stammen and Peter Waldmann, eds, *Vorgeschichte der Bundesre publik Deutschland. Zwischen Kapitulation und Grundgesetz* (Munich, 1979).

Beevor, Antony, *Stalingrad* (London, 1998).

Beevor, Antony, *Berlin: The Downfall, 1945* (London, 2002).

Behnken, Klaus, ed., *Deutschland-Berichte der Sozialdemokratischen Partei Deutschlands (Sopade) 1934–1940* (Vol. 5, Frankfurt am Main, 1980).

Bell, Norman W. and Ezra E. Vogel, eds, *A Modern Introduction to The Family* (London, 1960).

Norman W. Bell and Ezra E. Vogel, 'Toward a Framework for Functional Analysis of Family Behaviour' in Norman W. Bell and Ezra E. Vogel, eds, *A Modern Introduction to The Family* (London, 1960), 382–397.

Bellinghausen, Hans, *Koblenz am Rein und Mosel. Ein Handbuch* (Koblenz, 1950).

Benz, Ute and Wolfgang, *Sozialisation und Traumatizierung. Kinder in der Zeit des Nationalsozialismus* (Frankfurt, 1992).

Benz, Ute, '"Maikäfer, flieg! Dein Vater ist im Krieg." Aspekte der Heimkehr aus familiarier Sicht' in Annette Kaminsky, ed., *Heimkehr 1948. Geschichte und Schicksale deutscher Kriegsgefangener* (Munich, 1998), 176–191.

Benz, Wolfgang, ed., *Die Bundesrepublik Deutschland* (Vol. 2, Frankfurt, 1985).

Bergmeier, Horst J.P. and Rainer E. Lotz, *Hitler's Airwaves. The Inside Story of Nazi Radio Broadcasting and Propaganda Swing* (New Haven, 1997).

Bessel, Richard, ed., *Life in the Third Reich* (2nd edition, Oxford, 2001).

Bessel, Richard and Dirk Schumann, eds, *Life After Death. Approaches to a Cultural and Social History of Europe during the 1940s and 1950s* (Cambridge, 2003).

Bessel, Richard, *Nazism and War* (London, 2004).

Bessel, Richard, *Germany, 1945* (London, 2009).

Biess, Frank, 'Men of Reconstruction. The Reconstruction of Men. Returning PoWs in East and West Germany 1945–55' in Karen Hagemann and Stefanie Schüler-Springorum, eds, *Home/Front. The Military, War and Gender in Twentieth Century Germany* (Oxford, 2002), 335–358.

Biess, Frank, *Homecomings. Returning Prisoners of War and the Legacies of Defeat in Postwar Germany* (Oxford, 2006).

Bird, Gloria and Keith Melville, eds, *Families and Intimate Relationships* (McGraw-Hill, 1994).

Blank, Ralf, 'Kriegsalltag und Luftkrieg an der "Heimatfront"' in Jörg Echternkamp, ed., *Das Deutsche Reich und Der Zweite Weltkrieg*, Vol. 9/2 (Munich, 2004), 357–464.

Bock, Gisela, *Zwangssterilisation im NS: Studien zur Frauenpolitik* (Opladen, 1986).

Boehling, Rebecca, 'Stunde Null at the Ground Level: 1945 as a Social and Political Ausgangspunkt in Three Cities in the U.S. Zone of Occupation Germany' in Geoffrey J. Giles, ed., *Stunde Null: The End and the Beginning Fifty Years Ago* (Washington, 1997), 105–128.

Boelcke, Willi A., *Der Schwarz-Markt 1945–1948. Vom Überleben nach dem Kriege* (Braunschweig, 1986).

Bode, Sabine, *Die vergessene Generation. Die Kriegskinder brechen ihr Schweigen* (Munich, 2005).

Boeschoten, Riki von, 'The Impossible Return: Coping with Separation and the Reconstruction of Memory in the Wake of the Civil War' in Mark Mazower, ed., *After the War was Over. Reconstructing the Family, Nation and State in Greece, 1943–1960* (Oxford, 2000), 122–141.

Bohn, Helmut, *Die Heimkehrer aus russischer Kriegsgefangenschaft* (Frankfurt, 1951).

Böll, Heinrich, *The Stories of Heinrich Böll* (Trans. Leila Vennewitz, London, 1986).

Bouman, Pieter Jan, Gunther Beijer and Jan J. Oudegeest, *The Refugee Problem in Western Germany* (Trans. H.A. Marx, The Hague, 1950).

Borneman, John, *Belonging in the Two Berlins* (Cambridge, 1992).

Borsdorf, Ulrich and Mathilde Jamin, eds, *Über Leben im Krieg. Kriegserfahrungen in einer Industrieregion 1939–1945* (Hamburg, 1989).

Botting, Douglas, *In the Ruins of the Reich* (London, 1985).

Bourke, Joanna, 'Fear and Anxiety: Writing about Emotion in Modern History', in *History Workshop Journal*, No. 55, 2003, 111–133.

Bourke, Joanna, *Fear: A Cultural History* (London, 2005).

Bourke, Joanna, *Rape: A History from 1860 to the Present* (London, 2007).

Bracher, Karl Dietrich, *The German Dictatorship. The Origins, Structure and Effects of National Socialism* (Trans. Jean Steinberg, London, 1971).

Brandes, O. Jean, 'The Effect of War on the German Family', *Social Forces*, Vol. 29, No. 2, 1950, 164–173.

Brett-Smith, Richard, *Berlin '45. The Grey City* (London, 1966).

Bridenthal, Renate, Marion Kaplan and Atina Grossmann, eds, *When Biology Became Destiny. Women in Weimar and Nazi Germany* (New York, 1984).

Bridenthal, Renate and Claudia Koonz, 'Beyond Kinder, Küche, Kirche: Weimar Women in Politics and Work' in Renate Bridenthal, Atina Grossmann and Marion Kaplan, eds, *When Biology Became Destiny. Women in Weimar and Nazi Germany* (New York, 1984), 33–65.

Brockmann, Stephan, 'German Literature' in Geoffrey J. Giles, ed., *Stunde Null: The End and the Beginning Fifty Years Ago* (Washington, 1997), 59–74.

Broszat, Martin, Elke Fröhlich and Falke Wieseman, *Bayern in der NS-Zeit* (Oldenberg, 1977).

Broszat, Martin, Klaus Dietmar Henke and Hans Woller, eds, *Von Stalingrad zur Währungsreform. Zur sozialgeschichte des Umbruchs in Deutschland* (Munich, 1988).

Browning, Christopher, *Ordinary Men: Reserve Police Battalion 101 and the Final Solution* (New York, 1992).

Bruns, Ingeborg, *Als Vater aus dem Krieg heimkehrte. Töchter erinnern sich* (Frankfurt, 1991).

Bruss, Regina, *Mit Zuckersack und Heiße Getränke. Leben und Überleben in der Nachkriegszeit, Bremen 1945–1949* (Bremen, 1988).

Buchbender, Ortwin and Reinhold Sterz, *Das Andere Gesicht des Krieges* (Munich, 1982).

Bude, Heinz, *Bilanz der Nachfolge. Die Bundesrepublik und der Nationalsozialismus* (Frankfurt, 1992).

Burgess, Ernest W., Harvey J. Locke and Mary Margaret Thomas, eds, *The Family. From Traditional to Companionship* (4th edition, New York, 1971).

Burleigh, Michael, *Death and Deliverance. 'Euthanasia' in Germany, c. 1900–1945* (Cambridge, 1994).

Burleigh, Michael, ed., *Confronting the Nazi Past. New Debates on Modern German History* (London, 1996).

Burleigh, Michael, *The Third Reich. A New History* (London, 2001).

Butler, Judith and Joan W. Scott, eds, *Feminists Theorize the Political* (London, 1992).

Büttner, Ursula, ' "Gomorrha" und die Folgen der Bombenkrieg' in Forschungsstelle für Zeitgeschichte in Hamburg, ed., *Hamburg im 'Dritten Reich'* (Göttingen, 2005), 613–632.

Calder, Angus, *Britain at War* (London, 2002).

Calhoun, Arthur W., *A Social History of the American Family from Colonial Times to the Present* (Cleveland, 1917–1919).

Canning, Kathleen, 'Feminist History After the Linguistic Turn: Historicizing Discourse and Experience', *Signs*, Vol. 19, No. 2, 1994, 368–404.

Caplan, Jane, 'Foreword' in Carola Sachse, *Industrial Housewives: Women's Social Work in the Factories of Nazi Germany* (London, 1987), 1–9.

Carleton Mayer, Herbert, *German Recovery and the Marshall Plan* (New York, 1969).

Carr, William, 'Nazi Policy against the Jews' in Richard Bessel, ed., *Life in the Third Reich* (2nd edition, Oxford, 2001), 69–82.

Cohen, Stanley, *Folk Devils and Moral Panics. The Creation of the Mods and the Rockers* (2nd edition, Oxford, 1980).

Connor, Ian, *Refugees and Expellees in Post-War Germany* (Manchester, 2007).

Corrin, Chris, ed., *Superwoman and the Double Burden* (Toronto, 1992).

Coser, Lewis A., 'Some Aspects of Soviet Family Policy' in Rose Laub Coser, ed., *The Family. Its Structures and Functions* (2nd edition, London, 1974), 412–429.

Costello, John, *Love Sex and War. Changing Values 1939–45* (London, 1985).

Crew, David F., *Nazism and German Society, 1933–1945* (New York, 1994).

Dahrendorf, Ralf, *Society and Democracy in Germany* (London, 1967).

Daniel, Ute, *The War from Within. German Working-Class Women in the First World War* (Oxford, 1997).

Davidson, Elizabeth, *The Death and Life of Germany. An Account of the American Occupation* (London, 1959).

Demos, John, 'Developmental Perspectives on the History of Childhood' in Theodore K. Rabb and Robert I. Rotberg eds, *The Family in History. Interdisciplinary Essays* (London, 1971), 127–139.

Jacques Derrida, *Of Grammatology* (Baltimore, 1967).

Deutsches Rotes Kreuz-Suchdienst, ed., *Zur Geschichte der Kriegsgefangenen im Westen* (Bonn, 1962).

Diehl, James M., *The Thanks of the Fatherland. German Veterans after the Second World War* (North Carolina, 1993).

Dinter, Andreas, *Berlin in Trümmern. Ernährungslage und medizinische Versorgung der Bevölkerung Berlins nach dem II. Weltkrieg* (Berlin, 1999).

Dollinger, Hans, ed., *'Kain, wo ist dein Bruder?' Was der Mensch im Zweiten Weltkrieg erleiden musste – dokumentiert in Tagebüchern und Briefen* (Munich, 1983).

Dollinger, Hans, 'Beitragen, den Krieg zu ächten' in Hans Dollinger, ed., *'Kain, wo ist dein Bruder?' Was der Mensch im Zweiten Weltkrieg erleiden musste – dokumentiert in Tagebüchern und Briefen* (Munich, 1983), 391–394.

Dörr, Margarete, ed., *'Wer die Zeit nicht miterlebt hat...' Frauenerfahrungen im Zweiten Weltkrieg und in den Jahren danach. Band I – Lebensgeschichten* (New York, 1998).

Dörr, Margarete, ed., 'Wer die Zeit nicht miterlebt hat...' Frauenerfahrungen im Zweiten Weltkrieg und in den Jahren danach. Band II – Kreigserfahrung (New York, 1998).

Dörr, Margarete, ed., 'Wer die Zeit nicht miterlebt hat...' Das Verhältnis zum Nationalsozialismus und zum Krieg. Band III – Frauenerfahrungen im Zweiten Weltkrieg und in den Jahren danach (New York, 1998).

Downs, Laura Lee, 'If "Woman" is Just an Empty Category, Then Why Am I Afraid to Walk Alone at Night? Identity Politics Meets the Postmodern Subject', Comparative Studies in Society and History, Vol. 35, No. 2, 1993, 414–437.

Downs, Laura Lee, 'Reply to Joan Scott', Comparative Studies in Society and History, 35, 1993, 445–451.

Downs, Laura Lee, Writing Gender History (London, 2004).

Doyle McCarthy, E., 'Emotions Are Social Things' in David D. Franks and E. Doyle McCarthy, eds, The Sociology of Emotions: Original Essays and Research Papers (London, 1989), 51–72.

Drechsler, Hannelore, Mamatschi schenk mir ein Pferdchen. Die Geschichte einer wahren Liebe (Essen, 1997).

Ebert, Jens, ed., Stalingrad – eine deutsche Legende. Zeugnisse einer verdrängten Niederlage (Hamburg, 1992).

Echternkamp, Jörg, Das Deutsche Reich und Der Zweite Weltkrieg 1939 bis 1945 (Vol. 9/2, Munich, 2004).

Echternkamp, Jörg, ed., Die Deutsche Kriegsgesellschaft 1939 bis 1945 (Vol. II, Munich, 2005).

Echternkamp, Jörg, Kriegsschauplatz Deutschland 1945 (Paderborn, 2006).

Echternkamp, Jörg, 'Im Schlagschatten des Krieges. Von den Folgen militärischen Gewalt und nationalsozialisitischer Herrschaft in der frühen Nachkriegszeit' in Rolf Dieter Müller, ed., Das Deutsche Reich und der Zweite Weltkrieg (Vol. 10/2, Munich, 2008), 657–698.

Eckstädt, Anita, Nationalsozialismus in der 'zweiten Generation' (Frankfurt, 1989).

Edmunds, June and Bryon S. Turner, Generations, Culture and Society (Philadelphia, 2002).

Eher, Franz, 'Darüber lache ich heute noch.' VB-Feldpost. Soldaten erzählen heitere Erlebnisse (Berlin, 1943).

Ehlers, Jürgen, Feldpost. Mein Kriegstagebuch (und mehr) (Braunschweig, 2005).

Elder, Glen H., Children of the Great Depression. Social Change in Life Experience (Chicago, 1974).

Engelmann, Berndt, In Hitler's Germany: Everyday Life in the Third Reich (New York, 1986).

Engert, Jürgen, Heimatfront. Kriegsalltag im Deutschland 1939–1945 (Berlin, 1999).

Entwistle, Charles R. and A.M. Entwistle, An Introduction to German Censorship, 1939–45 (Perth, 1993).

Erikson, Erik, Childhood and Society (2nd edition, London, 1965).

Erker, Paul, Ernährungskrise und Nachkriegsgesellschaft. Bauern und Arbeiterschaft in Bayern 1943–1953 (Stuttgartt, 1990).

Evans, Richard J. and William Robert Lee, eds, The German Family. Essays on the Social History of the Family in Nineteenth and Twentieth Century Germany (London, 1981).

Evans, Richard J., *Comrades and Sisters. Feminism, Socialism and Pacifism in Europe 1870–1945* (Sussex, 1987).

Evans, Richard J., *In Defence of History* (London, 1997).

Evans, Richard J., *The Third Reich in Power* (New York, 2005).

Evans, Richard J., *The Third Reich at War* (London, 2008).

Farquharson, John E., *The Plough and the Swastika. The NSDAP and Agriculture in Germany, 1928–1945* (London, 1976).

Lucian Febvre, *A New Kind of History and Other Essays*, ed., Peter Burke (New York, 1973 [1941]).

Lucian Febvre, 'Sensibility and History: How to Reconstitute the Emotional Life of the Past' in Lucian Febvre, *A New Kind of History and Other Essays*, ed., Peter Burke (New York, 1973 [1941]), 12–26.

Fehrenbach, Heide, 'Rehabilitating Fatherland: Race and German Remasculinization', *Signs. Journal of Women in Culture and Society*, Vol. 24, 1998, 107–127.

Fehrenbach, Heide, 'Of German Mothers and Negermischlingskinder. Race, Sex and the Postwar Nation' in Hanna Schissler, ed., *The Miracle Years. A Cultural History of West Germany, 1949–1968* (Princeton, 2001), 164–186.

Fehrenbach, Heide, *Race after Hitler. Black Occupation Children in Postwar Germany and America* (Oxford, 2005).

Fehrenbach, Heide, 'Afro-German Children and the Social Politics of Race after 1945' in Neil Gregor, Nils Roemer and Mark Roseman, eds, *German History from the Margins* (Indiana, 2006), 226–251.

Feltz, Nina and Johanna Meyer-Lenz, 'Franz P. "Sei stark, werde nicht schwach – Du kannst noch einsamer sein, als Du denkst!" Zu den Einflüssen des nationalsozialistischen Männlichkeitsbildes in der Nachkriegszeit' in Johanna Meyer-Lenz, ed., *Die Ordnung des Paares ist unbehaglich. Irritationen am und im Geschlechterdiskurs nach 1945* (Hamburg, 2000), 295–318.

Filmer, Werner and Heribert Schwan, eds, *Besiegt, befreit…Zeitzeugen erinnern sich an das Kriegsende 1945* (Munich, 1995).

Finckh, Renate, *Mit uns zieht die neue Zeit* (Baden Baden, 1978).

Fitzpatrick, Sheila and Michael Geyer, eds, *Beyond Totalitarianism* (Cambridge, 2009).

Fitzpatrick, Sheila and Alf Lüdtke, 'Energizing the Everyday: On the Breaking and Making of Social Bonds in Nazism and Stalinism' in Sheila Fitzpatrick and Michael Geyer, eds, *Beyond Totalitarianism* (Cambridge, 2009), 266–301.

Flemming, Jens, Klaus Saul and Peter-Christian Witt, eds, *Familienleben im Schatten der Krise. Dokumente und Analysen zur Sozialgeschichte der Weimarer Republik* (Düsseldorf, 1988).

Foitzik, Doris, ed., *Von Trümmerkind zum Teenager. Kindheit und Jugend in der Nachkriegzeit* (Bremen, 1992).

Forschungsstelle für Zeitgeschichte in Hamburg, ed., *Hamburg im 'Dritten Reich'* (Göttingen, 2005).

Förster, Jürgen, 'Geistige Kriegsführung in Deutschland 1919 bis 1945' in Jörg Echternkamp, ed., *Das Deutsche Reich und Der Zweite Weltkrieg*, Vol. 9/2 (Munich, 2005), 469–640.

Foucault, Michel, *Discipline and Punish* (New York, 1975).

Foucault, Michel, *The Will to Knowledge* (New York, 1978 [1976]).

Franck, Norbert, ed., *Heil Hitler, Herr Lehrer. Volksschule 1933–1945. Das Beispiel Berlin* (Hamburg, 1983).

Franks, David D. and E. Doyle McCarthy, eds, *The Sociology of Emotions: Original Essays and Research Papers* (London, 1989).

Frei, Norbert, *Karrieren Im Zwielicht: Hitlers Eliten Nach 1945* (Frankfurt, 2001).

Frei, Norbert, *1945 und Wir. Das Dritte Reich im Bewusstsein der Deutschen* (Munich, 2005).

Frevert, Ute, *Women in German History. From Bourgeois Emancipation to Sexual Liberation* (Trans. Stuart McKinna-Evans, Oxford, 1989).

Frevert, Ute, *A Nation in Barracks. Military Conscription and Civil Society* (Oxford, 2004).

Frevert, Ute, *Vertrauen: eine historische Annäherung* (Göttingen, 2003).

Freud, Anna, and Dorothy T. Burlingham, *War and Children* (New York, 1943).

Friedrich, Carl J. and Zbigniev K. Brzezinski, *Totalitarian Dictatorship and Autocracy* (Cambridge, 1956).

Friedrich, Jörg, *The Fire* (Trans. Allison Brown, New York, 2006).

Fritz, Stephen G., *Frontsoldaten. The German Soldier in World War II* (Kentucky, 1995).

Fritzsche, Peter, *Life and Death in the Third Reich* (London, 2008).

Fulbrook, Mary, *German National Identity after the Holocaust* (Oxford, 1999).

Fussell, Paul, *The Great War and Modern Memory* (3rd edition, Oxford, 2000).

Geiger, Kent, 'Changing Political Attitudes in Totalitarian Society: A Case Study of the Role of the Family' in Norman W. Bell and Ezra E. Vogel, eds, *A Modern Introduction to The Family* (London, 1960), 219–234.

Gellately, Robert, *The Gestapo and German Society. Enforcing Racial Policy 1933–1945* (Oxford, 1990).

Gellately, Robert, *Backing Hitler. Consent and Coercion in Nazi Germany* (Oxford, 2001).

Gellately, Robert, 'Die Gestapo und die deutsche Gesellschaft: Zur Entstehungsgeschichte einer selbstüberwachenden Gesellschaft' in Detlef Schmiechen-Ackermann, ed., *Anpassung, Verweigerung, Widerstand: Soziale Milieus, Politische Kultur und der Widerstand gegen den NS in Deutschland im regionalen Verleich* (Berlin, 1997), 109–122.

Gerstenberer, Heide and Dorothea Schmidt, eds, *Normalität oder Normalisierung? Geschichtswerkstätten und Faschismusanalyse* (Münster, 1987).

Giles, Geoffrey, ed., *Stunde Null: The End and the Beginning Fifty Years Ago* (Washington, 1997).

Gillen, Otto, *'Ich will das Lied der Liebe singen'. Feldpostbriefe an meine Braut 1943–1946. Kriegstagebuch 1945* (Stein am Rhein, 1999).

Gimbel, John, *A German Community under American Occupation. Marburg, 1945–52* (Stanford, 1961).

Glaser, Hermann, *The Rubble years. The Cultural Roots of Postwar Germany* (New York, 1986).

Glaser, Hermann, *1945 Ein Lesebuch* (Frankfurt, 1995).

Goldstein, Joshua S., *War and Gender. How Gender Shapes the War System and Vice Versa* (Cambridge, 2001).

Gollancz, Victor, *In Darkest Germany* (London, 1946).

Gollancz, Victor, *Our Threatened Values* (London, 1946).

Golovchansky, Anatoly, *'Ich will raus aus diesem Wahnsinn.' Deutsche Briefe von der Ostfront 1941–1945 aus Sowjetischen Archiven* (Wuppertal, 1991).

Grass, Günter, *Im Krebsgang* (Göttingen, 2002).

Grau, Günter, *Hidden Holocaust? Gay and Lesbian Persecution in Germany 1933–45* (London, 1995).

Grayzel, Susan R., *Women's Identities at War. Gender, Motherhood, and Politics in Britain and France during the First World War* (North Carolina, 1999).

Gries, Rainer, *Die Rationen-Gesellschaft. Versorgungskampf und Vergleichsmentalität: Leipzig, München und Köln nach dem Kriege* (Münster, 1991).

Grossman, Atina, 'A Question of Silence: The Rape of German Women by Occupation Soldiers' in Robert G. Moeller, ed., *West Germany under Construction* (Michigan, 1997), 33–52.

Grossmann, Atina, *Jews, Germans, and Allies. Close Encounters in Occupied Germany* (Princeton, 2007).

Grube, Frank and Gerhard Richter, *Die Schwarzmarktzeit. Deutschland zwischen 1945 und 1948* (Berlin, 2006).

Grull, Günter, *Radio und Musik von und für Soldaten. Kriegs- und Nachkriegsjahre 1939-1960* (Cologne, 2000).

Grunberger, Richard, *A Social History of the Third Reich* (London, 1971).

Hagemann, Karen and Stefanie Schüler-Springerum, eds, *Home/Front. The Military, War and Gender in Twentieth Century Germany* (Oxford, 2002).

Hall, Catherine, *White, Male and Middle-Class. Explorations in Feminism and History* (Oxford, 1992).

Hammer, Ingrid and Susanne zur Nieden, eds, *'Sehr selten habe ich geweint.' Briefe und Tagebücher aus dem Zweiten Weltkrieg von Menschen aus Berlin* (Zürich, 1992).

Hardach, Karl, *The Political Economy of Germany in the Twentieth Century* (London, 1980).

Hareven, Tamara K., 'The History of the Family as an Interdisciplinary Field' in Theodore K. Rabb and Robert I. Rotberg, eds, *The Family in History. Interdisciplinary Essays* (London, 1971), 211–226.

Harsch, Donna, *The Revenge of the Domestic: Women, the Family and Communism in the German Democratic Republic* (Princeton, 2007).

Hausen, Karin, 'Historische Familienforschung' in Reinhard Rürup, ed., *Historische Sozialwissenschaft* (Göttingen, 1977), 59–95.

Heimannsberg, Barbara and Carl Schmidt, *The Collective Silence. German Identity and the Legacy of Shame* (San Francisco, 1993).

Heimkes, Heinrich, *Ein Münchener als Soldat der 1. Gebirgsdivision im Kaukasus und auf dem Balkan* (Self-published, 2002).

Heineman, Elizabeth, 'The Hour of the Woman: Memories of Germany's "Crisis Years" and West German National Identity', *American Historical Review*, Vol. 101, No. 2, 1996, 354–395.

Heineman, Elizabeth, *What Difference Does a Husband Make? Women and Marital Status in Nazi and Postwar Germany* (London, 1999).

Helwig, Gisela, 'Familienpolitik in der SBZ' in Ugo Wengst, ed., *Geschichte der Sozialpolitik in Deutschland seit 1945* (Vol. 2/1, Munich, 2001), 664–665.

Herbert, Ulrich, 'Die guten und die schlechten Zeiten. Überlegungen zur diachronen Analyse lebensgeschichtliche Interviews' in Lutz Niethammer, ed., *'Die Jahre weiss man nicht, wo man die Leute hinsetzten sol'. Lebensgeschichte und Sozialkultur im Ruhrgebiet 1930–60* (Vol. I, Berlin, 1983), 67–98.

Herbert, Ulrich, 'The Real Mystery in Germany' in Michael Burleigh, ed., *Confronting the Nazi Past. New Debates on Modern German History* (London, 1996), 23–36.

Herbert, Ulrich, *Hitler's Foreign Workers* (Cambridge, 1997).

Herzog, Dagmar, 'Desperately Seeking Normality. Sex and Marriage in the Wake of the War' in Richard Bessel and Dirk Schumann, eds, *Life After Death: Approaches to a Cultural and Social History of Europe during the 1940s and 1950s* (Cambridge, 2003), 161–192.

Herzog, Dagmar, ed., *Sexuality and German Fascism* (Texas, 2005).

Herzog, Dagmar, 'Hubris and Hypocrisy, Incitement and Disavowal' in Dagmar Herzog, ed., *Sexuality and German Fascism* (Texas, 2005), 1–21.

Herzog, Dagmar, *Sex after Fascism. Memory and Morality in Twentieth Century Germany* (Oxford, 2005).

Highmore, Ben, *Everyday Life and Cultural Theory* (London, 2002).

Hill, Reuben, *Families under Stress. Adjustment to the Crises of War Separation and Reunion* (New York, 1949).

Hillmann, Jörg and John Zimmermann, eds, *Kriegsende 1945 in Deutschland* (Munich, 2002).

Hoecker, Beate and Renate Meyer-Braun, eds, *Bremerinnen bewältigen die Nachkriegszeit* (Bremen, 1988).

Hoff, Joan, 'Gender as a Postmodern Category of Paralysis', *Women's History Review*, Vol. 3, No. 2, 1994, 149–168.

Höhn, Maria, 'Stunde Null der Frauen? Renegotiating Women's Place in Postwar West Germany' in Geoffrey J. Giles, ed., *Stunde Null: The End and the Beginning Fifty Years Ago* (Washington, 1997), 75–87.

Höhn, Maria, *GIs and Fräuleins. The German-American Encounter in 1950s West Germany* (North Carolina, 2002).

Hoffmann, David L. and Annette F. Timm, 'Utopian Biopolitics. Reproductive Policies, Gender Roles, and Sexuality in Nazi Germany and the Soviet Union' in Sheila Fitzpatrick and Michael Geyer, eds, *Beyond Totalitarianism* (Cambridge, 2009), 87–129.

Hoffmann, Stephanie, ' "Darüber spricht man nicht"? Die öffentliche Diskussion über die Sexualmoral in der 50er Jahren im Spiegel der Frauenzeitschrift "Constanze" ' in Johanna Meyer-Lenz, ed., *Die Ordnung des Paares ist unbehaglich. Irritationen am und im Geschlechterdiskurs nach 1945* (Hamburg, 2000), 54–84.

Homsten, Georg, *Die Berliner-Chronik. Daten. Personen. Dokumente. 1939–1949* (Düsseldorf, 1984).

Horkheimer, Max, 'Authoritarianism and the Family' in Ruth Nanda Anshen, ed., *The Family: Its Function and Destiny* (New York, 1949), 359–374.

Hughes, Michael L., *Shouldering the Burdens of Defeat. West Germany and the Reconstruction of Social Justice* (North Carolina, 1999).

Humburg, Martin, 'Deutsche Feldpostbriefe im Zweiten Weltkrieg' in Wolfram Wette and Detlev Vogel, eds, *Andere Helme – andere Menschen? Heimaterfahrung und Frontalltag im Zweiten Weltkrieg. Ein internationaler Vergleich* (Stuttgart, 1995), 13–36.

Humburg, Martin, *Das Gesicht des Krieges. Feldpostbriefe von Wehrmachtssoldaten aus der Sowjetunion 1941–1944* (Wiesbaden, 1998).

Humburg, Martin, 'Feldpostbriefe am Ende des Krieges' in Jörg Hillmann and John Zimmermann, eds, *Kriegsende 1945 in Deutschland* (Munich, 2002).

Humburg, Martin, 'Feldpostbriefe aus dem Zweiten Weltkrieg – Werkstattbericht zu einer Inhaltsanalyse' in *Methodische Vorüberlegungen zur Briefanalyse*, at: http://hsozkult.geschichte.hu-berlin.de/beitrag/essays/feld.htm. Last accessed 14 February 2008.

Jarausch, Konrad H., 'Towards a Social History of Experience: Postmodern Predicaments in Theory and Interdisciplinarity', *Central European History*, Vol. 22, No. 3/4, 1989, 427–443.

Jarausch, Konrad H., '1945 and the Continuities of German History: Reflections on Memory, Historiography and Politics' in Geoffrey J. Giles, ed., *Stunde Null: The End and the Beginning Fifty Years Ago* (Washington, 1997), 9–24.

Jarausch, Konrad H., *After Hitler. Recivilizing Germany, 1945-1995* (Trans. Brandon Hernziker, Oxford, 2006).

Jeffords, Susan, 'The "Remasculinization" of Germany in the 1950s: Discussion', *Signs*, Vol. 24, No. 1, 1998, 107–127.

Jenk, Gabriele, *Steine gegen Brot: Trümmerfrauen schildern den Wiederaufbau in der Nachkriegszeit* (Bastei-Lübbe, 1988).

Jerome, Roy, ed., *Conceptions of Postwar German Masculinity* (New York, 2001).

Jolly, Margaretta, '"Briefe, Moral und Geschlecht."' Britische und amerikanische Diskurse über das Briefeschreiben im Zweiten Weltkrieg' in Wolfram Wette and Detlev Vogel, eds, *Andere Helme – andere Menschen? Heimaterfahrung und Frontalltag im Zweiten Weltkrieg. Ein internationaler Vergleich* (Stuttgart, 1995), 173–204.

Joosten, Astrid, *Die Frau, das 'segenspendende Herz der Familie.' Familienpolitik als Frauenpolitik in der Ära Adenauer* (Bamberg, 1990).

Jordan, Ulrike, ed., *Conditions of Surrender. Britons and Germans Witness the End of the War* (London, 1997).

Judt, Tony, 'A Clown in Regal Purple: Social History and the Historians' in *History Workshop*, No. 7, 1979, 66–94.

Judt, Tony, *Postwar. A History of Europe since 1945* (London, 2005).

Kaminsky, Annette, ed., *Heimkehr 1948. Geschichte und Schicksale deutscher Kriegsgefangener* (Munich, 1998).

Kaplan, Marion, *Between Dignity and Despair. Jewish Life in Nazi Germany* (Oxford, 1998).

Kaplan, Marion, *Jewish Daily life in Germany, 1618–1945* (Oxford, 2005).

Kershaw, Ian, *Popular Opinion and Political Dissent in the Third Reich, Bavaria 1933–1945* (2nd edition, Oxford, 1993).

Kershaw, Ian, 'Hitler and the Germans' in Richard Bessel ed., *Life in the Third Reich* (2nd edition, Oxford, 2001), 41–55.

Kettenacker, Lothar, ed., *Volk von Opfern?* (Berlin, 2003).

Kienitz, Sabine, 'Body Damage. War Disability and Constructions of Masculinity in Weimar Germany' in Karen Hagemann and Stefanie Schüler-Springerum, eds, *Home/Front. The Military, War and Gender in Twentieth Century Germany* (Oxford, 2002), 181–203.

Kilian, Katrin Anja, Das Medium Feldpost als Gegenstand interdisziplinärer Forschung. Archivlage, Forschungsstand und Aufbereitung der Quelle aus dem Zweiten Weltkrieg (PhD Dissertation, Berlin, 2001).

Kilian, Katrin A., 'Kriegsstimmungen' in Jörg Echternkamp, ed., *Die Deutsche Kriegsgesellschaft 1939 bis 1945* (Vol. II, Munich, 2005), 251–288.

Kindleberger, Charles P., *The German Economy, 1945–1947. Charles P. Kindleberger's Letters from the Field* (London, 1989).

Kirkpatrick, Clifford, *The Family as Process and Institution* (New York, 1955).

Kitchen, Martin, *Germany at War* (London, 1995).

Kleindienst, Jürgen, 'Feldpost im Zweiten Weltkrieg' in Gerwin Udke, ed., *'Schreib so oft Du kannst'. Feldpostbriefe des Lehrers Gerhard Udke. 1940–1944* (Berlin, 2002).

Klemperer, Victor, *I Shall Bear Witness. The Diaries of Victor Klemperer 1933–1941*, Martin Chalmers, ed. (2nd edition, London, 1998).

Klessmann, Christoph, ed, *Nicht nur Hitlers Krieg. Der Zweite Weltkrieg und die Deutschen* (Düsseldorf, 1989).

Klönne, Arno, ' "Wieder Normal werden?" Entwicklungslinien politischer Kultur in der Bundesrepublik' in Hans-Uwe Otto and Heinz Sünker, eds, *Soziale Arbeit und Faschismus. Volkspflege und Pädagogik im Nationalsozialismus* (Bielefeld, 1986), 467–476.

Klönne, Arno, *Jugend im Dritten Reich. Die Hitler-Jugend und ihre Gegner* (Düsseldorf, 1982).

Knoch, Peter, ed., *Kriegsalltag. Die Rekonstruktion des Kriegsalltags als Aufgabe der historischen Forschung und der Friedenserziehung* (Stuttgart, 1989).

Knoch, Peter, 'Kriegsalltag' in Peter Knoch, ed., *Kriegsalltag. Die Rekonstruktion des Kriegsalltags als Aufgabe der historischen Forschung und der Friedenserziehung* (Stuttgart, 1989), 222–251.

Knopp, Guido, *Das Ende 1945. Der verdammte Krieg* (Munich, 1995).

Knopp, Guido, *Damals 1945. Das Jahr Null* (Stuttgart, 1996).

Kocka, Jürgen, *Geschichte und Aufklärung* (Göttingen, 1989).

Kolinsky, Eva, *Women in West Germany. Life, Work and Politics* (Oxford, 1989).

Kolling, Hubert, ed., *'Wenn nur der Krieg bald zu Ende ist...'. Die Feldpostbriefe des Johann Theodor Schirra aus Illingen/Saar (1944–1945) nebst einer biographischen Skizze* (Illingen, 2001).

König, Rene, *Materialien zur Soziologie der Familie* (Bern, 1946).

König, Rene and Reuben Hill, eds, *Families in East and West. Socialisation Process and Kinship Ties* (Paris, 1970).

König, Rene, 'Family and Authority: The German Father in 1955', *The Sociological Review*, Vol. 5, No. 1, 1957–58, 107–127.

König, Rene and Rosemarie Nave-Herz, eds, *Familiensoziologie* (Opladen, 2002).

Koonz, Claudia, 'The Competition for a Women's Lebensraum, 1928–34' in Renate Bridenthal, Marion Kaplan and Atina Grossmann, eds, *When Biology Became Destiny. Women in Weimar and Nazi Germany* (New York, 1984), 199–236.

Koonz, Claudia, *Mothers in the Fatherland. Women, the Family and Nazi Politics* (London, 1986).

Kressel, Carsten, *Evakuierungen und Erweiterte Kinderlandverschickung im Vergleich. Das Beispiel der Städte Liverpool und Hamburg* (Frankfurt, 1996).

Kruse, Peter, ed., *Bomben, Trümmer, Lucky Strikes. Die Stunde Null in bisher unbekannten Manuskripten* (Berlin, 2004).

Kuhn, Annette and Jörn Rüsen, eds, *Frauen in der Geschichte* (Vol. III, Düsseldorf, 1983).

Kuhn, Annette and Anna-Elisabeth Freier, eds, *Frauen in der Geschichte V. 'Das Schicksal Deutschlands liegt in der Hand seiner Frauen.' Frauen in der deutschen Nachkriegsgeschichte* (Düsseldorf, 1984).

Kuhn, Annette, 'Power and Powerlessness: Women after 1945, or the Continuity of the Ideology of Femininity', *German History*, Vol. 7, No. 1, 1989, 35–46.

Kühne, Thomas, *Kameradschaft: Die Soldaten des nationalsozialistischen Krieges und das 20. Jahrhundert* (Göttingen, 2006).

Kundrus, Birthe, 'Geschlechterkriege. Der Erste Weltkrieg und die Deutung der Geschlechterverhältnisse in der Weimarer Republik' in Karen Hagemann and Stefanie Schüler-Springerum, eds, *Home/Front. The Military, War and Gender in Twentieth Century Germany* (Oxford, 2002), 171–187.

Kundrus, Birthe, 'Forbidden Company: Romantic Relationships between Germans and Foreigners, 1939 to 1945' in Damar Herzog, ed., *Sexuality and German Fascism* (Texas, 2005), 201–222.

Lakowski, Richard and Hans-Joachim Büll, *Ein Lebenszeichen! 1945. Feldpost zwischen Oder und Elbe* (Berlin, unpublished).

Lamprecht, Gerald, *Feldpost und Kriegserlebnis. Briefe als historisch-biographische Quelle* (Innsbruck, 2001).

Lange, Herta and Benedikt Burkard, eds, *'Abends wenn wir essen fehlt uns immer einer'. Kinder schreiben an die Väter, 1939–1945* (Tübingen, 2000).

Laslett, Peter and Richard Wall, *The Household and Family in Past Times* (Cambridge, 1969).

Latzel, Klaus, *Vom Sterben im Krieg. Wandlungen in der Einstellung zum Soldatentod vom siebenjährigen Krieg bis zum II. Weltkrieg* (Warendorf, 1988).

Latzel, Klaus, 'Die Zumutungen des Krieges und der Liebe – zwei Annäherungen an Feldpostbriefe' in Peter Knoch, ed., *Kriegsalltag. Die Rekonstruktion des Kriegsalltags als Aufgabe der historischen Forschung und der Friedenserziehung* (Stuttgart, 1989), 204–221.

Latzel, Klaus, *Deutsche Soldaten – Nationalsozialistischer Krieg? Kriegserlebnis, - Kriegserfahrung, 1939–1945* (Bielefeld, 1996).

Latzel, Klaus, 'Vom Kriegserlebnis zur Kriegserfahrung. Theoretische und methodische Überlegungen zur erfahrungsgeschichtlichen Untersuchung von Feldpostbriefen', *Militärgeschichtliche Mitteilungen*, Vol. 56, 1997, 1–30.

Latzel, Klaus, 'Wehrmachtsoldaten zwischen "Normalität" und NS-Ideologie, oder: Was sucht die Forschung in der Feldpost' in Rolf-Dieter Müller and Hans-Erich Volkmann, eds, *Die Wehrmacht. Mythos und Realität* (Munich, 1999), 573–588.

Latzel, Klaus, 'Der "Krieg von unten" in Soldatenbriefen', *Rhein-Reden. Texte aus der Melanchthon-Akademie Köln*, Vol. 2, 1999, 33–51.

Laub Coser, Rose, ed., *The Family. Its Structures and Functions* (2nd edition, London, 1974).

Leh, Almut and Alexander von Plato, *Ein unglaublicher Frühling. Erfahrene Geschichte im Nachkriegsdeutschland, 1945–48* (Bonn, 1997).

Lehmann, Albrecht, *Gefangenschaft und Heimkehr. Deutsche Kriegsgefangene in der Sowjetunion* (Munich, 1986).

Lehmann, Albrecht, 'Die Kriegsgefangenen', *Aus Politik und Zeitgeschichte*, Vol. 7–8, 1995, 13–19.

Lindner, Ulrike, 'Rationalisierungsdiskurse und Aushandlungsprozesse. Der moderne Haushalt und die traditionelle Hausfrauenrolle in den 1960er Jahren' in Matthias Frese, Julia Paulus and Karl Teppe, eds, *Demokratisierung und gesellschaftlicher Aufbruch. Die sechziger Jahre als Wendezeit der Bundesrepublik* (Paderborn, 2003), 83–106.

Lipp, Christine, ed., *Kindheit und Krieg* (Frankfurt am Main, 1992).

Loehlin, Jennifer A., *From Rags to Riches. Housework, Consumption and Modernity in Germany* (Oxford, 1999).

Lohalm, Uwe, 'Für eine leistungsbereite und "erbgesunde" Volksgemein schaft Selektive Erwerbslosen-und Familienpolitik' in Forschungsstelle für Zeitgeschichte in Hamburg, ed., *Hamburg im 'Dritten Reich'* (Göttingen, 2005), 379–431.

Löhr, Brigitte and Rita Meyhöfer, 'Wandel in Ehe und Familie' in Lutz Niethammer, ed., *Bürgerliche Gesellschaft in Deutschland. Historische Einblicke, Fragen, Perspektiven* (Frankfurt, 1990), 601–611.

Lott, Sylvia, *Die Frauenzeitschriften von Hans Huffzky und John Jahr. Zur Geschichte der deutschen Frauenzeitschriften zwischen 1933 und 1970* (Berlin, 1985).

Löwenthal, Richard and Patrik von zur Mühlen, *Widerstand und Verweigerung in Deutschland 1933 bis 1945* (Berlin, 1982).

Löwenthal, Richard, 'Widerstand im totalen Staat' in Richard Löwenthal and Patrik von zur Mühlen, *Widerstand und Verweigerung in Deutschland 1933 bis 1945* (Berlin, 1982), 11–24.

Lüdtke, Alf, "Formiergung der Massen" oder: Mitmachen und Hinnehmen? "Alltagsgeschichte" und Faschismusanalyse' in Heide Gerstenberer and Dorothea Schmidt, eds, *Normalität oder Normalisierung? Geschichtswerkstätten und Faschismusanalyse* (Münster, 1987), 15–34.

Lüdtke, Alf, ed., *The History of Everyday Life. Reconstructing Historical Experiences and Ways of Life* (Trans. William Templer, Princeton, 1995).

Lüdtke, Alf, 'What Is the History of Everyday Life and Who Are Its Practitioners?' in Alf Lüdtke, ed., *The History of Everyday Life. Reconstructing Historical Experiences and Ways of Life* (Trans. William Templer, Princeton, 1995), 3–40.

Lukas, Richard C., *Did the Children Cry? Hitler's War against Jewish and Polish Children, 1939–1945* (New York, 1994).

Lutz, Catherine A. and Lila Abu-Lughod, eds, *Language and the Politics of Emotion* (Cambridge, 1990).

Macardle, Dorothy, *Children of Europe. A Study of the Children of Liberated Countries: Their Wartime Experiences, Their Reactions, and Their Needs, with a Note on Germany* (London, 1949).

Manoschek, Walter, *Die Wehrmacht im Rassenkrieg: Der Vernichtungskrieg hinter der Front* (Vienna, 1996).

Martel, Gordon, ed., *Modern Germany Reconsidered, 1870–1945* (London, 1992).

Marten, James, ed., *Children and War. A Historical Anthology* (New York, 2002).

Marwick, Arthur, Clive Emsley and Wendy Simpson, eds, *Total War and Historical Change: Europe 1914–1955* (Philadelphia, 2001).

Marwick, Arthur, *The Deluge. British Society and the First World War* (2nd edition, London, 1991).

Mason, Timothy, *Social Policy in the Third Reich: The Working Class and the National Community*, Jane Caplan, ed. (Oxford, 1993).

Matschenz, Andreas, 'Der Onkel da ist Dein Vater'. Die Heimkehr der Kriegsgefangenen nach Berlin bis 1948 in Annette Kaminsky, ed., *Heimkehr 1948* (Munich, 1998), 117–140.

Mazower, Mark, ed., *After the War was Over. Reconstructing the Family, Nation and State in Greece, 1943–1960* (Oxford, 2000).

Meade, Teresa A. and Merry E. Wiesner-Hanks, eds, *A Companion to Gender History* (Oxford, 2004).

Medick, Hans and David. W. Sabean, eds, *Emotionen und materielle Interessen* (Göttingen, 1984).

Merritt, Richard and Anna, *Public Opinion in Occupied Germany* (Illinois, 1970).

Merritt, Richard, *Democracy Imposed* (Yale, 1996).

Meyer, Sibylle and Eva Schulze, eds, *'Wie wir das alles geschafft haben': Alleinstehende Frauen berichten über ihr Leben nach 1945* (Munich, 1984).

Meyer, Sibylle and Eva Schulze, eds, *'Von Liebe Sprach Damals Keiner': Familienalltag in der Nachkriegszeit* (Munich, 1985).

Meyer, Sibylle and Eva Schulze, ' "Als wir wieder zusammen waren, ging der Krieg im Kleinen weiter": Frauen, Männer und Familien in Berlin der vierziger Jahre' in Lutz Niethammer and Alexander von Plato, eds, *'Wir kriegen jetzt andere Zeiten': Auf der Suche nach der Erfahrung des Volkes in nachfaschistischen Ländern* (Bonn, 1985), 305–326.

Meyer, Sibylle and Eva Schulze, 'Krieg im Frieden. Veränderungen des Geschlechterverhältnisses untersucht am Beispiel familiärer Konflikte nach 1945' in Klaus Bergmann, Annette Kuhn, Jörn Rüsen and Gerhard Schneider, eds, *Frauenmacht in der Geschichte. Beiträge des Historikerinnentreffens 1985 zur Frauengeschichtsforschung* (Düsseldorf, 1986), 184–193.

Meyer-Lenz, Johanna, ed., *Die Ordnung des Paares ist unbehaglich. Irritationen am und im Geschlechterdiskurs nach 1945* (Hamburg, 2000).

Meyer-Lenz, Johanna, 'Interview mit Karin C. "Weil ich immer gegen meinen Vater gekämpft hab, und heute ja immer noch!" ' in Johanna Meyer-Lenz, ed., *Die Ordnung des Paares ist unbehaglich. Irritationen am und im Geschlechterdiskurs nach 1945* (Hamburg, 2000), 357–424.

Michalka, Wolfgang, *Das Dritte Reich. Dokumente zur Innen- und Aussenpolitik. Band 2. Weltmachtanspruch und nationaler Zusammenbruch 1939–1945* (München, 1985).

Mierzejweski, Alfred C., *Hitler's Trains: The German National Railway in the Third Reich* (Stroud, 2005).

Militärgeschichtlichen Forschungsamt, eds, *Das Deutsche Reich und der Zweite Weltkrieg*, Vol. 5, No. 1, *Organisation und Mobilisierung des Deutschen Machtbereichts* (Stuttgart, 1988).

Miller, John, 'Dangerous Women and Naughty Girls: Fraternization and the American Occupation of Germany, 1945–47,' in *Women's and Gender History Symposium* (Illinois, 2003), 1–7.

Minnaard, Gerard and Werner Steinbrecher, eds, *Eine Kiste im Keller. Das Schicksal eines 'guten' deutschen Soldaten im Zweiten Weltkrieg – eine künstlerische und theologische Verarbeitung* (Knesebeck, 2002).

Mitscherlich, Alexander, *Society without the Father* (Trans. E. Mosbacher, London, 1969).

Mitterauer, Michael and Reinhard Sieder, eds, *The European Family* (Trans. Karla Oosterveen and Manfred Hoerzinger, Oxford, 1982).

Mitterauer, Michael, 'The Family as an Historical Social Form' in Michael Mitterauer and Reinhard Sieder, *The European Family* (Trans. Karla Oosterveen and Manfred Hörzinger, Oxford, 1982), 1–23.

Mitterauer, Michael, 'The Myth of the Large Pre-industrial Family' in Michael Mitterauer and Reinhard Sieder, *The European Family* (Trans. Karla Oosterveen and Manfred Hoerzinger, Oxford, 1982), 24–47.

Mitterauer, Michael, *A History of Youth* (Frankfurt, 1986).

Mitterauer, Michael, *The European Family* (Trans. Karla Oosterveen and Manfred Hoerzinger, Munich, 2003).

Möding, Nori, 'Die Stunde der Frauen?' in Martin Broszat, Klaus-Dietmar Henk and Hans Woller, eds, *Von Stalingrad zur Währungsreform. Zur Sozialgeschichte des Umbruchs in Deutschland* (Munich,1988), 619–648.

Moeller, Robert G., *Protecting Motherhood. Women and the Family in the Politics of Postwar West Germany* (Oxford, 1993).

Moeller, Robert G., ed., *West Germany under Construction* (Michigan, 1997).

Moeller, Robert G., '"The Last Soldiers of the Great War" and Tales of Family Reunions in the Federal Republic of Germany', *Signs*, Vol. 24, No. 1, 1998, 126–46.

Moeller, Robert G., *War Stories. The Search for a Useable Past in the Federal Republic of Germany* (Berkeley, 2001).

Moeller, Robert G., 'The Politics of the Past in the 1950s: Rhetorics of Victimization in East and West Germany' in Bill Niven, ed., *Germans as Victims. Remembering the Past in Contemporary Germany* (London, 2006), 26–42.

Moller, Sabine, Karoline Tschuggnall and Harald Welzer, eds, *Opa war kein Nazi. Nationalsozialismus und Holocaust im Familiengedächtnis* (Frankfurt, 2002).

Mooser, Josef, *Arbeiterleben in Deutschland 1900–1970: Klassenlagen, Kultur und Politik* (Frankfurt, 1984).

Mosse, George L., *Nazi Culture. Intellectual, Cultural and Social Life in the Third Reich* (London, 1966).

Mouton, Michelle, *From Nurturing the Nation to Purifying the Volk. Weimar and Nazi Family Policy, 1918–1945* (Cambridge, 2007).

Mühlen, Patrik von zur, 'Sozialdemokraten gegen Hitler' in Richard Löwenthal and Patrik von zur Mühlen, eds, *Widerstand und Verweigerung in Deutschland 1933 bis 1945* (Berlin, 1982), 57–75.

Müller, Sven Oliver, 'Nationalismus in der deutschen Kriegsgesellschaft' in Jörg Echternkamp, ed., *Die Deutsche Kriegsgesellschaft 1939 bis 1945* (Vol. II, Munich, 2005).

Müller, Rolf Dieter, ed., *Das Deutsche Reich und der Zweite Weltkrieg* (Vol. 10/2, Munich, 2008).

Müller, Rolf Dieter, 'Der Zusammenbruch des Wirtschaftslebens und die Anfänge des Wiederaufbaus' in Rolf Dieter Müller, ed., *Das Deutsche Reich und der Zweite Weltkrieg* (Vol. 10/2, Munich, 2008), 55–200.

Naimark, Norman, *The Russians in Germany. A History of the Soviet Zone of Occupation, 1945–1949* (Harvard, 1995).

Nanda Anshen, Ruth, ed., *The Family: Its Function and Destiny* (New York, 1949).

Narr, Wolf-Dieter and Dietrich Thränhardt, eds, *Die Bundesrepublik Deutschland. Entstehung-Entwicklung-Struktur* (Königstein, 1979).

Naumann, Klaus, ed., *Nachkrieg in Deutschland* (Hamburg, 2001).

Neumann, Vera, *Nicht der Rede Wert. Die Privatisierung der Kriegsfolgen in der frühen Bundesrepublik* (Münster, 1999).

Newton, Judith L., Mary P. Ryan and Judith R. Walkowitz, *Sex and Class in Women's History* (London, 1983)

Nieden, Susanne zur, *Alltag im Ausnahmezustand. Frauentagebücher im zerstörten Deutschland 1943 bis 1945* (Berlin, 1993).

Niehuss, Merith, 'Kontinuität und Wandel der Familie in den 50er Jahren' in Axel Schildt and Arnold Sywottek, eds, *Modernisierung im Wiederaufbau. Die westdeutsche Gesellschaft der 50er Jahre* (Bonn, 1993), 316–334.

Niehuss, Merith, *Familie, Frau und Gesellschaft. Studien zur Strukturgeschichte der Familie in Westdeutschland 1945–1950* (Göttingen, 2001).

Niethammer, Lutz, ed., *Lebenserfahrung und kollektives Gedächtnis. Die Praxis der Oral History* (Frankfurt, 1980).

Niethammer, Lutz, 'Privat-Wirtschaft. Erinnerungsfragmente einer anderen Umerziehung', in Lutz Niethammer, ed., *'Hinterher merkt man, dass es richtig war, dass es schiefgegangen ist ': Nachkriegs-Erfahrungen im Ruhrgebiet* (Vol. II, Bonn, 1983).

Niethammer, Lutz and Alexander von Plato, eds, *'Wir kriegen jetzt andere Zeiten': Auf der Suche nach der Erfahrung des Volkes in nachfaschistischen Ländern* (Bonn, 1985).

Niethammer, Lutz, 'War die bürgerliche Gesellschaft in Deutschland 1945 am Ende oder am Anfang?' in Lutz Niethammer, ed., *Bürgerliche Gesellschaft in Deutschland. Historische Einblicke, Fragen, Perspektiven* (Frankfurt, 1990), 515–532.

Niethammer, Lutz, ed., *Bürgerliche Gesellschaft in Deutschland. Historische Einblicke, Fragen, Perspektiven* (Frankfurt, 1990).

Niethammer, Lutz, *Ego-Histoire? Und andere Erinnerungs-Versuche* (Cologne, 2002).

Niven, Bill, ed., *Germans as Victims. Remembering the Past in Contemporary Germany* (London, 2006).

Noelle, Elisabeth and Erich Peter Neumann, *Jahrbuch der öffentlichen Meinung* (Allensbach am Bodensee, 1957) .

Noakes, Jeremy, 'Social outcasts in the Third Reich' in Richard Bessel, ed., *Life in the Third Reich* (Oxford, 2001), 83–96.

Nussbaum, Martha C., *Upheavals of Thought. The Intelligence of Emotions* (Cambridge, 2001).

Oatley, Keith and Jennifer M. Jenkins, *Understanding Emotions* (Oxford, 1996).

Oatley, Keith, *Emotions: A Brief History* (Toronto, 2004).

Oertzen, Christine von, *The Pleasure of a Surplus Income. Part-Time Work, Gender Politics, and Social Change in West Germany, 1955–1969* (London, 2007).

Orgel-Purper, Liselotte, *Willst Du meine Witwe werden? Eine deutsche Liebe im Krieg* (Berlin, 1995).

Ötzina, Dieter, Werner Abelshauser and Anselm Faust, *Sozialgeschichtliches Arbeitsbuch III. Materialien zur Statistik des Deutschen Reiches 1914–1945* (Munich, 1978).

Overmans, Rüdiger, *Deutsche militärische Verluste im Zweiten Weltkrieg* (Munich, 1999).

Overmans, Rüdiger, *Soldaten hinter Stacheldraht. Deutsche Kriegsgefangene des Zweiten Weltkrieges* (Munich, 2002).

Overmans, Rüdiger, 'Das Schicksal der deutschen Kriegsgefangenen des Zweiten Weltkriegs' in Dieter Müller, ed., *Das Deutsche Reich und der Zweite Weltkrieg* (Vol. 10/2, Munich, 2008), 379–508.

Overy, Richard, *The Penguin Historical Atlas of the Third Reich* (London, 1996).

Owings, Alison, *Frauen: German Women Recall the Third Reich* (New Brunswick, 1993).

Padover, Saul. K., *Psychologist in Germany. The Story of an American Intelligence Officer* (London, 1946).

Peukert, Detlev J.K., *Volksgenossen und Gemeinschaftsfremde. Anpassung, Ausmeize und Aufbegehren unter dem Nationalsozialismus* (Cologne, 1982).

Peukert, Detlev J.K., *Inside Nazi Germany. Conformity, Opposition and Racism in Everyday Life* (Trans. Richard Deveson, London, 1989).

Peukert, Detlev J.K., *The Weimar Republic* (Trans. Richard Deveson, 2nd edition, London, 1993).

Peukert, Detlev J.K., 'Youth in the Third Reich' in Richard Bessel, ed., *Life in the Third Reich* (2nd edition, Oxford, 2001), 25–40.

Pfeil, Elisabeth, *Der Flüchtling* (Hamburg, 1949).

Pine, Lisa, *Nazi Family Policy, 1933–1945* (Oxford, 1999).

Pine, Lisa, 'Women and the Family', in Sheilagh Ogilvie and Richard Overy, eds, *Germany. A New Social and Economic History* (Vol. III, London, 2003).

Poewe, Karla, *Childhood in Germany During World War II* (New York, 1988).

Polm, Rita, *'Neben dem Mann die andere Hälfte eines Ganzen zu sein?!' Frauen in der Nachkriegszeit* (Münster, 1990).

Poiger, Uta G., 'A New "Western" Hero? Reconstructing German Masculinity in the 1950s', *Signs*, Vol. 24, No. 1, 1998, 147–162.

Poiger, Uta G., 'Krise der Männlichkeit. Remaskulinisierung in beiden deutschen Nachkriegsgesellschaften' in Klaus Naumann, ed., *Nachkrieg in Deutschland* (Hamburg, 2001), 227–266.

Pollock, Linda, *Forgotten Children: Parent-Child Relations from 1500-1900* (Cambridge, 1983).

Powell, Anthony, *Last Letters from Stalingrad* (London, 1956).

Prost, Antoine and Gerard Vincent, eds, *A History of Private Life* (Harvard, 1991).

Rabb, Theodore K. and Robert I. Rotberg, eds, *The Family in History. Interdisciplinary Essays* (London, 1971).

Rahden, Til van, Demokratie und väterliche Autorität. Das Karlsruher 'Stichentscheid' – Urteil von 1959 in der politischen Kultur der frühen Bundesrepublik, *Zeithistorische Forschungen/Studies in Contemporary History*, 2, 2005, 160–179.

Rainer, Tristine, *The New Diary. How to Use a Journal for Self-guidance and Expanded Creativity* (London, 1980).

Ranke, Winfried, Carola Jüllig, Jürgen Reiche and Dieter Vorsteher, eds, *Kultur, Pajoks und Care-Pakete. Eine Berliner Chronik 1945–1949* (Berlin, 1990).

Rapp, Rayna, Ellen Ross and Renate Bridenthal, 'Examining Family History' in Judith L. Newton, Mary P. Ryan and Judith R. Walkowitz, eds, *Sex and Class in Women's History* (London, 1983), 232–258.

Rass, Christoph, *'Menschenmaterial': Deutsche Soldaten an der Ostfront. Innenansichten einer Infanteriedivision 1939–1945* (Paderborn, 2003).

Rauschenbach, Brigitte, ed., *Erinnern, Wiederholen, Durcharbeiten. Zur Psycho-Analyse deutschen Wenden* (Berlin, 1992).

Recke, Marie-Luise, *Nationalsozialistische Sozialpolitik im Zweiten Weltkrieg* (Munich, 1985).

Reddy, William M., *The Navigation of Feeling. A Framework for the History of Emotions* (Cambridge, 2001).

Reddy, William M., *The Invisible Code. Honor and Sentiment in Postrevolutionary France, 1814–1848* (California, 1997).

Redding, Kimberly A., *Growing Up in Hitler's Shadow. Remembering Youth in Postwar Berlin* (London, 2004).

Reese, Dagmar, *Straff, aber nicht stramm – herb, aber nicht derb. Zur Vergesellschaftung von Mädchen durch den Bund Deutscher Mädel im sozialkulturellen Vergleich zweier Milieus* (Basel, 1989).

Reese, Dagmar, *Growing Up Female in Nazi Germany* (4th edition, Michigan, 2009).

Reulecke, Jürgen, *Rückkehr in die Ferne. Die deutsche Jugend in der Nachkriegszeit und das Ausland* (Munich, 1997).

Reulecke, Jürgen, *'Ich möchte so einer werden wie die'...Männerbünde im 20. Jahrhundert* (Frankfurt, 2001).

Ritter, Gerhard A., 'Continuity and Change. Political and Social Developments in Germany after 1945 and 1989/90' (Annual Lecture, German Historical Institute, London, 1999).

Roberts, Ulla, *Starke Mütter – ferne Väter. Über Kriegs- und Nachkriegskindheit einer Töchtergeneration* (Frankfurt, 1994).

Rodnick, David, *Postwar Germans* (Yale, 1948).

Roper, Lyndal, *Oedipus and the Devil* (London, 1994).

Roper, Michael, *Secret Battle: Emotional Survival in the Great War* (Manchester, 2009).

Roseman, Mark, 'World War II and Social Change in Germany' in Arthur Marwick, Clive Emsley and Wendy Simpson, eds, *Total War and Historical Change: Europe 1914–1945* (Philadelphia, 2001), 238–254.

Rosenbaum, Heidi, *Familie als Gegenstruktur zur Gesellschaft. Kritik grundlegender theoretischer Ansätze der westdeutschen Familiensoziologie* (Stuttgart, 1978).

Rosenbaum, Heidi, *Formen der Familie. Untersuchungen zum Zusammenhang von Familienverhältnissen, Sozialstruktur und sozialem Wandel in der deutschen Gesellschaft des 19. Jahrhunderts* (Frankfurt, 1982).

Rosenbaum, Heidi, *Proletarische Familien. Arbeiterfamilien und Arbeiterväter im frühen 20. Jahrhundert zwischen traditioneller, sozialdemokratischer und kleinbürgerlicher Orientierung* (Frankfurt, 1992).

Rosenberg, Charles E., ed., *The Family in History* (Pennsylvania, 1975).

Rosenberg., Charles E., 'History and Experience' in Charles E. Rosenberg, ed., *The Family in History* (Pennsylvania, 1975), 1–11.

Rosenhaft, Eve and Robert Lee, 'Introduction', *German History*, Vol. 7, No. 1, 1989, 1–4.

Rosenhaft, Eve, 'Women in Modern Germany' in Gordon Martel, ed., *Modern Germany Reconsidered, 1870-1945* (London, 1992), 140–158.

Rosenthal, Gabriele, ed., *'Als der Krieg kam, hatte ich mit Hitler nichts mehr zu tun'. Zur Gegenwärtigkeit des Dritten Reichs in Biographien* (Opladen, 1990).

Rosenwein, Barbara, 'Worrying about Emotions in History', *American Historical Review*, Vol. 107, No. 3, 2002, 821–845.

Rosenwein, Barbara H., *Emotional Communities in the Early Middle Ages* (Cornell, 2006).

Rottenberger, Karl-Heinz, *Die Hungerjahre nach dem Zweiten Weltkrieg. Ernährungs- und Landwirtschaft in Rheinland-Pfalz 1945–1950* (Boppard am Rhein, 1980).

Ruhl, Klaus-Jörg, ed., *Deutschland 1945. Alltag zwischen Krieg und Frieden in Berichten. Dokumenten und Bildern* (Darmstadt, 1984).

Ruhl, Klaus-Jörg, *Frauen in der Nachkriegszeit, 1945–1963* (Munich, 1988).

Ruhl, Klaus-Jörg, *Verordnete Unterordnung. Berufstätige Frauen zwischen Wirtschaftswachstum und konservativer Ideologie in der Nachkriegszeit 1945–1963* (Munich, 1994).

Rupp, Leila J., *Mobilizing Women for War; German and American Propaganda 1939–45* (Princeton, 1978).

Rusinek, Bernd, *Gesellschaft in Katastrophe. Terror. Illegalität. Widerstand. Köln 1944/45* (Essen, 1989).

Sabean, David Warren and Hans Medick, eds, *Interest and Emotion. Essays on the Study of Family and Kinship* (Cambridge, 1984).

Sabean, David Warren and Hans Medick, 'Interest and Emotion in Family and Kinship Studies: A Critique of Social History and Anthropology' in Hans Medick and David Warren Sabean, eds, *Interest and Emotion. Essays on the Study of Family and Kinship* (Cambridge, 1984), 9–27.

Sachse, Carola, *Industrial Housewives: Women's Social Work in the Factories of Nazi Germany* (London, 1987).

Saldern, Adelheid von, 'Victims or Perpetrators? Controversies about the Role of Women in the Nazi State' in David F. Crew, ed., *Nazism and German Society, 1933–1945* (New York, 1994), 141–165.

Samuel, Raphael, ed., *Village Life and Labour* (London, 1975).

Samuels, Diane, *Kindertransport* (London, 1992).

Sander, Helke and Barbara Johr, eds, *Befreier und Befreite: Krieg, Vergewaltigung, Kinder* (Frankfurt, 1995).

Sandland, Dianne, *Time to Write to Yourself. A Guide to Journaling for Emotional Health and Self-development* (London, 2007).

Sauermann, Elisabeth and Christa Halatscheff, *Zum Nachdenken blieb keine Zeit: Frauen in Lippe nach dem Zweiten Weltkrieg* (Bielefeld, 1995).

Schelsky, Helmut, 'The Family in Germany', *Marriage and Family Living*, Vol. 16, No. 4, 1954, 331–335.

Schelsky, Helmut, *Wandlungen der Deutschen Familie in der Gegenwart* (Stuttgart, 1955).

Scherer, Alice and Robert, and Julius Dorreich, eds, *Ehe und Familie. Grundsätze, Bestand und Fördernde Massnahmen* (Freiburg, 1956).

Schikorsky, Isa, 'Kommunikation über das Unbeschreibbare. Beobachtungen zum Sprachstil von Kriegsbriefen' in Heinz Röllecke, ed., *Wirkendes Wort*, Vol. 42. No. 2, 1992, 295–315.

Schildt, Axel and Arnold Sywottek, *Modernisierung im Wiederaufbau. Die westdeutsche Gesellschaft der 50er Jahre* (Bonn, 1993).

Schildt, Axel, 'Jenseits der Politik? Aspekte des Alltags' in Forschungsstelle für Zeitgeschichte in Hamburg, ed., *Hamburg im 'Dritten Reich'* (Göttingen, 2005), 249–304.

Schissler, Hanna, ed., *The Miracle Years. A Cultural History of West Germany, 1949–1968* (Princeton, 2001).

Schiwy, Marlene A., *A Voice of Her Own. Women and the Journal Writing Journey* (New York, 1996).

Schleberger, Horst, ed., *Kriegsbriefe eines jungen Lehrers 1941–1945* (Pössneck, 2004).

Schmiechen-Ackermann, Detlef, ed., *Anpassung, Verweigerung, Widerstand: Soziale Milieus, Politische Kultur und der Widerstand gegen den NS in Deutschland im regionalen Verleich* (Berlin, 1997).

Schmitz-Koster, Dorothee, *Der Krieg meines Vaters. Als deutscher Soldat in Norwegen* (Berlin, 2004).

Schmuhl, Hans-Walter, *Rassenhygience, Nationalsozialismus, Euthanasie* (Göttingen, 1987).

Schoenbaum, David, *Hitler's Social Revolution: Class and Status in Nazi Germany 1933–1939* (New York, 1980).

Schöttler, Peter, 'Mentalities, Ideologies, Discourses on the "Third Level" as a Theme in Social-historical Research' in Alf Lüdtke, ed., *The History of Everyday Life. Reconstructing Historical Experiences and Ways of Life* (Trans. William Templer, Princeton, 1995), 72–115.

Schubert, Doris and Annette Kuhn, *Frauen in der deutschen Nachkriegszeit. Band 1. Frauenarbeit 1945-1949* (Düsseldorf, 1984).

Schulze, Rainer, 'Growing Discontent: Relations between Native and Refugee Populations in a Rural District in Western Germany after the Second World War' in Robert G. Moeller, ed., *West Germany under Construction* (Michigan, 1997), 53–72.

Schumann, Frank, ed., *'Zieh dich warm an!' Soldatenpost und Heimatbriefe aus zwei Weltkriegen* (Berlin, 1989).

Schütze, Yvonne and Dieter Geulen, 'Die "Nachkriegskinder" und die "Konsumkinder". Kindheitsverläufe zweier Generationen' in Ulf Preuss-Lausitz and Peter Büchner, eds, *Kriegskinder, Konsumkinder, Krisenkinder. Zur Sozialisationsgeschichte seit dem Zweiten Weltkrieg* (Basel, 1983), 29–52.

Schwarz, Angela, 'Mit dem grösstmöglichen Anstand weitermachen. Briefe britische Kriegsteilnehmer und ihrer Angehörigen im Zweiten Weltkrieg' in Wolfram Wette und Detlev Vogel, eds, *Andere Helme, Andere Menschen? Heimaterfahrung und Frontalltag im Zweiten Weltkrieg. Ein internationaler Vergleich* (Stuttgart, 1995), 205–236.

Scott, Joan W., 'Experience' in Judith Butler and Joan W. Scott, eds, *Feminists Theorize the Political* (London, 1992), 22–40.

Scott, Joan W., 'The Tipp of the Volcano', *Comparative Studies in Society and History*, Vol. 35, 1993, 438–443.

Scott, Joan W., 'Gender: A Useful Category of Historical Analysis', *The American Historical Review*, Vol. 91, No. 5, 1986, 1053–1075.

Seeler, Angela, 'Ehe, Familie und andere Lebensformen in den Nachkriegsjahren' in Annette Kuhn and Anna-Elisabeth Freier, eds, *Frauen in der Geschichte V. 'Das Schicksal Deutschlands liegt in der Hand seiner Frauen.' Frauen in der deutschen Nachkriegsgeschichte.* (Düsseldorf, 1984), 90–111.

Semmens, Kristin, *Seeing Hitler's Germany* (New York, 2005).

Seward, Georgene H. and Robert C. Williamson, eds, *Sex Roles in Changing Society* (New York, 1970).

Sheridan Allen, William, *The Nazi Seizure of Power. The Experience of a Single German Town 1922–1945* (London, 1965).

Sichrovsky, Peter, *Born Guilty. Children of Nazi Families* (Trans. J. Steinberg, Cologne, 1987).

Sieder, Reinhard, *Sozialgeschichte der Familie* (Frankfurt, 1987).

Simons, George F., *Keeping Your Personal Journal* (New York, 1978).

Stargardt, Nicholas, 'German Childhoods: The Making of a Historiography', *German History*, Vol. 16, No. 1, 1998, 1–15.

Stargardt, Nicholas, *Witnesses of War. Children's Lives under the Nazis* (London, 2005).

Stargardt, Nicholas, 'Jeux de guerre. Les enfants sous le régime nazi' in *Vingtieme Siecle, Revue d'Histoire*, Vol. 89, No.1, 2006, 61–76.

Stargardt, Nicholas, 'The *Historikerstreit* Twenty Years On', *German History*, Vol. 24, No. 4, 2006, 587–607.

Stargardt, Nicholas, 'A German Trauma', *Schweizerische Zeitschrift für Geschichte*, Vol. 57, No. 1, 2007, 85–98.

Stearns, Carol and Peter, 'Emotionology: Clarifying the History of Emotions and Emotional Standards', *American Historical Review*, Vol. 90, No. 4, 1985, 813–836.

Stearns, Carol and Peter, *Anger: The Struggle for Emotional Control in America's History* (New York, 1989).

Steege, Paul, *Black Market, Cold War. Everyday Life in Berlin, 1946–1949* (Cambridge, 2007).

Stehmann, Siegbert and Gerhard Sprenger, eds, *'Die Bitternis verschweigen wir.' Feldpostbriefe 1940–1945* (Hannover, 1992).

Steinert, Marlis G., *Hitlers Krieg und die Deutschen. Stimmung und Haltung der deutschen Bevölkerung im Zweiten Weltkrieg* (Düsseldorf, 1970).

Steinhoff, Johannes, Peter Pechel and Dennis Showalter, eds, *Voices from the Third Reich. An Oral History* (London, 1991).

Stephenson, Jill, *Women in Nazi Society* (London, 1975).

Stephenson, Jill, 'Women, Motherhood and the Family in the Third Reich' in Michael Burleigh, ed., *Confronting the Nazi Past. New Debates on Modern German History* (London, 1996), 167–183.

Stephenson, Jill, *Women in Nazi Germany* (London, 2001).

Stephenson, Jill, *Hitler's Home Front. Württemberg under the Nazis* (London, 2006).

Stibbe, Matthew, *Women in the Third Reich* (Oxford, 2003).

Stierlin, Helm, 'The Dialogue between the Generations about the Nazi Era' in Barbara Heimannsberg and Carl J. Schmidt, eds, *The Collective Silence. German Identity and the Legacy of Shame* (Trans. C. Oudejans Harris and G. Wheeler, San Francisco, 1993), 143–161.

Stiftung Stadtmuseum Berlin, ed., *Berliner Kindheit zwischen 1945 und 2005* (Stiftung Stadtmuseum Berlin, 2005).

Stolper, Gustav, *German Realities* (New York, 1948).

Stolper, Gustav, Karl Häuser and Knut Borchardt, eds, *The German Economy 1870 to the Present* (New York, 1967).

Stone, Lawrence, 'The Rise of the Nuclear Family' in Charles E. Rosenberg, ed., *The Family in History* (Pennsylvania, 1975), 13–57.

Stone, Lawrence, *The Family Sex and Marriage in England, 1500–1800* (Oxford, 1977).

Summerfield, Penny, *Reconstructing Women's Wartime Lives. Discourse and Subjectivity in Oral Histories of the Second World War* (New York, 1998).

Szodrzynski, Joachim, 'Die "Heimatfront" zwischen Stalingrad und Kriegsende' in Forschungsstelle für Zeitgeschichte in Hamburg, ed., *Hamburg im 'Dritten Reich'* (Göttingen, 2005), 633–685.

Thamer, Hans-Ulrich, 'Es wird alles ganz verwandelt sein' in Jörg Echternkamp, ed., *Die Deutsche Kriegsgesellschaft 1939 bis 1945* (Vol. II, Munich, 2005).

Thane, Pat, 'Family Life and "Normality" in Postwar British Culture' in Richard Bessel and Dirk Schumann, eds, *Life after Death. Approaches to a*

Cultural and Social History of Europe during the 1940s and 1950s (Cambridge, 2003), 193–210.

Thurnwald, Hilde, *Gegenwartsprobleme Berliner Familien. Eine soziologische Untersuchung an 498 Familien* (Berlin, 1948).

Tooze, Adam, *The Wages of Destruction. The Making and Breaking of the Nazi Economy* (London, 2006).

Townsend, Colin and Eileen, *War Wives. A Second World War Anthology* (London, 1989).

Trampe, Gustav, ed., *Die Stunde Null* (Reinbek, 1986).

Trees, Wolfgang, Charles Whiting and Thomas Omansen, eds, *Drei Jahre nach Null. Geschichte der britischen Besatzungszone 1945–1948* (Düsseldorf, 1978).

Trevor-Roper, Hugh, ed., *Hitler's Table Talk 1941–44: His Private Conversations* (London 1953).

Tyrell, Hartmann, 'Helmut Schelsky's Familiensoziologie' in Horst Baier ed., *Helmut Schelsky – ein Soziologe in der Bundesrepublik. Ein Gedächtnisschrift von Freunden, Kollegen und Schülern* (Stuttgart, 1986).

Vogel, Detlev, '"...aber man muss halt gehen, und wenn es in den Tod ist." Kleine Leute und der deutsche Kriegsalltag im Spiegel von Feldpostbriefen' in Wolfram Wette and Detlev Vogel, eds, *Andere Helme, Andere Menschen? Heimaterfahrung und Frontalltag im Zweiten Weltkrieg. Ein internationaler Vergleich* (Stuttgart, 1995), 37–58.

Volkmann, Hans-Erich, *Ende des Dritten Reiches – Ende des Zweiten Weltkriegs. Eine perspektivische Rückschau. Im Auftrag des Militärgeschichtlichen Forschungsamtes* (Munich, 1995).

Wachsmann, Nikolaus, *Hitler's Prisons. Legal Terror in Nazi Germany* (Yale, 2004).

Waller, Jane and Michael Vaughan-Rees, *Women in Wartime. The Role of Women's Magazines, 1939-1945* (London, 1987).

Weber, Hermann, 'Die KPD in der Illegalität' in Richard Löwenthal and Patrik von zur Mühlen, eds, *Widerstand und Verweigerung in Deutschland 1933 bis 1945* (Berlin, 1982), 83–101.

Weber-Kellerman, Ingeborg, *Die Deutsche Familie: Versuch einer Sozialgeschichte* (Frankfurt am Main, 1974).

Weber-Kellerman, Ingeborg, 'The German Family' in Antoine Prost and Gerard Vincent, eds, *A History of Private Life* (Harvard, 1991), 503–537.

Wehler, Hans-Ulrich, *Deutsche Gesellschaftsgeschichte. Vierter Band. Vom Beginn des Ersten Weltkriegs bis zur Gründung der beiden deutschen Staaten 1914–1949* (Munich, 2003).

Wehr, Laura, *Kamerad Frau? Eine Frauenzeitschrift im Nationalsozialismus* (Regensburg, 2002).

Welzer, Harald, ed., *Nationalsozialismus und Moderne* (Tübingen, 1993).

Welzer, Harald, Robert Montau and Christine Plass, eds, *'Was wir für böse Mensche sind.' Der Nationalsozialismus im Gespräch zwischen den Generationen* (Tübingen, 1997).

Welzer, Harald, ed., *Auf der Trümmern der Geschichte. Gespräche mit Raul Hilberg, Hans Mommsen und Zygmunt Baumann* (Tübingen, 1999).

Wendel, Else, *Hausfrau at War. A German Woman's Account of Life in Hitler's Reich* (London, 1957).

Wengst, Ugo, ed., *Geschichte der Sozialpolitik in Deutschland seit 1945* (Vol. 2/1, Munich, 2001).

Werner, Emmy E., *Through the Eyes of Innocents* (Oxford, 2000).

Westernhagen, Dörte von, ed., *Die Kinder der Täter. Das Dritte Reich und die Generation danach* (Munich, 1987).

Wette, Wolfram and Detlev Vogel, eds, *Andere Helme – andere Menschen? Heimaterfahrung und Frontalltag im Zweiten Weltkrieg. Ein internationaler Vergleich* (Stuttgart, 1995).

Wette, Wolfram, '"In Worte gefasst." Kriegskorrespondenz im internationalen Vergleich' in Wolfram Wette and Detlev Vogel, eds, *Andere Helme – andere Menschen? Heimaterfahrung und Frontalltag im Zweiten Weltkrieg. Ein internationaler Vergleich* (Stuttgart, 1995), 329–348.

Wette, Wolfram, Ricarda Bremer and Detlef Vogel, *Das letzte halbe Jahr. Stimmungsberichte der Wehrmachtpropaganda 1944/45* (Cologne, 2001).

Wierling, Dorothee, 'Mission to Happiness: The Cohort of 1949 and the Making of East and West Germans' in Hanna Schissler, ed., *The Miracle Years. A Cultural History of West Germany, 1949–1968* (Princeton, 2001), 110–126.

Wilde, Barbara, 'Das Interview mit Bettina S. Geschlechterdifferenz nach 1945: Keine Zeiten im Umbruch' in Johanna Meyer-Lenz, ed., *Die Ordnung des Paares ist unbehaglich. Irritationen am und im Geschlechterdiskurs nach 1945* (Hamburg, 2000), 105–132.

Wildt, Michael, *Am Beginn der 'Konsumgesellschaft'. Mangelerfahrung, Lebenshaltung, Wohlstandshoffnung in Westdeutschland in den fünfziger Jahren* (Hamburg, 1994).

Wilharm, Irmgard, 'Wiederaufbaudynamik und Wertewandel' in Lutz Niethammer, ed., *Bürgerliche Gesellschaft in Deutschland. Historische Einblicke, Fragen, Perspektiven* (Frankfurt, 1990), 561–576.

Wilke, Gerhard and Kurt Wagner, 'Family and Household: Social Structures in a German Village between Two World Wars' in Richard J. Evans and William Robert Lee, eds, *The German Family, Essays on the Social History of the Family in Nineteenth and Twentieth Century Germany* (London, 1981), 120–147.

Wilke, Gerhard, 'Village Life in Nazi Germany' in Richard Bessel ed., *Life in the Third Reich* (2nd edition, Oxford, 2001), 17–24.

Willenbacher, Barbara, 'Zerrütung und Bewährung der Nachkriegs-Familie' in Martin Broszat, Klaus-Dietmar Henke and Hans Woller, eds, *Von Stalingrad zur Währungsreform. Zur Sozialgeschichte des Umbruchs in Deutschland* (Munich,1988), 595–618.

Winkel, Harald, *Die Wirtschaft im geteilten Deutschland 1945–1970* (Wiesbaden, 1974).

Wirrer, Bärbel, ed., *'Ich glaube an den Führer'. Eine Dokumentation zur Mentalitätsgeschichte im nationalsozialistischen Deutschland 1942–1945* (Bielefeld, 2003).

Wurzbacher, Gerhard, *Leitbilder gegenwärtigen deutschen Familienlebens* (Stuttgart, 1969).

Wurzbacher, Gerhard, Gudrun Cyprian, Dietrich Hänsch, Martin Koschorke, Rainer Mackensen, Armin Tschoepe and Helgard Ulshoefer, eds, *Probleme der Familie und der Familienpolitik in der BRD* (Koblenz, 1973).

Wurzbacher, Gerhard, 'Wandel und Bedeutung der Familie in der modernen Gesellschaft', *Kirche im Volk*, Vol. 13, 1954, 4–21.

Zentner, Kurt, ed., *Aufstieg aus dem Nichts. Deutschland von 1945 bis 1953* (Vol. I, Berlin, 1954).

Ziemann, Benjamin, 'Feldpostbriefe und ihre Zensur in den zwei Weltkriegen' in Klaus Beyer and Hans-Christian Täubrich, eds, *Der Brief. Eine Kulturgeschichte der schriftlichen Kommunikation* (Frankfurt, 1997).

Ziehmann, Benjamin, 'Geschlechterbeziehungen in deutschen Feldpostbriefen des Ersten Weltkrieges' in Christa Hämmerle and Edith Saurer, eds, *Briefkulturen und ihr Geschlecht. Zur Geschichte der privaten Korrespondenz vom 16. Jahrhundert bis heute* (Vienna, 2003), 261–282.

Index

abortion, 30
Adenauer, Konrad, 96
adjustment, 2, 8, 59, 80–2, 84, 86, 92, 117, 122, 125, 139–43
adultery
  by servicemen, 68, 101
  by wives, 67–8, 114–15
  wartime anxiety about, 42–3, 65–7
  see illegitimacy
advice centres, 34, 116
agency
  individual, 9, 21, 150, 154
air raids *see* bombing
allies, 1, 4, 17, 18, 38, 46, 63, 64, 88, 95, 100, 123, 169
Alltagsgeschichte, 6, 8, 9
anti-semitism *see* jews
Ariès, Philippe, 6
Armed Forces, 1, 23, 39, 40, 43, 44, 51, 65, 93, 103, 113, 117, 135
asocials, 33–5

Baden Württemberg, 76
BDM (*Bund Deutsche Mädel*) *see* League of German Girls
Berlin, 3, 4, 11, 12, 13, 14, 15, 34, 38, 41, 42, 47, 49, 55, 66, 67, 69, 70, 71, 72, 73, 74, 76–7, 87, 90, 94, 98, 103, 107, 109, 115, 118, 119, 120, 123, 124, 125, 127, 134, 140, 146
Besatzungskinder (children fathered by occupation soldiers), 151
Bielenberg, Christabel, 70
birth control, 31
birth rate, 3, 30, 31, 68
Black Market, 71, 131
  see also food shortages
Böll, Heinrich, 37, 41, 45, 64, 78, 81, 84
bombing, 1, 17, 52, 56, 64–5, 67, 88, 123, 124, 125, 128
  air raid shelters, 38, 39, 88

destruction, 72–4, 129
worry about relatives, 38–9, 56, 65
Bourke, Joanna, 9
Bray, Charles, 107
brothels, 44, 66, 68
Bruns, Ingeborg, 9
Burkhard, Benedikt, 11

camaraderie, 12, 84
casualties, 17, 36, 62–4, 153
Catholics, 27, 37, 51, 76, 111
censorship, 11–12, 17, 43–6, 54–6, 59, 80
children
  and evacuation, 125–7
  and food shortages, 71, 130–1
  and Nazi loan program, 30
  and their absent fathers, 129–30, 136–9
  and their understanding of war, 128–9, 142–3
  and war games, 128
  long-term effects of war on, 148
  Nazi organization of, 1, 2, 16, 23–7
class, 16, 25, 26, 37, 75, 78, 95, 104, 131, 134, 154
communication *see* letters
Communists, 14, 15, 27, 97
concentration camps, 32
conscription
  domestic effects of, 1, 93, 124
  of men, 1, 23, 36, 103
  of women, 31
Constanze, 82, 86, 94, 96, 102, 104, 107
contraception *see* birth control
currency reform, 70, 77
correspondence *see* letters

DAF (*Deutsche Arbeitsfront*) *see* German Labour Front
Das Blatt der Hausfrau, 69, 77, 90, 99, 101, 106, 146

death, 17, 30, 62–4, 84–5, 114, 153
defeat, 3, 17, 18, 20, 32, 56, 63, 70, 99, 114, 115, 151
denazification, 95, 102
denunciations, 26
demobilization, 1, 116–17, 120–1, 139–40
diaries, 7–10, 13
disability, 64, 118–19
divorce, 2, 3, 29, 30, 76, 83–6, 99–101, 120
Dörr, Margarete, 3, 9
Downs, Laura Lee, 9
dystrophy, 116

East Germany (German Democratic Republic), 14–15, 97
Eastern Front, 38, 40, 44, 56, 58, 63, 65, 67, 95, 117
economy
    in recovery, 76–7
    in wartime, 70, 95
    post-war, 46, 89, 94, 98, 110
education
    children's interrupted by war, 148
    see also Indoctrination
Eintopfsonntage see one pot Sundays
emancipation *see* women and independence
emotionology, 8
employment
    of men *see* unemployment
    of women, 85, 93, 98–9, 101–3
estrangement, 2, 11, 18, 37, 80, 126, 140–2
euthanasia, 32
evacuation, 125–7
expellees, 50

family
    crisis discourse, 1, 2, 4, 82–3, 85–7, 150, 151
    difficulties in wartime, 36–9, 42, 46, 48, 62, 69, 71, 72, 75–6, 79, 81–3, 104–6, 124–5, 131, 134, 150
    difficulties post-war, 2, 14, 48–9, 53, 69, 70, 76–8, 81, 83–5, 87, 89, 94–5, 103, 107–8, 110, 112, 114–17, 123, 143–5, 148, 152, 154–5

East German, 14–15
    incomplete, 84–5
    Jewish, 32
    Ministry, 96–7, 122
    Minister *see* Würmeling, Franz-Josef
    Nazi policy for, 28
    pre-1933, 15–16
    refugee, 50–1, 53, 74, 77, 89
    sociological studies of, 13, 72, 74, 83, 87, 89, 91, 103, 146, 155
    West German, 3, 5, 13, 14–15, 18
    and class *see* Class
fatherhood, 1, 16
    changing role of, 145–9
    from afar, 131–8, 153
    see also children
Federal Republic of Germany, 14, 96
Feldpostbriefe see letters
feminist historians, 3, 7–9
Ferntrauungen (long-distance marriages), 100
First World War, 20, 32, 34, 70, 99, 100
foraging *see* shortages
foreign workers, 67
fraternization, 67, 109, 114–15
Frauenüberschuss see surplus of women
Friedrich, Jörg, 4

gender relations, 1–2, 5, 14, 16, 17–18, 93, 95–113, 120–2, 146
German Democratic Republic, 14–15, 97
German Labour Front, 23
Gestapo, 21, 26
Goebbels, Joseph, 70
Gollancz, Victor, 107
government
    East German, 14–15, 97
    West German, 14, 96
    Nazi, 17, 22, 24, 26, 27, 28, 31, 32, 33, 34
gypsies, 32–3

Hamburg, 39, 52, 53, 74, 76, 99, 116, 125, 126
Hareven, Tamara, 7
health, 77, 80, 102, 114, 116, 119–21, 132, 135
Heineman, Elizabeth, 3, 5, 9

Himmler, Heinrich, 29–30
history
  from below, 6
  of emotions, 8, 10
  of everyday life, 5, 6, 7, 9
  of the family, 6–7, 15–16
  of women, 3–4,
Hitler, Adolf, 24, 56, 113
Hitler Youth (HJ), 1, 2, 16, 23–6
home
  as a haven, 28, 84, 150–1
home front, 2, 11, 20, 36, 38, 43, 61,
    62, 63, 65, 70, 82, 83, 114, 115,
    121, 124, 125
homecoming
  anxiety about, 49, 53, 54, 60, 64,
    78, 140
  longing for, 12, 18, 48, 49, 56, 59, 67,
    78, 102, 111, 113, 126, 127, 135,
    136, 139, 140, 150, 152, 155
  uncertain timing of, 49, 54
  See reunion
homosexuals, 32
Hour of the Woman, 2, 3, 4, 5, 93
housing *see* shortages
Humburg, Martin, 11
husbands
  see adultery
  see divorce
  see family
  see gender relations
  see marriage
  see men

illegitimacy, 2, 29–30, 68, 85
impotence, 115
indoctrination
  in schools, 24, 26
  in youth organizations, 16–17,
    24–5, 126–7
infant mortality, 77
infidelity *see* adultery

Jarausch, Konrad, 6
Jews, 4, 15, 20, 32, 51, 53, 107

Kleindienst, Jürgen, 9, 14
Klemperer, Victor, 32
KLV (*Kinderlandverschickung*) *see*
  evacuation

Krockow, Christian von, 4

Lange, Herta, 11
Latzel, Klaus, 11
Law
  Against Malicious Attacks on State
    and Party, 21, 26
League of German Girls (BDM), 2, 16,
    25, 27
  See also Hitler Youth
Lebensborn, 30
Lebensraum, 20
letters, 7–13, 17–18, 37–43, 46–7, 50,
    54–7, 59, 63–4, 80, 91–2,
    151–2, 154
Ley, Robert, 33
Lili Marlene (song), 60
longing, 12, 18, 48, 49, 56, 59, 67,
    78, 102, 111, 113, 126, 127, 135,
    136, 139, 140, 150, 152, 155
Lüdtke, Alf, 6, 9

mail *see* letters
malnutrition *see* shortages
marriage, 3, 17, 26, 29, 30, 31, 36, 59,
    68, 72, 75–6, 79–80, 82–7, 91,
    96, 98–101, 146, 151
masculinity, 1, 113–19, 152
Medick, Hans, 6
memory, 10
men
  and masculinity, 1, 113–19, 152
  as fathers, 1, 16, 131–9, 145–9, 153
  as soldiers, 2, 4, 12, 17, 18, 29, 31,
    37–47, 49, 51, 53, 55, 56, 57, 58,
    60, 61, 63, 65, 67, 68, 78, 79,
    81, 82, 83, 86, 87, 91, 93, 95,
    99, 109, 111, 113, 114, 115, 116,
    117, 120, 121, 129, 130, 131,
    134, 135, 139, 142, 143, 144,
    146, 159–62
  returning from war, 1, 14, 17,
    48, 53–4, 69, 85, 87, 90, 115,
    116–17, 119, 120–1, 139, 116–7,
    120–1, 139–45, 147–8
  scarcity of, 98, 99, 101
Meyer, Sibylle, 3, 5, 9
militarism, 20, 22–4, 29, 34, 113–14
Mischlingskinder (children of mixed
    race), 86

missing relatives, 49–50, 51–4, 111
mobilization, 2, 16, 20, 22, 28, 31, 34,
    114, 150
Moeller, Robert, 3, 5
morale, 17, 33–4, 36–7, 57, 62–3,
    69–70, 126
motherhood
    according to the Nazi ideal, 29–31
    on the home front: 107–10, 124–6,
        127, 130–1
Mouton, Michelle, 5

National Socialist Womanhood, 23, 27
National Socialism *see* Nazism
Nazi Party *see* Nazism
Nazi Security Service, 36, 63,
    103, 126
Nazism
    and children, 23–7, 126–7
    and masculinity, 1, 113–19, 152
    and opposition, 21, 27–8, 33
    and passivity in the face of, 22,
        28–9, 33–4
    and persecution, 32–3
    and propaganda, 17, 31, 70, 113
    and racial ideology, 29, 31
    and the law, 21–2
    and women
        child rearing, 28, 29
        divorce, 30, 100
        employment, 31
        illegitimate children, 29–30
        marriage loan scheme, 30
        motherhood, 29–31
        population policy, 29–31
        welfare, 30
    and youth
        see Youth organizations
Niehuss, Merith, 2, 3, 5
Niethammer, Lutz, 6
NS-Frauenschaft see National Socialist
    Womanhood

occupation
    Allied, 15, 17, 74, 77, 86, 95, 109,
        114, 115, 151
one pot Sundays, 20–1
Onkel-Ehen, 99, 151
oral history, 3, 9–10

Orgel-Purper, Liselotte, 12–13
orphans, 53

patriarchy, 2, 16, 18, 96, 97
Peukert, Detlev, 6, 28
Pine, Lisa, 2, 5
post *see* letters
post-structuralism, 7–9
Post Traumatic Stress Disorder (PTSD)
    see dystrophy
prisoners of war (POWs), 2, 8, 45,
    79, 116
    correspondence from, 48–9, 50, 79,
        84, 127, 133–4, 136
    disability, 69, 118–19
    missing, 41, 48, 49, 51, 64, 108,
        112, 151
    numbers of, 47
    Post Traumatic Stress
        Disorder, 116
    returning, 14, 17, 48, 53–4, 69,
        85, 87, 90, 115, 116–17, 119,
        120–1, 139, 141, 142, 143,
        144, 145, 147, 148
    soviet, 8, 15, 44, 48, 50, 78, 81,
        87, 116–17, 121
private sphere, 1, 2, 3, 4, 5, 7, 9, 10, 11,
    12, 13, 14, 15, 17, 22, 26, 27, 28,
    29, 30, 32, 33, 34, 70, 72, 79, 86,
    96, 97, 98, 102, 110, 112, 114,
    115, 121, 139, 150, 151, 152, 155
public sphere, 8, 18, 28, 29, 86, 98,
    110, 150, 151

race
    Nazi ideology on, 29, 31
radio, 60–1
rape, 4, 15, 115
rationing *see* shortages
reconstruction, 3, 14, 15, 18, 19, 94,
    97, 150
Red Army, 73
Red Cross, 48, 51–3, 111
refugees (from East to West), 50–1, 53,
    74, 77, 89
returnees *see* prisoners of war
reunion, 53–4, 69, 80–2, 86–7, 90–1,
    107, 113, 116–17, 120,
    139–49

Roberts, Ulla, 9
Roper, Lyndal, 9
Ross, Ellen, 6
Russia *see* Soviet Union

SA (Storm Troopers), 23
Schelsky, Helmut, 13, 83, 87, 89, 91,
    103, 155
Schulze, Eva, 3, 5, 9
Scott, Joan, 7, 8, 9
search services, 51, 111
    International Refugee
        Organization, 52
    Red Cross, 51–3, 111
self-mutilation, 44
separation, 41–3, 45–6, 60–1, 62, 78–9,
    91, 131–38, 149, 151, 152–3
sex, 44, 67, 75, 114–16
shell shock *see* dystrophy
Shirer, William, 34, 62
shortages
    general, 46–7, 69–70, 87, 89, 90,
        91, 107
    food, 70–2, 103, 123, 130, 131
    housing, 72–7, 89
Sicherheitsdienst (SD) *see* Nazi Security
        Service
Social Democratic Party, 27, 33
    See persecution
soldiers, 2, 4, 12, 17, 18, 29, 31, 37–47,
    49, 51, 53, 55, 56, 57, 58, 60, 61,
    63, 65, 67, 68, 78, 79, 81, 82,
    83, 86, 87, 91, 93, 95, 99, 109,
    111, 113, 114, 115, 116, 117, 120,
    121, 129, 130, 131, 134, 135,
    139, 142, 143, 144, 146, 159–62
Sopade (Social Democratic Party in
    exile), 22
Soviet PoWs, 8, 15, 44, 48, 50, 78, 81,
    87, 116–17, 121
    See also prisoners of war
Soviet Union, 1, 4, 8, 15, 37, 38, 40,
    42, 44, 46, 48, 49, 50, 51, 56,
    57, 58, 59, 62, 63, 64, 65, 67, 79,
    86, 87, 95, 112, 113, 115, 116,
    117, 119, 121, 123, 130, 132,
    136, 151
SS (Nazi Protective Squadron), 29–30
Stalingrad, 40, 55, 56, 70, 79, 80, 151

Stargardt, Nicholas, 10
sterilization, 32
Stunde Null see Zero Hour
Sturmabteilung see SA
Stuttgart, 127
suffering
    German, 4, 45, 48, 82, 114,
        121, 143
surplus of women, 98, 99, 101

The Strong Woman, 5, 93–5, 97,
    101, 152
Third Reich *see* Nazism
Thurnwald, Hilde, 13, 72, 74,
    89, 146
total war, 36, 70, 174
trauma, 115, 148
Trümmerfrauen see Women of the
    Rubble

unemployment, 34, 95

veterans, 14, 17, 48, 53–4, 69, 85,
    87, 90, 115, 116–19, 120–1,
    139, 141, 142, 143, 144,
    145, 147, 148
victimhood
    sense of, 4, 5, 154
victories
    early, 62
Volksgemeinschaft, 32
Volkssturm, 127

war brides, 99–100
war games
    children's, 128
war widows, 84–5
Weimar, 34
Wette, Wolfram, 11
wives
    see adultery
    see divorce
    see family
    see gender relations
    see marriage
    see women
Wolff-Mönckeberg, Mathilde, 39
women
    and adultery, 67–8, 114–15

women – *continued*
  and divorce, 2, 3, 29, 76, 83–6,
    99–101, 120
  and employment, 85, 93, 98–99, 101–3
  and family, 1, 2, 4, 14–16, 18,
    28, 82–3, 85–7, 96–7, 122, 150–1
  and fraternization, 67, 109, 114–15
  and gender relations, 1–2, 5, 14,
    16–18, 93, 95–113, 120–2, 146
  and the Hour of the Woman, 2, 3,
    4, 5, 93
  and independence, 1, 3, 4, 18,
    93–6, 103–13, 121–2, 152, 154–5
  and marriage, 3, 17, 26, 29, 30, 31,
    36, 59, 68, 72, 75–6, 79–80,
    82–7, 91, 96, 98–101, 146, 151

  and motherhood, 16, 124–6, 127,
    130–1
  and Nazism, 23, 27–31
  and rape, 4, 15, 115
  and war work, 31
  standing alone, 3, 101, 104,
    108, 112
Women of the Rubble, 93, 94,
  98, 108
Wunschkonzert, 60–1, 132
Würmeling, Franz-Josef, 86, 96,
  151, 154

yellow star, 32

Zero Hour, 70